Webster Division, McGraw-Hill Book Company
St. Louis New York San Francisco Dallas Toronto London Sydney

HOW YOU PLAN AND PREPARE MEALS

About the Authors

Byrta Carson teaches homemaking in Sidney Lanier Junior and Senior High School, San Antonio, Texas. She received her B.S. degree in home economics from Mary Hardin-Baylor College and her M.A. degree from Colorado State University. She also studied at Texas Women's University, St. Mary's University, and the University of Texas. Miss Carson is the author of *How You Look and Dress.*

MaRue Carson Ramee taught homemaking at Poe Junior High School, San Antonio, Texas. At present, she is a full-time homemaker. Mrs. Ramee received her B.S. degree in home economics from Texas College of Arts and Industries. She also studied at Texas Technological College.

How You Plan
and Prepare
Meals

Second Edition

Byrta Carson

MaRue Carson Ramee

AMERICAN HOME AND FAMILY SERIES

Barclay-Champion: Teen Guide to Homemaking
Carson: How You Look and Dress
Carson-Ramee: How You Plan and Prepare Meals
Hurlock: Child Growth and Development
Landis: Your Marriage and Family Living
Morton: The Home and Its Furnishings
Shank-Fitch-Chapman: Guide to Modern Meals
Sturm-Grieser: Guide to Modern Clothing
(Other Titles in Process)

HOW YOU PLAN AND PREPARE MEALS

ISBN 07-010161-2

9 10 11 12 13   KPKP   7 9 8

Cover photograph: Courtesy American Dairy Association
Front matter photographs: Courtesy Stix, Baer, and Fuller, St. Louis, Mo., Jack Kelleher, Photographer

FOREWORD

The Second Edition of *How You Plan and Prepare Meals* is an updated edition of this visual foods textbook, which has been so well received in the classroom. The findings of teachers who have used the First Edition and the latest research in the foods field are reflected in this new edition, which has been changed in the following ways: introduction of color throughout; new front and back matter; and many new illustrations depicting modern styles, equipment, and furniture.

The general organization and plan of the book remain as follows:

1. *Reality:* By *showing how* through photographs, rather than merely *telling how* with words, and by using numerous pictures of actual situations in which young students are models, the authors give examples which are realistic and within possibility.

2. *Format:* By combining specific illustrations with simple wording, the authors develop a clear and graphic way of communicating the most recent information about all aspects of the beginning foods course.

3. *Organization:* By its organization into 4 parts and 29 chapters, the book includes all necessary detail, without breaking up or interrupting the discussion of main subjects.

4. *Content:* By presenting subject matter from the standpoint of meal planning, as well as by giving details about the kinds of foods, the authors include a great deal of general information and offer it from different viewpoints.

5. *Research:* By developing the content and organization from a study of the foods courses in all sections of the country, by obtaining or taking photographs for the best presentation of the idea to be illustrated, by having the chapters and the recipes tested in classrooms in many sections of the country, the authors have organized a text which is both adaptable to the foods course and comprehensible to the student.

6. *Coverage:* Methods of planning, preparing, and serving meals—from simple party refreshments to a full-course dinner—are included. Nothing is taken for granted; even simple equipment is pictured and labeled, elementary procedures are explained, and the most common situations are considered.

7. *Up-to-dateness:* Latest equipment and products, the many varieties of the most common foods, and quickly prepared meals are all pictured.

8. *Enjoyment:* With the basic goals of the foods course always in mind, and without sacrificing content, the authors give the student information in a form that is easy to comprehend and enjoyable to study and apply.

We hope the Second Edition will be even more useful for the students than the First Edition.

ACKNOWLEDGEMENTS

How You Plan and Prepare Meals is dedicated to the friends whose contributions made this book possible. The authors are indebted to so many that it would be difficult to name all. However, they wish to express their sincere appreciation to:

Margarete Schuette, Tura Cressey, Payton Kennedy, Elizabeth Thomas, Martha Mussett, Johnie Riggs, Katie Elder, Elia Tamez, Vada Belle Zellner, Lucille Cole, Nell Reed, Grace Voges, Gladys Eddy, and Lucille Cooper for the many ways in which they helped.

Erwin Wesp and Julius Patteson for their work on the illustrations.

The magazines, stores, manufacturers, and others who loaned photographs.

The girls who, in class and on their own time, worked to simplify and clarify the material, and the girls and boys who posed for photographs.

The following homemaking teachers in San Antonio, Texas, who helped with the illustrations: Elaine T. Carol and Albertine W. Gibson, Alamo Heights Senior High School; Althea Le Sage, Edgewood High School; and Lou Pyka, Thomas Jefferson High School.

The test kitchen of Mrs. Tucker's Shortening for allowing Albertine Berry to test the recipes.

Special acknowledgment is made to the homemaking teachers, supervisors, homemaking educators, professional home economists, and homemakers who gave constructive criticism on the outline and the manuscript, who helped in compiling the recipes, or who tested the recipes in class:

Dorothy Glane, Los Angeles City Schools, Los Angeles, California

Virginia Bonnefon, George Churchill Junior High School, Galesburg, Illinois

Albertine Berry Castle, Nutrition Consultant, Texas Gulf Bakers Council, Houston, Texas

Betty Forsythe Chamness, former homemaking teacher, Quincy, Illinois

Lucille Harrison Cole, homemaking teacher, Houston, Texas

Alethea Moore, Maxine Resseguie, Marilyn Margo, Daravene Thomas, and Alice Doningues, Sidney Lanier Junior and Senior High School, San Antonio, Texas.

Irene A. Dougherty, K. D. Waldo Junior High School, Aurora, Illinois

Helen Evans, Roosevelt Junior High School, San Diego, California

Clydine Baldwin, John Marshall High School, San Antonio, Texas

Clara N. Flemington, former homemaking teacher, Ellendale, North Dakota

Hazel Hopkins, Van Horn High School, Kansas City, Missouri

Elizabeth Harvey, Edgemont High School, Scarsdale, New York

Jean Kallenberger and Marjory Moravek, Home Economics Education, Mankato State College, Mankato, Minnesota

Rhea Keeler, Associate Professor, Vocational Education, University of Nebraska, Lincoln, Nebraska

Marjorie King, West Seattle High School, Seattle, Washington

June Krebs, Fort Hays Kansas State College, Hays, Kansas

Ruth Marcum Leitzke, Washington Junior High School, Dinuba, California

Marion Lowery, Everett High School, Everett, Washington

Madalynne McKague, former homemaking teacher, Salt Lake City, Utah

Ramona Montgomery, Edison High School, San Antonio, Texas

Joyce Nance, Nixon High School, Nixon, Texas

Frances Rast, Byars-Hall High School, Covington, Tennessee

Martha L. Rast, Head, Home Economics Department, Chester County High School, Henderson, Tennessee

Fern E. Ruck, Rangely High School, Rangely, Colorado

Helen Scheve, State Supervisor, Homemaking Education, Topeka, Kansas

Sue Stephens, Wheatland High School, Wheatland, Wyoming

Mary Eloise Stone, Head, Home Economics Department, Madison Junior High School, Syracuse, New York

Juanita Stutsman, Head, Home Economics Department, Bozeman High School, Bozeman, Montana

Esther Veen Huis, E. E. Fell Junior High School, Holland, Michigan

The authors hope that students will find this book stimulating and interesting and that the information obtained from it will be of lasting value.

BYRTA CARSON
MARUE CARSON RAMEE

CONTENTS

x

Part 3: YOUR MEALS IN THE SCHOOL KITCHEN

Part 4: YOUR RECIPES AND HOW TO USE THEM

Bland

1

YOUR MEALS—HOW YOU SERVE THEM

Parties should be fun for everyone. Invite those who enjoy being together. Entertain your guests while they are present. Attend to clean-up duties after they have gone home.

Chapter 1 | LET'S HAVE A PARTY

Although the main reason for having a party is to have a good time, there are other reasons. You may have a party to return a social obligation, to have your friends meet each other, to have your friends meet your parents, or to bring your friends into your home to enjoy an evening with your family.

The person who is giving a party is called a "hostess," if it is a girl or woman, or a "host," if it is a boy or man. Part of the success of any party is the spirit of the group and the attitude of the hostess. A good hostess greets the guests at the door and makes them feel welcome. She sees that the guests' wraps are taken care of. She introduces all guests to her parents and to all the other guests. She should also be sure that all the guests are having a good time and that no one is neglected as long as the party lasts.

Before you start planning a party, talk to your mother to be sure that she is going to be at home. Find out also whether your ideas meet with her approval and fit in with her plans as well as with those of the other members of the family. Your mother will probably help you with the party, but you should do as much as you can yourself because it is your party.

HOW TO PLAN A PARTY

For a well-planned party, you should consider all these items:

1. *The amount of money you have to spend and how to get the most for it:* The best parties are not always the ones that cost the most money.

2. *The kind of party you will have and the type of entertainment:* In deciding this, you will want to consider the number of people you are inviting, the amount of room and the facilities you have in your home, the season of the year and the weather, the time of day, and the likes and dislikes of your friends, as well as their age and personality.

3. *The place, date, and time:* If you cannot have the party in your home, be sure that your parents approve the place that you select for it. Also be sure that your guests will be able to reach the place easily. In setting the date, consider school activities and other events in the community and avoid conflict with them. The time of day you choose may depend on the kind of party, the distance your friends have to travel, and the convenience of the time for your guests.

4. *Whom you will invite and how you will invite them:* Try to invite people who get along well together or will be interesting to each other. Make a complete list of those you intend to ask. As they accept or decline, indicate it on your list so that you will know how many guests to prepare for.

5. *What decorations you will have:* If you have decorations and favors, they should be suited to the theme of the party. For example, if you are having a Valentine party, consider using hearts, cupids, and arrows as decorations and favors.

6. *What you will have to eat and how you will serve it:* See pages 9 and 10.

Photos Courtesy Stix, Baer, and Fuller, St. Louis

2

Courtesy Lawry's Foods, Inc.

The refreshments for parties at which active games are played are
usually hearty. Any of these simple dishes could be easily prepared.
All are popular with young people.

When deciding what to serve at a party, consider the season of the year, the place, the amount of money to be spent, and the number of people to be invited. The best parties are not always the ones that cost the most money.

Courtesy Melmac Dinnerware

To make any party a success, you will need to do some planning ahead of time and to have all the supplies and equipment conveniently arranged when the guests arrive. Then you can relax and enjoy yourself.

Sunsweet Growers, Inc., San Jose, California

If you make your own decorations, you will have more money to spend for other things, such as refreshments, for your party. You will also find that you can more easily carry out a color scheme or a party theme when you make your own decorations than when you buy them.

Whether you extend the invitation by word of mouth or in writing, be sure to tell your guests the place, the time, the date, and the kind of party so that they will know what to wear.

You might write or say something like this: "I am having a few friends over Sunday afternoon, February 24, at 3:30 to meet friends from Canada, and I would like to have you come."

For a special party, it is a good idea to invite your guests at least a week in advance so that they can make their plans for the party.

WHAT TO DO BEFORE THE PARTY

Several Days Before

1. Look over books, pamphlets, and magazines for ideas on invitations, decorations, entertainment, and refreshments.
2. Make a list of what you have to do and what you have to buy.
3. Invite the guests.
4. Make or buy the decorations, favors, and napkins.
5. Decide what you will need for the entertainment you have planned, such as materials for games, new records, and wax for the floor if you are going to dance.
6. Check to see that the dress you are going to wear is clean and pressed.
7. Buy whatever groceries you can from the list of foods needed for the refreshments.
8. Check to see that the tablecloth and napkins you are using are clean and well pressed. (If paper napkins are used, be sure that they follow the party theme.)
9. If small TV tables are to be used, check to see that you have enough.
10. Decide what chairs you are going to use. Be sure that you have plenty for the number of people you have invited.

The Day Before

1. Make sure that the house is clean and in order. Provide extra chairs or rearrange furniture if necessary.
2. Check supplies in the bedroom and the bathroom to be sure that you have enough cleansing tissue, toilet paper, soap, guest towels, and similar things that will be needed.
3. Make sure that a place is provided for taking care of the guests' wraps and that there are plenty of hangers.
4. Recheck the grocery list to make sure that you have not forgotten anything.
5. Prepare as much of the food as possible.
6. Check dishes, silver, and glassware that will be needed, and see that they are clean and ready for use.

The Day of the Party

1. Check the house carefully to see that all furniture is freshly dusted and all dirt and marks are removed from the floors.
2. Clean the bathroom and see that fresh towels are out.
3. Use a room deodorant so that the house will smell clean and fresh.
4. Arrange the decorations, set the table, and put out materials for games, favors, and prizes.
5. Complete the preparations for the refreshments.
6. Dress in plenty of time so that you will be ready when your guests arrive.

Courtesy "Farm Journal" and Black Star

Kitchen parties: A kitchen party, or a "cook-it-yourself" party, is most successful if there are just a few guests and if each one has a special job. One couple might be responsible for preparing the main dish, another for making the salad and setting the table, another for preparing the beverage, and so on. At such a party you might serve noodle goulash, tossed salad, buttered French bread, ice cream, cookies, and milk. You can have a simple kitchen party in this way:

1. Arrange milk, ice cream, and sirup on the table so that each guest can make his own milk drink or sundae.

2. Place bread, meat, butter, lettuce, and relishes on the table so that each guest can make his own sandwich to his liking.

3. Have everything ready for the group to make popcorn balls or candy.

4. Use electric appliances at the table to make grilled sandwiches or waffles as they are needed.

As for all other parties, when you have a kitchen party, you will need to plan the menu ahead of time, buy the groceries, and have all the supplies and equipment conveniently arranged when the guests arrive.

Potluck suppers, or covered-dish suppers, are similar to kitchen parties except that the guests prepare the food at home and each guest brings a special dish. One might bring a meat dish, another the salad, still another the dessert, and so on. The hostess usually provides the beverage and arranges the table.

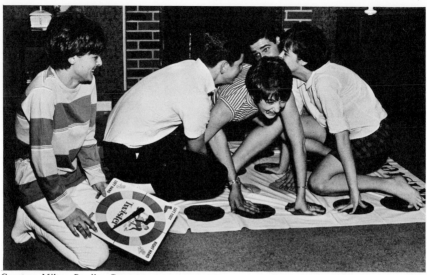

Parties at which active games are played: Serve hearty refreshments because everyone will be hungry after the activity. For example, you might serve pizzas, hamburgers, hot dogs, or meat sandwiches.

Parties after a game or an outdoor activity: If you and your friends have been to a game or have been participating in an outdoor activity, you will be hungry. A hot meat sandwich with a favorite relish can be served quickly and easily if you have prepared everything beforehand. All that you will have to do is cook the meat.

Courtesy Fostoria Glass Company

To make the party something special, plan it in relation to an idea or a party theme. If you are entertaining after a football game, you might carry out a football theme. Examine the centerpiece above. The players are made of photographs cut from newspapers and pasted on cardboard. The field is made of ready-to-eat cereal. The goal posts were made by tying ribbon to candles. You might make invitations in the shape of a football. For favors you might buy small footballs in the dime store and attach ribbons in the school colors. Arrange the food on the table so that each guest can serve himself with perhaps some help from members of the family or friends.

7

Courtesy Las Cruces, New Mexico Public Schools

Whatever you serve at a party should be attractive. A cold drink is more appealing served in glasses than in bottles, and cookies look better served on a plate than in a box.

Plan to have foods that go well together. For instance, sandwiches or coconut cake go better with a chocolate drink than chocolate cake does. If you are serving a plain drink, you can have fancy cookies. But you should not serve fruit cookies with a fruit punch that contains a lot of chipped fruit.

Courtesy General Foods Corporation

THE REFRESHMENTS

1. Consider the kind of party. For example, you would have more food for a party at which active games are played and which lasts several hours than you would for a tea.
2. Consider the amount to be spent. If you have only enough money for hamburgers, do not plan to have a steak. It is a good idea to compare prices of foods before deciding what to have.
3. Consider the number of people you are having and the number of servings you want to have for each.
4. Think about the guests you are having. For example, if the party includes boys, the refreshments should, of course, be different from those you would serve to, say, your mothers.
5. Plan to have food that you are sure that you know how to prepare — that is, food that you have prepared before.
6. Try to plan a party that will result in a minimum of clean-up problems.
7. Serving refreshments will be easy if you plan to have foods that can be entirely or partially prepared ahead of time.
8. The time of day that you are having your party might affect what you serve. For instance, your refreshments should not interfere with the guests' regular meals or be too heavy if served late at night.
9. If you are having a party for a special occasion or with decorations, plan your refreshments to fit in with the party theme.
10. The kind of food you have will also depend upon the way you plan to serve it — that is, whether you plan to have your guests eat standing up, sitting at a table, or from a plate on their laps.

Even a family snack can become a party if you take time to serve foods in a pleasing manner.

Courtesy Wellco Foamtread Slippers

Shrimp cocktail is made of whole cooked shrimp. The shrimp are speared, dipped into the cocktail sauce, and eaten with the cocktail fork.

Fried chicken is cut from the bone with the knife. It is eaten from the fork as the fork is held in the right hand.

Spaghetti is eaten after it is rolled around the fork. Sometimes a large spoon is held in the left hand to help roll the spaghetti on the fork.

Photos courtesy Stix, Baer, and Fuller, St. Louis

Pizza is cut into pie-shaped pieces and eaten with the fingers.

Grapes are taken in bunches from the serving dish and eaten individually with the fingers. Seeds from grapes and other similar foods may be removed from the mouth with the fingers and placed on the side of the plate.

Corn on the cob is held in both hands and eaten directly from the cob. Butter, salt, and pepper are added to only a portion at a time.

Photos courtesy Stix, Baer, and Fuller, St. Louis

11

GIVING A TEA

At a tea the food you serve should be simple and dainty. Ordinarily the refreshments consist of a beverage, cookies or cakes, and sandwiches. The attractiveness of the food and the way it is served, rather than the amount of food, are important. When giving a tea, the following suggestions will be helpful:

1. Cover the table with a plain or fancy tablecloth: linen, rayon, lace, organdy, or a fabric with metallic threads.
2. Be sure to have a centerpiece that is colorful and that harmonizes with the china, silver, and glassware.
3. Arrange the cups or glasses in a semicircle near the person who is serving so that she can reach them easily.
4. Place the plates in stacks of 6 to 10 near the person who is serving, or stack them along the side of the table if the guests are to serve themselves.
5. Place the silver in a row with the handles toward the edge of the table so that they can be picked up easily.
6. Arrange the napkins in a row so that they slightly overlap each other.
7. The beverage should be served at one end of the table or, when two beverages are served, at both ends of the table. The lemon, sugar, cream, or whatever is needed for the beverage should be nearby.
8. When a large sheet cake is served, it should be placed at one end of the table and served first.
9. Small cakes and cookies which can be picked up easily and eaten with the fingers are better than large ones.
10. Sandwiches, which should be small and dainty, may be cut into various shapes.
11. Salted nuts and colored mints may also be placed on the table.
12. All foods should be attractively arranged on plates or trays and placed near the edge of the table so that they are within easy reach of the guests.

Courtesy Stix, Baer, and Fuller, St. Louis

12

A guest should hold the plate low enough for the hostess to place the food on it easily.

If You Are a Hostess

When a group of girls gives a tea, each girl is a hostess who is responsible for one or more of the following duties:

1. Greet the guests at the door.
2. Show the guests where to put their wraps.
3. Introduce guests to each other.
4. See to it that the guests are served.
5. Serve the beverage or cake at the table.
6. Bring extra dishes or silver from the kitchen when needed.
7. Bring new plates of cookies or sandwiches as needed.
8. Pick up soiled dishes, and take them to the kitchen.

If You Are a Guest

As a guest at a tea, you should follow these suggestions:

1. Arrive at any time between the hours given on the invitation.
2. Help yourself to one or two sandwiches, cookies, nuts, or whatever else is on the table.
3. Take a napkin and any silver you may need before leaving the table.
4. Visit and chat with friends or other guests while you eat.
5. When you finish eating, crumple your napkin slightly, put it on your plate, and hand the plate to the hostess who is picking up the soiled dishes. (*NOTE:* Do not put soiled dishes back on the tea table.)
6. It is not necessary to stay at a tea more than 30 minutes. Before you leave, you should express your appreciation to a hostess or sponsor.

13

COOKING OUTDOORS

1. Plan to have plenty of food because the outdoor air stimulates the appetite.

2. If your time is limited, do not have foods that take a long time to cook, such as baked potatoes and stews.

3. When building a fire, use paper, kindling (small pieces of wood), or commercial fluid to start the fire. Never use gasoline or kerosene.

4. Start the fire about 30 minutes to an hour before you put the food on the grill so that the food will be cooked over glowing coals rather than over a flame.

5. Be sure that the preparation of other food is timed so that it will be ready to serve when the meat is done.

When Cooking in the Park

1. Check beforehand to be sure that the park where you are planning to go has tables and cooking facilities.

2. Pack perishable foods, such as fresh vegetables and meat, in ice or ice containers to keep them fresh if they are not to be used for several hours.

3. Take plenty of drinking water unless you are positive that good drinking water is available.

Courtesy Reynolds Metals Company

4. Make sure that you take all necessary equipment for cooking and serving: old newspapers, matches (in a metal container), bottle and can openers, sharp knives, paper plates and cups, knives and forks, a plastic or a paper tablecoth, paper towels, and a dishcloth.

5. Before leaving, be sure to pick up all wastepaper and trash and to put out the fire.

For outdoor cooking, food may be seasoned and wrapped in aluminum foil and then cooked over an open grill.

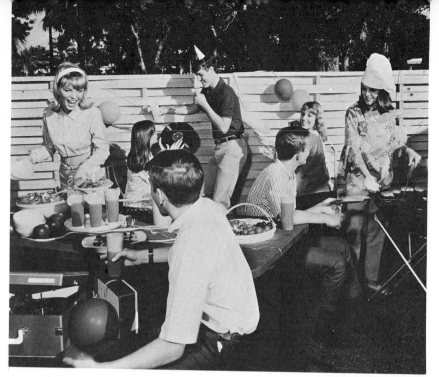

Courtesy Tupperware

You can do outdoor cooking in your own back yard or at a camp site. Pots used directly over open flames should be coated with a paste made of detergent and water so they can be washed easily. Favorite foods are ribs, hamburgers, frankfurters, chicken, and corn.

Courtesy Camp Fire Girls, Inc.

15

Shelton from Monkmeyer

For picnics, all the food is usually prepared at home and is ready to eat. It may consist of any cold foods, such as sandwiches (see Chapter 16), potato salad, hard-cooked eggs, pickles, olives, potato chips, cookies or cupcakes, and fruit. Or, it may consist of one hot main dish, such as a stew or a chowder, pot roast with vegetables, baked beans, meat loaf, or a casserole. The hot food can be carried in the container in which it was cooked. The container should be wrapped in several layers of newspaper to keep the food hot. Stews and soups may be taken in large-mouthed thermos bottles. Fresh vegetables for salads to go with the hot dish, such as carrot strips, tomatoes, and celery, may be taken in plastic bags or placed in jars with a few pieces of ice to keep them fresh and crisp.

Courtesy Associated Pimiento Canners

ACTIVITIES

Deciding what makes a good party:
1. Describe the best party you ever attended. Did you enjoy yourself because of the other guests, the kind of party, the refreshments, the entertainment, or for some other reason?

Getting ideas for parties:
2. Make a scrapbook of magazine clippings with ideas for decorations, entertainment, and refreshments for parties.
3. Bring to class party invitations and favors which you have received at parties, and exchange ideas.

Planning a party:
4. Have the class plan a wiener roast in the park. Appoint committees, each with a chairman, to: *(a)* plan the menu, *(b)* decide on the amount of food to buy, *(c)* prepare the food, *(d)* serve the food, and *(e)* clean up afterward.

Learning to be a good hostess:
5. Select one girl in the class to be a hostess, and have her appoint four assistant hostesses. The other girls in the class will act as guests. The hostesses will practice: *(a)* greeting guests, *(b)* helping them with their wraps, *(c)* introducing them to each other, *(d)* serving the refreshments, and *(e)* saying good-by, at the end of the party.

Serving refreshments in various ways:
6. Discuss the kinds of party refreshments that might be served when the guests are to eat: *(a)* standing up, *(b)* from their laps, and *(c)* sitting at a small table.
7. Plan the refreshments for a party: *(a)* after the movies and *(b)* at which active games will be played.

Giving a tea after school:
8. Have an informal tea after school to which each girl will invite a guest. When the party is over, discuss it. Did everyone have a good time? Were the place, date, and time of the party suitable? If there was a party theme, was it well carried out? Were the refreshments enjoyed, and were they attractive? Could any money have been saved?

Having parties with your family:
9. Plan a surprise party for a member of your family.
10. Tell about a family you know that has fun together and why you think they do.
11. Describe some games that your family enjoys playing.
12. Tell how you help your mother when she entertains.

For an attractive and well-set table, everything should be spotlessly clean and placed so that the table as a whole appears well balanced. The centerpiece may be placed in the center, to the side, or at one end of the table.

Courtesy Russel Wright Associates

When serving foods outdoors, you can set the table and serve in the same ways as indoors. For a buffet meal, arrange all food, silver, dishes, and linen on the table so that each person can help himself.

Courtesy Haviland and Company

The centerpiece should be in proportion to the size of the table. A large arrangement may be used on a large table, but it should be placed to the side or at one end of the table so that the diners will be able to see each other. For a small table, an arrangement of three or four flowers or a small growing plant is appropriate.

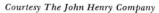

A WELL-SET TABLE

For an attractive and well-set table, everything should be spotlessly clean and placed so that the table as a whole appears well balanced:

1. The silver, china, and glassware should be placed in straight lines both lengthwise and across the table. All pieces should be placed parallel with even spacing between them.
2. The linen — tablecloth or place mats and napkins — should be free of wrinkles and should match or harmonize with each other. When a tablecloth is used, a silence cloth or pad should be placed under it to protect the table, to make the table look better, and to deaden the noise of the dishes and silver. The tablecloth should be placed so that the center fold is exactly in the center of the table and the sides are the same distance from the floor.
3. The centerpiece may be placed in the center, to the side, or at one end of the table, but its position should be considered in arranging a well-balanced table.
4. The chairs should be placed so that the center of the chair is in line with the center of the plate. The front of the chair should come just under the edge of the table so that a person may sit down or rise without having to move the chair too much.

Courtesy The Gorham Company

The silver, china, glassware, and napkin to be used by each person, called a "cover" or "place setting," should take up about 20 to 24 inches of space. Note that the plate, silver, and napkin are aligned at the bottom about 1 inch from the edge of the table. (See page 400.) Note also these points:

1. *The plate* is directly in the center of the space allowed for the entire cover.

2. *The silver* is placed in the order in which it is to be used . . .

   . . . the knife to the right, with the cutting edge toward the plate.

   . . . the spoon to the right of the knife, with the bowl turned up.

   . . . the forks to the left with the prongs turned up. However, when no knife is to be used, the fork may be placed on the right with the spoons. An oyster, or cocktail, fork is always placed to the right of the spoons. The salad fork may be placed outside or inside the dinner fork, depending upon when the salad is to be served.

3. *The goblet, or glass,* is just above the tip of the knife.

4. *The napkin* is usually at the left, with either the open or the folded side next to the forks. It may also be placed in the center of the plate (see page 21).

5. *The bread-and-butter plate* is just above the forks. The butter spreader may be laid across the top of the plate or along the side, with the cutting edge turned inward.

6. *The cup and the saucer,* if placed with the setting, should be to the right and just below the glass or goblet, with the handle of the cup parallel to the edge of the table.

20

An individual salad plate may be placed to the left of the plate, or it may be placed to the right when no coffee or tea is served with the meal. When a bread-and-butter plate is also used, the salad plate is placed slightly lower, and the napkin is put in the center of the plate or cover.

A soup bowl should be placed in the center of a serving plate. The soup spoon should be on the extreme right because it will be used first.

An extra glass for milk, juice, or an iced drink should be on a coaster to the right and just below the water glass. Iced drinks should be placed on coasters, and an iced-tea spoon should be placed to the right of the teaspoon.

CENTERPIECES

Courtesy The Gorham Company

A centerpiece need not be expensive or complicated. For a small table, a few flowers in a simple vase are quite enough. For a larger table, a bowl of fresh fruit, some wild flowers, or colorful vegetables are appropriate. Centerpieces may also be made of dried grasses and weeds; odd-shaped cones, pods, and gourds; potted plants; or branches with brightly colored berries. Figurines of glass, pottery, or metal may be added to make the arrangement more attractive (see page 19). All centerpieces should be low enough for people to see each other across the table.

Courtesy The Cambridge Glass Company

ARRANGING FLOWERS

Courtesy Kelly-Scherrer Flower Shop

The container in which flowers are arranged should be so simple that it does not take attention away from the flowers. It is easy to arrange flowers if you use a flower holder that is fastened to the container with modeling clay. The following suggestions will help you to arrange flowers attractively:

1. Pick the flowers the night before you make the arrangement. Place them in water overnight so that they will last longer and the stems will be erect.

2. Place the tallest flower in the flower holder first in order to get an idea of the height of the arrangement and to make sure that it is fastened securely.

3. Add other flowers of different heights, placing dark ones near the bottom and lighter ones near the top.

4. An odd number of flowers — say, 3, 5, 7, or 9 — will make a more interesting arrangement than an even number.

5. Using some buds, some flowers partly in bloom, and some in full bloom will also add interest.

6. A few well-placed flowers are better than too many.

7. The flower holder should be concealed when the arrangement is complete.

8. Be sure that the arrangement is attractive on all sides unless it is to be placed against a wall or at the end of a table.

Bland

In many homes, all or most of the food is placed on the table in platters or large serving dishes before the family sits down. The serving dishes are then passed to the right, allowing each person to help himself. When this style of service is used, the following points should be kept in mind:

1. The main dish is placed in front of the father, or host, and is usually passed first.
2. The vegetables are placed on either side of the host.
3. The salad and the bread are usually placed near the mother, or hostess, at the end of the table opposite the host.
4. Sugar, butter, jelly, pickles, and similar dishes are placed along the sides of the table.
5. All dishes and silver should be placed so that they can be easily reached by the person who is to start passing.
6. The spoon or the fork needed for serving the food is usually placed to the right of the dish, never in the dish, before the meal is served.

In many busy families today, all the food is put on individual plates in the kitchen to be served to each person at the table. This service saves time in setting the table and in washing the dishes. It is also a convenience for families that have limited space at the table or for families in which someone is on a diet.

Courtesy Texas Hereford Association

In some families — especially when there are guests or when the main dish is a roast or a fowl that has to be carved — the father, or host, carves and serves the meat. The mother, or hostess, may serve the salad and the beverage from the other end of the table. The potatoes and other vegetables may be served by the father with the meat, passed in serving dishes, or served by the mother.

Bland

Serve and remove food on the left side, using your left hand. Never reach in front of the person you are waiting on. Hold the plate or the dish so that you do not put your thumb over the rim.

Serve and remove the beverage on the right side, using your right hand. Hold the glass by the lower part so that your fingers do not touch the top or the inside of the glass. Glasses or cups should be filled to within ½ or ¾ inch of the top. This leaves room for adding sugar and cream or for stirring without spilling.

Hold foods low enough so that the person being waited on can help herself easily.

Photos Courtesy Winn's Stores, Inc

THE TABLE

In clearing the table, remove the serving dishes before the individual plates. Remove all soiled dishes in front of one person before you go to the next person on his right. Never stack the dishes. Sugar, lemon, and cream for the beverage are the only foods remaining on the table. Silver needed for eating the dessert or stirring the beverage is also left.

Use a folded napkin to brush any crumbs from the table before serving the dessert.

When the silver is brought in on the dessert plate, be sure that it is placed so that it will not fall off.

Photos Courtesy Winn's Stores, Inc.

Bland

Buffet style is an ideal way to serve a meal when there is not enough room for everyone to sit around the table or when you are eating out of doors. For a buffet meal, arrange all the food, silver, dishes, and linen on the table so that each person can help himself. The following points will be helpful:

1. Plan the kind of menu you would for any other meal — that is, have a main dish, one or two vegetables, a salad, bread, a dessert, and a beverage — but have food that is easy to serve and easy to eat. For example, casseroles, creamed dishes, and meat loaf, which do not require the use of a knife, are appropriate.

2. Push the table against a wall if the room is small and more space is needed. If the room is large, you may leave the table in the center so that guests may serve themselves from both sides of the table.

3. Place the main dish and the plates at one end of the table.

4. Put vegetables, salads, relishes, and bread along the side of the table, close enough to the edge to be reached easily.

5. Place the beverage, the silver, and the napkins at the other end of the table to be picked up last.

6. Provide a small table or a tray for each guest when possible.

7. Place the dessert on the table later, allowing each person to serve himself, or have the dessert served to each guest.

ACTIVITIES

Comparing types of table service:

1. Describe the way in which you set the table and serve meals at home. What other ways are there, and what are the advantages of each?
2. Practice setting the table for each type of table service described on pages 24 and 25.
3. Bring to class three pictures of attractively arranged tables, and discuss how the hostess probably intended to serve the meal.

Deciding what the cover should include:

4. Plan a simple menu. Then make a list of the glasses, silver, and china that will be needed by each person to be served. Next, make a drawing of the cover, showing where each item is to be placed on the table.
5. Bring to class pictures of linens, glassware, china, and silverware that seem to belong together.
6. Demonstrate how to fold napkins of different sizes. Then show various ways in which napkins may be placed on the table.

Placing the china, glassware, and silver on the table:

7. Demonstrate where the following are usually placed: *(a)* dinner plate, *(b)* bread-and-butter plate, *(c)* salad plate, and *(d)* cup and saucer. When they may be placed elsewhere, explain.
8. Demonstrate where the following are usually placed: *(a)* goblet or water glass, *(b)* glass for fruit juice, iced drink, or milk, *(c)* cup and saucer, and *(d)* napkin. When they may be placed elsewhere, explain.

Deciding what makes a good centerpiece:

9. Arrange on the bulletin board pictures of attractive but simple and inexpensive centerpieces.
10. Have a demonstration of flower arrangements. Then have each girl make an attractive arrangement using whatever she wishes. Ask judges to select the best arrangements, and display them.
11. Take turns making simple flower arrangements for the homemaking department. See if you can get new ideas for centerpieces or arrangements.

Learning to wait on the table correctly:

12. Practice waiting on the table and removing the dishes. Ask friends to act as host, hostess, and two guests.

Bland

Chapter 3 | **MEALTIME MANNERS**

Understanding good table manners and using them at all times will help you to avoid embarrassment and give you poise.

Mealtime manners are important not only when you are a guest at someone's home but also when you are eating in the school cafeteria, in a public restaurant, or in your own home.

Mealtime is usually one of the few times that the family is together, and it should be one of the most enjoyable times of the day. Some of the ways in which you can help to make it pleasant are these:

1. Be on time for meals, and go to the table as soon as the meal is ready. If you are delayed away from home for some reason that cannot be helped, telephone your mother.

2. Be careful about your appearance. See that your hair is combed, that your hands and nails are clean, and that you are dressed neatly and presentably.

3. Be courteous by not starting to eat until all have been served, by observing the rules of good manners, and by not leaving the table until you have asked to be excused.

4. Be cheerful and interested in what other people have to say, and share with them your own experiences of the day.

GIVING THANKS

Many families say grace — that is, ask a blessing and give thanks — before eating. Grace is usually said after everyone is seated. The following are three forms which are widely known and used.

Protestant

Bless, O Lord, this food to our use, and us to Thy service, and make us ever mindful of the needs of others, in Jesus' Name. Amen.

Catholic

Bless us, O Lord, and these Thy gifts, which we are about to receive from Thy bounty, through Christ our Lord. Amen.

Jewish

Lift up your hands toward the sanctuary and bless the Lord. Blessed art Thou, O Lord our God, Ruler of the Universe, Who bringest forth bread from the earth. Amen.

Elicson

WHERE PEOPLE SHOULD SIT

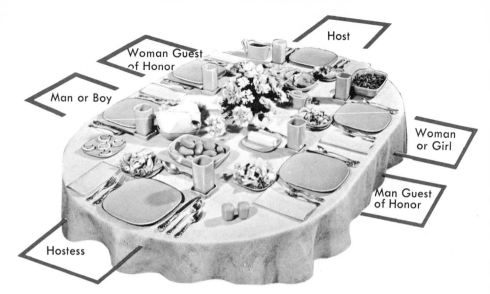

Design Studio

For family meals, each person in the family usually sits at the same place at the table. Thus there is no problem about seating.

When the family has guests for a meal, the hostess, or mother, decides ahead of time where each person is to sit. The above illustration shows the usual arrangement of places at the dining table when guests are present. Note the places of the host, the hostess, the woman guest of honor, the man guest of honor, the girl or the woman guest, and the boy or the man guest.

When there are guests, the mother, or hostess, announces that dinner is ready and leads the way into the dining room. She directs each person to his place at the table as he enters.

Usually the girl or the woman guests follow the hostess into the dining room. Naturally, however, an older woman or a guest of honor is the first to follow the hostess.

The host is last to enter the dining room.

As people are assigned their places at the table, they stand behind their chairs until everyone is at his place and the host and hostess start to sit down. Then each man and boy assists the woman or the girl nearest to him in being seated before he himself sits down.

When the meal is over, the hostess rises. At this signal, the men and the boys rise immediately to assist the women and the girls next to them. Then they stand aside to allow the women and the girls to leave the dining room ahead

of them.

PASSING FOOD

When possible, all food should be passed to the right. The person to whom it is passed should take the dish with her right hand. However, if it is more convenient to pass food to the left, then all food should be passed in that direction.

The main dish should be passed first, followed by the potatoes and other vegetables.

After taking a dish with your right hand, transfer it to your left hand in order to serve yourself. Then pass the dish on with your left hand to the next person.

If you are asked to pass something, put the serving spoon or fork in the dish so that the handle is toward the person who is to receive it.

When passing a pitcher or any other dish with a handle, turn the handle toward the person on your right who is to receive it. In this way, she can take it with her right hand and pour from it easily.

USING SILVER

When you are undecided about which piece of silver to use in eating something, watch your hostess for cues. These general rules may also help:

1. A knife should be used only when the food cannot be cut with a fork.
2. A spoon should never be used when you can use a fork.
3. Only very dry or firm foods should be eaten with the fingers.

Bland

Knife Foods	Fork Foods	Spoon Foods	Finger Foods
Steaks, chops, other meat, and fowl*	Vegetables (unless very liquid)	Soups	Bread and rolls
		Stewed tomatoes	Crackers
Fish that has to be boned	Potatoes	Ice cream	Toast
	Seafood	Creamed vegetables	Most sandwiches
Butter, jelly, cheese, and food that has to be spread	Croquettes	Cantaloupe	Cookies
	Waffles and griddlecakes	Fruit cocktail	Small cakes
	Eggs	Citrus fruits	Nuts
	Large pieces of cake or small pieces that are too soft to be picked up with the fingers	Puddings	Celery
			Olives
		Custards	Crisp bacon
		Cereals	Potato chips
		Cooked fruits	Radishes
	Shortcakes		Corn on the cob
	Pies		Grapes
	Watermelon		Cherries
	Hamburger patties		Candy
	Meat loaf		

*At informal social events, at some restaurants, or at home, it is permissible to eat fried chicken with the fingers if everyone else does.

From Beery: "Manners Made Easy," McGraw-Hill Book Company, Inc. Photo by Robert K. Waldron

In cutting meat with a knife and a fork, hold the prongs of the fork down. The ends of the handles of both the knife and the fork should touch the palms of your hands. Hold your hands in such a position that your elbows do not stick out to bother the people seated on either side of you. Cut only one or two bite-sized pieces of meat at one time.

Shift the fork to your right hand after cutting, and lift the food to your mouth with the prongs of the fork up.

The European custom is to leave the fork in the left hand and to raise the fork to the mouth with the prongs down.

From Beery: "Manners Made Easy," McGraw-Hill Book Company, Inc. Photo by Robert K. Waldron

HOW TO USE SPOONS

When Eating Soup

1. Dip the spoon away from you.

2. Fill the spoon about two-thirds full. Allow the spoon to drip before raising it to your mouth.

3. Bring the spoon up to your mouth. Never bend your head down to the spoon.

4. Eat the soup from the side of the spoon noiselessly.

5. When you finish, leave the spoon in the dish.

When Taking Sugar

Use the spoon in the sugar bowl to put sugar in a beverage. Never use your own spoon.

Courtesy Stix, Baer, and Fuller, St. Louis

When Stirring a Beverage

1. When it is necessary to stir a beverage, do so quietly and only two or three times around.

2. If you wish to taste a beverage, sip it from the side of the spoon rather than from the tip.

3. When you remove the spoon, place it on the coaster or the saucer — never on the tablecloth.

Bland

Bland

When you lift a glass:

This   Not This

When you lift a goblet:

This   Not This

When you lift a cup:

This   Not This

When you have finished using a beverage spoon:

38 This   Not This

WHEN EATING

When you take bread:

This   Not This

When you butter bread:

This   Not This

When you are not using your knife and fork:

This   Not This

When you have finished using a dessert spoon:

This   Not This

DURING THE MEAL

Always . . .

. . . sit well back in your chair so that you do not touch the table with your body.

. . . keep your left hand in your lap when you are not using it.

. . . keep your mouth closed when chewing food.

. . . chew your food well.

. . . contribute to the conversation.

. . . compliment your mother when she serves something that you especially like.

Never . . .

. . . put your feet on the chair or cross your knees. Instead, keep both feet close together on the floor or cross your ankles.

. . . play or motion with the silver.

. . . draw in when eating soup or a hot beverage.

. . . blow on your food to cool it.

. . . hold your head down over the plate when you eat. Instead, bring the food up to your mouth.

. . . hold a piece of bread in one hand while you eat with the other. Instead, lay the bread on the bread-and-butter plate or on the rim of the dinner plate when eating another food.

. . . put too much food in your mouth at one time.

. . . speak while you have food in your mouth.

. . . put your elbows on the table.

. . . put a knife in your mouth.

. . . reach across the table.

. . . stretch, yawn, or belch.

. . . pick your teeth or roll your tongue to dislodge food.

. . . argue or quarrel at the table.

. . mention that you have eaten too much or that you feel full or uncomfortable at the end of a meal.

From Beery: "Manners Made Easy," McGraw-Hill Book Company, Inc. Photo by Robert K. Waldron

When you have finished eating the main course, place your knife and fork across the center of the plate to indicate that you have finished.

Fold a cloth napkin when you are in your own home or when you are visiting and you expect to be back for the next meal. But you should crumple it when you are eating out or when you are a guest for only one meal.

Paper napkins should always be crumpled.

Bland   *From the McGraw-Hill Filmstrip "Table Talk"*

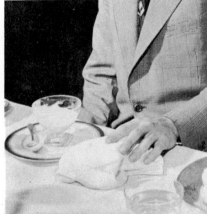

At what time should I arrive? Plan to arrive about 10 minutes before the meal is to be served.

Where should I sit at the table? Your hostess will tell you where to sit. (See page 32.)

What should I do when I am not sure that grace is to be said? When you are not sure that grace is to be said, watch your hostess. Do not start to talk until you are sure that it will not be said.

When should I open my napkin? When the hostess picks up her napkin, open yours. Then spread it over your lap. Do not tuck it in your clothing.

When should I begin to eat? You may begin anytime after your hostess has started to eat.

How should I pass the food? When the hostess suggests that you help yourself first before passing food, do so. Otherwise, you should pass the food to the person on your right. (See page 34.)

Bland

Accidents are embarrassing, of course, but they should not disturb you so much that you do not enjoy **42** the meal.

What should I do if there is no serving spoon? Ask your hostess for one. Never use your own spoon to take food from a general serving dish.

What should I do when asked for my choice of food? Tell your hostess honestly if you have a preference. Do not say, "It doesn't matter," unless you mean it.

What should I do when I do not like a food that is served? By the time you become a teen-ager; you should be able to eat all foods. Even though you may like some things better than others, take a small amount of all foods served. At least taste everything.

Is it all right to ask for a second helping? Yes, provided the hostess suggests it or the food is passed to you. If it is necessary to pass your plate to the head of the table for a second helping, be sure that your knife and fork are placed across the plate so that they will not fall off.

FOR A DINNER GUEST

How do I refuse food when I have had enough? Merely say, "No thank you." Never decline by saying, "I am full" or "I am stuffed already."

What should I do if I want something on the table that has not been offered? Merely say, "Will you please pass the . . ." or "Please pass the. . . ." Never reach for a food unless it is directly in front of you.

What should I do if I have to remove something from my mouth? Use your thumb and first finger to remove the object from your mouth, and put it on the rim of your plate.

What should I do if I have an accident at the table? Apologize sincerely but briefly by saying, "I am sorry." Then do not mention the accident again during the meal. If, however, you have damaged or broken something, you should later offer to replace it or have it repaired. If you drop a piece of silver, leave it on the floor. Your hostess will give you another.

What should I do if I have to cough or sneeze at the table? Turn your head, and use your napkin to shelter your face. If you are choking or have a fit of coughing, ask to be excused from the table.

What should I talk about? Talk about anything that will be of interest to everyone present. Be careful, though, not to monopolize the conversation, and listen to others with interest. Avoid getting into an argument, talking about anything unpleasant, or discussing your diet.

How should I indicate that I have finished eating? See page 41.

How will I know when to leave the table? When the hostess puts her napkin on the table, it is a signal that the meal is over and that you may leave the table.

How long should I stay after the meal? Stay for a reasonable length of time unless your hostess indicates that she has something else planned for the evening.

Courtesy Stix, Baer, and Fuller, St. Louis

Before you leave, thank both your hostess and her mother. When the visit is ended, leave without delay.

43

MANNERS IN PUBLIC EATING PLACES

Courtesy Stix, Baer, and Fuller, St. Louis

In the School Cafeteria . . .

. . . take your time in line, and do not push or crowd. Remember that good manners are contagious.

. . . select your food quickly, and have the correct change ready so that you do not hold up the other students.

. . . be friendly with everyone, and do not sit with the same group every day unless you have been assigned to a definite table.

. . . try to keep the conversation pleasant and interesting.

. . . do not be so childish as to show off, throw things, or create a lot of noise.

. . . put used straws, bottle tops, and napkins on the tray or in the wastebasket instead of stuffing them in the bottles.

. . . leave the table clean when you finish eating.

In a Snack Bar or Drugstore . . .

. . . your manners should be the same as they would be in a nice restaurant. (See page 45.)

. . . be careful not to become so interested in other people or what is going on at another table that you neglect the person you are with.

. . . avoid making a nuisance of yourself by performing tricks, calling across the room, talking loudly, or damaging or misusing property.

. . . it is all right to stay at the table for a while after you finish eating if other people are not waiting for a table.

In a Restaurant . . .

. . . a boy removes his hat and topcoat as soon as he enters.

. . . the waiter or the escort should lead the way to the table and assist the girl in being seated.

. . . the girl should remove her coat and gloves as soon as she is seated. She should leave her purse and gloves in her lap, never on the table.

. . . it is all right to ask the waiter to explain anything you do not understand on the menu and to describe dishes with which you are not familiar.

. . . a considerate girl will not order the most expensive dishes on the menu.

. . . the girl usually tells the boy what she would like to have. The boy gives the order to the waiter for both of them. However, it is all right for the girl to give her order directly to the waiter if he asks for it.

. . . the boy should always rise whenever it is necessary for the girl to leave the table.

Courtesy Stix, Baer, and Fuller, St. Louis

When a boy seats a girl at the table, he pulls out her chair in such a way that she can sit down easily from the left side. As she sits down, he gradually pushes the chair in closer to the table. On leaving the table, he helps her in much the same way. He pulls the chair back gradually as she rises and leaves from the left side.

ACTIVITIES

Learning the importance of good table manners:

1. Discuss the importance of: *(a)* knowing what to do in order to have good table manners and *(b)* using good table manners at home.
2. Plan ways in which girls in the homemaking class can help other students to improve their table manners in the school cafeteria. Consider making posters, planning a program for a school assembly, and setting a good example.
3. Have a contest for the best composition on the importance of good table manners.

Learning to have good table manners:

4. Set a table in the laboratory, and demonstrate the following: *(a)* helping someone to be seated in a chair at the table, *(b)* sitting down from the left of the chair so that everyone can be seated at the same time, *(c)* unfolding the napkin and using it, *(d)* eating soup, *(e)* passing food, *(f)* cutting meat with a knife and fork, *(g)* eating with a fork, *(h)* taking a drink of water, *(i)* using a bread-and-butter plate and a butter spreader, and *(j)* leaving the knife, fork, and spoon correctly at the end of the meal.

Discussing problems of mealtime manners:

5. Describe the table manners of various people you have seen on TV.
6. Name as many foods as you can, in addition to the ones listed on page 35, which may be eaten with the fingers.
7. Describe a time when you were embarrassed because of an accident at the table, and tell what you did about it.
8. Make a list of points in table manners which you and your classmates need to improve. Discuss ways of forming good table manners.
9. List do's and don't's for carrying on a conversation at the table.

Sharing the responsibilities at mealtime:

10. Discuss ways in which you and your brother or sister may help during a meal.
11. Arrange on the bulletin board pictures of families enjoying a meal.

Eating out:

12. Plan a project for improving table manners in the school cafeteria. For example, you may prepare posters with pictures and slogans. Ask a home economics teacher to evaluate your selections.
13. With the help of some of your classmates, give a skit in class on how to order in a restaurant.
14. Plan a program for assembly showing good and bad manners in a snack bar, a drugstore, or a restaurant.

Chapter 4 | # YOUR FOOD NEEDS

In the United States, there is more than enough food for everyone. Yet studies show that nearly half of the teen-agers are undernourished, not because they do not get enough to eat, but because they do not eat the right kinds of food. Boys and girls who do not eat enough of the right kinds of food may become nervous and irritable. They may also tire easily, have poor complexions, or develop tooth decay.

In order to be healthy, you must eat a variety of foods so that your body will be supplied with all the nutrients: carbohydrates, fats, proteins, minerals, and vitamins. In general, your body needs the nutrients for the following purposes: (1) to give you energy and to keep you warm (see page 55), (2) to help you grow and to repair parts of your body (see page 57), and (3) to regulate the processes of your body and to protect it from disease (see page 59).

In order to help you easily plan meals that include foods with the necessary nutrients, the U.S. Department of Agriculture has developed *A Daily Food Guide,* in which foods are divided into four groups: the Milk Group, the Meat Group, the Vegetable–Fruit Group, and the Bread–Cereal Group.

A DAILY FOOD GUIDE*

A *Daily Food Guide,* offered by the United States Department of Agriculture, includes four food groups. You should eat a certain amount of each group daily. The four groups are:

Milk Group

Foods Included
Milk . . . fluid whole, evaporated, skim, dry, buttermilk.
Cheese . . . cottage; cream; cheddar-type — natural or processed.
Ice cream.

Contribution to Diet
Milk is our leading source of calcium, which is needed for bones and teeth. It also provides high-quality protein, riboflavin, vitamin A, and many other nutrients.

Amounts Recommended
Some milk every day for everyone: children, 3 to 4 cups; teen-agers, 4 or more cups; adults, 2 or more cups. Part or all of the milk may be fluid skim milk, buttermilk, evaporated milk, or dry milk. Cheese and ice cream may replace part of the milk. The amount of either it will take to replace a given amount of milk is figured on the basis of calcium content. Common portions of various kinds of cheese and of ice cream and their milk equivalents are:

1-inch cube cheddar-type cheese = ⅔ cup milk
½ cup cottage cheese = ⅓ cup milk
2 tablespoons cream cheese = 1 tablespoon milk
½ cup ice cream = ¼ cup milk

*Source: USDA Leaflet 424.

Courtesy National Dairy Council

Meat Group

Foods Included

Beef; veal; lamb; pork; variety meats, such as liver, heart, kidney.
Poultry and eggs.
Fish and shellfish.
As alternates — dry beans, dry peas, lentils, nuts, peanuts, peanut butter.

Contribution to Diet

Foods in this group are valued for their protein, which is needed for growth and repair of body tissues — muscle, organs, blood, skin, and hair. These foods also provide iron, thiamine, riboflavin, and niacin.

Amounts Recommended

Choose 2 or more servings every day. Count as a serving: 2 to 3 ounces of lean cooked meat, poultry, or fish — all without bone; 2 eggs; 1 cup cooked dry beans, dry peas, or lentils; 4 tablespoons peanut butter.

Courtesy National Dairy Council

Vegetable-Fruit Group

Foods Included

All vegetables and fruit. This guide emphasizes those that are valuable as sources of vitamin C and vitamin A.

Sources of Vitamin C

Good sources. — Grapefruit or grapefruit juice; orange or orange juice; cantaloup; guava; mango; papaya; raw strawberries; broccoli; green pepper; sweet red pepper.

Fair sources. — Honeydew melon; tangerine or tangerine juice; watermelon; asparagus tips; brussels sprouts; raw cabbage; collards; garden cress; kale; kohlrabi; mustard greens; potatoes and sweetpotatoes cooked in the jacket; spinach; tomatoes or tomato juice; turnip greens.

Sources of Vitamin A

Dark-green and deep-yellow vegetables and a few fruits, namely: Apricots, broccoli, cantaloup, carrots, chard, collards, cress, kale, mango, persimmon, pumpkin, spinach, sweetpotatoes, turnip greens and other dark-green leaves, winter squash.

Contribution to Diet

Fruits and vegetables are valuable chiefly because of the vitamins and minerals they contain. In this plan, this group is counted on to supply nearly all the vitamin C needed and over half of the vitamin A.

Vitamin C is needed for healthy gums and body tissues. Vitamin A is needed for growth, normal vision, and healthy condition of skin and other body surfaces.

Amounts Recommended

Choose 4 or more servings every day, including:

1 serving of a good source of vitamin C or 2 servings of a fair source.
1 serving, at least every other day, of a good source of vitamin A.

If the food chosen for vitamin C is also a good source of vitamin A, the additional serving of a vitamin A food may be omitted. The remaining 1 to 3 or more servings may be of any vegetable or fruit, including those that are valuable for vitamin C and vitamin A.

Count as 1 serving: ½ cup of vegetable or fruit; or a portion as ordinarily served, such as 1 medium apple, banana, orange, or potato, or half of a medium grapefruit or cantaloup.

Courtesy "What's New In Home Economics"

Bread-Cereal Group

Foods Included

All breads and cereals that are whole grain, enriched, or restored; *check labels to be sure.*

Specifically, this group includes: Breads, cooked cereals; ready-to-eat cereals; cornmeal; crackers; flour; grits; macaroni and spaghetti; noodles; rice; rolled oats; and quick breads and other baked goods if made with whole-grain or enriched flour.

Contribution to Diet

Foods in this group furnish worthwhile amounts of protein, iron, several of the B-vitamins, and food energy.

Amounts Recommended

Choose 4 servings or more daily. Or, if no cereals are chosen, have an extra serving of breads or baked goods, which will make at least 5 servings from this group daily.

Count as 1 serving: 1 slice of bread; 1 ounce ready-to-eat cereal; ½ to ¾ cup cooked cereal, cornmeal, grits, macaroni, noodles, rice or spaghetti.

Other Foods

Everyone uses some other foods — such as butter, margarine, other fats, oils, and sugars — which supply calories and add to the total nutrients in meals.

A DAILY FOOD GUIDE*

FOOD GROUP	DAILY REQUIREMENT

Meat Group

Beef, veal, pork, lamb, poultry,
    fish, eggs

Alternates: dry beans, dry peas, nuts

2 or more servings

Milk Group

Milk, cheese, ice cream

Children	3 to 4 cups
Teen-agers	4 or more cups
Adults	2 or more cups

Vegetable-Fruit Group

Include: A citrus fruit or other fruit
or vegetable important for vitamin C

A dark-green or deep-yellow vegetable for vitamin A at least every
other day

Other vegetables and fruits, including potatoes

4 or more servings

Bread-Cereal Group

Whole grain, enriched, or restored

4 or more servings

NOTE: *A Daily Food Guide* does not include butter and margarine because it is
assumed that adequate amounts will be obtained if meals are well balanced.

---

*Source: USDA Leaflet 424.

Courtesy Personal Products, Inc.

Foods which contain carbohydrates, fats, and proteins give you energy to work and to play. They also help to keep you warm. People who are active or do hard physical work need more energy foods than those who are less active.

Carbohydrates are divided into two groups: sugars and starches, as shown in the chart on page 55. It is better to get the sugar (energy) your body needs from milk or fruit than to get it from candy, pies, or jellies because milk and fruit supply your body with minerals and vitamins as well. (See pages 59 and 60.)

Fats furnish more energy than do carbohydrates. But because more foods in our diet contain carbohydrates than contain fats, we get most of our energy from carbohydrates.

Proteins furnish some energy. But since the chief function of proteins is to build and repair the body (see pages 56 and 57), it is better to get energy from the foods that contain carbohydrates and fats.

Bob Taylor

54

THE ENERGY FOODS

NUTRIENTS	FOODS WHICH CONTAIN THESE NUTRIENTS	WHAT THESE NUTRIENTS DO FOR YOU
Carbohydrates Sugars	Cakes, pies, candy, and other sweets	Give you energy to work and play. Help to keep you warm.
Starches	Breads Cereals Cereal products Potatoes	
Fats	Butter Margarine Salad oils Shortening Fat meats	Give you energy to work and play. Help to keep you warm.
Proteins High-quality (complete)	*Foods which come from animals:* Meat, fish, and poultry Eggs Milk and milk products *Foods which come from plants:* Seeds, especially soybeans and peanuts	Give you energy to work and play. Help to keep you warm. Build and repair the body.
Incomplete	*Foods which come from plants:* Vegetables such as peas, beans and corn Breads Cereals and cereal products *Foods which come from animals:* Gelatin	

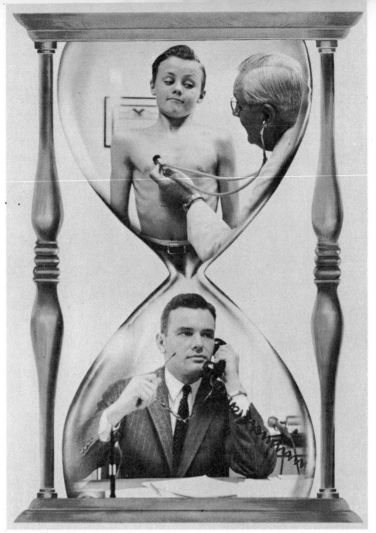

Courtesy New York Life Insurance Company

The foods which contain proteins and minerals help to build and repair your body. Since boys and girls are growing, it is very important that they get enough proteins. Those who do not get enough proteins may be stunted in growth or have weak muscles and bones.

Proteins come from animals (meat, poultry, fish, eggs, and milk) and plants. "Complete proteins" have all the essential amino acids your body needs. Large amounts of them are found in animal products. Seeds contain some complete proteins because baby plants need them in their early growth period.

Most plants contain some protein, but the proteins found in any single plant are likely to contain only part of the amino acids your body needs. They are said to contain "incomplete protein."

Minerals are found in the soil. As various plants grow, they absorb these minerals. Then by eating these plants and by eating meat from animals that

have eaten these plants, we obtain the minerals we need for our bodies.

FOODS THAT BUILD AND REPAIR

NUTRIENTS	FOODS WHICH CONTAIN THESE NUTRIENTS	WHAT THESE NUTRIENTS DO FOR YOU
Proteins High-quality (Complete)	*Foods which come from animals:* Meat, fish, and poultry Eggs Milk and milk products *Foods which come from plants:* Seeds, especially soybeans and peanuts	Build and repair the body. Furnish energy. Keep the body warm.
Incomplete	*Foods which come from plants:* Vegetables such as peas, beans, and corn Breads Cereals and cereal products *Foods which come from animals:* Gelatin	Build and repair the body. Furnish energy. Keep the body warm.
Minerals Calcium Phosphorus Iron Iodine	See the chart on page 59.	See the chart on page 59.

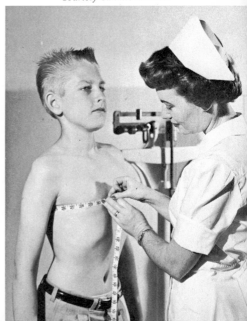

Foods which contain minerals and vitamins help to regulate the body processes, such as elimination, digestion, and circulation.

Minerals help to build and repair the body, but they also help to regulate the body (see page 59). For example, iron is used in the blood to help carry oxygen to all parts of the body. Without calcium the blood would not clot when you cut yourself.

Vitamins help to keep you healthy and to make you grow and develop. Without the help of vitamins the body cannot use proteins and minerals to build and repair. Each vitamin has specific ways in which it helps to regulate the body. One vitamin cannot replace another, but in some cases their work is very similar.

FOODS THAT REGULATE THE BODY

NUTRIENTS	FOODS WHICH CONTAIN THESE NUTRIENTS	WHAT THESE NUTRIENTS DO FOR YOU
Minerals Calcium	Milk and milk products Green, leafy vegetables, such as turnip greens and kale Molasses Legumes (dry peas and dry beans)	Builds strong bones, teeth, and fingernails. Aids in keeping various muscles working, such as the heart. Aids the nervous system. Helps blood to clot.
Phosphorus	If you eat enough foods that contain proteins and calcium, you will have enough phosphorus in your diet.	Helps calcium to build bones and teeth.
Iron	Liver and other variety meats, such as heart, brains, sweetbreads Egg yolk Lean meat (especially beef) Dried yeast Molasses Green, leafy vegetables Fresh and dried fruit	Builds hemoglobin, which carries oxygen to all parts of the body through the blood stream.
Iodine	Salt-water fish and seafood Iodized salt Vegetables and fruits grown in soil which contains iodine	Helps the thyroid gland to work properly and the body cells to use their food at the correct rate of speed.
Vitamins Vitamin A	Dark-green and deep-yellow vegetables, namely, broccoli, carrots, chard, collards, cress, kale, pumpkin, spinach, sweetpotatoes, turnip greens and other dark-green leaves, winter squash A few fruits, namely, apricots, cantaloupe, mangoes, persimmons Liver and other variety meats Fish-liver oils Whole milk, cream, and butter Egg yolk	Helps to keep the eyes in good condition. Helps the eyes to adjust to dim light. Prevents infections by keeping the linings of the nose, throat, and stomach in healthy condition. Helps in the development of teeth, especially the enamel. Improves health in general.

NUTRIENTS	FOODS WHICH CONTAIN THESE NUTRIENTS	WHAT THESE NUTRIENTS DO FOR YOU
Vitamin B B₁ (thiamine)	Liver and other variety meats Pork (lean) Milk Egg yolk Dry beans and soybeans Whole-grain and enriched cereals Yeast	Promotes growth and good health in general. Helps to stimulate the appetite. Aids in digesting food. Helps to steady the nerves. Improves the morale. Helps the body to obtain energy from carbohydrates.
B₂ (riboflavin)	Liver and other variety meats Lean meat Eggs Milk Dark-green vegetables	Stimulates growth and is necessary for good health. Keeps skin, hair, and eyes in good condition. Helps to prevent infection. Aids the digestive and nervous systems. Helps thiamine to obtain energy from carbohydrates.
Niacin	Liver and other variety meats Lean meat Fish Peanut butter Whole-grain and enriched cereals	Promotes growth and good health in general. Aids the digestive and nervous systems. Helps thiamine to make the best use of carbohydrates. Aids the health of the skin.
Vitamin C	Grapefruit or grapefruit juice Orange or orange juice Cantaloupe, guava, mangoes, papaya, raw strawberries Broccoli, green peppers, and sweet red peppers	Promotes normal growth. Helps to develop bones, teeth, and gums. Builds strong body cells and blood vessels.
Vitamin D (the sunshine vitamin)	Fish-liver oils Egg yolk	Develops strong bones and teeth. Helps the body to use calcium and phosphorus.

The skins of such fruits as apples and grapes; the fiber or strings of celery; the membrane (white part) of oranges; the stringy material in pineapple, plums, and peaches; and the rough, woody part of whole-grain cereal are called "roughage." It is sometimes referred to as "bulk" or "cellulose."

Roughage is made up of carbohydrates. But since roughage is not digested in the body, it does not produce energy. However, as the roughage passes through the digestive tract, it acts like a small brush and takes with it the other foods which have not been digested or used by the body.

Bland

Water is not considered a food, but it plays a very important part in regulating the body. Water is used in the body to:

1. Help dissolve food so that it can be digested.

2. Take the digested foods to various parts of the body.

3. Remove the waste from the body.

4. Help regulate the temperature of the body.

From two-thirds to three-fourths of the weight of the body is made up of water. As this water is given off by the kidneys or by perspiration, it must be replaced. The average person should have from six to eight glasses of water each day.

Courtesy Personal Products, Inc.

ACTIVITIES

Learning about the nutrients:
1. What are the five important nutrients?
2. Besides the nutrients, what else is necessary for good health?
3. What do carbohydrates do for your body?
4. What foods did you eat today that contain carbohydrates (see chart on page 55) ? Were they sugar or starches?
5. What do proteins do for your body?
6. Name two foods that have high-quality (complete) proteins and two that have incomplete proteins.
7. Name five protein dishes which your family enjoys. Decide whether the proteins are high-quality (complete) or incomplete.
8. What do fats do for your body?
9. What foods did you eat today that contain fats?
10. What do minerals do for your body?
11. What foods did you eat today that contain minerals?
12. What do vitamins do for your body?
13. What foods did you eat today that contain vitamins?
14. Collect advertisements of vitamin pills. Discuss how these advertisements may sometimes leave the wrong impression.
15. Name four foods that are a good source of vitamin C.
16. With the help of your classmates, work out an attractive bulletin board with pictures cut from magazines illustrating what each of the nutrients does for the body.

Using *A Daily Food Guide:*
17. List 10 foods that you enjoy eating. Check to see in which groups of *A Daily Food Guide* each is found.
18. Keep a record of the foods you eat for 1 day, and compare them with the foods recommended in *A Daily Food Guide*. Tell what foods you should eat to improve your diet and make it adequate.
19. Select one menu each for breakfast, lunch, and dinner from a magazine or a newspaper. Then check to see whether they include the correct number of servings of foods according to *A Daily Food Guide*.

Developing good eating habits:
20. Make a list of things you and other members of your class might do to improve the food habits of the students in your school. For example, you might make posters or plan an assembly program about what food does for your body.
21. Tell about people you know who have improved their eating habits.
22. Report to the class on an article on nutrition that you have read in a newspaper or a magazine.

Chapter 5 | # PLANNING YOUR MEALS

In America, most people eat three meals a day: breakfast, lunch, and dinner (or breakfast, dinner, and supper). The heaviest meal of the day is called "dinner" whether it is served at noon or in the evening. When dinner is served in the evening, the noon meal is called "lunch." If dinner is eaten at noon, the evening meal is called "supper." It is not a good idea to have one or two very light meals and another very heavy meal. It is much better to keep all three meals about the same size.

A good meal, whether it is breakfast, lunch, or dinner, requires planning. A homemaker must know how to plan for, shop for, prepare, and serve meals so that they are nutritious, flavorful, and attractive.

Your mother may not write down what she plans to serve for each meal. However, since you have not had very much experience, you should write down your menus. A menu is a list of the foods to be served at any one meal. A course is the food served at any one time during a meal. For example, soup is a course, meat is another course, and dessert is still another. Most family meals consist of only two courses: the main course (meat, vegetables, salad, and bread) and the dessert course.

63

Bland

PLANNING

When planning menus, consider the following:

1. *Nutrition:* that is, the foods necessary for good health that are available. (See page 66.)

2. *The family:* the number of people, their ages, health, occupations, activities, likes and dislikes. (See page 67.)

3. *The budget:* how to get the most out of the amount of money allowed for food without exceeding that amount. (See Chapter 11.)

4. *Time:* how long it will take to prepare a meal, the amount of experience you have had, and the amount of time you have available. (See pages 68 and 69.)

5. *Variety:* in the kinds of food, the color, the size and shape, the texture, the flavor, and the methods of preparation. (See pages 70–73.)

WRITING

1. List the foods in the order in which they are to be served.
2. List together foods that are to be served together.
3. List the beverage last or with the dessert.

Courtesy Household Finance Corporation

MENUS

Planning menus in advance saves time, energy, and money and assures nutritious, flavorful, attractive meals because . . .

... it is a way to make sure that the family members get the foods they need each day, that is, by including the foods in *A Daily Food Guide.*

... it provides an opportunity to take advantage of the best buys reported in the newspapers.

... it allows time to look for new ideas in cookbooks, magazines, and newspapers.

... it usually results in variety in meals.

... it gives an opportunity to plan for the preparation of some foods for more than one meal and to make use of leftovers.

... it reduces the number of trips to the grocery store.

... it eliminates last-minute rush and the need to decide every night what to have for dinner.

A MENU

4. Capitalize the names of all dishes.
5. Leave a margin around the list.

For examples of menus, see page 74.

PLANNING MEALS FOR GOOD NUTRITION

Photos Courtesy National Dairy Council

1. Foods from each group of *A Daily Food Guide* should be included in meals every day. However, it is not necessary that each meal contain foods from all four groups. (See Chapter 4.)

2. To be sure that all foods needed for good health are included, it is usually best to plan all three meals at one time. The menu for one meal leads into the menu for another. For example, if you do not serve eggs for breakfast, you might serve deviled eggs for lunch or egg custard for dinner.

3. Meals that are eaten away from home should also be considered when planning meals for the day.

4. In planning lunch or dinner, first select a meat or a meat substitute as the main dish. Then choose the vegetables, that is, the potatoes and one or two other vegetables, preferably a dark-green or a deep-yellow vegetable (see page 50). A meal may be planned with the meat and the vegetables combined in one main dish, as in a stew or a casserole.

5. Sweets may be included in the meals, but they should not crowd out or take the place of foods which are essential. Whenever possible, it is wise to include such desserts as fruit, custard, and ice cream, which contain foods listed in *A Daily Food Guide*.

When planning meals, first select a meat or a meat alternate for the main dish. Then choose the salad, the vegetables, and other foods to add variety in color, size and shape, texture, and flavor. (See pages 70 and 71.)

Courtesy Evaporated Milk Association

Salads may be served: (1) at the beginning of a meal, (2) as the main dish of a light meal, (3) with the meat and potatoes of a heavy meal, (4) in place of a dessert, or (5) for a party refreshment. Regardless of when they are served, cool, colorful, crisp salads stimulate the appetite, brighten up a meal, and provide a contrast to the other foods served.

Courtesy United Fruit Company

Courtesy Ac'cent International

When selecting the vegetables for a meal, serve one or more watery vegetables, such as tomatoes, celery, lettuce or spinach, but no more than one starchy vegetable. Avoid, if possible, serving two vegetables of the same color, flavor, type, or shape.

Pies, cakes, and other rich desserts may be included in meals, but they should not crowd out or take the place of foods which are essential. Whenever possible, it is wise to include such desserts as fruits, custards, ice cream, and other foods which are listed in *A Daily Food Guide.*

PLANNING MEALS FOR FAMILY MEMBERS

1. The number of people in the family has some effect on the homemaker's decisions about what foods to have and how to prepare them. For example, for a large family a one-bowl salad or a large dessert takes less time to prepare than individual salads and desserts.

2. The ages and particular needs of the family members should be considered. Babies and small children need different types of food from those needed by older people. Growing teen-agers need more food than adults. Old people or people on a diet may need special foods.

3. **The kinds of work and activities of the members of the family make a difference in the planning. People who are engaged in outdoor work or are active in sports need more high-energy foods (potatoes, bread, and cereals) than do those who take little exercise.**

4. Of course, the homemaker should remember the likes and dislikes of the different family members as she plans her menus. However, no one person should be catered to at the expense of the other members of the family. An effort should be made to encourage young people and children to like all foods.

5. Naturally, the homemaker should keep in mind any family customs, traditions, or religious observances in planning the meals.

6. The amount of time that the homemaker has and the amount of help she can depend on from the other members of the family make some difference in the kinds of meals she plans and how she prepares the food.

Courtesy Sunkist Growers

SAVING TIME BY PLANNING

Preparing a meal is somewhat like running a three-ring circus because several things are going on at once and all must be finished at the same time. Much of this last-minute rush can be avoided if everything is planned ahead of time. For example . . .

. . . the menu should be carefully planned.

. . . supplies should be checked to see that everything needed to prepare the meal is on hand.

. . . the steps in the preparation of the meal should be thought through ahead of time and carried out. For instance, what jobs can be done ahead of time? What foods can be prepared ahead of time — which first, second, and so on? Can several jobs be done at the same time?

Although you may have helped your mother prepare meals, do you think you could prepare a meal by yourself and have everything ready on time? Why not try it with a simple breakfast menu, such as the following:

Prunes and Ready-to-eat Cereal

Buttered Toast

Milk

HINTS: Cook the prunes the night before, and put them in the refrigerator to chill. Set the table the night before, and see that the sugar bowl has been filled. Then all you will have to do in the morning is make the toast and put it on the table with the prunes, cereal, and milk.

Courtesy National Dairy Products Corporation

Preparing a meal is much easier for the homemaker if everyone in the family helps. Sometimes the father in the family has some special dish that he likes to prepare. Other tasks can be done by other members of the family. With some help, even the youngest children can be assigned something to do in preparing the meals.

In some families one person takes care of setting the table for a week, washing the dishes the next week, and helping in the kitchen the next. Thus, tasks are rotated.

Often the father or a teen-age son or daughter does most or all of the shopping. The teen-age girl whose mother works may prepare the entire meal or start the foods which will take a long time to cook. Thus, a part of the planning of a meal in any family is the carrying out of the various tasks necessary for preparing and serving a healthful and satisfying meal.

PLANNING MEALS WITH VARIETY

Variety in the foods served for a meal stimulates interest and appetite. Color, size and shape, texture, and flavor of foods should be considered when planning a meal. Variety can also be achieved by balancing heavy with light foods and by preparing the foods in different ways.

Variety in color: In planning meals, some thought should be given to how the colors of the foods are going to look together. For example, a meal consisting of ham with a parsley garnish, green beans, carrots, a relish dish, and corn sticks is colorful, attractive, and appetizing. A meal with all colorless foods — such as creamed chicken, mashed potatoes, cole slaw, and white bread — is not very appealing to the appetite.

Courtesy American Can Company

Variety in size and shape: A meal is attractive when the foods are of different sizes and shapes. Avoid having more than one diced, chopped, or mashed food at the same meal. The roast, mashed potatoes, green peas, and congealed salad shown below are more attractive than the same meal would be with, say, diced carrots instead of peas and diced potatoes instead of mashed potatoes. Do the other meals shown on these pages have variety in size and shape?

USDA Photo

Courtesy Texas Agricultural Extension Service

Variety in texture: When we speak of the "texture" of a food, we mean whether it is soft or hard, crisp or chewy, fibrous or smooth, dry or moist. In this meal of macaroni (soft and moist), cooked carrots (neither soft nor crisp), fruit salad (crisp as well as fibrous), bread (soft but dry), custard (soft and moist), and cookies (crisp and dry), texture has been taken well into account.

Variety in heavy and light foods: Meals are enjoyable when heavy, rich foods are balanced with light foods. Foods are considered "heavy" when they contain a large amount of sugar or fat. In this meal, the pie (a heavy food) is all right for dessert because the creamed dish with carrots and the grapefruit salad are light foods.

Courtesy Wheat Flour Institute

71

Courtesy Texas Agricultural Extension Service

Variety in flavor: Balancing mild and strong flavors in foods adds to the appeal of a meal. Not more than one strongly flavored food—such as onions, cabbage, cauliflower, or turnips—should be served at a meal. Here, onions (strongly flavored) are served with liver, mashed potatoes, and corn bread — all mildly flavored foods. There should also be a balance between sweet and acid foods. For example, the grated-carrot-and-celery salad in this meal is better with the lemon pie than a grapefruit salad would be. Variety in flavor can also be achieved by not repeating the same kind of food or the same flavor. For example, if, as here, a fruit salad is served, then the dessert should be something other than fruit. It would not be good to serve pineapple juice and pineapple salad or pineapple cake at the same meal.

Courtesy Wheat Flour Institute

Variety in ways of preparation: The cream of corn soup, the creamed tuna casserole, and the asparagus with a cream sauce shown in the pictures look delicious, and each is nutritious. But they would not be very enjoyable if served together at any one meal because all are either made with or served with a cream sauce. Buttered whole-kernel corn and asparagus salad would be much better with the creamed tuna casserole.

When meat is served with a sauce over it, the vegetables should be plain.

All the foods at any one meal should not be cooked in the same way — such as fried hamburgers, fried potatoes, and fried tomatoes. Mashed potatoes and sliced tomatoes would be much better with fried hamburgers.

There are so many ways to prepare foods—creamed, baked, boiled, broiled, scalloped, mashed, au gratin, stuffed, fried, and glazed, for instance — that it should not be necessary to use the same method over and over again.

PLANNING MEALS FOR THE DAY

Breakfast

Half Grapefruit
Poached Egg on Toast
Toast   Butter or Margarine
Milk

Lunch or Supper

Baked Beans   Frankfurters
Carrot Sticks with Green Pepper Strips
Brown Bread   Butter or Margarine
Banana Cream Pudding
Milk

Dinner

Baked Ham
Candied Sweetpotatoes
Buttered Broccoli
Lettuce Wedge with Thousand Island
Dressing
Roll   Butter or Margarine
Chocolate Cake
Milk

USDA Photos

Now that you have read what is involved in planning meals that are healthful, interesting, within the budget, and enjoyable for all members of the family, check the three meals for a day shown on page 74.

1. Do the meals meet the requirements of A *Daily Food Guide*? (See pages 48-52.)
2. Do the meals as a whole seem well balanced (see page 63)? Your lunch or supper should include about one-third of the foods that are needed daily. Your breakfast should include less than one-third, and your dinner, a little more than one-third.
3. Does each of the meals fulfill the requirements as to variety:
   a. Are they colorful ?
   b. Are the sizes and shapes of the foods varied at each meal?
   c. Is there a difference in the textures of the foods served?
   d. Is there a variety of flavor in each meal?
   e. Are the heavy and the light foods well balanced for each meal?
   f. Is there variety in the ways the different foods are prepared?
4. Can the food for the meals be bought with the amount of money that you have to spend? If not, what changes would you make?
5. In preparing each of these meals, what could you prepare the night before? Then in what order would you prepare the other foods for each meal—first, second, and third?
6. Would these meals be suitable for the members of your family? If not, why? What changes would have to be made?
7. If you were helping your mother with any one of these meals, which of the foods could you prepare?

ACTIVITIES

Helping to plan, prepare, and serve meals:

1. Make a list of the ways in which you help at home in planning, preparing, and serving the meals. Compare your list with the ones made by your classmates. In what ways could you help your mother more?
2. Tell about the first time you ever prepared a meal all by yourself. What did you find most difficult to do?
3. What are the biggest problems you have when cooking at home?
4. Suppose that your mother is to be away from home until almost dinnertime. Plan a menu with foods that you and your brother or sister could have almost ready by the time she arrives. List the things that would have to be done after she arrives.

Learning to check your food needs:

5. Keep a record of the foods you eat for 3 days. Then study your record, and ask yourself the following questions: (a) Have I eaten the correct amount of food from each of the groups of *A Daily Food Guide?* (b) In what ways could the meals I ate have been changed in order to have more variety? (c) Were my between-meal snacks necessary? Could I have made a better choice in the foods I ate between meals?

Deciding what to consider when planning meals:

6. After studying the top picture on page 70, which illustrates variety in color, check the other picture on page 70 and the pictures on page 73 for variety in color. Then check all the pictures on pages 70–73 for variety in texture, flavor, and so on.
7. Discuss how age, sex, type of work, and health affect the planning of meals.

Planning meals to be served in class:

8. Plan four simple menus with one of the following meat substitutes as a main dish: (a) Welsh rabbit, (b) creamed eggs in toast cups, (c) salmon loaf, or (d) tuna-and-noodle casserole.
9. Plan a menu to be served in class. Then review the recipes, and check the foods laboratory to see which supplies are on hand and which will need to be bought. Make a market order (see page 395) and a time schedule (see page 396).

Deciding how to evaluate your work:

10. Plan, prepare, and serve a meal for a guest in class.
11. Give a report on the work in preparing the meal you served the guest. Evaluate the plans you made for the menu, your method of working, and the enjoyment of the occasion.

Chapter 6 | BREAKFAST

Breakfast is usually the easiest meal of the day to prepare. In many ways, it is the most important meal. Yet, unfortunately, many people do not take the time to eat breakfast. Others do not eat enough food for breakfast.

A person who goes without breakfast may not realize that the tired feeling that he has during the middle of the morning is caused by the lack of food. He may have a headache or become weak, nervous, restless, or cross because he is hungry, but he may not realize it. The person who eats a good breakfast has more energy, does better work, and is better natured than the person who has not had enough food to start the day.

When a person gets up in the morning, he probably has not had any food for 12 to 14 hours. Therefore, his body is very much in need of food.

By eating three or four of the foods that are needed daily for breakfast, it is easier to get a well-balanced diet for the day. Nutritionists say that from one-fourth to one-third of the amount of food required by the body for the day should be eaten at breakfast. Foods served for breakfast should be ones that have value for the body, are easily digested, and are not so heavy that they cause discomfort.

Merrim from Monkmeyer

EXCUSE: "I do not have time."

REMEDY: You will have time to eat a good breakfast if you will: (1) get all your clothes and school things ready the night before, (2) get up a few minutes early, and (3) set the table or do part of the work the night before.

EXCUSE: "I am not hungry" or "I do not feel well after I eat breakfast."

REMEDY: Maybe you do not think that you are hungry at breakfast time. But by the middle of the morning you will know that you are hungry when you become weak, nervous, restless, irritable, or when you feel ill. The reason that you are not hungry at breakfast time may be that you are not in the habit of eating breakfast. Try eating a little breakfast every morning. Your health, appearance, and disposition are bound to improve.

Courtesy Personal Products, Inc.

NOT EATING BREAKFAST

Courtesy Stix, Baer, and Fuller, St. Louis

EXCUSE: "I do not like the foods that are served for breakfast."

REMEDY: You will enjoy your breakfast if you will help to see that: (1) a variety of food is served rather than the same thing day after day (see page 80), (2) the food is attractive and properly prepared, and (3) the food is served at the proper temperature.

EXCUSE: "I want to lose weight."

REMEDY: When you are trying to lose weight, be careful to eat all three meals. Your weight is controlled by the total number of calories you eat — not by how many times you eat. If you skip meals you may injure your health. Also, skipping meals may cause you to become so hungry that you will overeat at the following meal. Be certain that your diet has plenty of meat, milk, vegetables, fresh fruits, and cereals. Avoid such fattening foods as potato chips, cake, and pie.

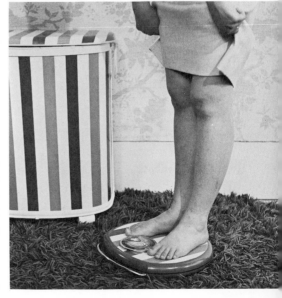

Courtesy Stix, Baer, and Fuller, St. Louis

GIVING VARIETY TO
THE BREAKFAST MENU

Fruit Cup
Ready-to-eat Cereal
Coffeecake
Milk

Courtesy Kellogg Company

Tomato Juice
Hot Cereal with Dates
Nut Bread
Milk

Courtesy Cereal Institute, Inc.

Stewed Dried Fruit
Hot Cereal
Scrambled Eggs   Sausage
Toast   Milk

Courtesy Evaporated Milk Association

Griddlecakes
Sausage
Cocoa

Courtesy Processed Apples Institute, Inc.

KINDS OF FOODS FOR BREAKFAST

The kinds of foods that are eaten for breakfast vary according to the person's needs, the section of the country in which he lives and its climate, the season of the year, and the habits or preferences of the family.

In many homes the breakfast menu is more likely to be the same from day to day than is the menu for any other meal. Unfortunately, most families do not have as much variety in breakfast foods as they could. For example, consider the many variations that are possible with foods that are usually served for breakfast.

Fruits

Orange or grapefruit juice, halves, and sections
Dried fruits, such as prunes and apricots
Applesauce
Melons, berries, bananas, or other fresh fruit
Tomato juice and many other fruit and vegetable juices

Cereals

Numerous ready-to-eat or hot cereals served
plain or in combination with various fruits

Eggs

Fried, scrambled, soft-cooked, baked, omelet, and so on

Meats

Bacon, ham, and various kinds of sausages

Breads

White, whole-wheat, and raisin bread or toast
Muffins, biscuits, sweet rolls, coffeecake, and nut breads
Waffles and griddlecakes

Beverages

Milk, cocoa, hot chocolate, tea, or coffee

TYPES OF BREAKFASTS

1. A *light breakfast* is usually composed of fruit, a bread or a cereal, and a beverage. This type of breakfast is adequate for people who do not use a great deal of energy.

2. A *medium breakfast* may include fruit, cereal or eggs, bread, and a beverage. Most adults and growing boys and girls who are only moderately active usually eat a medium breakfast.

3. A *heavy breakfast* should include fruit, cereal, eggs alone or with a meat, bread, and a beverage. Growing boys and girls who are very active and adults who do heavy, active work should eat a breakfast of this type every day. They use a great deal of energy.

Using the following breakfast patterns as a guide, plan menus for two light, two medium, and two heavy breakfasts. To have variety in your menus, try not to have the same fruit or cereal twice.

Breakfast Patterns

Light

Fruit	Fruit
Cereal	Bread
Beverage	Beverage

Medium

Fruit	Fruit
Cereal	Eggs
Bread	Bread
Beverage	Beverage

Heavy

Fruit	Fruit
Cereal	Cereal
Eggs	Eggs
Bread	Breakfast Meat
Beverage	Bread
	Beverage

Regardless of your age you must have certain foods every day. Some of them may be included in between-meal snacks. For example, many people enjoy an orange juice break.

Courtesy Ralston Purina Company

Breakfast is usually the easiest meal of the day to prepare, and in many ways it is the most important. Foods served for breakfast should have high food value. Select foods that can be easily digested, and avoid heavy foods that may cause discomfort.

Courtesy United Fresh Fruit and Vegetable Association

Courtesy National Dairy Council

Lunch is usually served at noon. In some families this light meal is served in the evening and is called "supper." At lunch, meat and vegetables may be combined into one main dish, such as a stew or a casserole. Meat alternates, such as cheese and eggs, may also be served as the main dish with a salad, a fruit, or a vegetable.

Courtesy United Fresh Fruit and Vegetable Association

Courtesy National Dairy Council

Dinner, the heartiest meal of the day, may be served at noon or in the evening. When planning dinner, include at least four foods from A Daily Food Guide as shown here and consider the foods that will be eaten for breakfast and lunch. It is desirable to have all three meals about the same size. Avoid having one of the three meals very light and another very heavy.

Courtesy United Fresh Fruit and Vegetable Association

WAYS OF SERVING BREAKFAST

Courtesy Cereal Institute, Inc.

An attractive breakfast is just as easy to prepare as, and costs no more than, an unattractive breakfast. Many people do not realize how important the appearance of food is in stimulating the appetite and in making the meal more enjoyable. An attractive breakfast table should be a pleasant meeting place for the family to start the day off right.

If all members of the family cannot eat together, arrangements might be made so that each one can pepare his own breakfast and clean up his own dishes. For instance, the fruit or fruit juice could be prepared and left in the refrigerator. The toaster and egg poacher could be left on the stove. Cocoa or a hot cereal could be kept hot in the top part of a double boiler.

Courtesy American Institute of Baking

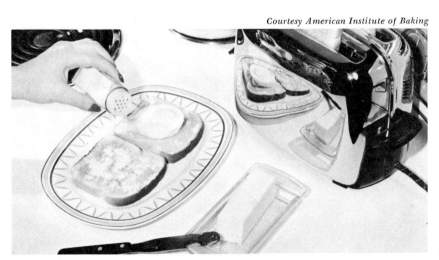

Breakfast is a very important meal and time is often a factor.

Setting the table and doing as much of the other work as possible the night before are time-savers for most people.

Having supplies, equipment, and ingredients set out conveniently for use is another help.

If you are sure ahead of time that all the necessary food is on hand, you will avoid last-minute shopping or changes in plans, thus saving time.

Courtesy Stix, Baer, and Fuller, St. Louis

Some families like to have breakfast in the kitchen. Others do not. If the food is to be taken to another room, it can be served on a tray in order to save steps as well as time. Fill glasses and cups only three-quarters full to prevent spilling. You may also arrange the silver, china, napkins, and so on, on the tray to save trips.

Courtesy Ralston Purina Company

84

AT BREAKFAST

Use of electric appliances can save
time at breakfast. They can be used
to cook some foods at the table while
the members of the family drink
their fruit juice or eat their cereal.

Courtesy National Presto Industries, Inc.

Serve foods that do not require too much time to cook or foods that may
be cooked while you eat something else. For example, toast can be prepared more quickly than waffles. Scrambled eggs or soft-cooked eggs can
be prepared more quickly than baked eggs or an omelet. Poached eggs
might be put on to cook while the cereal is being eaten.

Courtesy Kellogg Company

ACTIVITIES

Realizing the importance of eating breakfast:

1. Take turns with classmates in arranging on the bulletin board pictures of foods that are often served for breakfast.
2. Write a page on why it is important for everyone to eat a good breakfast.
3. Have each member of the class make a time schedule of her meals. Note the time between meals, and discuss why it is important to have regular meals. Study the breakfast menu of each girl, and determine whether or not it seems adequate for her needs.
4. Discuss reasons why some boys and girls do not eat breakfast and what might be done about it.
5. With the help of your student council, health department, or science department, sponsor a better-breakfast campaign.

Making breakfast more enjoyable:

6. Arrange on the bulletin board pictures of attractive breakfast tables.
7. Show pictures of colorful place mats made of fabric, oilcloth, straw, or cork which would be suitable for the breakfast table.
8. Discuss what can be done to a potted plant to make it an attractive centerpiece for the breakfast table. Demonstrate how to make attractive flower arrangements for the breakfast table.

Preparing breakfast at home:

9. Discuss how family members may share in the responsibilities of preparing breakfast.
10. Plan the menu for your family's Sunday breakfast. Prepare the food and serve it. Report to the class on the problems you had, and discuss ways of solving them.
11. Mary's mother and father have to go to work early. Therefore, it is necessary for Mary to prepare and serve breakfast for her eleven-year-old brother and her nine-year-old sister. Discuss what she might serve for 1 week without repeating the same foods.

Preparing breakfast at school:

12. Plan a breakfast menu that might be prepared in class.
13. Select recipes, and make out a market order according to the directions on page 395.
14. Work out a time schedule for each member according to the directions on page 396.
15. Ask your teacher to check your work.
16. Prepare and serve the meal.
17. Discuss what could have been done to improve your time schedule and your working habits.

Courtesy Campbell Soup Company

Chapter 7 | # LUNCH OR SUPPER

The light meal usually eaten at noon is called "lunch." In some families this light meal is served in the evening and is called "supper." Whether the light meal is eaten at noon or at night makes no difference in the types of food served. The luncheon menu should be made up of a few simple dishes that can be prepared without too much trouble and served and eaten in a short time.

When meat is the main dish at lunch or supper, the servings are smaller than they would be for dinner. Sometimes the meat is served in combination with other foods.

The main dish at lunch may be any one of the following: a sandwich, a soup, a salad, a vegetable plate, a fruit plate, a cold-meat plate, cheese, eggs, dry peas, or dry beans. One-hot-dish meals, such as a meat pie, a scalloped or creamed dish, or a casserole, are also popular for lunch or supper.

When meat substitutes, such as macaroni and cheese, baked beans, or an omelet, are the main dish, variety is given to the day's menu. The cost of the meal is less than it would be for meat. At the same time, much of the protein needed in the day's diet is provided.

87

Courtesy Edgewood High School, San Antonio

The food for a luncheon may be placed on the table in serving dishes before the people are seated, or it may be served on plates and brought in from the kitchen. Luncheon may also be served buffet style.

People often entertain at lunch or supper because they can prepare the meal easily and serve it casually.

Bland

Courtesy Alamo Heights High School

MAIN DISHES FOR LUNCH

Hearty Sandwiches

Chicken, eggs, cheese, meat, or bacon
on bread, toast, buns, or hot-dog rolls
See Chapter 16.

Hearty Salads

Chicken, meat, eggs, or seafood with
bread-and-butter sandwiches, hot rolls,
biscuits, crackers, or French bread
See Chapter 14.

Hearty Soups

Cream soups, meat and vegetable
soups, fish or seafood chowders, or
gumbos with crackers, muffins, or bread
See Chapter 15.

Photos Courtesy Blue Bonnet Margarine

A *meat pie* is made of meat or poultry cut into small uniform pieces, combined with vegetables, and simmered in a thickened, seasoned gravy. Then it is put into a baking dish and topped with baking powder biscuits, pastry, or mashed potatoes, and baked. Meat pie is frequently made from leftover pot roast or stew. (See pages 517 and 528.)

A *scalloped dish* is made by arranging alternate layers of meat, poultry, fish, shellfish, or eggs with bread crumbs or cracker crumbs and a well-seasoned white sauce. It is then topped with buttered bread crumbs and baked.

Photos Courtesy Blue Bonnet Margarine

Photos Courtesy Blue Bonnet Margarine

A *casserole* is usually made of a small amount of meat combined with vegetables, rice, macaroni, or potatoes, and it is baked in a casserole dish. Frequently part or all of the food has been cooked before it is baked. Usually a white sauce or gravy is added. Macaroni and cheese and baked beans are also referred to as casseroles.

ADVANTAGES OF ONE-HOT-DISH MEALS

Meat pies, scalloped dishes, and casseroles are all generally referred to as "one-hot-dish meals" because they are usually served as the only hot dish at a meal. There are several advantages in having a one-hot-dish meal:

1. It is not necessary to prepare many different foods. A salad, a bread, and a beverage are usually all that need to be added to complete a one-hot-dish meal.
2. A one-hot-dish meal requires only a small amount of effort since the food does not have to be watched while it cooks.
3. The food may be prepared several hours before serving time.
4. Only a small amount of meat is needed to make a flavorful yet inexpensive dish.
5. A one-hot-dish meal is an excellent way to use leftovers and low-cost foods. Sometimes foods left from other meals can be made into new dishes which are more attractive and flavorful than they were when first cooked. (See page 146.)

91

Courtesy Poultry and Egg National Board

A creamed dish is made of meat, fish, cheese, eggs, or vegetables which have been added to white sauce and heated. Parsley, pimento, green pepper, peas, celery, or onion may be added for color and flavor. Creamed dishes may be served over crisp toast, waffles, rice, pastry shells, or crisp noodles.

Courtesy The Borden Company

A top-of-the-stove dish, such as goulash (page 7), spaghetti and meat balls, chop suey, chicken and spaghetti (page 520), and other skillet dishes, may also be served as a one-hot-dish meal.

LUNCHEON PLATES

Fruit Plate

Fresh, frozen, dried, and canned fruit arranged on salad greens and served with hot cinnamon rolls, nut bread, or crackers (Cottage cheese or a sherbet is sometimes included.)

Bland

Bland

Cold-meat Plate

Cold cuts of meat, cheese, and sometimes potato salad and deviled eggs, served with rye or garlic bread, rolls, or biscuits

Courtesy General Foods Kitchens

Vegetable Plate

Several kinds of cooked vegetables, sometimes with cole slaw, carrot strips, or hard-cooked egg, served with rolls, muffins, corn bread, or biscuits

Shelton from Monkmeyer

Whether you buy lunch in the school cafeteria or take a packed lunch, you will want to . . .

. . . consider what you had for breakfast and the type of meal you will have for dinner to be sure that you get the foods you need daily. (See *A Daily Food Guide* on pages 48-52.) For example, if your other meals do not include enough fruit, vegetables, and milk, you will want to have these for lunch.

. . . plan your meals so that you will get the most for your money. The most expensive foods are not always the most nutritious. If you can afford to buy only three items, a bowl of soup, a sandwich, and a glass of milk would be a better choice than a piece of chocolate pie, potato chips, and a soft drink. You may take part of your lunch from home and buy the rest in the school cafeteria. For example, if you bring sandwiches and fruit from home, you can have a well-balanced meal by buying milk and a salad or, on a cold day, hot soup or stew in the school cafeteria.

96

Courtesy Personal Products, Inc.

Courtesy Chicago Public Schools

A good lunch for school contains meat or a meat substitute, a vegetable and/or fruit, whole-wheat bread, and milk. Eating such a lunch every day will help to keep you well, give you pep, and enable you to do your schoolwork more easily.

When you eat only a hot dog, potato chips, and a bottle of pop for lunch, it is almost impossible to get all the vitamins and minerals that your body needs for the day in the foods of the other two meals.

Courtesy Associated Pimiento Canners

Courtesy Alcoa Wrap

Courtesy Dow Chemical Company

Sandwiches made with meat, cheese, or eggs are perhaps the most popular main dish for a packed lunch. Fried chicken, hard-cooked eggs, deviled eggs, or other food which may be eaten with the fingers may also be included in a packed lunch.

Just as you need raw vegetables and fruits in other meals because of the minerals and vitamins, so do you need them in your lunch box. Fruits and vegetables, such as oranges and tomatoes, add something moist or juicy to your lunch. Carrot strips, celery, lettuce, apples, grapes, or pears add something crisp or chewy.

To save time when packing a lunch, you can do things the night before. For example, wash raw fruits or vegetables, peel if necessary, and cut them into convenient pieces so that they can be eaten easily.

Also to save time, keep all articles needed in packing the lunch in a particular place. Napkins, wax paper, foods which do not need to be kept in the refrigerator, and any jars or containers needed may be placed near the lunch box.

Another method of saving time is to prepare sandwiches and freeze them (see page 230). Lettuce and other foods which cannot be frozen should not be added to sandwiches until the day they are to be eaten. Cookies or cake which is to be eaten with the sandwich may be wrapped with it.

A LUNCH

Another timesaver is making sandwich fillings in amounts large enough to be used for several days.

Food which is wrapped in plastic film, wax paper, or aluminum foil does not dry out easily.

Use plastic containers for carrying foods that cannot be wrapped easily.

Place very moist foods in tightly covered paper cartons or in glass or plastic jars, and arrange them in the lunch box so that they will not turn over.

Place heavy foods, such as apples, on the bottom of the lunch box and lighter and easily crushed foods on top. The food which will be eaten first should naturally be placed on top unless it is too heavy.

Include two napkins, one to spread on the table and the other to use as a napkin.

Hot soup, hot cocoa, cold milk, chocolate milk, fruit juice, or tomato juice may be carried in a thermos bottle. Stews, vegetable soup, and similar foods may be eaten with a spoon from a wide-mouthed thermos bottle.

The lunch box, thermos bottle, and all jars used to carry food should be washed in hot soapy water, rinsed in boiling water, and left open to the air or sun when not in use.

Courtesy General Foods Corporation

Courtesy Dow Chemical Company

Courtesy Campbell Soup Company

ACTIVITIES

Learning to plan interesting, well-balanced meals:

1. List foods frequently served in your home for lunch or supper.
2. Clip three lunch or supper menus from papers or magazines. Discuss the following in class: *(a)* Is there variety? What can be done to improve the menus? *(b)* Are the meals well balanced? If not, why? *(c)* Which dish should you start to prepare first? *(d)* What will have to be done at the last minute?

Deciding on the main dish at lunch:

3. Plan a menu with creamed ham and egg on toast as the main dish. Compare your menu with others prepared by classmates.
4. Plan a lunch menu with a main dish that requires very little meat.
5. Ask each student to bring to class a recipe for a one-hot-dish meal which includes both meat and vegetables. Select one, and then decide on a salad and a beverage to make and serve in class.

Planning the meals for the day:

6. Write down what you had for dinner last night and for breakfast this morning. Then plan a lunch menu to go with the breakfast and dinner you had. Include the foods required in *A Daily Food Guide* (pages 48–52).
7. Plan menus for a day's meals — breakfast, lunch, and dinner. Then prepare the lunch menu in class.

Preparing meals at home:

8. Make arrangements with your mother to allow you to plan, prepare, and serve at least one meal a week.
9. Prepare a Sunday-night supper at home. Report to the class on how you planned for it, what you served, how you prepared the food, and how well the family enjoyed it.
10. Collect magazine pictures of foods that are usually served in the school cafeteria. Allow each girl to make a list of the foods she would include in a lunch menu. Compare menus as to cost and balanced diet.
11. Consider the appearance of the cafeteria and the behavior of the students. Discuss ways in which both could be improved. Invite the manager of the cafeteria and the principal to meet with a committee of the class to consider ways in which the situation could be improved.

Packing a school lunch:

12. Plan a packed lunch for each day in the week without repeating any one food more than necessary.
13. Figure the costs of three different kinds of sandwiches.
14. Discuss ways of keeping lettuce and carrot strips crisp in a packed lunch.

Courtesy Extension Service, University of Maine

Chapter 8 | **DINNER**

The heartiest meal of the day is called "dinner" whether it is served at noon or in the evening. As a rule, dinner is the most expensive meal of the day, and the homemaker spends more time planning and preparing it than she does for any other meal.

When planning a dinner menu, ask yourself these questions:

1. Have I included at least four foods from *A Daily Food Guide?* (See pages 48–52.)
2. Have I considered the foods to be eaten at the other meals during the day?
3. Have I considered whether or not the foods are available?
4. Have I considered the amount of money to be spent? (See Chapter 11.)
5. Have I selected foods suited to the people to be served — their age, occupation, activities, likes and dislikes, and so on? (See page 67.)
6. Do I have variety in color, size and shape, texture, flavor, and so on? (See pages 70–73.)
7. Have I considered the time it will take to prepare each dish? (See pages 68 and 69.)
8. How will I serve the food? (See pages 24 and 25.)

DINNER MENUS

Dinner differs from the other two meals in that the main course is usually meat, poultry, or fish and more kinds of foods are served. A complete dinner menu consists of the following dishes, although most American families do not have this many:

Appetizer or soup: See page 104.
Main dish: See pages 106 and 107.
Starchy vegetable: Potatoes are preferable, but other starchy vegetables or rice may be served. (See page 110.)
One other vegetable: A dark-green or a deep-yellow vegetable is preferable. (See pages 108 and 109.)
Salad: See page 111.
Bread and butter: See page 112.
Dessert: See page 113.
Beverage: See Chapter 25.

Dinner Patterns

Light	Example
Main Dish	Broiled Hamburger Steak
Vegetable	Baked Stuffed Potato
Salad	Combination Salad
Bread	Hard Rolls Butter
Dessert	Ambrosia
Beverage	Milk Coffee

Medium	Example
Main Dish	Braised Steak
1 Starchy Vegetable	Mashed Potatoes Green Beans
1 Dark-green or Deep-yellow Vegetable	Grated Carrot Salad
Salad	Whole-wheat Bread Butter
Bread	Lime Sherbet Sugar Cookies
Dessert	Milk Coffee
Beverage	

Heavy	Example
Appetizer and/or Soup	Consommé
Main Dish	Meat Loaf
1 Starchy Vegetable	Scalloped Potatoes Broccoli
1 Nonstarchy Vegetable	Peach Half on Lettuce
Salad	Corn Bread Butter
Bread	Lemon Chiffon Pie
Dessert	Milk Tea
Beverage	

FOR A SUCCESSFUL DINNER

The enjoyment of a family dinner depends upon these factors:

1. *The attractiveness of the table:* A table can be attractive without being elaborate. Chapter 2 gives some suggestions on how to set the table, how to select a centerpiece, and how to serve.
2. *The kind of food you have:* The appeal of food depends on how well it has been prepared and how it is served.
3. *Your appearance and behavior:* The meal is more pleasant when everyone is clean and neat and uses good manners.
4. *Your attitude:* Since dinner is often the only time in the day when all the family are together, it should be as pleasant as possible.
5. *Your mood:* Relaxing and taking adequate time to eat will add to the enjoyment of the meal.
6. *Your cooperativeness as a member of the family:* Do you try to help your mother prepare and serve the dinner? Do you help yourself at the table, or do you expect your mother to "wait on you"? Do you let your mother know when you enjoy something instead of criticizing something that you do not like? Do you help to clear away the dishes?

Courtesy Texas Hereford Association

Courtesy Towle Manufacturing Company   *Bland*   *Bland*

Appetizers, such as fruit juice, tomato juice, fruit cocktail, seafood cocktail with a highly seasoned sauce, or canapés, may be served at the beginning of a dinner to stimulate the appetite. Fruit or fruit juice which is served as an appetizer should be tart to stimulate the appetite.

Courtesy Best Foods, Inc.

Soup for dinner should be light, such as a clear soup, bouillon, or consommé. (See page 213.) In restaurants, the menu often includes both soup and an appetizer, but seldom are both included in the menu for a family dinner. Various kinds of crackers or melba toast are served with appetizers.

RELISHES

Courtesy Alethea Moore

Such relishes as celery, radishes, and olives may be served as an appetizer as well as with the main course. Either way, they add a crisp texture to the meal. A relish tray is sometimes served instead of a salad. Such relishes as pickles, chowchow, cranberry sauce, tart jellies, and catsup, which have a sweet-sour taste, often accompany the meat. Because many relishes are colorful, they are used as a garnish as well as a relish. (See pages 470–472.)

Courtesy H. J. Heinz Company

MAIN DISHES FOR DINNER

Beef, veal, pork, and lamb are the meats served for dinner. When planning menus, consider the foods that go well with the different meats.

1. *Beef* may be served with any vegetable. Mashed or baked potatoes go especially well with broiled steak, hamburger patties, and meat loaf. Tossed green salads are particularly enjoyable with beef.
2. *Veal* served with potatoes au gratin, green beans, and tomato aspic salad makes an interesting menu.
3. *Pork* goes nicely with applesauce, sweetpotatoes, spinach, and a pineapple salad or with buttered corn, Brussels sprouts, and Waldorf salad.
4. *Lamb* goes well with creamed or mashed potatoes, yellow squash, and a grapefruit-and-avocado salad. Another combination might be buttered rice, peas, and lettuce with a tart dressing.

For information on buying, preparing, and serving meat, see Chapter 19.

Variety meats, such as liver, heart, kidney, and tongue, are very nutritious and, when properly cooked, make excellent main dishes. (See page 281.) Mashed potatoes, buttered carrots, and a combination vegetable salad go well with liver and bacon.

Courtesy Ac'cent

For holidays and other special occasions roast turkey with dressing is frequently the main dish. Cranberry sauce, candied sweetpotatoes, buttered broccoli, gelatin salad, hot rolls with butter, and lime sherbet go well with poultry.

Courtesy National Biscuit Company

Fish and shellfish may be fried, broiled, baked, or stuffed. Parlsey potatoes, Harvard beets, and wedges of lettuce salad or baked potatoes, green beans, and cole slaw might complete the menu when fish is the main dish. For information on buying, preparing, and serving fish, see Chapter 20.

U.S. Fish and Wildlife Service

Courtesy Hazel-Atlas Glass Company

Dark-green vegetables (spinach, broccoli, chard, collards, kale, turnip greens) and deep-yellow vegetables (carrots, pumpkin, sweetpotatoes, winter squash) are all excellent sources of vitamin A as well as other vitamins and minerals. (See page 50.)

For detailed directions on how to buy, prepare, and serve vegetables, see Chapter 13.

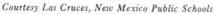

Courtesy Las Cruces, New Mexico Public Schools

Courtesy West Bend Aluminum Company

There is no need to have the same vegetable day after day. There are many kinds of vegetables, and the ways in which they can be prepared are varied. For example, vegetables may be buttered, mashed, baked, broiled, creamed, scalloped, au gratin, pickled, creoled, stuffed, fried, or glazed. When properly cooked, vegetables are rich in minerals and vitamins. They add variety in color, flavor, and texture to the meal.

Courtesy Snow Crop Frozen Foods

POTATOES

Mashed Potatoes

Parsley Potatoes

Browned Potatoes

Creamed Potatoes with Chives

Riced Potatoes

Scalloped Potatoes

Courtesy National Presto Industries, Inc.

Irish potatoes or sweetpotatoes are preferable for the starchy vegetable in a meal because they contain many minerals and vitamins. If another starchy vegetable (corn, dry beans, or dry peas) or starchy cereal (rice, noodles, or spaghetti) is served at dinner, then potatoes should be included at some other time during the day. Serving such starchy foods at the same meal with potatoes would include too much starch in one meal.

Courtesy Maine Extension Service, University of Maine

SALADS

Courtesy Libby, McNeill and Libby

Salads for dinner usually consist of vegetables, fruits, or salad greens. Meat or seafood salads are too heavy to be served at dinner. Salads are usually served with the main course. But they are sometimes served before or after the main course. Salads may be served in a bowl and passed at the table so that each person may help himself. They may also be put in individual salad bowls, which are placed to the left of the plate.

Courtesy Wesson Oil and Snowdrift Sales Company

BREADS

Most families like to have some type of bread for dinner, and often they prefer hot bread. Rolls, biscuits, and muffins are popuar because they can be made easily from mixes or bought partially prepared to be heated shortly before serving time. Bread can be kept hot at the table by putting it in a folded napkin.

For more ideas about breads and how to make bread, see Chapter 22.

DESSERTS

For dinner, light desserts, such as puddings, custards, sherbets, gelatin, and fruit cups, are appropriate. Fresh fruit in season, such as berries, melons, pineapple, and peaches, are always a pleasing finish to a meal. Cheese and crackers with fresh fruits are becoming an increasingly popular dessert.

For more ideas on dinner desserts and how to make them, see Chapters 23 and 24.

Courtesy The Borden Company

Courtesy The Borden Company

Courtesy American Dairy Association

ACTIVITIES

Helping Mother:
1. Prepare a "surprise dish" to serve at dinner in your home. Discuss the results in class.
2. Tell about some problems that you and your mother have had in preparing an evening meal.
3. List five things that Mary and her brother might do to help with dinner when their mother has to work until 6 o'clock.

Having enjoyable meals:
4. Plan to do three things to make dinner in your home more enjoyable.
5. List five subjects you might talk about at the dinner table in your home.
6. Plan, prepare, and serve the meals for 1 day in your home. Evaluate the results, and discuss ways of improving your methods of work.

Planning the dinner menu:
7. Using the dinner patterns on page 102, plan a light, a medium, and a heavy dinner.
8. Discuss how the work plans on page 392 will help you in planning and preparing dinner.

Deciding what to serve:
9. List five foods usually served as the main dish for dinner. Then plan a menu around each main dish.
10. Demonstrate how to prepare fruit juice and fruit combinations which may be used as appetizers at dinner.
11. Discuss various ways in which vegetables can be prepared and served for dinner.
12. Arrange on the bulletin board pictures of attractive dinner salads. Bring to class a recipe for one of your favorite salads that could be served for dinner.
13. Describe six light desserts which may be served at dinner.

Planning interesting classwork:
14. Plan a dinner menu to be served in class. Then make a work plan for each girl according to the directions on pages 393 and 396.
15. Describe three ways of making plain foods attractive and appetizing.
16. Bring to class three pictures of garnishes that are used to make food attractive. (See pages 470–472.)
17. Describe a meal which was made attractive by the use of garnishes. Describe another meal which had too many garnishes.

Courtesy Cereal Institute, Inc.

Chapter 9 | SPECIAL MEALS

For one reason or another, special meals are often required by certain members of a family: infants and small children, persons who are ill or have certain food requirements, and those who want either to gain or to lose weight. Therefore, this chapter is concerned with special meals for each group.

Pages 116–121 deal with food and meals for infants and small children. At your age, you will not have full responsibility for feeding a baby or a small child. However, if you have a young brother or sister or if you are a baby sitter, you will be expected to help with the feeding. For this reason, you should know something about the foods that babies and children require, as well as how they should be fed.

Pages 122–124 discuss food for the sick. Knowing how to plan diets for sick people and how to prepare and serve the meals will make it possible for you to help out when someone in your home is ill.

Pages 125–131 take up the problem of weight control. Some boys and girls want to gain weight, and others want to lose. If you are one of them, the information given on these pages should help you.

MEALS FOR INFANTS AND SMALL CHILDREN

Every child's growth depends to a great extent upon the kind and the amount of food that he eats. Food habits, likes, and dislikes are usually formed in early childhood. Therefore, the food in the diets of infants and small children should be as varied as possible. In addition, the food should be prepared with care so that it will be attractive in appearance as well as tasty in order to encourage them to eat and to enjoy all food that is served to them.

A baby grows more during the first year of its life than at any other time. By the time a child is one year old, he should weigh three times more than he did at birth.

Since the food for a baby is very important, most babies are fed under the direction of a doctor during the first year. A baby's stomach is small. Therefore, it is necessary for him to eat often. Most young babies are fed about every 4 hours. Some may need to be fed more often than others.

The mother's milk is better for her child than any other milk. If for some reason the mother's milk cannot be given to the baby, the doctor will recommend a formula which is usually made of cow's milk. Although milk is an almost perfect food, it does not supply everything that is needed for a balanced diet and good health. For this reason, several foods are added to the young child's diet. Among those which are generally added first are orange juice, cereals, egg yolk, and strained fruits, vegetables, and meats.

A child begins to have teeth between one and two years of age. He is then ready to eat chopped or mashed foods. It is at this age that a child learns how to chew and develops his food habits.

Infants have to be fed. A young child can feed himself, but he has to have help in learning how to drink from a cup and how to use a spoon.

116

GETTING THE BOTTLE READY

If a mother for whom you are baby-sitting expects you to feed the baby, she should have the milk formula made and stored in bottles in the refrigerator.

Just before it is time to feed the baby, you should do the following:

1. Get the baby ready for feeding by putting dry diapers on him and washing his hands and face.

2. Wash your hands with soap and water, and dry them with a clean towel.

3. Both glass and plastic bottles are used. If you are using a glass bottle, remove it from the refrigerator about five minutes before heating, to prevent cracking. Shake the bottle to mix the milk formula.

4. Remove the cap very carefully. Place the nipple on the bottle, taking care not to touch the part that goes into the baby's mouth.

5. Follow the mother's specific directions for heating the bottle.

6. Heat the milk to the temperature the mother suggests. Some babies are fed cold milk, but usually the formula is warmed slightly.

7. Test the temperature of the milk by shaking a few drops onto the inside of your wrist. If it feels neither hot nor cold, the temperature is correct for most babies.

Courtesy Davol Rubber Company

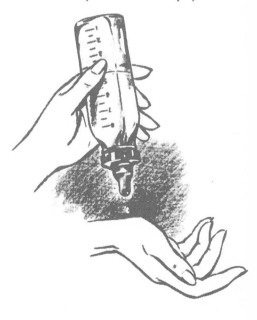

FEEDING MILK

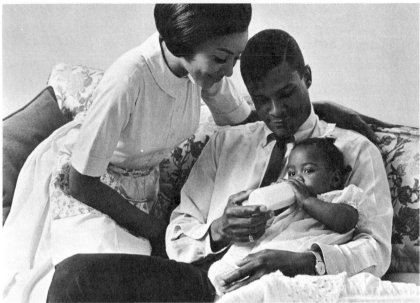

Courtesy Prudential Insurance Company

A baby should be comfortable and feel that he is loved while he is being fed.

If you are required to feed a baby his bottle while baby-sitting, keep the following points in mind:

1. Hold the baby in your arms so that he will feel loved.

2. Seat yourself in a comfortable chair, and hold the baby in such a way that he will feel secure and that you will be able to feed him easily.

3. Hold the bottle high enough for the nipple to be filled with milk at all times. This should be done to prevent the baby from sucking in too much air with the milk.

4. Hold the baby against your shoulder, and pat him gently on the upper part of his back when he has finished his feeding or when he stops to rest. This is called "burping." It brings up any air that the baby has swallowed and prevents him from spitting up the milk.

5. Put the baby in his crib to sleep or allow him to lie quietly as soon as he has finished his milk. It is not a good idea to play with a baby after he has been fed.

6. Throw out any milk that is left in the bottle after the feeding.

7. Rinse the nipple and the bottle in cold water so that they can be washed easily.

FEEDING SOLID FOOD

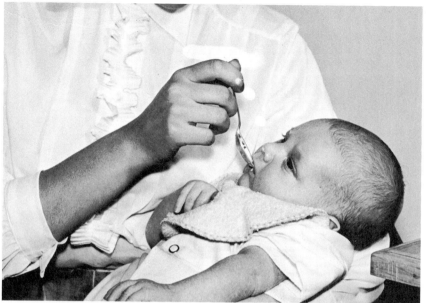

Courtesy Heinz Baby Foods

When you are a baby sitter, the mother will tell you which strained foods to feed the baby and how much he is expected to eat. Then when feeding time comes, you should proceed as follows:

1. Place the amount of food that the baby is expected to eat in a small bowl or in a food warmer to which hot water has been added. Heat the bowl in a pan of warm water until the food is lukewarm. Be sure to test the temperature of the food as you did the milk (see page 117).

Courtesy Gerber Baby Foods

2. Put a bib on the baby.

3. Put a small amount of food on the tip of a spoon, and place it well back in the baby's mouth. Do not rush him. He needs time to get acquainted with the taste of the food and the experience of eating.

4. Take the food away from the baby as soon as he seems to have lost interest. Do not force him to eat.

5. Throw away any remaining food, and rinse the dish.

LEARNING TO EAT

Courtesy Heinz Baby Foods

Children enjoy trying to feed themselves, and they should be encouraged to do so even though they make mistakes. Here are some suggestions for helping a child to feed himself when you are baby-sitting:

1. Be sure that you know what and how much the child should eat.
2. Allow him to rest and relax by looking at a book or drawing pictures while you are getting the food ready.
3. Help him to wash his face and hands. Then put a bib on him to protect his clothing in case of an accident. It might be wise to put a few newspapers under his chair and to wear an apron.
4. See that he has proper eating utensils. He will be able to feed himself more easily if he has a short-handled spoon which is small enough for him to hold firmly, a cup that he can hold and that will not turn over easily, a broad-rimmed dish which is heavy enough not to slide around, and a comfortable chair.
5. Be patient with him and encourage him, no matter how poorly he does. When the child is learning to eat, he may be messy and he may not get very much food into his mouth. Therefore, it is a good idea for you to feed him occasionally with another spoon to make sure that he gets enough to eat.
6. Be calm in case of an accident. Sometimes children will repeat an accident if they get attention the first time.
7. Help him to wash his face and hands, and encourage him to take a nap or to play quietly when he has finished eating.

DEVELOPING GOOD FOOD HABITS

The development of good food habits in young children should be stressed because the habits that they form in early years generally remain with them throughout their lives. The regularity of meals, the kinds of foods served, the way the food is prepared and served, and the attitudes of the other members of the family are all important to the child who is learning to eat among older people.

1. *Regularity:* Children should have a regular time to eat. They should also be given enough time so that they will chew their food properly. However, they should not be allowed to dawdle or to play with their food.

2. *Kinds of food served:* Very young children need the same basic foods as older people except that their food should be chopped or cut into small pieces. Small children have to be taught to like a variety of foods. New foods should be added to the diet one at a time and served in small amounts. Young children should never be given highly seasoned foods, such as spaghetti, mustard, and catsup; rich foods, such as pastries and pies; fat foods, such as fat meats, pork, ham, and sausage; foods that are difficult to chew and digest, such as nuts, popcorn, and cooked dry peas and dry beans; or hot breads, such as griddlecakes, waffles, and biscuits.

3. *How the food is prepared:* Food for young children should be simply prepared with very little seasoning so that they will learn to enjoy its natural flavor. Between-meals snacks for young children should be light foods, such as fruits, milk, crackers, or small, simple sandwiches.

4. *How the food is served:* Children are more likely to eat if they are given food in small servings on a small plate. Young children like bright-colored foods, such as beets, spinach, and carrots. They also enjoy foods in special shapes, such as animal cookies and gingerbread men, and they like gay dishes that have color and design or pictures.

Courtesy Gerber Baby Foods

5. *Attitude of the family:* Mealtime should be one of the happiest times of the day for everyone because a child in the family assumes the attitude of those around him. When a child eats at the table with the rest of the family, he will imitate the older people and learn from them. Therefore, the adults should set a good example by eating some of all foods served and by using correct table manners.

MEALS FOR THE SICK

When there is illness in the family and the doctor prescribes the diet for the patient, it will probably be one of three kinds: liquid, soft, or light.

Liquid Diet

Fruit and vegetable juices
Milk drinks
Ice cream, milk sherbets, and junket
Cereal gruels (strained, whole-grain cereals)
Broth or beef tea
Clear soup or light cream soup

Soft Diet

All foods on the liquid diet plus the following:

Thin crisp toast or milk toast
Well-cooked cereals
Soft-cooked or poached eggs
Mashed or strained fruits or vegetables (with little or no seasoning)
Vegetable soup or chicken broth with rice
Strained baby food
Plain gelatin desserts
Desserts made with milk or milk and eggs, such as ice cream, custard, cornstarch pudding, and junket

Light Diet

All foods on the liquid diet and the soft diet plus the following:

Lean meats, fish, and poultry (which have been roasted, broiled, or creamed if they are not too rich)
Easy-to-digest vegetables, such as baked potatoes, beets, carrots, and peas
Raw and cooked fruit (with little or no seasoning)
Plain salads without rich dressings
Bread or toast
Cottage cheese
Any kind of simple dessert that is not too sweet or too rich

All of the foods in the light diet should be prepared so that they can be easily digested, that is, without too much fat or sugar.

Following the doctor's orders about diet is as important as following his instructions about medicine.

ARRANGING THE TRAY

Bland

The meals for a sick person should be as attractive as possible so that he will be tempted to eat. These suggestions should help you to arrange the food on the tray conveniently and attractively:

1. Cover a large tray with something pretty. Paper place mats or napkins are inexpensive and can be discarded after use.

2. Use colorful dishes and glasses that do not tip over easily.

3. Arrange the dishes and silver so that they will be convenient.

4. Serve foods that are easy to cut and easy to eat.

5. Serve small portions of food because they are more tempting to a sick person than large portions.

6. Fill bowls, glasses, or cups no more than two-thirds full.

7. Use covered dishes for hot food, or cover the dishes with a plate or a saucer to keep the food from cooling.

8. Use garnishes on the food.

9. Place a flower on the tray when possible.

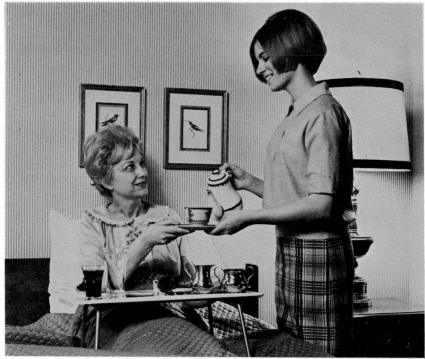

Courtesy Stix, Baer, and Fuller, St. Louis

Special attention should always be given to a person who is ill. Although the doctor prescribes the diet, you should keep the following suggestions in mind when planning, preparing, or serving the patient's meals:

1. The patient should be made as comfortable as possible before she is given her food. She should be helped to wash her hands and face and comb her hair. If there is no armrest, the pillows should be arranged so that she can sit up.

2. Some kind of arrangement should be made to hold the tray so that the patient can sit up in bed to eat. A bed table, a cutout cardboard box, or a small pillow may be used.

3. No one who has a cold or a cough or who is otherwise in poor health should be allowed to handle the food.

4. The person who prepares the meals should wash her hands before and after handling any food or dishes used by the patient.

5. The meals should be served at regular times each day.

6. All linens, dishes, and utensils should be: (a) removed from the sickroom as soon as the patient has eaten, (b) washed thoroughly in hot, soapy water, scalded, and allowed to drain dry, and (c) kept separate from those used by other members of the family.

124

OVERWEIGHT AND UNDERWEIGHT

Correct weight is very important to good health. Many young people talk about their weight without really knowing whether they have a problem or not. Each person has a weight range which is correct for him. This correct weight is in proportion to his body build and height.

It is natural for some boys and girls who have small bones and are small of build to be below average in weight. Others weigh more because they have large bones. Your doctor can tell you which body build you have. He can also tell you what you should weigh.

It is up to you to maintain your correct weight. If you really have a problem, get help from your doctor and your mother. You are growing and need good-sized servings of meat, potatoes, fruit, vegetables, and milk. You should eat these foods every day. Your doctor can tell you which other foods to eat or not to eat. Your mother can help by daily serving the foods which your doctor recommends.

Your weight is measured in pounds, and your height is measured in inches. The amount of heat and energy that you get from the food you eat is measured in calories. Each calorie gives you a certain amount of energy to work and play or to keep you warm just as a car runs a certain number of miles on a gallon of gasoline.

Most boys and girls are too thin or too fat because they do not eat properly. The calorie chart on pages 128-131 lists the number of calories found in various foods. As you study the chart, you will notice that foods which have a large amount of fat or carbohydrates (sugars and starches) are high in calories. If you eat too many foods which are high in calories, the extra amount is stored in your body as fat, causing you to gain weight. In order to reduce, then, you should see a doctor, eat foods which are low in calories, and exercise, but do not overexercise.

When you exercise, your body will use up the fat that is stored. If, at the same time, you eat low-calorie foods, you will lose weight. Even on a reducing diet, you should be sure to eat the foods that are needed daily for good health (see *A Daily Food Guide*, pages 48-52). For example, when you studied about the food group on page 49, you learned that you need two or more servings of meat each day. If you are trying to lose weight, select lean meat rather than fat meat. Notice in the calorie chart that one small apple (2½ inches in diameter) has 64 calories but that one serving of apple pie has 355 calories. If you were trying to lose weight, which would be a better choice for a snack after school: an apple or a piece of apple pie?

Girls between the ages of thirteen and fifteen need about 2600 calories each day. Boys of the same age need about 3200 calories each day. Growing boys and girls naturally need more calories than older people. The larger you are, the more calories your body needs. A football player needs more calories than someone who only sits and reads or watches TV. In the winter, when it is cold, you need more calories to keep you warm.

IF YOU ARE UNDERWEIGHT

Many boys and girls who are underweight do not realize that they would feel better and be more attractive if they gained a little weight. People who are underweight are inclined to be tense, nervous, restless, and irritable. In many cases, they tire easily. A real danger that results from being underweight is that infections are likely to occur.

If you find it too difficult to gain weight, it may be wise to consult a doctor. Being underweight is sometimes the result of some physical disturbance. However, the following general suggestions should help you to gain weight:

1. Eat a well-balanced diet. (See Chapter 4.) Include plenty of foods which are high in calories, such as fats (butter, margarine, cream, and fat meats), sweets (candy, cakes, pastries, and other rich desserts), starches (potatoes, cereals, and bread), whole milk, mayonnaise, rich sauces, and gravies.

Courtesy American Dairy Association

2. Learn to like many different kinds of food. This will be easy to do if the food is well prepared and attractively served.

3. Chew your foods well so that your body will be able to digest them easily.

4. Limit the amount of liquids at mealtime because liquids fill your stomach and prevent you from eating the foods you need.

5. Enjoy yourself during mealtime by eating in a pleasant atmosphere.

6. Slow down and be less active. Rest and sleep more than usual. If possible, rest before and after eating.

7. Eat more between meals provided this practice does not prevent you from wanting to eat at regular mealtimes.

8. A snack before going to bed will also help to increase the amount of food eaten each day.

IF YOU ARE OVERWEIGHT

Boys and girls who are overweight probably do not realize that they eat as many fattening foods as they do. Some eat too rapidly without chewing their food properly and, thus, eat far more than they should. Others skip meals but nibble away at fattening snacks all day long. Some do both!

If you weigh more than most of your friends, you may think that you should reduce. But, since a little extra weight is desirable during the teens, be sure that you are really overweight before going on a diet of any kind. The best way to find this out in your particular case is to consult a doctor.

Perhaps the best-recognized, safest, and most scientific way of losing weight is to eat foods which are low in calories. (See pages 128–131.) Other suggestions that may be helpful are these:

1. Eat three well-balanced meals each day. Even though you should include all the foods required by *A Daily Food Guide*, it is especially important to include ample amounts of meat, eggs, fruits, vegetables, and milk. Eat moderately of foods in the Bread-Cereal Group, and avoid sweets and rich foods.

2. Take smaller servings than you usually do, and never ask for a second helping. It is best to eat a hearty breakfast that includes cereal or eggs, or both, as well as some fruit and milk. Eating a good breakfast will help you to have a balanced diet, even when you are losing weight.

3. Eat at regular times each day. Do not eat between meals. If you must eat between meals, select fruits or raw vegetables, such as celery, carrot sticks, or apples.

4. Increase your amount of exercise by participating in outdoor sports.

Remember that calories in foods that you eat between meals count just as much as those in foods that you eat at mealtimes.

Courtesy Lever Brothers Company

FOOD	CALORIES	FOOD	CALORIES
Milk and Milk Products		Margarine, 1 tablespoon	100
Buttermilk, cultured, 1 cup	85	Oils, salad or cooking,	
Milk, cow: Fluid, whole, 1 cup	165	1 tablespoon	125
Fluid, nonfat (skim), 1 cup	85	Salad dressings, 1 tablespoon	
Evaporated (undiluted),		French	60
1 cup	345	Cooked	30
Condensed (undiluted),		Mayonnaise	90
1 cup	980		
Dry, whole, 1 tablespoon	40	**Eggs**	
Dry, nonfat solids,		1 whole medium egg: Raw	75
1 tablespoon	30	Fried	117
Cheese, 1 ounce		Scrambled	118
Cheddar (1-inch cube)	115		
Cheddar, processed	105	**Meat, Poultry, and Fish**	
Cheese foods, Cheddar	90	Beef, without bone, cooked	
Cottage, from skim milk	25	Chuck, 3 ounces	265
Cream	105	Hamburger, 3 ounces	315
Swiss	105	Sirloin, 3 ounces	255
Cream, 1 tablespoon: Light	30	Beef, dried, 2 ounces	115
Heavy	50	Beef-and-vegetable stew,	
Beverages, 1 cup		1 cup	250
Chocolate (all milk)	240	Chicken, canned, boned,	
Cocoa (all milk)	235	3 ounces	170
Chocolate-flavored milk	185	Crab meat, canned, 3 ounces	90
Malted milk	280	Halibut, broiled, 1 steak	
Desserts:		(4x3x½ inches)	230
Blanc mange, 1 cup	275	Heart, beef, raw, 3 ounces	90
Custard, baked, 1 cup	285	Lamb, leg roast, cooked,	
Ice cream, plain		3 ounces	230
⅐ quart brick	165	Liver, beef, fried, 2 ounces	120
8 fluid ounces	295	Mackerel, canned, solid	
		and liquid, 3 ounces	155
Fats, Oils, and Related Products		Oysters, meat only, raw,	
Bacon, medium fat, broiled or		1 cup	200
fried, 2 slices	95	Pork loin or chops, cooked,	
Butter, 1 tablespoon	100	3 ounces without bone	285
Fats, cooking (vegetable fats),		Pork, cured ham, cooked,	
1 tablespoon	110	3 ounces without bone	340

CHART*

FOOD	CALORIES	FOOD	CALORIES
Pork luncheon meat, canned, spiced, 2 ounces	165	Beans, snap, green, cooked, 1 cup	25
Salmon, canned, pink, 3 ounces	120	Beets, cooked, diced, 1 cup	70
Sardines, canned in oil, drained solids, 3 ounces	180	Broccoli, cooked, 1 cup	45
Sausage: Bologna, 1 slice (⅛ inch thick, 4½-inch diameter)	65	Brussels sprouts, cooked, 1 cup	60
Frankfurter, 1 cooked	125	Cabbage, 1 cup	
Shrimp, canned, 3 ounces	110	Raw, shredded	25
Soups, canned, ready-to-serve		Cooked	40
Beef, 1 cup	100	Carrots	
Chicken, 1 cup	75	Raw, grated, 1 cup	45
Clam chowder, 1 cup	85	Cooked, diced, 1 cup	45
Tongue, beef, raw, 4 ounces	235	Cauliflower, cooked, 1 cup	30
Tuna fish, drained, 3 ounces	170	Celery, raw, diced, 1 cup	20
Veal cutlet, cooked, 3 ounces	185	Corn, sweet	
		Cooked, 1 ear (5 inches long)	85
Dry Beans, Dry Peas, and Nuts		Canned, 1 cup	170
Almonds, shelled, 1 cup	850	Cucumbers, raw, 6 slices	5
Beans, canned or cooked, 1 cup		Lettuce, headed, raw, 2 large or 4 small leaves	5
Red kidney	230	Okra, cooked, 8 pods (3 inches long)	30
Navy or other varieties with:		Onions, raw: Mature, 1 onion (2½-inch diameter)	50
Pork and tomato sauce	295	Young, green, 6 small	25
Pork and molasses	325	Peas, green, cooked, 1 cup	110
Coconut, dried and shredded, 1 cup	345	Peppers, green, raw, 1 medium	15
Peanuts, roasted, shelled, 1 cup	805	Potatoes: Baked, medium (2½-inch diameter)	95
Peanut butter, 1 tablespoon	90	Boiled in skin, 1 medium	120
Pecans, halves, 1 cup	750	French-fried, 8 pieces (2x½x½ inches)	155
		Potato chips, 10 medium	110
Vegetables		Radishes, raw, 4 small	5
Asparagus		Spinach, cooked, 1 cup	5
Cooked, cut spears, 1 cup	35	Squash, 1 cup	
Canned, green, 6 spears	20	Summer, cooked, diced	35
Beans, lima, green, cooked, 1 cup	150	Winter, baked, mashed	95

*Adapted from "Food Values in Common Portions," U.S. Department of Agriculture

FOOD	CALORIES	FOOD	CALORIES
Sweetpotatoes, peeled		Lime juice, fresh, 1 cup	60
Baked (5x2 inches)	185	Oranges, 1 medium (3-inch	
Boiled (5x2½ inches)	250	diameter)	70
Tomatoes		Orange juice: Fresh, 1 cup	110
Raw, 1 medium (2x2½ inches)	30	Canned, unsweetened,	
Canned or cooked, 1 cup	45	1 cup	110
Tomato juice, canned, 1 cup	50	Frozen concentrate,	
Turnips, cooked, diced, 1 cup	40	6-ounce can	300
Turnip greens, cooked, 1 cup	45	Peaches: Raw, 1 medium	45
		Canned in sirup, 1 cup	175
Fruits		Dried, cooked, unsweetened,	
Apples, raw, 1 medium		1 cup	225
(2½ inches)	75	Pears	
Apple Betty, 1 cup	345	Raw, 1 pear (3x2½ inches)	95
Applesauce, canned, sweetened,		Canned in sirup, 2 medium halves	
1 cup	185	and 2 tablespoons sirup	80
Apricots: Raw, 3 apricots	55	Pineapple	
Canned in sirup, 4 medium		Raw, diced, 1 cup	75
halves, 2 tablespoons sirup	95	Canned in sirup, 1 large slice	
Dried, cooked, unsweetened,		and 2 tablespoons sirup	95
fruit and liquid, 1 cup	240	Pineapple juice, canned, 1 cup	120
Avocados, raw, peeled, half	280	Prunes, cooked, unsweetened,	
Bananas, raw, 1 medium	90	1 cup	310
Cantaloupes, raw, ½ melon	35	Raisins, dried, 1 cup	430
Cherries, pitted, 1 cup: Raw	65	Raspberries, red, raw, 1 cup	70
Canned, red, sour	120	Strawberries: Raw, 1 cup	55
Cranberry sauce, sweetened,		Frozen, 3 ounces	90
1 cup	550	Watermelons, ½ slice	
Dates, fresh and dried, pitted		(¾x10 inches)	45
and cut, 1 cup	505		
Fruit cocktail, canned, 1 cup	180	**Grain Products**	
Grapefruit, raw, sections, 1 cup	75	Biscuits, baking powder, 1 biscuit	
Grapefruit juice		(2½-inch diameter)	130
Canned, unsweetened, 1 cup	90	Bran flakes, 1 cup	115
Frozen concentrate,		Breads, 1 slice	
6-ounce can	295	Boston brown	105
Grapes, 1 cup	85	Rye	55
Grape juice, bottled, 1 cup	170	White, enriched	65
Lemon juice, fresh, 1 cup	60	Whole wheat	55

FOOD	CALORIES	FOOD	CALORIES
Cakes: Angel food, 2-inch sector ($1/12$ cake, 8-inch diameter)	110	Rice, cooked, 1 cup	205
		Rolls, 1 plain roll	120
		Spaghetti, cooked, 1 cup	220
Doughnuts, 1 cake-type	135	Waffles, 1 baked ($4\frac{1}{2} \times 5\frac{5}{8} \times \frac{1}{2}$ inches)	215
Foundation, 1 square (3x2x1¾ inches)	230		

Cakes: Angel food, 2-inch sector
 ($1/12$ cake, 8-inch
     diameter) 110
Doughnuts, 1 cake-type 135
Foundation, 1 square
  (3x2x1¾ inches) 230
Foundation, plain icing, 2-inch
sector, layer cake ($1/16$ cake,
  10-inch diameter) 410
Fruit cake, dark, 1 piece
  (2x2½ inches) 105
Gingerbread, 1 piece
  (2x2x2 inches) 180
Plain cake and cupcakes, 1
  cupcake (2¾-inch
    diameter) 130
Sponge, 2-inch sector ($1/12$
  cake, 8-inch diameter) 115
Cookies, plain and assorted,
  1 3-inch cookie 110
Corn bread or muffins 105
Corn flakes, 1 cup 95
Crackers
  Graham, 4 small or 2 medium 55
  Soda, plain, 2 medium 45
Macaroni, cooked, 1 cup 210
Muffins, 1 muffin (2¾-inch
  diameter) 135
Noodles, cooked, 1 cup 105
Oatmeal or rolled oats, cooked,
  1 cup 150
Pancakes, baked, wheat, 1 cake
  (4-inch diameter) 60
Pies, 4-inch sector (9-inch diameter)
  Apple 330
  Custard 265
  Lemon meringue 300
  Mince 340
  Pumpkin 265

Rice, cooked, 1 cup 205
Rolls, 1 plain roll 120
Spaghetti, cooked, 1 cup 220
Waffles, 1 baked
  ($4\frac{1}{2} \times 5\frac{5}{8} \times \frac{1}{2}$ inches) 215

Sugars and Sweets
Candy, 1 ounce
  Caramels 120
  Chocolate, sweetened, milk 145
  Fudge, plain 115
  Hard 110
  Marshmallows 90
Chocolate sirup, 1 tablespoon 40
Honey, strained, 1 tablespoon 60
Jams, marmalades, preserves,
  1 tablespoon 55
Molasses, cane, 1 tablespoon 50
Sugar, 1 tablespoon
  Granulated, cane or beet 50
  Brown 50

Miscellaneous
Beverages, carbonated, cola type,
  1 cup 105
Chocolate, unsweetened,
  1 ounce 140
Gelatin dessert, plain, ready-
  to-serve, 1 cup 155
Olives, pickled, "mammoth" size
  Green, 10 olives 70
  Ripe, 10 olives 105
Pickles
  Dill, cucumber, 1 large 15
  Sweet, cucumber or mixed,
    1 medium 20
Sherbet, ½ cup 120
White sauce, medium, 1 cup 430

ACTIVITIES

Learning to be a better baby sitter:

1. Find out how many girls in your class have younger brothers or sisters. How many have earned money for baby sitting outside their homes?
2. List the definite information that you should get from the mother about feeding a child when you baby-sit.
3. Invite a mother of small children to talk to your class about what parents expect when they hire someone to take care of their children.
4. Arrange pictures of children of different ages on the bulletin board. Under each photograph make a list of foods you might expect a child of that age to eat.
5. Tell about a child who refused to eat when you tried to feed him. Discuss what might have been the reason for his refusal and what you might have done to encourage him to eat.
6. Plan and give a party for preschool children.

Learning to take care of the sick:

7. Find out how many girls in your class have helped to take care of someone who was ill for several days. How many girls have been in a hospital? Discuss the food that was served in the hospital.
8. List six ways in which you might help your mother when a member of the family is ill.
9. Describe four things you might do to make a tray for a sick person interesting and attractive.
10. Plan a day's menu for someone who is on a liquid diet. Then plan a soft diet for the next day and a light diet for the third day.
11. Discuss what you might take to a friend who is ill. Discuss advantages and disadvantages of taking food to a person who is ill.
12. If it can be conveniently arranged, invite a dietitian to tell your class about the various diets which are given to people in a hospital.

Learning about overweight and underweight:

13. Keep a record of the food that you eat for 3 days. With the help of the calorie chart on pages 128–131, figure out how many calories you had each day.
14. Plan meals for 3 days for a person who is underweight. Plan meals for 3 days for a person who is overweight. Discuss the differences between the two menus.
15. Bring to class a reducing diet that you have seen in a magazine or newspaper. Note the good points as well as the poor ones about each diet.
16. Compare your weight with the average given on a height-weight chart for a person of your height, sex, and age.

From "Better Living." Courtesy DuPont

Chapter 10 | # MEALS IN A HURRY

In the past, many women had to spend from 6 to 8 hours each day in preparing and serving meals. Today many wives and mothers work outside the home or are engaged in some activity in addition to homemaking. Most women are looking for ideas on how to prepare and serve nutritious and attractive meals in a short time. As a result, ways are constantly being devised to help families prepare meals in a minimum of time and with a minimum of effort.

For example, food manufacturers are preparing many foods in ready-to-eat, frozen, powdered, dehydrated, and partially prepared forms (see page 136). Equipment manufacturers are making many new kinds of large and small equipment (see pages 143 and 380). Home economists in schools, colleges, and businesses are doing research and giving out information constantly in an effort to help homemakers plan, prepare, and serve meals quickly and easily.

If you are responsible for all or some of the meals in your home, you, too, will be interested in learning ways to prepare nutritious, enjoyable, and attractive meals quickly and easily so that you can have time for other activities.   **133**

PLANNING TO SAVE TIME AND ENERGY

By planning ahead, you can prepare meals quickly and easily. That is, you should plan what you are going to have, what you need to buy, how you are going to prepare the food, how much time the preparation will take, what you can do ahead of time, and how you are going to serve the meals. The plans will, of course, be affected by the situation. For instance, . . .

. . . Marie's mother has a full-time job, and Marie has to prepare the evening meals. Therefore, over the week end Marie and her mother do most of their shopping for the week, prepare what foods they can ahead of time, and plan the evening meals for each day.

. . . Martha's family is having company over the week end. What can Martha and her mother do about the meals so that they will be able to spend more time with the guests and less in the kitchen?

. . . All of Katie's family are going to a play in which she is taking part, and they have to arrive early. What kind of dinner should they have so that they will not have to rush through the meal?

. . . Janie and her family have a great deal of work to do about the house because they are redecorating. What kind of lunches, which can be prepared quickly and served without too much trouble, might they have?

Courtesy Corning Glass Works

FOODS FOR AN EMERGENCY

Many homemakers have two or three favorite menus for meals which they can prepare quickly when unexpected company drops by. They usually keep a supply of foods for such menus in the freezer or on an "emergency shelf."

Each homemaker probably has her own ideas about what should be kept on hand for an emergency, but these general suggestions might be helpful:

1. *For appetizers and soups:* Fruit juice, tomato juice, fruit or seafood cocktails, canned and dehydrated soups

2. *For main dishes:* Canned chicken, hash, tuna fish, salmon, stew, ham, sausages, chipped beef, spaghetti, chili, baked beans

3. *For creamed dishes or casseroles:* Mushroom and chicken soups, commercial sauces, evaporated milk

4. *For vegetables:* Canned peas, corn, tomatoes, beans

5. *For salads:* Canned peaches and pears, canned peas and beans (It is a good idea always to keep lettuce, celery, carrots, and tomatoes in the refrigerator because they can be used as the base for many kinds of salads.)

6. *For desserts:* Canned fruits, boxes of gelatin and puddings, ice-cream mixes, pie mixes, cake mixes

7. *For breads:* Biscuit and muffin mixes, canned brown bread

8. *For an extra touch:* Jellies, jams, pickles, olives, relishes

Such foods are bread, butter, potatoes, rice, onions, and fresh milk are used so frequently that they should be kept on hand at all times.

It is a good idea to check emergency supplies at regular times.

Courtesy National Canners Association

Courtesy Household Finance Corporation

Today foods are available in a great many forms that are particularly adaptable for preparing meals in a short time:

1. *Ready-to-eat foods,* which can be placed on the table as they come from the store (cold cereals, cold meats, cheese, milk, bakery goods, and some canned foods)

2. *Precooked foods,* which need only to be heated before they are served (canned vegetables and meats)

3. *Powdered* or *dehydrated foods,* to which only water has to be added (orange juice, coffee, tea, soups, and mashed potatoes)

4. *Frozen foods,* some of which need only to be defrosted (fruits and cakes), some of which need only to be heated (plate dinners and prepared dishes), and some of which need to be cooked (meat pies and vegetables)

5. *Partially cooked foods,* which need further cooking (quick-cooking cereals and brown-and-serve rolls)

6. *Partially prepared foods,* which need to be mixed or combined with other ingredients (cake, pie, and bread mixes)

These forms of foods have the added advantage of resulting in a good product for the beginning cook as well as being quick and easy to prepare. There is no doubt that the homemaker who buys these foods will save time and energy. However, she will probably spend more money because the more ready to eat a product is, the more it is likely to cost.

Courtesy Libby, McNeill and Libby

A great many foods may be bought ready to be served: cold cuts, baked ham, roast beef, sliced turkey, barbecued meats, cheese, potato salad, gelatin salads, cereals, frozen desserts, milk and milk beverages, bakery products (breads, cakes, cookies, and pies), and some canned foods (fruit, meat, and sauces).

Courtesy National Dairy Council

Courtesy Associated Blue Lake Canners, Inc.

Canned foods are usually the least expensive of all ready-to-eat or partially prepared foods. Since they have been seasoned and cooked, canned foods may be served immediately after heating. The efficient homemaker will improve the flavor of canned foods by adding special seasoning or by combining them with another food. Here are some ideas for improving and "dressing up" canned foods:

1. Add ½ cup tomato juice as part of the liquid and a few drops of Worcestershire sauce to cream of tomato soup.
2. Add 2 tablespoons sour cream to a cream soup, and stir slightly just before serving.
3. Add about ½ cup vegetables to a cream-style soup, for example, English peas to pea soup and raw cauliflower to chicken soup. Add celery salt, a pinch of sugar, and 1 tablespoon butter to improve the flavor of many canned cream soups.
4. Add a small onion to soup while heating. Remove it before serving.

Main Dishes

1. Combine canned beef stew with additional cooked vegetables, such as peas, carrots, and onions. You may bake the mixture in a casserole topped with biscuits, pastry dough, or mashed potatoes.
2. The flavor of canned hash may be improved by adding any of the following: chopped onions, green peppers, or celery. (NOTE: Many other canned foods can be improved in flavor by the addition of onions, green peppers, celery, bacon, and canned tomatoes.)
3. Make a creamed dish out of chipped beef, grated cheese, canned mushrooms, and a can of cream of mushroom soup. Serve on crisp toast or freshly baked waffles.
4. Make a casserole of chipped beef, sliced turkey, or sliced chicken and a can of spaghetti with tomato sauce, and bake.

Vegetables

1. Put melted cheese on top of green beans, broccoli, or asparagus.
2. Add a pinch of sugar to such canned vegetables as peas or corn. Brown sugar is sometimes added to carrots.
3. Add onion rings, butter, and salt to canned beans. Heat and serve.
4. Combine a can of peas with a small can of mushrooms. Heat, and season with butter and garlic salt.

Courtesy Best Foods, Inc.

DEHYDRATED FOODS

Dehydrated foods, such as milk (page 243), chocolate beverages (page 364), orange drinks (page 362), vegetables (page 190), soups (page 214), and desserts (page 348), are foods from which the water has been removed before packaging. They require no refrigeration if they are kept in their moistureproof packages.

To prepare most dehydrated foods, add hot or cold milk or water according to the directions on the package.

Not only are dehydrated foods easy to prepare, but most of them are inexpensive. Some, such as dehydrated potatoes, cost more than fresh food, but there is no waste involved in preparation.

Courtesy Campbell Soup Company

Courtesy Birds Eye

Courtesy Armour and Company

FROZEN FOODS

Some frozen foods (such as fruits, fruit juices, and some pies and cakes) need only to be defrosted before serving. Complete meals (such as TV dinners) and complete dishes (such as broccoli with hollandaise sauce) may be bought in frozen form and merely heated before serving. Other frozen foods that have been only partly prepared and cooked (such as meat pies and fruit pies) need to be cooked or baked for a short time before they are served. Frozen foods which have been prepared ready for cooking (such as minute steaks and breaded shrimp) may also be obtained.

For more information on frozen foods, see pages 160, 170, 176, 185, 189, 214, 280, and 350.

MIXES

Mixes may be bought, or they may be made in the home for less money.

Some of the commercial mixes for biscuits, pancakes, waffles, muffins, gingerbread, cookies, and cakes require only the addition of a liquid. Others require the addition of an egg as well.

Mixes for gelatin desserts, cornstarch puddings, and ice cream may be prepared in a few minutes, but time must be allowed for them to chill or freeze.

Foods made from mixes are virtually foolproof. Therefore, almost anyone can count on having good results. Many a homemaker who would not attempt to make cakes and pies with her own ingredients makes them with mixes. For this reason, many families now have homemade cakes and pies. However, some families prefer the baked products which the homemaker makes with her own ingredients.

In most instances, a cake made with a mix costs a little more than a cake that a homemaker makes with her own ingredients. But there are times when a cake mix costs less. For example, when eggs are expensive, an angel food cake made with a mix will be cheaper than a cake made entirely in the home. However, this would not be true of a mix which requires the addition of fresh eggs.

When buying any mix, always check the label to be sure that the flour used has been enriched. (See page 315.)

Courtesy Betty Crocker of General Mills

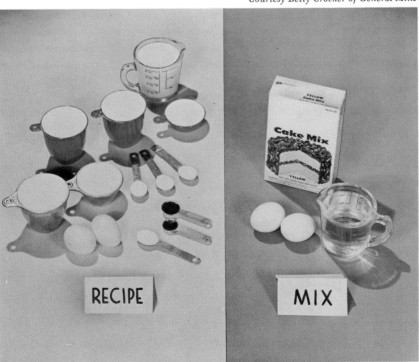

FOODS THAT CAN BE PREPARED QUICKLY

Courtesy New York State College of Home Economics, Cornell University

There are some fresh foods that can be prepared just as quickly and as easily as packaged, canned, or frozen foods. For instance, egg dishes, such as omelets and scrambled, poached, and fried eggs, can be used for any quick meal as well as for breakfast. Many kinds of meat, such as meat patties, chops, and steaks, can be broiled or fried in a short time. Frankfurters cooked with other foods, such as bacon and cheese (see recipe on page 516), can be prepared and cooked quickly as a main dish for lunch or supper.

Courtesy Libby, McNeill and Libby

Courtesy Wilson and Company, Inc.

Courtesy National Presto Industries, Inc.

Vegetables can be cooked in a few minutes in a pressure saucepan. Meats, such as stew, braised chicken, meat balls, Swiss steak, and pot roast, can be cooked more quickly in a pressure saucepan than in any other way (see page 379).

Electric griddles and other electric appliances are timesavers because they can be set for doneness and the food does not have to be watched.

See pages 374 and 380 for other ideas on use of equipment to save time.

Courtesy "Electrical Merchandising"

Courtesy American Sheep Producers Council, Inc.

When all the food for a meal is combined in one hot dish — as in a casserole, a stew, or a meat pie — or when the meat, the vegetable, and the potato are cooked together in aluminum foil, a meal takes less time to prepare than when each of the foods is cooked separately.

Courtesy Reynolds Metals Company

Courtesy Ac'cent

The ingredients for meat loaf (see recipe on page 518) may be combined and shaped into loaves one day and stored in the refrigerator to be baked the next. Many recipes in this book state how to do part one day and finish it the next.

Meat loaf will bake quickly if shaped into individual loaves or baked in muffin pans.

Such foods as gelatin desserts or salads and refrigerator puddings can be prepared the day before they are to be served. This is a particularly helpful timesaver when entertaining.

Courtesy Abbott Laboratories

Courtesy Reynolds Wrap

Certain kinds of foods can be prepared over the week end and stored in the refrigerator for use during the week. For instance, a roast or baked ham that is served hot the first time may be sliced and served cold for another meal. Then whatever is left may be used for a meat pie, a casserole, croquettes, or sandwiches. Leftover stewed chicken may be made into chicken and dumplings or chicken and spaghetti for a second serving. The rest may be used to make chicken à la king or chicken salad.

If the food is to be kept longer than 2 or 3 days, however, it should be properly wrapped and stored in the freezing compartment of the refrigerator or in a food freezer. Of course, there are many foods that can be prepared and put in the food freezer to be served later, such as soups, stews, casseroles, breads, cookies, cakes, and pies.

Some cookie dough (see recipe on page 541) may be kept in the refrigerator or the food freezer until it is to be baked.

USDA Photo

Bland

There are many ways of saving time and energy in serving meals. For example, if the plates are served in the kitchen, time will be saved in passing or serving the food at the table. Energy will be saved because there will be no serving dishes to wash.

For a large group, serve the food buffet style (page 28).

For the family or a small informal group, place the food on a table or a cabinet in the kitchen, and allow each person to make his own sandwich or to serve his own plate.

If electric appliances are used, part or all of the food may be prepared at the table.

Place mats are less trouble than a tablecloth. Those made of straw or plastic are timesavers because they do not have to be laundered.

Courtesy "Electrical Merchandising"

147

ACTIVITIES

Using prepared foods:

1. List three advantages of using ready-to-eat and partially prepared foods. Then list three disadvantages of using them.
2. Describe the ready-to-eat foods and the partially prepared foods that your mother uses.
3. Describe an embarrassing situation you and your mother have had when you did not have food on an emergency shelf for unexpected company.

Learning to use equipment which saves time:

4. Describe two gadgets, such as a parer, which your mother uses that save time. Describe two other gadgets which are seldom used in your home.
5. What kinds of electrical appliances may be used at the table?

Planning ahead:

6. Plan menus for the evening meals for 1 week. List foods which may be prepared during the week end and kept until needed.
7. Susie and her family are going out for the evening, but they wish to eat at home before they go. Plan a menu of foods that can be prepared in a hurry or partially prepared the day before.
8. Plan menus that might be served by each of the families described on page 134.

Learning to use canned foods:

9. Plan four menus using as many of the suggestions for canned foods on pages 138 and 139 as possible.
10. List canned foods which can be improved in flavor by the addition of one or more of the following: onions, green peppers, celery, bacon.
11. Bring five suggestions to class on how to add variety to, and improve the flavor of, canned goods, similar to the suggestions on pages 138 and 139.

Preparing part of the food one day:

12. Select from cookbooks three recipes which may be partially prepared one day and then finished the next day.
13. List five dishes, such as a gelatin salad, which may be prepared one day and served the next.

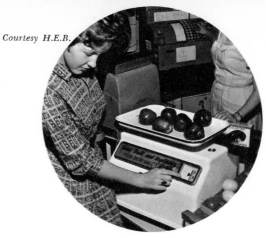

Courtesy H.E.B.

part **2**

YOUR FOODS–
HOW YOU BUY
AND PREPARE THEM

Chapter 11 | BUYING YOUR FOOD

Homemakers who spend a great deal of money for food do not necessarily serve the best meals. The reason that one family can have better meals for less money than another depends largely upon the knowledge of the homemaker in the following situations:

1. *When planning to shop:* Before going to the food stores, tentatively plan the menus for the coming week. Next, check the supplies on hand, and read the current food advertisements. Finally, make a list of what you need. Then, when you know what you need and have checked the prices, you can make a more definite plan for the menus.

2. *When buying foods:* Every time you go to the food stores, it is your business to get the best value that you can for the money that you have to spend. However, you must remember that the cheapest food is not always the best buy. It is the amount of food value that you get for your dollar that counts. Consider it a challenge to learn how to be a better buyer each time you shop.

3. *When preparing and serving food:* The amount of money that is spent for a family's food can be cut if: (*a*) the homemaker takes pride in eliminating waste as well as in preparing and serving low-cost foods so that they are tasty and nutritious and (*b*) the family will learn to eat and enjoy all food that the homemaker serves.

150

DECIDING ON THE AMOUNT TO SPEND

The homemaker who decides on a certain amount of money that she will spend each week for food and spends no more than that amount usually manages better than those who buy in a hit-and-miss fashion. The amount to be spent for food depends upon the following factors:

1. The income of the family.
2. The size of the family and the ages as well as the food likes and dislikes of the members.
3. The community in which the family lives.
4. The amount of food that is produced at home and the amount that is canned or frozen by the family.
5. The activities of the family and the amount of entertaining. The family that does a lot of entertaining will naturally spend more for groceries than one that does very little.
6. The amount of time that the homemaker has for shopping and cooking.
7. The experience that she has had in preparing meals.

For the homemaker who works outside the home, it may be best to buy pre-cooked, premixed, prepackaged, frozen, and instant foods because she does not have much time to prepare meals. Most studies show that food which is prepared entirely in the home is less expensive than that which is partially prepared when purchased. Food which is partially prepared is less expensive than that which is ready to serve. For example, homemade biscuits are a little cheaper than biscuits which are made with a biscuit mix. Biscuits made with a mix are cheaper than canned biscuits. The homemaker who is at home all day can and should prepare foods which, although they may take longer to cook, are less expensive than partially prepared and ready-to-serve foods. Also, she has time to compare prices and to watch for food specials.

Koos from Black Star

151

PLANNING MEALS TO SAVE MONEY

There are many ways to save money when buying food and yet serve tasty as well as nutritious meals.

1. Plan meals and make out a market list for the week to avoid extra trips to the food stores. The fewer your trips to the stores, the less temptation you will have to buy unnecessary foods or to overbuy.

2. Check the newspapers, watch television, and listen to the radio for weekly food specials. Plan your meals with these specials in mind. But remember that the purpose of advertising is to make you want to buy the product advertised (see page 153).

3. Plan to serve foods that are in season because they are usually cheap, plentiful, and of good quality.

4. Plan the week's market order with *A Daily Food Guide* in mind (see pages 48-52). Plan first for the foods that are needed to maintain good health. Then, if you have extra money, you may include in your menus nonessential foods, such as mushrooms, pimentos, olives, nuts, ice-cream sundaes, cookies, sweet rolls, potato chips, and carbonated drinks. In order to have enough money for nonessential foods, you may prefer to buy less-expensive foods in each group of *A Daily Food Guide*. If you do, the following suggestions should be helpful even though conditions vary in different sections.

Milk Group: Nonfat dry milk costs less than evaporated milk. Evaporated milk costs less than whole fresh milk. Cottage cheese costs less than cream cheese. Coffee cream costs less than whipping cream. Processed and blended cheeses are often less expensive than some natural cheeses. However, some cheese spreads are very expensive.

Meat Group: Round steak costs more than hamburger. Lamb chops are more expensive than veal chops. Shrimp is more expensive than most fish. Grade B eggs are less expensive than Grade A eggs. Canned meats and poultry usually cost more than fresh, but most canned fish is less expensive than fresh fish. Of course, as in many other instances, the price depends upon the location. Dry beans, dry peas, and lentils all cost less than meats. Yet all contain proteins and may be served in place of meat part of the time. Peanuts are less expensive than pecans and many other nuts.

Vegetable-Fruit Group: Grapefruit is cheaper than strawberries but may not be as cheap as cantaloupe during certain seasons of the year. All three contain vitamin C. Raw cabbage is cheaper than lettuce and other salad greens. Carrots are cheaper than broccoli. Both are important sources of vitamin A. Fresh fruits and vegetables which are in season are cheaper as well as better than those which are not in season. Idaho potatoes are excellent for baking, but they may be more expensive than potatoes grown near your home.

Bread-Cereal Group: Oatmeal and other cooked cereals are less expensive than ready-to-eat cereals. Day-old bread is cheaper than fresh bread. Bread made at home is cheaper than bread which merely needs to be heated or baked.

ADVERTISEMENTS

Food advertisements in newspapers often give special prices for certain brands which are being offered. If the homemaker uses this information properly, she may save on her food purchases. If it is necessary to ride a bus or to drive across town to buy the food that is on special sale, she should consider the cost of transportation. She should also note whether the can or the container of the item which is being sold at the special price is of the same size as the one which sells at the regular price.

One of the duties of the Federal Trade Commission of the United States government is to check claims made in advertisements. Its regulations encourage accuracy and help to maintain high standards in advertising.

Do not be satisfied because someone on a radio or a television commercial or in a newspaper or a magazine advertisement says that a certain brand of food is the best buy. Check for yourself. The many glamorous advertisements and catchy slogans may make it difficult to tell if something is a good buy. For example, whether to buy fresh, frozen, canned, or dried food can become a problem. An advertisement put out by a canning company might lead one to believe that canned food not only is cheapest but also contains the most nutrients. On the other hand, a manufacturer of frozen foods might indicate in advertisements that his products are the best buys.

Some companies make special offers in order to get you to try their product. It may be a good idea to take advantage of a special offer if you have use for the product. The following are examples of special offers:

1. A can or a package may contain a coupon which allows you to save a certain amount the next time you buy that same product.

2. A special price is offered if two or more of the product are bought.

3. Sometimes, in order to introduce a new product, an offer is made to refund some or all of the purchase price for a limited time.

Courtesy New York Life Insurance Company

Courtesy Household Finance Corporation

Even though a homemaker keeps a grocery list in the kitchen and jots down supplies which are getting low, she should check the cabinets and the refrigerator before going to the food stores.

When you make a shopping list after you have planned the menus for the week, it is helpful to list possible substitutes. Then, if the store does not have the food that you had planned to serve or if you find that it is too expensive, you can easily select something else.

If you group similar things together on your shopping list, as shown below, you will save a great deal of time when shopping. Note that canned and bottled groceries, which are the heaviest items, should be placed in the bottom of the cart or the basket. Staples, such as flour and sugar, should be put in the cart or the basket next. Fresh fruits and vegetables should be selected toward the end of your shopping so that they will not be crushed. Frozen foods should, of course, be selected last so that they will have less chance to thaw before you get home.

Food Groupings for Shopping List

Canned and bottled groceries
Staples, such as flour, sugar, and salt
Meat, fish, and poultry
Dairy products and eggs
Bread and bakery foods
Fresh fruits and vegetables
Frozen foods

Courtesy Weber Showcase and Fixture Company, Inc.

The type of store in which you shop depends mostly upon where you live. Perhaps the most common places in which to shop are supermarkets, chain stores, independent stores, public markets, roadside markets, cooperatives, and delicatessens. It is wise to shop around to learn where you can get the most for your money. If you are in the habit of shopping at one place, you may find it helpful to go to other stores just to compare prices and to see what they have to offer. Of course, the homemaker who goes from store to store looking for specials may be surprised at the amount of time she spends in doing it. Then, too, she must also consider the quality of food sold at very low prices. Even though the vegetables may be much cheaper in one store than they are in another, if they are wilted and part of them cannot be used, they are not a good buy.

Courtesy Farmers Market

Our federal, state, and city governments have laws to protect the food we eat. The federal and state governments have pure food laws and laws concerning food weights and measures and food containers. They also set standards for grading and labeling food. On page 252 you will learn how eggs are graded. How meats are inspected and graded is discussed on page 266. Federal and state inspectors visit food manufacturing plants to make sure that food is prepared and packaged under sanitary conditions. Federal regulations apply to food which is shipped from state to state. Regulations of the individual states apply only to food that is prepared and sold within the state. State and city health departments set standards for milk, require medical examinations for food handlers, and inspect restaurants to see that food is prepared under sanitary conditions.

Every shopper who is interested in getting the most for her money should read food labels carefully. Some of the information on labels is required by law. Other information, including recipes, is supplied by the manufacturer because he wants to interest the shopper so that she will choose his product and buy it often. Regardless of what information is on a label, federal law requires that it be truthful and not misleading.

Information which federal law requires on labels includes the following: the name of the manufacturer and the distributor, the common name of the product, the weight in ounces or pounds or the liquid measurement of the contents, and a list of the ingredients used in making the product. If the product is an imitation of another product, this must be stated on the label. The label must also state if any chemical preservative, artificial flavoring, or artificial coloring has been added to the food. Most manufacturers also include on the labels the style of pack (sliced, whole, cream style), the size (tiny, small, medium, large, extra large), the variety or type (cling or freestone peaches), the type of sirup used with fruits (light, heavy, extra heavy), the amount (number of pieces, cups, or servings), suggestions for using the product, and the grade.

Courtesy H. E. B.

USDA *Photo*

Grades A, B, and C are United States government grading standards for canned foods. Canned tomatoes of all three grades are shown above and described below.

U.S. Grade A (Fancy): Tomatoes are whole; practically uniform; good red, typical color; practically free of defects; normal tomato flavor and odor.

U.S. Grade B (Extra Standard): Most of the tomatoes are whole; reasonably good red, typical color; reasonably free of defects; normal tomato flavor and odor.

U.S. Grade C (Standard): The tomatoes are in pieces; fairly good red, typical color; fairly free of defects; normal tomato flavor and odor.

It is not always necessary to buy the best grade. Grade C will serve the purpose just as well for tomato soup as would Grades A or B since the tomatoes will be mashed anyway.

Government grading of canned goods is not required by law. Therefore, some manufacturers use their own grading systems, such as "super" and "super-super" grades.

The government does not require that the amount of moisture be stated on the can, but the homemaker who takes an interest in getting the most for her money soon learns that some brands contain more water than others.

Bland

BUYING FRESH FOODS

You can judge fresh foods by their general appearance, color, texture, size, and weight. See the following pages for specific directions on buying fresh foods: fruits, page 169; vegetables, page 184; milk, page 242; eggs, page 256; meat, pages 266-271; poultry, page 286; and fish, pages 293 and 294.

Most fresh food is sold by weight rather than by the dozen, head, bunch, or quart. When buying food by weight:

1. Look at the scale and check the weight yourself.
2. Request that a thin layer of paper or none at all, not a large paper sack, be placed under the food being weighed.
3. Notice if the scale bears a government seal showing that it has been checked for accuracy.

Food that is sold by weight is usually priced by unit of weight — ¼ pound, ½ pound, 1 pound, 2 pounds, and so on. Usually it is economical to buy the full unit.

BUYING PACKAGED FOODS

Patteson

Many fruits and vegetables are packaged so that they will retain their freshness. Packaging protects food from bruising, handling, and dirt. In addition, packaged fruits and vegetables are a convenience for shoppers in self-service markets.

Spinach that has been washed before it is packaged saves time for the homemaker. Packaged vegetables for soup are economical because it is unnecessary to buy several different kinds of vegetables. Vegetables that have been cut, trimmed, and shredded for salads are great timesavers. But they are usually more expensive than the whole vegetable, and they cannot be kept very long. When comparing prices, however, consider that there is no waste in prepared packaged vegetables.

A large box of food is less expensive per serving than a small box. Food that is sold in plastic bags is usually cheaper than the same food sold in boxes. Food sold in boxes is cheaper than the same food sold in cans.

Patteson

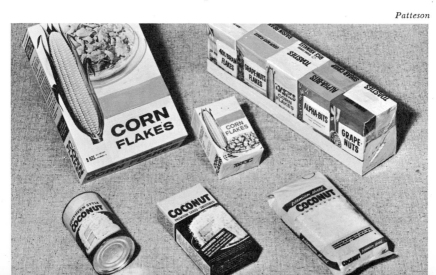

Courtesy H. E. B.

BUYING FROZEN FOODS

For frozen food to be at its best, it must be kept solidly frozen from the time it is shipped from the processing plant until it is to be used. Hence, you should take these special precautions in buying frozen food:

1. Buy only in stores in which frozen food is kept below the food line in the frozen food case. The temperature of the frozen food case should be 0 degrees or less.

2. Buy frozen food last, or just before you leave the store.

3. Select packages that are firm and solidly frozen. However, this is not a guarantee that the food has been cared for properly. Packages that are torn, misshapen, or stained with fruit juice may have thawed and may have been refrozen.

4. Buy only the amount that you can store properly even if you must forego a bargain. Frozen food can be kept for several months in a food freezer but for only 2 or 3 weeks in the freezing compartment of a refrigerator.

5. Put frozen food in an insulated freezer bag, which many stores have near the frozen food, or in two small paper bags.

6. Ask the clerk who packs your groceries to put the frozen food on top of the other food so that you can put it in the freezing compartment as soon as you get home.

7. When you have your groceries delivered, take the frozen food with you.

8. Take frozen food home at once so that there will be no chance of its defrosting.

9. When you store frozen food, write the date on packages that are to be kept more than a few days.

10. Never refreeze food once it has been allowed to thaw completely.

11. Follow the directions on the package when defrosting. Not all frozen foods are defrosted alike.

12. Inform the store manager if you see packages of frozen food in the case which seem to have been refrozen after thawing.

13. For specific directions for buying frozen food, see the following pages: fruit, page 170; vegetables, page 185; eggs, page 256; meat, page 272; poultry, page 287; and fish, page 294.

BUYING CANNED FOODS

SIZE OF CAN	SERVINGS	USES
6 ounces	4 to 6	Frozen concentrated juices
8 ounces	2	Fruits, vegetables, and specialties*
No. 1	2 to 3	Condensed soups, some fruits, vegetables, meat and fish products, and specialties*
12 ounces	4 to 5	Vacuum-packed corn
No. 300 (often called 1-pound can)	3 to 4	Pork and beans, baked beans, meat products, cranberry sauce, blueberries, and specialties*
No. 303 (often called 16- or 17-ounce can)	3 to 4	Fruits, vegetables, meat products, and specialties*
No. 2	4 to 5	Juices, fruits, vegetables, and specialties*
No. 2½	6 to 7	Fruits, such as peaches, pears, plums, and fruit cocktail; and some vegetables, such as pumpkin, spinach, other greens, and tomatoes
1 quart	5 to 8	Fruit and vegetable juices; whole chicken and fruits and vegetables for restaurant use
No. 10	35 to 50	Fruits and vegetables for restaurant use

*Specialties are usually food combinations, such as macaroni, spaghetti, Spanish-style rice, Mexican-type foods, Chinese foods, and tomato aspic.

Patteson

161

Photos Courtesy National Dairy Council

Before leaving the grocery store, check to make sure that you have something from each group in *A Daily Food Guide* pictured above. After you have bought sufficient foods from each of the groups in *A Daily Food Guide*, you may wish to use the remainder of your food money for nonessential foods, such as cold drinks, nuts, olives, mushrooms, and potato chips.

162

IGA Food Stores

MAKING THE MOST
OF WHAT YOU HAVE

Do not store foods which do not need to be refrigerated in the refrigerator. They take up the room that is needed for perishable foods. Also, they raise the cost of the electric bill.

Store such foods as potatoes, onions, garlic, and winter squash where cool air can circulate around them rather than in the refrigerator.

For proper storage of other foods, see the following pages: fresh fruits and vegetables, page 172; milk, page 244; eggs, page 256; and meat, page 272.

Courtesy St. Charles Custom Kitchens

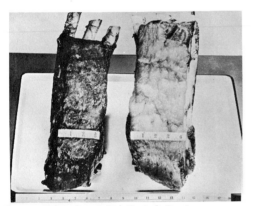

Courtesy Robertshaw-Fulton Controls Company

Courtesy Fire-King Casseroles

You can save money by preparing and cooking food properly. For example, meat which is cooked at a low temperature will not shrink nearly so much as meat which is cooked at a high temperature. As you study the following chapters, you will learn many other ways in which you can save money when preparing food.

Wise use of leftovers is a must when you are trying to save on the food budget. Place leftovers in tightly covered containers, and store them in the refrigerator until you are ready to use them. Avoid merely warming leftovers. Instead, change them as much as possible, and add a garnish. **163**

ACTIVITIES

Learning to save when planning meals:

1. List and compare the prices of each of the following: *(a)* individual boxes of cereal and a large box, *(b)* packaged rice and bulk rice in plastic bags, *(c)* fresh tomatoes and canned tomatoes, *(d)* tomato juice and orange juice, *(e)* frozen carrots and fresh carrots. Next, compare the food value of each. Then decide which would be the best buy in each case.

2. Make a list of the foods on page 152 which are similar even though one food is more expensive than the other. Then add other examples, such as cinnamon toast (page 524), which is less expensive than sweet rolls. Have a contest in class to see which girl can make the longest and best list.

Learning to use advertisements:

3. Select five food advertisements from magazines or a local newspaper. *(a)* Compare what the advertisements have to say. *(b)* Discuss how helpful each one is. *(c)* List the statements pertaining to nutrition that they contain.

4. Make a list of five new words that you have learned in this chapter. Use each word in a sentence.

Deciding how and where to shop:

5. Dramatize a scene in a grocery store. The leading character is a woman shopper who has no idea of what she wants to buy.

6. Make a market order according to the directions on page 154.

7. In several grocery stores, compare prices of a particular food, such as a certain brand of margarine. Compare prices again in 2, 4, and 6 weeks. Was the store which had the best price the first time also the cheapest at other times when you compared prices?

8. List the advantages of shopping at certain times on certain days.

Deciding to buy fresh, frozen, canned, or dried food:

9. Discuss when it is best to buy different foods in fresh, frozen, canned, or dried form in your community.

10. Bring to class three labels from canned food. With the help of your classmates, select the label which has the most helpful information.

11. Consult other chapters in this book, and discuss points to consider when buying fresh fruits, fresh vegetables, and fresh meats.

12. Give a skit showing the correct and incorrect ways to shop for fresh fruits and vegetables.

13. In your community, at what time of the year is it better to buy fresh rather than canned or frozen: *(a)* strawberries, *(b)* pineapple, *(c)* tomatoes?

Chapter 12 | FRUIT

Everyone likes some kind of fruit. The many varieties of fruit, with their colorful appearance, pleasing flavor, and many uses, add interest and appeal to any meal.

Besides having color, flavor, and usefulness, fruit is a food of great value:

1. Fruit contains a type of sugar that gives quick energy.
2. Fruit is rich in vitamins and minerals. Both are important to health. Citrus fruits, particularly oranges and grapefruit, are especially rich in vitamin C. Some citrus fruit should be eaten every day unless vitamin C is contained in other foods eaten.
3. Fruit contains little or no fat and very little protein.
4. Many fruits contain roughage, which is needed for normal elimination.

Fruit may be served for any part of any meal, between meals, or before going to bed. Because fruit is rich in vitamins and minerals and stimulates the appetite, it is a very good food to eat between meals. In fact, fruit makes a much better snack than a soft drink, candy, a piece of cake, or other sweets. **165**

Elicson

As an appetizer: Fruit juices are favorite breakfast appetizers. Because of its tart flavor, fruit stimulates the appetite. Therefore, various kinds of fruit — fruit juice, fruit cups, grapefruit halves, orange sections, and sliced fruit — are served as appetizers for all meals.

As a fruit plate or a salad: Fruit plates or large fruit salads are popular during the summer months. Small fruit salads are served the year round before the main course, with the main course, or as a dessert.

Courtesy Best Foods, Inc.

Courtesy Associated Pimiento Canners

As a garnish: Fruit adds not only to the attractiveness of a dish, but to its flavor as well. Some popular fruit garnishes are pineapple (with ham), cranberries (with poultry), lemon (with fish), and apples (with pork). Cherries, lemons, limes, pineapple, and oranges are also used as garnishes for various beverages.

As a dessert: Fruit pies, cobblers, tarts, shortcakes, gelatin, puddings, and whips are only a few of the many ways in which fruit may be used in desserts. Fresh fruit in season, such as peaches, berries, and melons, is also a favorite American dessert.

Courtesy Processed Apples Institute, Inc.

167

BUYING AND SELECTING FRESH FRUIT

There are many points to consider when selecting and buying fresh fruits:

1. Shop for fruit early in the morning. The selection will be better and the fruit will be fresher than later in the day.

2. Buy fruit in season. It is less expensive and has a better flavor than when out of season. Fruit grown near your home is better than that which is shipped from a distant place. Fruit that is to be shipped is usually picked before it is ripe to prevent it from spoiling.

3. Decide how the fruit is to be used before buying it. Is it to be served raw or cooked? Is it to be used for juice or salad? Navel oranges are best for eating. Valencia oranges are best for juice. Firm apples, such as Rome Beauty, are good for baking. On the other hand, Delicious apples are a favorite for eating. Fruit in fancy packages (specially selected) or select fruit may be attractive, but it has no more food value than fruit which costs less.

4. Do not order fruit by telephone. Only by seeing fruit can you make a good selection. It should be ripe, but not too ripe. Fruit should be firm and have a good color. A large size does not always mean quality. For example, a large grapefruit or orange that is lightweight might not be as good a buy for juice as a small one that is heavy. Melons and pineapple should be selected by their aroma.

5. Do not buy fruits which show signs of decay. Mere blemishes do not affect the quality of the inside of the fruit. Waste caused by cutting away decay often makes the price much higher than that of good-quality fruit.

6. When selecting fruit, handle it as little as possible. It should not be squeezed or handled much because it bruises easily. Bruised fruit spoils quickly. This loss to the retailer is passed on to you in higher-priced fruit.

7. Avoid buying too much fruit even when it is cheap. The amount of fruit bought should depend on the number of people in the family, the availability of storage space at home, and the kind of fruit. For example, apples can be kept much longer than bananas.

8. Fruit bought in containers should be uniform throughout. Examine berries in baskets before buying.

Fruit is sold by the dozen, by the piece, by the pint or quart, or by the pound. Buying by weight (by the pound) is best in most instances.

BUYING FROZEN, CANNED, AND DRIED FRUIT

Courtesy Household Finance Corporation

Whether you buy fresh, frozen, canned, or dried fruit will depend upon what is available in your locality at a particular time of the year and the way in which you want to use it. Surely with the many kinds that are always available in some form, no one should have any trouble in including fruit in his diet at least twice a day.

Quick-frozen fruits often seem to be more expensive than fresh, canned, or dried fruit. However, when comparing the price of frozen fruits with the prices of other kinds, remember that frozen fruits have no waste, are easy to serve, are of high quality, and are higher in food value than some canned or dried fruit. When buying canned fruit, as in buying any other canned goods, read the label as discussed on pages 156 and 178.

Courtesy Sunsweet Growers Inc.

Dried fruit may be bought in transparent, moistureproof packages, in boxes, or in paper bags. Dried prunes are available in three sizes — large, medium, and small — and are priced accordingly. The pits weigh so much that medium prunes are usually a better buy than small ones even though small prunes may cost less per pound. Large prunes are a more luxurious item than small or medium ones. Apricots may be more expensive per pound than prunes. But they are not so expensive as they may seem because the pits have been removed. When you compare prices, also notice the net weight on the box or package.

FRUIT JUICE

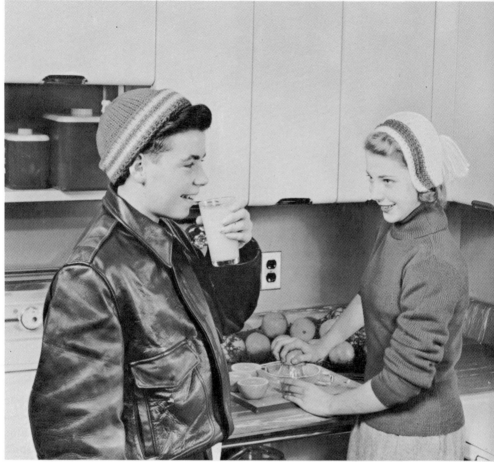

Courtesy Florida Citrus Commission

Fruit juice makes a refreshing and healthful between-meal drink or an appetizer. It may be squeezed from the fresh fruit or bought in canned, cartoned, powdered, or frozen forms.

Fresh orange juice has the best flavor when it is served soon after it is squeezed. If it must be kept for any length of time, it should be stored in an airtight container in the refrigerator. If it is allowed to stand too long, it becomes bitter and loses part of its valuable vitamins, especially vitamin C.

Canned fruit juice should be chilled. The can should not be opened until serving time. Concentrated canned fruit juice must be mixed with water before it can be served. Frozen fruit juice should be kept frozen until it is needed. When it is used immediately after being defrosted, it is as nutritious as fresh fruit juice. Powdered fruit juice may be quickly and easily prepared.

Courtesy Straus-Frank Company

Most fruit may be stored in the lower part of the refrigerator in a covered container, such as a hydrator. Bananas are the only fruit which should not be placed in the refrigerator. Chilling causes bananas to become discolored. Hardy fruits, such as apples and citrus fruits, will keep for days without being refrigerated. But once they have been chilled, they should be kept in the refrigerator. If refrigerated, these hardy fruits should be placed on the bottom of the hydrator. Grapes, cherries, and other small fruits should be kept in a separate container or put in a plastic bag on top of the hardy fruits. Berries should be left in the container in which they were bought until ready to be used.

To avoid bruising, handle fruit as little as possible. Fruit that is crowded into a small container will bruise easily. Bruised or fully ripe fruit should be eaten first. The hydrator should be checked daily so that any fruit which has started to spoil may be removed. One piece of spoiled fruit will cause others to spoil.

After fruit has been cut, it should be covered or wrapped with aluminum foil or transparent moistureproof paper. A grapefruit or orange half may be turned over on a plate to prevent it from drying out.

Courtesy Dow Chemical Company

Whether it has been cut or not, fruit with a strong odor — such as melons —must be wrapped to prevent the odor from spreading to other foods in the refrigerator. Melons may be pared and sliced and kept in a jar with a tight-fitting lid.

WASHING FRUIT

From "Better Living." Courtesy Du Pont

All fruit should be washed thoroughly before it is eaten. It is usually dusty, and it has been handled by many people. Besides, most fruit trees are sprayed with poison to destroy insects. All fruit should be washed as quickly as possible and not be allowed to stand in water. Fruit tends to spoil when wet. Therefore, it should not be washed until it is to be used. If it is washed, it should be dried thoroughly before it is put into the refrigerator. Various fruits should be washed in different ways.

Grapes should be cut into small bunches before being washed.

Apples and citrus fruits should be rubbed while being washed under running water. Special attention should be given to the stem end.

Berries should be washed in a colander or strainer just before they are to be used. After they have been drained, the stems and hulls should be removed. The berries should be washed again only if necessary.

Courtesy Vapocan

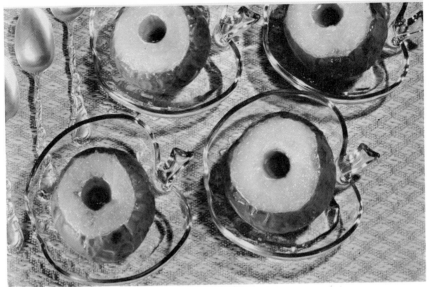

Courtesy H. F. Byrd, Inc.

Apples are the most popular baked fruit. Their heavy outer skin makes apples ideal fruit for baking.

Grapefruit, bananas, canned pineapple, and apricot and peach halves may be broiled.

Bananas and apples may be pan-fried in a small amount of fat.

Courtesy Florida Citrus Commission   *Courtesy United Fruit Company*

FRESH FRUIT

Whenever possible, fresh fruit should be served raw because fruit loses some of its vitamins when cooked. Cooked fruit, however, adds variety to meals. Also, some fruit, such as green apples, has a better flavor when cooked than when served raw. Some fruit, such as rhubarb, cannot be eaten raw. Fruit which has become too ripe will keep longer if cooked. Fruits may be stewed, baked, broiled, fried, sautéed, or glazed. They may be used in pies, tarts, and cobblers. Some fruits may be made into jellies, jams, and preserves. Regardless of which method you use when cooking fruit, the following suggestions should be considered:

1. Whenever possible, cook fresh fruit in the skins for better color and flavor as well as more food value.
2. If it is necessary to cut fruit before it is cooked, cut it into uniform pieces so that all the pieces will be tender at the same time.
3. Cook fruit in as small an amount of water as possible only until tender. This will prevent loss of vitamins and minerals which dissolve in boiling water. Little water is needed when fruit is cooked in a covered utensil. But if there is any liquid left after cooking, serve it with the fruit.
4. The amount of sugar needed depends on the sweetness of the fruit. For this reason recipes often say from ¼ to ⅓ cup sugar. If too much sugar or spice is added, it tends to destroy the delicate flavor of the fruit.

When making a fruit sauce, add sugar just before it is removed from the heat. If you wish fruit to hold its shape, add sugar when you start to cook it.

Courtesy Oregon-Washington-California Pear Bureau   *Courtesy Processed Apples Institute, Inc.*

When buying frozen fruit, select a package that is solidly frozen. Immediately after arriving home, put the frozen fruit in the freezing compartment of the refrigerator or in the food freezer. Because not all frozen fruits are defrosted alike, follow the directions on the package. In most cases, however, frozen fruits may be thawed in 2 or 3 hours at room temperature. They may also be thawed in the refrigerator over a longer period of time. Frozen fruits should never be refrozen after they have been thawed.

Quick-frozen fruits are fruits which were gathered at the peak of their flavor and frozen quickly. The fruits are frozen so rapidly that they retain much of the flavor, food value, and color of fresh fruit. A sugar sirup is usually added to help preserve the fruit.

Frozen fruits may be bought at practically all grocery stores. They may also be prepared at home from home-grown fruit or fruit bought in large quantities during the season. They may be stored in the family food freezer. Strawberries, raspberries, peaches, and blueberries are some of the most popular frozen fruits.

Quick-frozen fruits often seem to be more expensive than fresh, canned, or dried fruit. However, when comparing the price of frozen fruits with the prices of other kinds, remember that frozen fruits have no waste, are easy to serve, are of high quality, and are higher in food value than canned or dried fruit.

Courtesy Quick Frozen Foods

FRUIT JUICES

Frozen fruits may be used on short-cakes, in salads, as a sauce on desserts, or in any way that fresh or canned fruit is used. They may also be eaten plain as they come from the package, topped with sour cream (sprinkled with brown sugar) or sweet cream, or used in breakfast foods.

Courtesy Birds Eye

Most people prefer to eat frozen fruit just before it is completely defrosted, while there are still ice crystals in it. At this time the texture, flavor, and color are at their best. If frozen fruit is allowed to stand after it has been defrosted, it loses its bright color, has a flat taste, and becomes watery, soft, and shapeless.

When frozen fruit is to be used in cooking, it should be partly defrosted and then used as though it were fresh. Since sugar is usually added before the fruit is frozen, it is not necessary to add more sugar when the fruit is used in cooking.

Frozen fruit juices are the most popular of all frozen foods. (See page 171.) In addition to being used as beverages, they may be used undiluted as sauces on ice cream or fresh fruits.

Photos Courtesy Florida Citrus Commission

CANNED FRUIT

Applesauce
Fruit Cocktail
Sliced Peaches
Crushed Pineapple
Peach Halves
Pineapple Chunks
Whole Apricots

Julio G. Huante

Canned fruit may be bought whole, in halves, in chunks, sliced, crushed, or as a sauce. Most homemakers keep several cans of fruit on hand. Canned fruit takes up little storage space, is available all year round, and can be served easily in many ways at a moment's notice. Canned fruit may be chilled and served as a dessert just as it comes from the can. It may be drained and used in salads, fruit cups, gelatin desserts, puddings, pies, cobblers, and upside-down cakes. It may be used as a garnish or as a meat complement. From the label on canned fruit you should learn the following about the fruit you buy:

1. The size of the can, so that you can determine the amount that it holds, the number of servings, or the number of pieces.

2. The grade of the fruit, that is, whether the fruit is Fancy, Choice, or Standard.

3. The form of the fruit, that is, whether it is whole, cut in half, sliced, or made into a sauce.

4. If sugar has been added, whether the sirup is heavy or extra heavy.

5. Suggested recipes or ways to serve the fruit.

DRIED FRUIT

Dried fruits, such as prunes, apples, apricots, peaches, and raisins, may be cooked and served plain. They may also be combined with hot or cold cereal, or they may be used in salads, breads, cakes or cookies, and pie fillings.

If a box of dried fruit is labeled "tenderized," the fruit has been partially precooked. It may be cooked without being soaked if the directions on the box are followed. Dried fruit that is not labeled "tenderized" contains just as much food value as, and is less expensive than, tenderized fruit. But it is drier and harder. It should be soaked in warm water and then cooked in the same water to save the minerals and vitamins.

Ewing Galloway

Sweets (candies) made from dried fruits and candied fruits may be attractively arranged on a tray. In addition to being very colorful, dried fruit has a pleasing tartness. It is better to eat sweets made of dried fruit than to eat candy for between-meal snacks. Dried fruit contains valuable minerals and vitamins as well as natural fruit sugar to give quick energy.

Dates, figs, and prunes, which may be steamed until plump and soft, may be eaten plain. They may also be stuffed with nuts, panoche, fondant, peanut butter, marshmallows, preserved ginger, or candied fruit peelings. Dried fruit prepared in this manner may, if desired, be rolled in powdered sugar, granulated sugar, or granulated sugar to which a little cinnamon has been added.

Courtesy Alethea Moore

179

ACTIVITIES

Deciding which form of fruit to buy:

1. Compare the costs of fresh, frozen, canned, and dried peaches in your grocery stores.
2. Buy three thin-skinned and three thick-skinned oranges of about the same size. Compare the two types of oranges as to cost, flavor, and amount of juice.
3. Which three fruits would you consider the most economical to buy in your community this week?
4. Name 10 fruits which may be served for breakfast. Compare the costs.

Learning to give fruits the proper care:

5. Discuss the differences in methods of storing fresh, frozen, canned, and dried fruits.
6. To demonstrate what happens when you handle tomatoes, peaches, or other perishable foods too much in a grocery store, take two fruits which look very much alike and bruise one of them by mashing it. Place the two fruits in the refrigerator, and check their appearance in a couple of days.
7. Discuss ways in which cantaloupe and other strong-flavored fruits may be kept in the refrigerator without spoiling the flavor of the other foods.

Realizing the food value of fruits:

8. How many times should fruits be eaten every day?
9. Demonstrate how to prepare grapefruit or oranges according to the directions on page 469.
10. Select one group of girls to cook applesauce (see recipe on page 479). Have another group make "rosy apples." Have still another group bake apples. Then discuss the differences in the three dishes.
11. Make a list of fruits which can be bought in dried form. Describe ways of serving each. Which way do you prefer for each and why?
12. Describe five interesting fruit arrangements that you have seen, or collect pictures of arrangements that appeal to you.

Discussing ways of serving fruits:

13. Bring to class pictures of attractive fruit plates which may be served for lunch.
14. Discuss fruits which might be arranged on a fruit plate with variety in color, texture, and flavor.
15. Make a list of all the fruits sold in your local stores. Then suggest two ways of serving each.
16. Make a list of ways in which fruit may be served or used in cooking (page 175). Then name two fruits that you have eaten which were prepared according to each suggestion.

Chapter 13 | **VEGETABLES**

Vegetables are a valuable food for health because of the vitamins and minerals they supply. (See Chapter 4.) To obtain needed vitamins and minerals, try to include in your meals every day a dark-green vegetable (broccoli, spinach, turnip greens, and other dark-green leaves) or a deep-yellow vegetable (sweetpotatoes, carrots, winter squash, and pumpkin).

Besides selecting vegetables for their health value and appealing combination with the meat being served (page 106), consider the following suggestions in planning the vegetables for any one meal:

1. Avoid serving two vegetables of the same color, flavor, type, or shape.
2. Obtain variety by having one raw vegetable and one cooked vegetable or by preparing cooked vegetables in different ways.
3. Serve at least one or more watery vegetables (tomatoes, celery, lettuce, or spinach) but no more than one starchy vegetable (sweetpotatoes, Irish potatoes, corn, dry peas, or dry beans).
4. Serve one strong-flavored vegetable (cabbage, Brussels sprouts, broccoli, or cauliflower) and one or more mild-flavored vegetable (carrots, peas, potatoes, or green beans).

FOOD VALUE

Count the vegetables pictured above and on page 183. How many can you name? Which vegetables are grown in your part of the country? Which ones must be shipped in? There are many kinds of vegetables. Yet some people serve the same ones day after day. How much more interesting and attractive their meals would be if they served a variety of vegetables with bright colors of green, yellow, and red.

When vegetables are properly selected, prepared, and served, they can be very flavorful. Because vegetables are important in the diet, it is recommended that you eat four or more servings every day. Vegetables are valuable food because they contain vitamins, minerals, carbohydrates, proteins, and cellulose.

Vitamins: Vitamins A and C are the chief vitamins in vegetables. The fresher the vegetable, the more vitamins it contains. Dark-green and deep-yellow vegetables (broccoli, carrots, kale, spinach, pumpkin, and sweetpotatoes) are especially rich in Vitamin A. Broccoli and green peppers are good sources of vitamin C (see page 60).

Courtesy United Fresh Fruit and Vegetable Association

OF VEGETABLES

Minerals: Vegetables absorb calcium, phosphorus, iron, and iodine from the soil as they grow. When you eat vegetables, you benefit from these minerals. Minerals are especially important in building strong teeth and bones. Dark-green vegetables and dry peas and beans are rich in minerals.

Carbohydrates (sugars and starches): Potatoes, corn, and dry peas and beans provide us with carbohydrates as well as with minerals and vitamins. Carbohydrates supply the body with energy.

Proteins: Dry peas and beans, lentils, and soybeans are good sources of protein. Therefore, these vegetables are sometimes served as the main dish of a meal in place of meat, which is our chief source of protein. Proteins help to build and repair the body.

Cellulose: The stems and skins of vegetables, as well as the strings of celery, contain cellulose, which is sometimes called "roughage." It is important to include cellulose in the diet because it is needed by the body to aid in the digestion of food.

183

Courtesy Handy Andy

Fresh vegetables start to lose vitamins, tenderness, and flavor as soon as they are gathered. Therefore, locally grown vegetables are better buys than are vegetables which have been shipped from a distance. When buying fresh vegetables, check carefully to be sure that they are: (1) fresh and crisp, (2) bright in color and free of brown spots or decay, (3) clean and free of soil or sand, (4) reasonable in price for the season and in comparison with other forms.

The points listed on page 169 for buying fresh fruits also apply for buying fresh vegetables.

Canned vegetables have an advantage over fresh vegetables because they can be stored in the home and may be prepared for serving in a few minutes. Nearly all kinds of vegetables may be bought in cans. For suggestions on buying canned foods of all kinds, see page 161.

Courtesy "Forecast"

VEGETABLES

Patteson

Frozen vegetables compare favorably with fresh vegetables in appearance, flavor, and food value. When buying frozen vegetables, keep these suggestions in mind:

1. Be sure that the packages you select are firm and solidly frozen.

2. Do not buy more at any one time than you can store in your freezer or the freezing compartment of your refrigerator.

3. Buy frozen foods last, or just before you leave the store. Take them home immediately so that there will be little chance of their defrosting.

4. Store frozen foods as soon as you arrive home.

WHICH TO BUY — FRESH, FROZEN, OR CANNED?

When trying to decide whether to buy fresh, frozen, or canned food, consider the time that it will take to prepare the food, the amount of waste, and the cost. For example, frozen peas are often considered a better buy than fresh peas. On the other hand, fresh carrots are a better buy than frozen carrots. Fresh peas can be obtained only at a certain season of the year. A large amount of time is required for shelling the peas, and there is a great deal of waste. Fresh carrots, on the other hand, are available at a reasonable price most of the year. They can be prepared quickly, and there is very little waste.

In order to avoid making extra trips to the grocery store, some homemakers serve fresh vegetables the first part of the week and frozen or canned vegetables the latter part of the week.

185

Courtesy National Presto Industries, Inc.

Whether vegetables are to be served raw or cooked, wash them thoroughly and check for insects. If vegetables are allowed to stand in water, they lose some of their vitamins and minerals. Therefore, they should be washed quickly. Leafy vegetables should be dipped up and down in several waters or washed under running water to remove sand and grit. Root vegetables should be washed with a vegetable brush.

Dr. Quijano

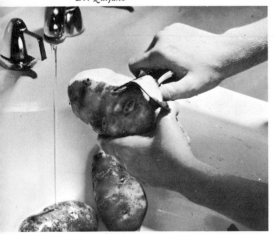

When paring vegetables, use a sharp knife or a vegetable parer so that you remove only the skin. Many important vitamins and minerals are just under the skin. Then cook the vegetable immediately because exposure to water or air causes vegetables to lose vitamins. Whenever possible, cook vegetables without removing their skins.

COOKING FRESH
VEGETABLES

Place vegetables whole or in large pieces in a small amount of boiling water in order to save vitamins.

Dr. Quijano

After placing the vegetables in the boiling water, cover, and let the water come to a boil again. To prevent green vegetables from turning dark, do not cover for the first 2 or 3 minutes.

Dr. Quijano

When the water comes to a boil again, reduce the heat and cook until tender, without stirring. Vegetables will cook as quickly at a slow, even boil as in rapidly boiling water.

Patteson

187

Dr. Quijano

When a vegetable can be easily pierced with a fork or a toothpick, it is done. When done, the vegetable should have the same shape as when raw. It should also have some crispness and a good color. Overcooked vegetables are soft and unattractive. They have an unpleasant odor and flavor. Also, they have lost much of their food value. Liquid that is left after cooking should not be thrown away because it contains valuable minerals and vitamins. Serve it with the vegetable, or place the uncovered saucepan over high heat, and cook quickly until the liquid has evaporated. You may wish to save the liquid for gravies, soups, or sauces.

Watch vegetables carefully while cooking to prevent them from burning. If a vegetable boils dry and starts to burn, place the saucepan in cold water for 1 minute. Then remove the vegetable from the saucepan, and cut off the burned sections. Place the vegetable in fresh, boiling, salted water in another sauce-

pan, and continue cooking until done.

COOKING FROZEN VEGETABLES

Patteson

All frozen vegetables, except corn on the cob, should be cooked without being thawed. The best method of cooking a frozen vegetable is stated on the package. Use only the amount that will be served at one meal, and keep the rest in the freezer. Cook frozen vegetables in the same way as fresh vegetables with the following exceptions.

1. Use a pan that is large enough for the vegetable to lie flat.
2. Use slightly less boiling water than for fresh vegetables because defrosting supplies some water.
3. Break the vegetable with a fork when it starts to defrost so that all parts will be cooked evenly.
4. If the vegetable has been defrosted, less cooking time is required.

Dr. Quijano

Photos Courtesy Libby, McNeill and Libby

Because canned vegetables have already been cooked, they need only to be heated and seasoned. Drain the liquid from the can into a saucepan, and boil it rapidly to reduce the amount. Then add the vegetable, and cook 3 or 4 minutes. Some of the vitamin value of vegetables is lost in canning, but there is little loss of minerals. To retain vitamins and flavor, do not open canned vegetables until you are ready to use them.

PREPARING DEHYDRATED VEGETABLES

To prepare dehydrated vegetables, add water and cook according to the directions on the package.

Dehydrated vegetables are fresh vegetables that have been cleaned, trimmed, and cut into pieces. The water is removed from the vegetables before they are packaged. There is no waste in dehydrated vegetables, and most of them are inexpensive and easy to use.

Bland

COOKING DRY VEGETABLES

Dry vegetables, called "legumes," include many varieties of beans, peas, and lentils. They are produced by allowing the fresh vegetable to stay in the field until it becomes mature, or dry.

Most legumes are available already cooked in cans. They are cheaper when sold uncooked in packages or boxes. Legumes will keep for a long time provided they are stored in a cool, dry place in a container with a tight-fitting lid to protect them from moisture and insects.

Dry vegetables are tasty as well as economical and are often served in place of meat.

To cook dry beans, peas, and lentils . . .

. . . follow the directions on the package or in the recipe for the amount per serving. (*NOTE:* Most dry vegetables increase in size two or three times when cooked.)

. . . wash thoroughly, and remove any stems, stones, or imperfect pieces.

. . . soak for several hours or overnight in enough water to cover. The length of time is usually indicated on the package.

. . . bake or boil slowly, in the same water in which they were soaked, until tender.

. . . flavor as desired or according to the recipe with fat meat, molasses, tomatoes, garlic, onion, spices, or herbs.

Patteson

Courtesy National Presto Industries, Inc.

Courtesy National Dairy Council

Vegetables may be boiled (cooked in a small amount of water until tender), steamed (cooked in steam from water), or pressure-cooked (cooked in a pressure saucepan according to the directions). They may be served with butter, margarine, or white sauce.

Vegetables may be panned (cooked in a small amount of fat in a tightly covered saucepan), deep-fat-fried (cooked in a large amount of fat), or pan-fried (cooked in a small amount of fat).

Courtesy Cooperative Extension Service, University of Arizona

USDA Photo

Courtesy Reynolds Wrap

Courtesy Reynolds Metals Company

Vegetables may be baked in the oven, either whole or in pieces, with or without aluminum foil.

To stuff vegetables, remove the center portion and fill with meat, bread crumbs, another vegetable, or a combination of these foods.

There are other ways of baking vegetables. Scalloped vegetables are cut into thin slices and arranged with alternate layers of medium white sauce. Au gratin vegetables are scalloped vegetables with bread crumbs or grated cheese sprinkled over the top. Vegetables may also be broiled (cooked under direct heat).

Courtesy National Canners Association

Courtesy Reynolds Metals Company

ACTIVITIES

Realizing the importance of eating vegetables:

1. Discuss why the following statement is true: From a health standpoint, it is more important to know how to cook vegetables than to know how to make desserts.

2. Keep a record of the vegetables you eat for 1 week. Check your list against *A Daily Food Guide* to see whether you have eaten the correct amount from each group each day.

Learning to recognize and enjoy different vegetables:

3. Name as many vegetables as you can which are grown in your community at some time during the year. Name vegetables which are always shipped in.

4. How many vegetables can you name that are: *(a)* dark green, *(b)* deep yellow, *(c)* white, *(d)* red?

5. Tell about learning to enjoy a vegetable that you once disliked.

Comparing the costs of vegetables:

6. Compare the costs and the food values of: *(a)* fresh carrots and frozen carrots, *(b)* fresh peas and frozen peas, *(c)* fresh green beans and frozen green beans, *(d)* fresh potatoes and dehydrated potatoes.

Preparing vegetables in different ways:

7. List the vegetable dishes that you know how to prepare. List the vegetable dishes that you would like to learn to prepare.

8. Prepare buttered English peas from fresh, frozen, and canned peas. Compare the appearances, flavors, and costs.

9. Arrange for each group in class to prepare a different kind of dry beans or peas. Then allow each girl to sample all kinds prepared.

10. Bring to class pictures of vegetables prepared in several different ways: baked, scalloped, au gratin, buttered, and creamed.

Serving vegetables:

11. List five vegetable dishes which would be suitable to serve at dinner.

12. Name five raw vegetables which might be included in a school lunch. Describe how each should be prepared and packed. (See page 98.)

13. Describe how parsley, hard-cooked eggs, and cheese can be used as garnishes to make vegetable dishes colorful.

14. With the help of your teacher and classmates, work out a chart or score card for judging the vegetables you prepare in class. When you do, keep in mind that well-cooked vegetables should: *(a)* lose little food value, *(b)* retain their natural flavor and be as tasty as possible, *(c)* be tender, yet firm, *(d)* have an attractive shape, and *(e)* keep as much of their natural color as possible.

Chapter 14 | **SALADS**

Courtesy Abbott Laboratories

Cool, colorful, crisp salads stimulate the appetite, brighten up a meal, and provide a contrast to the other foods served.

Salads are very healthful. If they are made of fresh fruits and vegetables, they furnish minerals and vitamins. Salads made of meat, seafood, chicken, and eggs are rich in protein. Those made of potatoes, dry beans, or other starchy foods furnish carbohydrates. Salads also supply a large amount of roughage.

The kind of salad served depends to some extent upon when it is to be eaten. For example, salad served . . .

. . . *at the beginning of a meal* should be small, colorful, and slightly tart so that it will stimulate the appetite.

. . . *with the meat and potatoes* should be light and crisp, such as a tossed green salad, a small vegetable salad, or a tart fruit salad. In American homes, salad is usually served with this course.

. . . *as the main dish* for lunch or supper should be large, such as a fruit plate, or should be made of a heavy food, such as meat, seafood, chicken, or eggs.

. . . *in place of a dessert* after a heavy meal should be small, colorful, and sweet.

. . . *for party refreshments* should be colorful, tasty, and appetizing.

195

KINDS OF SALAD GREENS

Photos Courtesy W. Atlee Burpee Company

Curly Endive   Head Lettuce   Romaine

Photos Courtesy Associated Seed Growers, Inc. *Courtesy Household Finance Corp.*

Cabbage   Water Cress   Leaf Lettuce

Photos Courtesy W. Atlee Burpee Company *Courtesy United Fresh Fruit and Vegetable Assn.*

Parsley   Chinese Cabbage   Spinach

If you keep a variety of salad greens in the refrigerator, you can make many interesting salads. Head lettuce is perhaps the most popular, but leaf lettuce and other salad greens which are a darker green in color are more nutritious. Cabbage is perhaps the cheapest of all salad greens. It is usually served as a slaw or in combination with other vegetables and fruits rather than as a base **196** to the salad. Red cabbage, which is also inexpensive, adds color to salads.

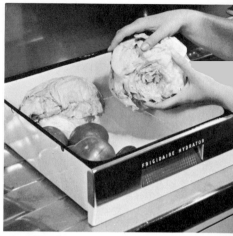

Photos Courtesy Wesson Oil and Snowdrift Sales Company

To keep salad greens crisp and avoid crushing them:

1. Place them in the refrigerator in a plastic bag or wrapped in a damp cloth, aluminum foil, or moistureproof transparent paper.

2. Place them in the hydrator or vegetable crisper of the refrigerator with or without wrapping.

To keep vegetables very crisp, wrap them in moistureproof transparent paper or put them in a plastic bag before placing them in the hydrator. Such a plan also helps to keep pieces of small vegetables together. Wrap such things as pieces of chives, onion, and garlic separately, or store them in covered containers with tight-fitting lids. For directions on washing and drying salad greens and removing the core from head lettuce, see page 467.

Courtesy Dow Chemical Company

Courtesy Libby, McNeill and Libby

An individual salad is more attractive if the lettuce or other salad greens do not cover the entire plate. The main part, or body, of an individual salad may be made of vegetables or large pieces of fruit which have been chilled and well drained. Arrange the fruits or vegetables attractively on salad greens.

The body of a salad may be made of a number of fruits or vegetables which have been tossed together with a salad dressing. Loosely pile the mixture in the center of the salad greens so that the fruits or vegetables have a natural look. Do not smooth the top.

Courtesy United Fruit Company

Courtesy Fruit Dispatch Company

Sometimes an unusual arrangement of fruits or vegetables on a plate adds interest to the salad. The salad dressing may be passed separately so that each person can help himself to as much as he chooses. It may also be added to the side of the salad or put on top when all persons being served like the dressing.

You may make gelatin salads the day before you intend to serve them. If you wish, you may unmold the salads and store them in the refrigerator until serving time. Be sure not to remove them from the refrigerator too far in advance.

Courtesy Libby, McNeill and Libby

SALADS TO BE PASSED

Courtesy New York State College of Home Economics, Cornell University

A salad made of a number of vegetables or fruits which have been tossed together with a salad dressing may be loosely piled in a bowl and passed at the table so that each person may serve himself.

Various kinds of cool, crisp vegetables may be attractively arranged on a large platter from which everyone selects what he likes. The foods may overlap slightly, but they should not appear crowded.

Courtesy Kraft Foods Company

MAIN-DISH SALADS

A salad can be a meal in itself when it is made of foods that are rich in proteins, such as shrimp, fish, meat, eggs, or cheese (above). Salads made of potatoes or macaroni are sometimes used with other foods (below). Since the main-dish salad is served cold, it may often be prepared in advance. Thus, it is the answer to easy entertaining or to meals which need to be served quickly.

Courtesy John Joyce, Inc.

The ingredients for a tossed green salad should be cut or sliced into large pieces. However, lettuce or other salad greens should be torn.

The flavor of a salad may be improved by rubbing the bowl with garlic before placing the ingredients in it. You may prefer either to use a garlic press to squeeze a garlic clove over the ingredients or to add a commercially prepared garlic juice to the salad.

Courtesy Swift and Company

If you add onion to a salad, it should be finely chopped so that the flavor will be distributed throughout.

The dressing should not be added until just before you serve the salad. Use only enough dressing to moisten the ingredients.

Mix the dressing with the salad by tossing the ingredients lightly in a large bowl with two forks or with a fork and a spoon until all parts are evenly coated. Avoid too much handling. The salad greens may become crushed and bruised and, therefore, cause the salad to be unattractive.

MAKING A MAIN-DISH SALAD

Courtesy Kraft Foods Company

Chicken and meat should be cut into uniform pieces, and fish should be flaked (page 295). To improve the flavor of meat, fish, or some cooked vegetables, moisten with French dressing and allow to marinate (to stand) for an hour or more. Then drain.

Vegetables may be sliced or cut into uniform pieces ahead of time and placed in the refrigerator to chill. For best results, do not combine the vegetables with the meat until just before the salad is served.

Use only enough mayonnaise or cooked salad dressing to flavor the salad and to hold the ingredients together.

You may serve the ingredients on lettuce or other salad greens or on avocado slices. Another idea is to make stuffed tomato salad. Tomatoes stuffed with cottage cheese may also be used as a main-dish salad. (See page 493.)

Courtesy Calavo Growers of California   *U.S. Fish and Wildlife Service*

MAKING A GELATIN SALAD

1. Whether you use sweetened or unsweetened gelatin (page 434), chill until it is about as thick as an unbeaten egg white. Then carefully fold in well-drained fruits or vegetables. If gelatin is not allowed to chill first, the solid foods will either sink to the bottom of the mold or float.

Julio G. Huante

2. Unmold gelatin by loosening the edge with a knife which has been dipped in warm water. Then dip the mold quickly into hot water, taking care that none of the hot water gets into the salad.
Some people find that, if the mold is very slightly greased with oil before the gelatin is poured in, the salad is easy to unmold.

Patteson

3. To remove the salad, shake the mold gently, yet quickly, over the salad plate. If the gelatin does not come out easily, dip the mold into hot water again or place a hot towel over it for a short time. Return the salad to the refrigerator until you are ready to serve it.

Patteson

WHAT MAKES A GOOD SALAD

The Ingredients
1. Select foods for a pleasing combination of colors and flavors.
2. Use crisp, raw vegetables or fruits if other foods in the meal are soft to give a contrast in texture.
3. Combine light foods with dark foods for a pleasing color combination. For example, leave part or all of the skin on apples to add color to a salad. Use pimentos, green peppers, or olives to add color as well as flavor to a meat or fish salad.

The Preparation
4. Wash, dry, and chill fresh vegetables or fruits.
5. Chill and drain canned vegetables or fruits.
6. Cook vegetables to be used in a salad only until barely tender. Over-cooked vegetables lose their shape.
7. Rinse leftover vegetables in hot water to remove butter or margarine. Then chill.
8. Be sure that pieces of chicken, meat, or fish to be used in a salad are free of skin, gristle, or bones.
9. When you use lettuce in a salad, tear, do not cut, it apart.
10. Cut salad ingredients into large pieces so that the food is easily recognized and so that the salad does not become mushy.
11. If you use raw apples, bananas, pears, or peaches in a salad, sprinkle them with lemon or orange juice to keep them from turning dark.
12. When you use nuts or raisins in a salad, add them just before serving so that the salad will not turn dark.
13. Combine ingredients gently by either tossing or lightly mixing. Do not overstir or overmix.

The Dressing
14. Do not add salad dressing until just before serving unless the directions state otherwise.
15. Use only enough dressing to moisten the ingredients, not so much that it drains onto the salad plate.

The Serving
16. Select individual salad plates that are large enough to allow for easy eating.
17. Pile tossed salad loosely in the center of a bowl or on individual salad plates so that the greens look natural.
18. When you serve salads on salad greens, be sure that the greens are neatly arranged and that the salad is attractively placed.
19. Brighten the salad with a garnish, but avoid having too much.
20. Keep the salad in the refrigerator until serving time.

Courtesy Wesson Oil and Snowdrift Sales Company

French dressing is a mixture of an oil, an acid — such as vinegar or lemon juice — and seasonings which have been shaken or beaten together. The seasonings, such as salt, pepper, paprika, mustard, and herbs, vary with the kind of salad on which the dressing is to be used. French dressing may be used on fresh vegetable salads and on tart fruit salads when it is made with lemon juice. Meat, chicken, and fish are sometimes moistened with French dressing and allowed to marinate (to stand).

Mayonnaise is a thick, rich, uncooked salad dressing made of oil, vinegar or lemon juice, egg, and seasoning. The main caution to remember in making mayonnaise is that the oil should be added very slowly to the beaten egg. Since mayonnaise is a richer salad dressing than French dressing, it is used more often on heavy salads, such as those made of chicken, meat, shrimp, egg, and potatoes.

Courtesy Stix, Baer, and Fuller, St. Louis

206

DRESSINGS

Courtesy Corning Glass Works

Cooked salad dressing is similar to mayonnaise in appearance and taste. However, because it does not contain oil, it is not so rich as mayonnaise. When bought in the store, it is called "salad dressing." It is less expensive than mayonnaise. It is made of milk or water, cornstarch, egg, butter or cream, and vinegar, lemon juice, or some other fruit juice, plus seasonings.

Courtesy Kraft Foods Company

Variations of French dressing, mayonnaise, and cooked salad dressing are easy to make, and they add new interest to meals. For example, mayonnaise or cooked salad dressing may be thinned with broth from cooked meat, cream, or fruit juice, depending on how it is to be used. Mayonnaise to which chili sauce, chopped hard-cooked egg, and chopped olives are added is Thousand Island dressing. It may be used on a salad made of only one ingredient, such as a wedge of head lettuce. French dressing flavored with onion and garlic may be used on a vegetable salad but not on a fruit salad.

For other variations of salad dressings, see the recipes on page 500.

Courtesy Alethea Moore

When an individual salad is served as a separate course, crisp salt wafers, crackers, cheese straws, bread strips, or melba toast are usually served with it.

When a salad is served as the main dish, hot rolls, biscuits, muffins, toasted sliced buns topped with cheese, or small sandwiches may be served with it.

When trying to decide what kind of bread to serve with a salad, plan to have flavors and textures that will blend well. Orange, date, and banana bread go well with a fruit salad but not with a vegetable salad. Garlic bread goes well with meat and crisp vegetable salads but not with fruit salads.

208

ACTIVITIES

Considering the importance of salads:

1. Tell how salads can improve a meal.
2. Make a bulletin-board picture display of salads that might be served as: *(a)* an appetizer, *(b)* an accompaniment to the main course, and *(c)* a dessert. What foods included in salads contain vitamin C? Tell what vitamin C does for your body.
3. Describe two ways in which carrots might be used in a salad. Discuss the importance of eating carrots.

Making a salad:

4. Demonstrate and discuss how to cut various fruits and vegetables for different salads. For example, which should be sliced, chopped, diced, or shredded? For what kind of salad should each be used?
5. Give a demonstration on how to keep bananas or apples from turning dark after they have been cut.
6. Some companies make mayonnaise and cooked salad dressing which look alike. Bring to class examples of each. Read the ingredients, and note the differences. Then compare their costs and flavors.
7. Discuss the following statement in detail: Salads made of fresh fruits or vegetables should not be combined until just before serving time.
8. Discuss ways of adding color to a fruit salad. For example, cubes of firm, bright-colored gelatin may be added to a mixed fruit salad.
9. Discuss ways in which the salad recipes in this book might be varied.

Arranging a salad:

10. Make an attractive bulletin-board display of pictures of salads: *(a)* in a large wooden bowl all ready to be passed at the table so that each person may serve himself, *(b)* in small individual bowls, *(c)* in individual salad plates, and *(d)* on a large platter.
11. Show how a salad containing the same ingredients can be arranged in four different ways. Then decide which arrangement is the most attractive.
12. Describe a salad that you have found difficult to eat.

Getting experience:

13. Prepare a different salad each evening at home for 1 week. Report the comments that were made by various members of your family.
14. Demonstrate how to peel a tomato by one of the following methods: *(a)* Put a fork in the stem end of a tomato. Turn the fork as you hold the tomato over a flame for about 1 minute. *(b)* Dip the tomato into boiling water for 1 minute. Remove and peel. Then chill.
15. With the help of the list on page 205, work out a chart for judging salads in class.

Chapter 15 | SOUPS AND SAUCES

On a chilly day nothing is more satisfying than a tasty, piping hot soup. Cold soups are popular during the summer months. Not only are soups well liked, but they are also inexpensive and easy to prepare. Making soup is an ideal way to make a small amount of low-cost meat go a long way. Also, vegetables and milk can be added to the menu in soup. Persons who do not make their own soup may buy it in cans or in frozen or dehydrated form.

Soups may be divided into two groups: (1) those made with stock, such as meat, fish, and vegetable soup and (2) those made with milk, such as cream soups and most chowders, bisques, and oyster stew which is made with milk and a seafood. Some soups are a combination of both milk and stock.

The right sauce can add as much to meat, poultry, fish, vegetables, or dessert as accessories add to a dress. Besides food value, sauces add color to colorless foods, flavor to foods lacking in flavor, moisture to dry foods, and new interest to leftovers. However, it is unwise to serve sauces with too many dishes at any one meal.

Some sauces are simple to make. For example, a little lemon juice with salt and pepper added is a good sauce for basting broiled fish. Other sauces are more difficult to make.

KINDS OF SOUPS

Hearty meat-and-vegetable soup: The first step in making vegetable-beef soup is to start the meat and bones to cook in cold water. This method of cooking will improve the flavor of the soup and extract most of the minerals, vitamins, proteins, and fat from the meat and bones. The liquid made by slowly cooking the meat and bones in water is called "stock." Remove the bones after the stock has cooked (simmered) for 2 or 3 hours. Then add chopped vegetables to the stock, and cook until tender. Such soups require long, slow simmering, but not boiling.

Just as the liquid left from cooking beef and bones is called "stock," so is the liquid left from cooking poultry, fish, or vegetables called "stock." When poultry or fish is used instead of beef, the soup is cooked in the same way as vegetable-beef soup.

The kind and the amount of seasoning used in soup are determined to some extent by the individual taste. Salt, pepper, bay leaf, thyme, and onions are the most common seasonings.

Piping hot, hearty soups, such as thick meat-and-vegetable soups, fish and clam chowders, and gumbos, may be served as the main dish for lunch or supper. Many times, a salad and some type of bread or a sandwich are added to complete the meal.

Courtesy Swift and Company

Courtesy National Dairy Council

Cream soup: A large bowl of a rich cream soup may be served as the main dish for lunch or supper. A small amount of cream soup, if not too rich, may be served as the first course of an otherwise light meal.

Cream soups may be made from chicken, seafood, mashed vegetables, or vegetables cut into small pieces and combined with white sauce (page 216). Nearly all vegetables can be used in making cream soups, but tomatoes, mushrooms, split peas, corn, spinach, and asparagus are used most frequently. Freshly cooked, frozen, canned, or leftover vegetables may be used. Liquids left from the cooking of fresh vegetables and liquids drained from canned vegetables should be saved and used in soup because they contain valuable minerals and vitamins as well as flavor.

Vichyssoise is a cream soup made from potatoes, leeks, and white sauce. It is usually served cold.

Most chowders are thick cream soups to which some type of seafood and/or coarsely cut vegetables have been added. Bisque is a thick, rich, smooth soup which is made with shellfish. Oyster stew is the most common of the stews made with milk and a seafood. Clams and lobster may also be used in stew.

Cream soups are usually garnished with sprigs of parsley, croutons (pieces of toasted bread), whipped cream, or sour cream.

Certain kinds of crackers and bread are usually served as an accompaniment with soup: soda crackers, rye crackers, melba toast, toasted bread strips, **212** corn bread, and hard rolls.

Courtesy H. J. Heinz Company

Light, clear soups: Bouillon and consommé are light, clear soups. They are ordinarily served at the beginning of a heavy meal. Such soups are highly seasoned to stimulate the appetite, but they have little food value compared with heavier soups.

Bouillons and consommés are served more often in restaurants than in the home because they are time-consuming and expensive to make. Therefore, when served in the home, they are generally made from bouillon cubes or from canned or frozen forms.

Bouillon is made from a brown meat stock (beef) which is highly seasoned and cleared. Consommé is made from a light meat stock (veal, poultry, or a combination of both) which is highly seasoned and cleared. For directions on making a stock, see page 211.

Courtesy Campbell Soup Company

Jellied soups: Consommé or bouillon may be chilled for several hours and served as jellied soup. Canned bouillon will usually become firm if placed in the refrigerator overnight. However, sometimes it is necessary to add gelatin according to the directions on the can. Before serving jellied soup, break up the jelly lightly with a fork, and garnish with lemon and parsley or salted whipped cream.

213

Bland

Canned, frozen, and dehydrated soups frequently take the place of homemade soup in family meals because they are easy to prepare, inexpensive, and, in many cases, just as flavorful as homemade soup. Many interesting soups can be made by combining two or three different kinds of canned soups. To give variation to canned vegetable or chicken noodle soup, add a few pieces of stewed chicken, and use the liquid in which they were cooked instead of water.

Canned cream soups may be served as sauces after they have been thinned with milk or light cream. They may also be used in creamed dishes, or they may be combined with other foods for casseroles. In fact, canned cream soups may be used in any way that white sauce is used (pages 216 and 217). Some suggested combinations are cream of mushroom soup with tuna fish, chopped ham, or vegetables; cream of tomato soup with fried fish fillets, fish cakes, macaroni or spaghetti casserole, meat loaf or other ground meat dishes; and cream of asparagus soup with salmon loaf.

Frozen soups are tasty and easy to prepare. But they are more expensive than canned and dehydrated soups. Some dehydrated soups may be used in dips for appetizers besides being made into soups. They are very inexpensive.

Bouillon cubes are made from stock that has been seasoned and then dried into firm ½-inch cubes. The directions for using bouillon cubes are found on the small jar or can in which they are sold. When served as bouillon, the cubes require no cooking, merely the addition of hot water to dissolve them. Bouillon cubes may also be used to add flavor to soups, sauces, gravies, and similar dishes.

MAKING BROWN GRAVY

1. Remove the meat from the roasting pan, and pour the fat drippings into a bowl. Then add part or all of the water to be used in making the gravy. Heat the roasting pan and scrape the sides to loosen the brown pieces which have stuck to the pan. These pieces add to the flavor of the gravy.

2. Make gravy in a skillet if the roasting pan is large. Put 1½ tablespoons flour and 1½ tablespoons fat drippings into the skillet for each cup of water or liquid to be used. Heat the mixture, stirring constantly until it is well blended and the flour is lightly browned.

3. Pour the brown liquid from the roasting pan into a skillet. Stir while heating to prevent lumps from forming. Boil 2 or 3 minutes to thicken. Season with salt and pepper.

Photos Courtesy Swift and Company

USES OF WHITE SAUCE

The use for which a white sauce is intended determines how thick it should be. White sauce may be thin, medium, thick, or very thick, depending upon the amount of flour used in making it. The thicker you wish a white sauce to be, the greater is the amount of flour that you should use for each cup of milk or liquid. This is shown in the following table.

Proportion of Ingredients for White Sauce

KIND	BUTTER OR MARGARINE	FLOUR	MILK OR LIQUID	USE
Thin	1 tablespoon	1 tablespoon	1 cup	Cream soups
Medium	2 tablespoons	2 tablespoons	1 cup	Creamed dishes, casseroles, scalloped dishes, and gravies
Thick	3 tablespoons	3 tablespoons	1 cup	Soufflés or salad dressing
Very thick	4 tablespoons	4 tablespoons	1 cup	Croquettes

Thin white sauce is used in cream soups and macaroni and cheese casserole. However, some people prefer macaroni and cheese with a medium white sauce.

Courtesy National Dairy Council

Creamed Shrimp on Rice

Chicken à la King

Creamed Chipped Beef in Toast Cups

Courtesy National Dairy Council

Medium white sauce is used for creamed vegetables. It is either poured over the vegetable (page 216) or combined with it. Medium white sauce may be combined with shrimp, chicken, or meat to make a creamed dish to be served in toast cups; on plain toast, corn bread, or waffles; or over rice, crisp noodles, or crisp cereals. Medium white sauce may also be used in combination with vegetables, meat, poultry, or fish and baked in a casserole. Scalloped dishes (page 90) are made with a medium white sauce in alternate layers with meat, poultry, fish or vegetables, topped with bread crumbs, and baked in the oven.

Thick white sauce is used in making soufflés and cooked salad dressings.

Very thick white sauce is used in making croquettes.

Courtesy National Dairy Council

Casserole

Scalloped Dish

Croquettes

Method I

Photos Courtesy National Dairy Council

1. Melt the butter or margarine in the upper part of a double boiler.

2. Add the flour and salt. Then stir until the mixture makes a smooth paste.

Photos Courtesy National Dairy Council

3. Add the milk slowly, continuing to stir to avoid lumps. The stock from cooking meat, chicken, or vegetables may be used instead of part of the milk.

4. Cook until thick and smooth, constantly stirring and scraping the bottom and sides of the pan. Cooking causes the sauce to thicken and destroys the raw starch flavor.

Method II

Melt the butter or margarine in a heavy saucepan over direct heat, turned low, **218** and follow steps 2 through 4 above. This method is used by experienced cooks.

WHITE SAUCE

Method III	Method IV

Patteson	*Patteson*

For Method III, pour ½ cup milk or other liquid into a shaker or small glass jar. Add the flour. Put the lid on tightly, and shake.

For Method IV, slowly add an equal amount of cold milk or liquid to the flour. Make a smooth paste which is free of lumps. Slowly stir in enough additional milk to make the mixture pour easily.

Pour one of the above mixtures into the remainder of the liquid, and cook, stirring constantly to prevent lumps. Since the flour and the liquid are well blended in both methods described above, the mixture may be slowly stirred into: (1) milk which has been heated, (2) a hot liquid as in stews, or (3) meat broth for gravy.

Patteson

MAKING CREAM GRAVY

You may make gravy by the methods used in making white sauce. (See recipe on page 501.) The chief difference is that drippings instead of butter or margarine are used in making gravy.

For thin gravy, use 1 tablespoon flour and 1 tablespoon drippings for each cup of milk or liquid, as for thin white sauce.

For medium gravy, use 2 tablespoons flour and 2 tablespoons drippings for each cup of milk or liquid, as for medium white sauce.

Cocktail sauce is used for seafood cocktails—shrimp, crab meat, lobster, oyster, and clam, for example. It is usually made of chili sauce, catsup, horseradish, Worcestershire sauce, lemon juice, Tabasco, and other seasonings.

Bland

Barbecue sauce is used for basting meat or chicken from time to time while it cooks slowly. It is also sometimes served with the meat. Most outdoor cooks have their own special recipes for barbecue sauce. Other sauces which are frequently applied to food as it cooks are lemon sauce, butter sauce, and garlic sauce.

Courtesy Kraft Foods Company

Tartar sauce is especially delicious with fish and other seafoods. Tartar sauce consists of mayonnaise, chopped pickles, parsley, olives, and onions.

Courtesy Wesson Oil and Snowdrift Sales Company

Hollandaise sauce is served on vegetables and fish. True hollandaise sauce is a golden rich sauce, composed largely of butter and egg yolks. It is somewhat difficult to make. Mock hollandaise sauce can be made with white sauce (page 502) or mayonnaise.

Courtesy Best Foods, Inc.

Tomato sauce is served on meat loaf, salmon loaf, chops, stuffed green peppers, and croquettes. Other sauces which are often served with meat are raisin sauce (with ham), cranberry sauce (with turkey), mint jelly (with lamb), and applesauce (with pork).

Courtesy Paper Cup and Container Institute

Miscellaneous sauces may be bought ready to use at a moment's notice. Recipes for using commercial sauces are often given on the label, or they can be obtained free of charge from the manufacturer.

Courtesy Piggly Wiggly

DESSERT SAUCES

Courtesy Best Foods, Inc.

A sauce can do much to improve the appearance and flavor of a simple dessert. Chocolate sauce and butterscotch sauce may be made at home or bought in cans or jars. They may be served on plain cake, ice cream, or puddings. Such sauces should be thin enough to pour easily but thick enough not to soak into the food. The sauce should not cover the entire dish. If a sauce is to be served hot, it should be piping hot. Cold sauces should be thoroughly chilled.

Ready-to-serve sauces should be kept on hand for use when a special dessert is needed at a moment's notice. Some kinds of canned fruit, such as crushed pineapple, sweet cherries, and fruit cocktail, may also be used as sauces on desserts. When frozen fruit is used as a sauce, it should be only partially thawed, just enough to be icy cold.

Courtesy Glass Container Manufacturers Institute

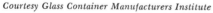

ACTIVITIES

Planning menus with soup:
1. Using the suggestions for planning meals on page 66, select a salad, a bread, and a beverage to serve with each of the following: (a) vegetable-beef soup, (b) cream of tomato soup, and (c) any cold soup.
2. Consult the information on planning meals on page 66. Discuss why it would be unwise to serve a cream soup and a soft custard at the same meal even though both are very nutritious.

Discussing ways of using canned soup:
3. On the bulletin board display pictures of food in which canned soup has been used in different ways.
4. Find two recipes using canned soup as a sauce on a meat dish.

Learning to prepare soup:
5. Judge the soup prepared in class on the following qualities: (a) pleasing appearance, (b) appetizing aroma, (c) good flavor, (d) proper amount of seasoning, (e) lack of fat floating on top, and (f) temperature — piping hot or cold, depending upon the kind.
6. Demonstrate how most of the fat can be removed from meat stock or soup by brushing the surface with a paper towel or paper napkin.
7. Compare canned vegetable-beef soup as to flavor and cost with vegetable-beef soup made in the home.

Serving soup:
8. Demonstrate: (a) how the serving dishes for hot soup may be heated either by placing them in the warming oven or by pouring very hot water over them and (b) how the serving dishes for cold soup may be chilled in the refrigerator.
9. Discuss the rules for serving and eating soup given on page 37.

Learning to use sauces in different ways:
10. Plan three different menus with: (a) a sauce used on the main dish, (b) a sauce used on the vegetables, and (c) a sauce served on the dessert.
11. Plan a menu based on each of the following: (a) cream soup made with thin white sauce, (b) scalloped dish made with medium white sauce, and (c) croquettes made with thick white sauce.
12. Discuss why you must stir white sauce constantly while cooking.
13. Look through cookbooks, and find three recipes for sauces which are made in the same way as, or similarly to, white sauce.
14. Have each group in class prepare a meal with meat loaf (page 276) as the main dish. Instruct each group to prepare a different sauce made from canned soup, such as cream of tomato or cream of mushroom, to serve with it.

223

Chapter 16 | **SANDWICHES**

There are so many kinds of sandwiches that, if you were to make a different kind every day of the year, you still would not have made all kinds. Sandwiches may be served for lunch or supper, as a between-meals snack, and at picnics, informal parties, dressy parties, and teas.

Most sandwiches fall into one of the following classifications:
1. *Hearty sandwiches,* often referred to as "lunch-box" sandwiches or "picnic" sandwiches, are perhaps the most common kind. (See page 225.)
2. *Finger sandwiches,* flat or rolled, are ordinarily served with another dish. Therefore, they are considered an accompaniment. (See page 227.)
3. *Small, dainty, tasty sandwiches* are served at dressy parties and teas. Many party sandwiches are open faced. (See page 234.)
4. *Hot sandwiches*—toasted or grilled sandwiches, hamburgers, hot dogs, and hot roast beef—may be served as the main dish at a meal. (See page 232.)

Regardless of the kind of sandwich you make, it should:
1. Be neat in appearance, tasty, and easy to eat.
2. Have a well-flavored filling which covers the bread but does not fall out when the sandwich is eaten.
224 3. Be moist, rather than dry, but not soggy.

KINDS OF SANDWICHES

Outdoor sports give anyone a good appetite. A hearty sandwich filled with meat, chicken, cold cuts, tuna fish, ham, egg, cheese, or a combination of these foods can be a meal in itself. Hearty sandwiches can also be served as the main dish for lunch or supper in the home. For example, a hearty sandwich served with a green salad, a beverage, and a dessert makes a simple, nutritious lunch. Another favorite menu for lunch consists of a sandwich served with hot soup, a beverage, and a fresh fruit.

Courtesy Gleem

Courtesy Wheat Flour Institute

Sandwiches may be made with various kinds of bread, such as enriched white, whole-wheat, rye, raisin, nut, and date. Unless otherwise stated in the recipe, bread for sandwiches should be a day or two old so that it can be spread and cut easily. Fresh bread is easier to slice or cut if it has been chilled.

The ingredients used in sandwich fillings may be sliced, chopped, ground, or mashed. Regardless of the filling used, it should be prepared so that the sandwich can be eaten easily. The sandwich should be of such kind, thickness, and size that it can be picked up easily. Meats should be evenly sliced, and the gristle, fat, and small bones should be removed. If greens are used with the filling, they should be crisp and proportioned to the size of the sandwich.

Courtesy Wheat Flour Institute

22

Courtesy David W. Evans and Associates

Sandwiches vary in size from small finger sandwiches (above) to large hearty sandwiches which are sometimes referred to as "hero" sandwiches, "Cuban" sandwiches, or "poor-boy" sandwiches. Finger sandwiches made with toasted or untoasted bread are often served when a heavy salad or a hearty soup is the main dish. Another favorite kind of sandwich is the rolled sandwich (page 235).

Club sandwiches (below) are made with three slices of bread instead of the usual two. They have two or more different fillings, such as chicken, bacon, and ham.

Courtesy Wheat Flour Institute

1. Take two slices of bread at a time from the wrapper. Lay them side by side in such a way that the edges will match when they are made into a sandwich.

2. Spread one side of each slice of bread with a thin layer of softened butter or margarine when a moist filling is to be used. The butter or margarine prevents the filling from soaking into the bread and making it soggy.

    Remove the butter or the margarine from the refrigerator about an hour before it is to be used so that it will be soft and easy to spread. You can also make butter soft and smooth by rubbing it against the side of a bowl with the back of a spoon.

3. Put the filling on the bread. Check to make sure that there is about the same amount of filling on each sandwich. Usually about 1 to 3 tablespoons of filling is needed for each sandwich.

Photos by Bland

SANDWICHES

4. Spread the filling all the way to the edges of the bread. Sliced meats or cheese should be cut or arranged to fit the piece of bread.

5. Before putting lettuce on a sandwich, remove the hard center part of the leaf, and use only the tender parts.

6. Sandwiches are usually cut in half for convenience in eating. They may also be cut into a variety of interesting shapes. Sandwiches are properly cut by using an easy back-and-forth sawing motion with a bread knife.

Design Studio

Above photos by Bland

229

WRAPPING SANDWICHES

To prevent sandwiches from drying out, wrap them in wax paper as shown at the left. You may also wrap them in aluminum foil or place them in plastic bags or cartons.

When you intend to keep sandwiches for any length of time, observe these precautions:

1. Be careful not to use a filling that is so soggy that it will soak into the bread.

2. Butter each slice of bread to prevent the filling from soaking into the bread.

3. Do not put crisp vegetables, such as celery or carrots, in the filling because they lose their crispness.

4. Wrap lettuce, sliced pickles, and radishes separately to keep them crisp. They should be added to the sandwiches at serving time.

Many kinds of sandwiches can be frozen if they are wrapped tightly in aluminum foil or freezer paper or put in a plastic freezer box.

For information on foods that do not freeze well, see page 98.

Photos Courtesy American Institute of Baking

Design Studio

If only a few sandwiches are to be served, arrange them on a tray and cover them with wax paper and a damp cloth. Store the sandwiches in the refrigerator until serving time.

To keep a number of unwrapped sandwiches:

1. Place a damp towel in a shallow pan, and cover the towel with wax paper.
2. Arrange layers of sandwiches with wax paper between each layer.
3. Put wax paper over the sandwiches, and cover it with a damp towel.
4. Keep the sandwiches in the refrigerator until serving time.

Design Studio

231

To make a hot meat sandwich, put a slice of bread or toast on a plate, and cover it with a slice of hot meat, such as pork, beef, or chicken. Pour gravy over the bread and meat. A tossed salad or a hot vegetable may be served with the sandwich.

To make a broiled sandwich, toast one side of a slice of bread. Then put a slice of cheese, luncheon meat, or other filling on the untoasted side of the bread, and return it to the broiler. Partly cooked bacon or sliced olives may be placed on top before the sandwich is returned to the broiler to give added flavor and make the sandwich more attractive.

To make a grilled sandwich, place a slice of cheese or other filling between two slices of bread. Toast the whole sandwich in a buttered skillet, a sandwich grill, or an electric fry pan. Serve immediately. A crisp vegetable salad or soup goes well with a grilled sandwich for lunch or supper.

Courtesy Wheat Flour Institute

Courtesy Kraft Foods Company

Bland

Hamburgers, cheeseburgers, and hot dogs are favorites among teen-agers as well as other members of the family. Hamburgers may be cooked in a skillet, under a broiler, or over an open fire. Hot dogs may be fried, broiled, or boiled. They may be served either plain or with mustard, pickles, chili sauce, relish, or whatever sauce is liked.

To make a stuffed roll, remove the center of a roll or a hamburger bun. Stuff the roll or bun with creamed dried beef, tuna fish, chopped chicken, meat, or a similar filling. Wrap it in aluminum foil, and heat it in a moderate oven.

OPEN-FACED SANDWICHES

Open-faced sandwiches are made with thinly sliced bread which is cut into various shapes. The bread is spread first with softened butter and then with a filling or spread. The top of the sandwich may be decorated with slices of stuffed olives, paprika, grated egg yolks, bits of cherry, nuts, small candies, sprigs of parsley, or strips of pimento or green pepper. Many different ideas for open-faced sandwiches are shown below, but for a party you might serve only two or three kinds. Since open-faced sandwiches do not stay fresh for long, they should be made shortly before they are to be served. If it is necessary to make the sandwiches well in advance, make small closed sandwiches.

Design Studio

ROLLED SANDWICHES

1. Use fresh bread, which will not crack when rolled. Trim the crust from the bread. Spread the bread first with softened butter or margarine and then with filling (page 228). Roll the slice of bread tightly.

2. Fasten each roll with a toothpick. Arrange the rolls in a shallow pan. Cover the pan with wax paper, and chill. Instead of fastening the ends with a toothpick after rolling, you may wrap the sandwiches tightly in wax paper before chilling.

3. Brush the rolled sandwiches with melted butter or margarine. Toast them in a broiler or a hot oven at 450° F. Remove the toothpicks, and serve the sandwiches piping hot. You may tuck a sprig of parsley, mint, or water cress in each end of the sandwich when it is served without being toasted. For a party, rolled sandwiches are usually cut in half.

Photos by Design Studio

PIN-WHEEL SANDWICHES

1. Cut fresh bread into extra-thin lengthwise slices. Remove the crust. Spread each slice thinly with softened butter or margarine. Then spread it with a smooth filling, or use one of the cheese spreads on page 506.

2. Starting at one end, roll up the slice of bread like a jelly roll. Spread a little soft butter on the end of the slice to make it stick. To add color, you may lay strips of green pepper and pimento about 1 inch apart over the entire slice of bread before rolling. If you lay stuffed olives across one end of the slice, you will be able to roll it easily and you will add color to the sandwich.

3. Wrap each roll in wax paper or aluminum foil, twisting the ends. Store in the refrigerator with the end of the slice of bread on the bottom of each roll. Chill for several hours or overnight. Cut the chilled roll into ¼- to ½-inch slices at serving time.

Photos by Bland

RIBBON AND CHECKERBOARD SANDWICHES

Ribbon sandwiches: Arrange two ½-inch-thick slices of white bread alternately with two slices of dark bread. Trim all the crusts at one time so that the slices will be the same size. Put the four slices together with softened butter, margarine, cream cheese, or any thinly spread filling that will hold the bread together. Press the slices lightly, and wrap them in wax paper or aluminum foil. Chill. Then cut into ½-inch slices. Serve them as ribbon sandwiches, or make them into checkerboard sandwiches.

Checkerboard sandwiches: Put ribbon sandwiches together with butter or cream cheese spread, stacking them so that every other sandwich is reversed to make a checkerboard. Wrap and chill. Cut with a sharp knife, using a sawing motion.

Photos by Design Studio

ACTIVITIES

Deciding what kind of sandwiches to serve:
1. Read the recipes for sandwich fillings on pages 504-506. Which would you use for each of the sandwiches described in Chapter 16?
2. Compare your favorite sandwich recipe with those of your classmates. Select one to prepare in class.

Deciding on the ingredients to buy for sandwiches:
3. In some places a 1-pound 1-ounce loaf of regular sliced bread contains about 16 ½-inch slices, and a 1-pound 1-ounce loaf of sandwich bread contains 24 ¼-inch slices. Compare these figures with those of breads that you buy.
4. If there are 24 slices of bread in a sandwich loaf, how many loaves of sandwich bread will be needed for 16 sandwiches?
5. A large roll of wax paper is 125 feet long. How many rolls will be needed to wrap 75 sandwiches if you use 12 inches for each sandwich?

Figuring the cost of sandwiches:
6. Compare the cost of the chicken sandwiches on page 504 with the cost of the pimento cheese sandwiches on page 505.
7. Decide on a sandwich that you and a friend might take to a party. Then figure how much the ingredients for 12 sandwiches would cost.

Making sandwiches:
8. Have a contest to see who can make the most attractive sandwiches.
9. Make rolled sandwiches, as described on page 235, but wrap each roll in wax paper instead of using toothpicks. Chill. Insert small pieces of parsley in the ends, and serve without toasting.
10. Review suggestions for a well-made sandwich on page 224. Then develop a score card for evaluating the sandwiches made in class.
11. Discuss what you can do when making many sandwiches to be sure that each has the same amount of filling. For example, you may divide the filling for 40 sandwiches into four equal amounts and then put the filling on the bread for sandwiches in groups of 10.
12. Discuss ways to use pieces of bread left after sandwiches are made.

Serving sandwiches:
13. Arrange on the bulletin board pictures of different kinds of sandwiches. Suggest how the various kinds of sandwiches might be served.
14. Plan six menus, using each of the hot sandwiches on pages 232 and 233 as the main dish. Decide what silver will be needed with each menu.
15. Make some sandwiches, and freeze them. Later, thaw the sandwiches, and compare their flavor with that of freshly made sandwiches.

MILK AND MILK PRODUCTS

Chapter 17

One of the ways in which most Americans might improve their diets is by increasing the amount of milk that they drink daily. Milk is such an important food that it is essential to everyone.

Nutritionists and doctors tell us that growing boys and girls should drink at least three to four glasses of milk a day and that adults should have at least a pint of milk daily. The easiest way to include milk in the diet is to drink a glass of milk at each meal. However, the milk that is used in preparing and cooking food is just as valuable as the milk that you drink. Milk may be used over cereals and fruits, in cream soups, in creamed casseroles, in creamed vegetables, and in sauces. It is an ingredient in many desserts, such as custards, puddings, cream pies, and ice cream, as well as in numerous and varied kinds of beverages, such as hot cocoa, chocolate milk, eggnog, and milk shakes.

Milk products — cream, ice cream, butter, and cheese — may be used in your diet as part of your daily milk requirement.

Cheese has the same high-quality (complete) protein as meat. Therefore, cheese may sometimes be served in place of meat to add variety. Also, it is a good substitute when meat is too expensive. (See page 249.) **239**

FOOD VALUE OF MILK

Milk is called "the almost perfect food" because it contains more of the nutrients needed by the body than any other food. It is also the easiest of all foods to digest.

The *proteins* found in milk are high-quality (complete) proteins, which help you to grow and help to keep your body in repair.

The *carbohydrates* (sugars and starches) in milk give you energy to work and play and help to keep your body warm.

The *fats* in milk also give you energy and help to keep you warm.

The *minerals* in milk (calcium and phosphorus) help to build strong bones and teeth. Milk contains more calcium than does any other food.

The *vitamins* in milk vary according to the kind of milk:

1. Vitamin A is found in the butterfat of whole milk. But skim milk, from which the cream has been removed, contains very little.
2. Vitamin B complex (thiamine, riboflavin, and niacin) is found in a fair amount in milk. Both whole milk and skim milk contain a large amount of riboflavin.
3. Vitamin D is found in only small amounts, but milk may be enriched by the addition of vitamin D.

Milk is not a "perfect food" because it contains only a small amount of iron and it contains no cellulose, or bulk. Vitamin C is found in raw milk, but some of it is lost when milk is heated, or pasteurized.

Courtesy National Dairy Council

Courtesy Cereal Institute, Inc.

Over cereals

Courtesy Nucoa Margarine

In cream soups

Courtesy National Dairy Council

In creamed casseroles

Courtesy Ac'cent

In sauces

Photos Courtesy American Dairy Association

In creamed vegetables

In baked custards

In cream pies

In milk drinks

Courtesy Mrs. Tucker's Shortening

Courtesy The Borden Company

FRESH MILK

Raw milk or *whole milk* is milk just as it comes from the cow. It is not changed in any way. When whole milk is allowed to stand, the butterfat rises, making cream at the top. This cream is sometimes called "top milk."

Skim milk is milk from which most of the cream, or butterfat, has been removed. It contains the same food value as whole milk except for vitamin A and butterfat.

Pasteurized milk is either whole milk or skim milk that has been heated to kill all harmful bacteria and make it safe for use. Over 90 percent of all milk is pasteurized.

Homogenized milk is pasteurized whole milk in which the fat has been so finely divided that it remains mixed with the milk and does not rise to the top as cream.

Vitamin D milk is pasteurized milk which has been enriched with vitamin D by exposing it to ultraviolet rays, by adding cod-liver oil, or by including vitamin D in the feed given to cows.

Two percent homogenized milk is pasteurized milk. About half the butterfat is removed from it. Vitamins are added to take the place of those removed with the butterfat. This milk is widely used by those wanting to eat less fat or to lose weight. It has far fewer calories than does whole milk.

Buttermilk is the liquid left from the cream after the making of butter. Cultured buttermilk, which is the kind of buttermilk sold by dairies, is made by adding a lactic acid to fresh skim milk or partly skimmed milk.

Chocolate milk and *chocolate-flavored milk* are milk drinks made by adding cocoa or chocolate sirup to whole or skim milk, depending upon the state regulations.

Courtesy Knowlton's Dairy

CANNED AND DRIED MILK

There are two kinds of canned milk.

Evaporated milk is whole milk that has been heated before canning to remove more than half the water. When evaporated milk is used just as it comes from the can, it is referred to in recipes as "undiluted milk." When it is mixed with an equal amount of water, it is referred to as "diluted milk." Diluted evaporated milk has almost the same food value as whole milk.

Sweetened condensed milk is evaporated milk to which about 40 percent sugar has been added.

There are also two kinds of dried milk.

Nonfat dry-milk solids, or dried skim milk, is made from fresh milk by the removal of the fat and the water. Nonfat dry milk has the same food value as skim milk or buttermilk.

Dried whole milk is whole milk from which only the water has been removed. It has the same food value as fresh whole milk.

Canned milk and dried milk are popular for cooking because they cost less than fresh milk and because they can be easily stored. Dried milk is the least-expensive kind. Canned milk can be stored with other canned foods until the can is opened. After the can has been opened it must be kept in the refrigerator. Nonfat dry milk will keep for several months if it is stored in an airtight container in a cool, dry place. Both canned milk and dried milk can be used in a variety of ways in their original forms. They can also be combined with water and used in place of fresh milk for cooking or, sometimes, for drinking. When you plan to use dried milk for drinking, mix it with water and allow it to stand in the refrigerator for a while before drinking.

Courtesy Davila's Grocery Store

Courtesy Kroger Company

Buying milk: Health regulations in most states require that all milk be pasteurized, have a certain amount of butterfat, and be handled under sanitary conditions. Find out what the regulations are where you live. Fresh milk usually sells for less in half-gallon or gallon containers than in pint or quart containers. Skim milk is cheaper than whole milk but contains the same nutrients, except fat and vitamin A.

Storing milk: Before storing milk in the refrigerator, wipe the bottle with a paper towel or a clean, damp cloth. Place the bottle in the coldest part of the refrigerator. Keep milk in the refrigerator at all times except when you are using it. Cover milk tightly because it absorbs flavors and odors. Do not mix new and old milk because the old milk will cause the new milk to spoil.

Courtesy Scott Paper Company

Courtesy Armour and Company

In order to prevent scorching, cook all milk dishes in a double boiler or in a heavy saucepan over very low heat. When milk is heated, a scum forms on top. Since this scum contains valuable proteins and fats, you should not remove it. You can prevent scum from forming by keeping the milk covered or by stirring or beating the milk while heating. For this reason, you should beat cocoa until a foam forms on top before you serve it. Homogenized milk forms very little, if any, scum because the fat is mixed with the milk when it is homogenized.

When you bake foods containing milk, use a slow oven. Some dishes containing milk, such as a baked custard, should be placed in a shallow pan of hot water before being put into the oven. (See recipe on page 536.)

Courtesy The Borden Company

Courtesy National Dairy Council

The most common milk products are cream, butter, ice cream, and cheese.

Cream is the butterfat that rises to the top of whole milk which has not been homogenized. Cream contains vitamin A. Because of its high butterfat content, cream is a good source of energy. Light cream is required to be at least 18 percent butterfat. It is used in coffee or on cereal. Heavy cream is required to be at least 36 to 40 percent butterfat. It is often used as whipping cream. Sour cream is used in salad dressings, sauces, baked foods, and meat dishes.

Butter is made from sweet or sour cream. When made from sweet cream, it is labeled "sweet cream butter." If salt is not added to butter, it is called "unsalted" or "sweet" butter. Butter is an excellent source of energy and is also rich in vitamin A.

Margarine is not a milk product since it is made from vegetable oil. However, if margarine is fortified with vitamin A, it is as nutritious as butter.

Ice cream is a milk product which is digested easily. It is an excellent substitute for milk. The quality of the ice cream depends on the quality of its ingredients and how it is made. Air is usually beaten into commercial ice cream to make it smooth.

Frozen desserts made from skim milk and a vegetable fat are similar to ice cream but are not so rich or nutritious. They are marketed under various trade names.

Sherbet may be made with or without milk and fruit. It is not so rich as ice cream.

246

PRODUCTS

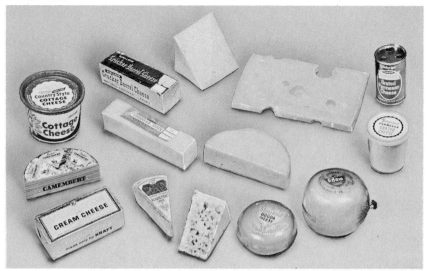

Courtesy Handy Andy

Cheese is a very valuable food in our diet because it is made from milk. There are hundreds of different kinds of natural cheeses, all of which can be divided into three groups, according to the degree of hardness:

1. *Soft cheeses:* Cottage cheese, cream cheese, Camembert
2. *Semihard cheeses:* Roquefort, Blue, Gouda, some Cheddar
3. *Hard cheeses:* Swiss, Edam, Parmesan, American, some Cheddar

Cheese furnishes the same kind of high-quality (complete) protein as meat. Therefore it may be used as a main dish instead of meat.

Processed cheeses are made by grinding, blending, and heating together one or more natural cheeses. Processed cheeses are sold in glasses, packages, or cartons and are labeled "cheese foods" and "cheese spreads."

Courtesy Handy Andy

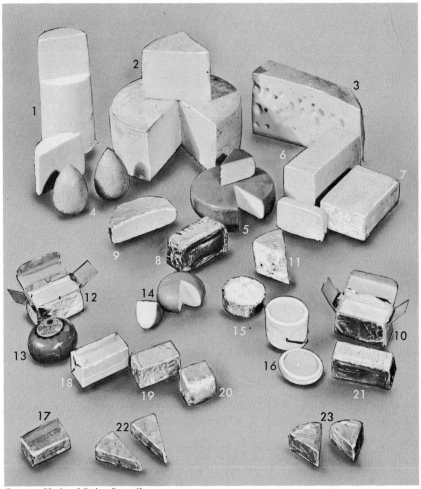

Courtesy National Dairy Council

How many of the cheeses pictured above do you recognize? The names are listed below with the corresponding number labels in the picture:

American, 10-pound print (6)	Brie (15)	Gouda (13)
American, flat style (2)	Camembert (23)	Hand (20)
American, longhorn style (1)	Cold Pack (16)	Limburger (8, 10, 12)
American, pasteurized process (18)	Cream (17)	Monterey (9)
Asiago (5)	Edam (14)	Pineapple (4)
Blue sectors (22)	Gjetost (21)	Primost (19)
Brick (7)	Gorgonzola (11)	Swiss (3)

CHEESE COOKERY

Courtesy The Borden Company

Cheese rabbit, which is melted cheese mixed with other ingredients and served over toast or crackers, is a popular main dish in which cheese is used instead of meat. There are three things to remember in cheese cookery:

1. Be sure to use the kind and the amount of cheese specified in the recipe.
2. Cook cheese at a low temperature to prevent it from becoming tough or rubbery.
3. Grate or cut cheese into small pieces before heating it or adding it to other ingredients so that it will melt quickly.

Campbell Hays from Monkmeyer

Toasted cheese sandwiches made with American cheese and topped with crisp bacon are a teen-age favorite. In addition to being used for sandwiches, cheese may be combined with other ingredients for dips and spreads, added to sauces for use over vegetables, served on a tray with crackers as a dessert, used as an accompaniment to pie or fruit, and used in salads.

ACTIVITIES

Learning the importance of milk:

1. Keep an account for 1 week of the number of glasses of milk that you drink as well as the amount that you get in other foods. Are you getting a sufficient amount?
2. Tell of people you have known who at one time disliked milk but have now learned to like it.
3. Study the food value of milk (page 240). Then discuss why babies are given the following at an early age: *(a)* orange juice, *(b)* vegetable juice, and *(c)* egg yolk.
4. For 2 weeks conduct an experiment with two white rats which weigh the same. Give one rat crackers and milk, and give the other crackers and water. Weigh the rats, and note the difference in weight as well as in smoothness and glossiness of fur. Then reverse the diets, and note the change.

Realizing what is meant by cleanliness:

5. List the regulations in your city and state concerning milk.
6. Visit a modern dairy. Discuss in class the cleanliness of the dairy and the methods used in handling the milk.

Including milk in the diet:

7. List five ways in which milk may be served for breakfast.
8. Have a class discussion on favorite milk drinks as well as milk desserts.
9. Bring 10 recipes to class which call for a large amount of milk.
10. List four ways in which milk may be included in the diet of a person who will not drink it.
11. Demonstrate: *(a)* how to open a can of milk and *(b)* how to close a package of nonfat dry-milk solids.

Deciding which is the best buy:

12. Study the illustration on page 242 to decide which kind of milk would be the best buy: *(a)* for your school lunch and *(b)* for a large family.
13. Compare the costs of 1 quart of: *(a)* fresh whole milk, *(b)* fresh skim milk, *(c)* diluted evaporated milk, and *(d)* nonfat dry milk to which water has been added.
14. Discuss why it would be unwise for a family to economize by reducing the amount of milk used.

Studying about milk products:

15. Place various kinds of cheese on a table with the correct name by each. Allow girls to taste each so that they will be able to recognize it and identify it when they taste it again.
16. List the various ways in which cheese is served or used in your home. Compare your list with those of your classmates.
17. Plan two menus in which cheese is used in the main dish.

Courtesy Poultry and Egg National Board

Chapter 18 | **EGGS**

Eggs are tasty and are good for you. In fact, they are almost as important as milk in your diet. Both eggs and milk are sometimes referred to as "the almost perfect food" because they contain so many of the food nutrients that are needed by the body—protein, fat, iron, phosphorus, calcium, and vitamins A, B, and D. (See page 47.) Because eggs are important for health, nutritionists recommend that everyone eat four or more eggs every week.

Eggs are easily digested if they are properly cooked. They should be cooked at a low temperature—never in boiling water. Eggs are often included in a light diet in place of meat because they are easily digested.

Eggs may be prepared in a variety of attractive and tasty ways. They may be served at any meal in the day to everybody in the family, from a baby to an elderly person. No longer are eggs thought of as breakfast food. They are often served as a main dish, as part of a vegetable dish, or as a salad. They may also be used in sandwiches, sauces, salad dressings, and desserts. Since egg dishes and many dishes containing eggs can be cooked quickly, eggs are frequently used for meals that need to be prepared and served in a short time.

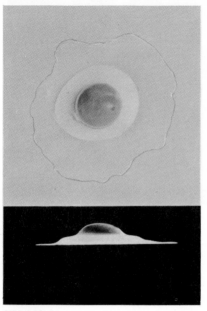 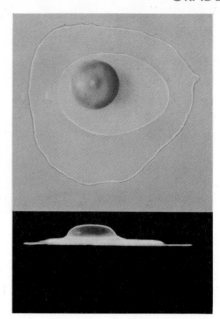

USDA Photos

Grade AA Egg   Grade A Egg

When broken, a Grade AA egg covers a small area, has a thick white that stands high, and has a yolk that is firm and high.

When broken, a Grade A egg covers a moderate area, has a reasonably thick white which stands fairly high, and has a yolk that is firm and high but not so high as that of a Grade AA egg.

The four grades of eggs which are pictured above and on page 253 have been established by the U.S. Department of Agriculture. Eggs may also be graded according to state or private standards.

According to the U.S. Department of Agriculture, Grade AA eggs are the freshest eggs and have the best flavor. Therefore, they are especially good for uses in which the flavor of the egg is important, as in poached, fried, soft-cooked or hard-cooked eggs or in egg drinks. Since Grade AA eggs generally cost very little more than other grades of eggs, many people buy only this grade when they are available.

Grade A is the best grade of eggs that is sold in many stores. Grade A eggs are used generally for the same purposes as Grade AA eggs.

252

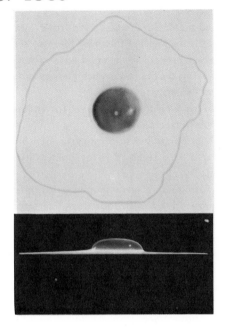 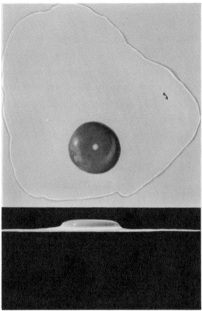

USDA Photos

Grade B Egg   Grade C Egg

When broken, a Grade B egg covers a wide area, has only a small amount of thick white, and has a yolk that is somewhat flattened and enlarged.

When broken, a Grade C egg covers a very wide area, has a white that is thin and watery, and has a yolk that is flat and enlarged and breaks easily.

Grade B eggs may be prepared and served in the same ways as are Grade AA and Grade A eggs. They may be scrambled, soft-cooked, or hard-cooked, and they may be used in making egg drinks. However, they are better suited for general cooking and baking. Grade B eggs are less expensive than Grade AA and Grade A eggs, and they are also less fresh. Therefore, their flavor is not so good as that of the better grades, and they do not look so appetizing.

Grade C eggs may be used for baking and cooking foods in which the flavor of the egg is not important. For example, they may be used in making gingerbread with good results since the spice flavor is strong. Grade C eggs are seldom sold in grocery stores.

253

FRESHNESS OF EGGS

The fresher the egg, the better its flavor and the easier the white separates from the yolk. The food which the hen eats will also affect the flavor of the egg she lays. Fresh eggs have little or no odor when broken. Stale eggs have a very bad odor. The food value of an egg is affected by the food which the hen eats, but it is not greatly affected by the age of the egg.

The freshness of eggs depends upon how well they are cared for by the farmer, the wholesaler, the grocer, and the homemaker.

Eggs that are taken from the nest soon after being laid and are then immediately refrigerated or brought to market are referred to as "newly laid eggs," "fresh eggs," or "fresh country eggs."

Eggs bought by wholesalers during the spring and summer months, when they are plentiful, and stored until winter are referred to as "storage eggs." In some states such eggs are labeled "storage," but in many states they are not labeled. For this reason, it is sometimes difficult to tell storage eggs from newly laid eggs. The shell of a newly laid egg has a slightly rough, chalky appearance. An old, or stale, egg or one that has been washed is smooth and shiny.

When properly stored, storage eggs differ only slightly in flavor from newly laid eggs. Unless newly laid eggs are put in the refrigerator, they lose their freshness in a short time. Hence, eggs that have been properly stored may be fresher than newly laid eggs that have not been refrigerated. Since eggs are graded at the time that they are put into the cartons, Grade A eggs that are not properly cared for may become Grade B eggs by the time they are ready to be used. So many things affect the true freshness of eggs that it is advisable to purchase eggs at a market where dependable standards are always maintained.

To promote good will and to encourage the sale of their eggs, many organizations and some states make special efforts to ensure that their eggs are properly graded as to quality, size, and so on, as well as properly cared for.

Courtesy Extension Service, University of Maine

254

JUMBO
5 Tablespoons
30 oz.

EXTRA LARGE
4½ Tablespoons
27 oz.

LARGE
4 Tablespoons
24 oz.

USDA Photos

Eggs come in different sizes. These pictures show the minimum weight per dozen required by the U.S. Department of Agriculture for each size. Study these pictures. Notice that there is a difference of 9 ounces in the weights of a dozen Extra Large eggs and a dozen Small eggs. Extra Large, Large, and Medium eggs are the sizes usually found in labeled cartons. The size does not affect the freshness, flavor, or food value of the egg, but it does affect the price.

Small eggs are usually cheaper by the dozen, but they may cost more by the ounce. Pullet eggs, which are the first eggs laid by a young chicken, are very small but are often a good buy.

Naturally, a small egg does not contain as much food value as a larger one. But ounce for ounce it is equal to a large egg in quality and nutritional value.

USDA Photos

MEDIUM
3½ Tablespoons
21 oz.

SMALL
3 Tablespoons
18 oz.

PEEWEE
2½ Tablespoons
15 oz.

255

BUYING EGGS

Eggs may be bought in the shell, frozen, or dried. Most eggs are bought in the shell. However, frozen eggs and dried eggs are becoming popular.

Eggs in the shell: To get the best quality when buying eggs in the shell, consider these factors:

1. The label on the carton should show: (a) the grade of the eggs, (b) the size of the eggs, and (c) the date the eggs were graded and the name of the person who packed the eggs or the name of the firm which is responsible for their freshness.

2. The source of the eggs is important. Whether you buy eggs in a store, from a producer, or from someone else, it is well to be sure that the dealer is dependable so that the same standards are always maintained.

3. The color of the shell has nothing to do with the flavor, the cooking quality, or the food value of the eggs. However, in some sections of the country, white eggs may be slightly higher in price than brown eggs. In other sections, brown eggs may cost more than white eggs.

Frozen eggs: Frozen eggs are used mostly by bakers and restaurants and in commercial mixes. They may be bought as whites alone, yolks alone, or as whites and yolks stirred together before they were frozen. One pound of frozen eggs is equal to about 10 medium fresh eggs.

Dried eggs: When eggs are dried, only the water is removed. What is left is made into a fine powder and sold as dried eggs, often called "egg solids." Dried eggs may be purchased whole, as egg yolks, or as egg whites. Although dried eggs do not contain all the vitamins of fresh eggs, the minerals and proteins are the same.

CARE OF EGGS

Since eggs spoil easily, observe the following precautions:

1. Buy eggs from a grocer who keeps them under refrigeration.

2. Put eggs in the refrigerator as soon as possible after you buy them.

3. Keep eggs in a covered container away from strong-flavored foods, such as onions and cantaloupe. Otherwise they will absorb the odor.

4. Do not wash eggs. Washing removes the film which seals the pores of the shell and prevents the egg from spoiling.

5. You can keep leftover egg yolks for a couple of days in the refrigerator if you cover them with a little water, milk, or cooking oil. You may keep them longer by freezing them. You may also hard-cook leftover egg yolks and use them in salads and sandwiches or as a garnish.

6. You can keep leftover egg whites for several days if you put them in a tightly covered container in the refrigerator.

7. Use cracked eggs immediately or store them as leftover eggs.

8. You can keep dried eggs for months if you store them in the refrigerator in a tightly covered container made of glass, metal, or plastic. However, you should use them within an hour after you have added water to them.

SERVING EGGS

Courtesy Poultry and Egg National Board

For breakfast or a light supper, eggs can be poached, scrambled, fried, soft-cooked, steamed, baked, or made into an omelet. Eggs have a mild flavor and are greatly improved when served with different kinds of breakfast meats, such as bacon, Canadian bacon, ham, or sausage.

For lunch or supper, egg sandwiches, deviled eggs, creamed eggs, scalloped eggs, and egg salad are a few of the many ways in which eggs can be served as the main dish. Hard-cooked eggs or deviled eggs are a stand-by for a packed lunch or a picnic basket. Hard-cooked eggs may also be used in chicken salad, meat salad, tuna salad, potato salad, and other vegetable salads. They may also be used as a garnish for salads.

For dinner, eggs are seldom served as a main dish. They are often used in making meat loaf, quick breads, and various kinds of desserts which are served for dinner.

For between-meal snacks, eggs may be added to milk drinks, such as egg-nog or egg-milk shakes, to make them smooth, improve their flavor, and add nutritional value.

Courtesy Poultry and Egg National Board

USES OF EGGS

To thicken food

To coat food

Eggs are used as a thickener in custards, sauces, puddings, and pie fillings.

Eggs are used to coat certain foods. For example, certain kinds of meat and fish are dipped into a beaten egg mixture and then into flour, bread crumbs, or meal before being fried. The crust on breaded veal cutlets is formed in this manner.

Eggs are used as a binder to hold ingredients together, as in meat loaf and croquettes.

Eggs are used to help make food, such as soufflés, rise. Beaten egg whites make angel food and sponge cakes rise.

Eggs are also used to add color, flavor, and texture to cakes, cookies, and muffins. They are also used as an emulsifier — that is, to hold oil and vinegar together, as in mayonnaise.

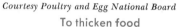

To bind ingredients

To make food rise

258

COOKING EGGS

Courtesy Sunkist Growers

When cooking eggs, you will find the following information helpful:

1. If eggs are cold, the yolk and the white can be separated easily.
2. If eggs are at room temperature, the white will take up air and beat up to a large amount, as in meringue (page 358) and the shell will be less likely to crack when the egg is put into hot water.
3. Each egg should be broken into a cup or a saucer before it is added to other eggs or other ingredients.
4. A hot mixture, such as that shown above, should be added to the beaten eggs very slowly and beaten constantly. Otherwise there will be little **specks** of cooked egg throughout, and the mixture will not thicken.
5. Eggs or mixtures containing eggs should be removed from the heat a few seconds before they appear to be done. Eggs continue to cook after being removed from the heat because they cook at a low temperature.
6. Eggs prepared alone or in combination with other foods should be served immediately while they are still hot and freshly cooked.

Eggs should be cooked at a low temperature (left) to prevent them from becoming tough and rubbery (right).

Photos Courtesy Robertshaw-Fulton Controls Company

1. Have the eggs at room temperature. Put water in a saucepan, and bring it to a boil. Reduce the heat so that the water will simmer. Lower the eggs into the water on a large spoon one at a time. Cook from 20 to 25 minutes. Do not boil.

2. Cool the eggs in cold water immediately to stop the cooking and to make it easy to remove the shells.

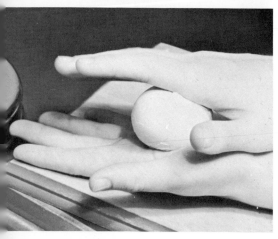

3. Crack the shell of each by gently tapping all sides of the egg on a hard surface. Then roll the egg between your hands to loosen the shell. Start peeling the shell at the large end of the egg while holding it under running water or in a bowl of water. (To cook eggs by the cold-water method, see page 510.)

Photos Courtesy Swift and Company

Courtesy Swift and Company   *Courtesy Poultry and Egg National Board*

Method I

Heat fat over low heat. Break the eggs one at a time into a saucer. Lower the saucer over the skillet, and slip each egg gently into the skillet. Cook slowly 3 to 4 minutes, or until the whites are firm. To cook the top of the eggs, dip the hot butter or fat over the eggs with a spoon until a thin white film forms.

Method II

Follow the directions above for heating the fat and putting the eggs into the skillet. Cook the eggs over low heat about 1 minute, or until the edges turn white. Then add a teaspoon of water. Cover the skillet immediately with a tight-fitting lid. Cook about 1 to 2 minutes if a soft yolk is desired or about 2 to 3 minutes for a well-cooked egg yolk.

Photos Courtesy Swift and Company

Photos Courtesy The Borden Company

Break the eggs into a mixing bowl, and beat slightly with a fork. Add milk, salt, and pepper, and mix only until well blended. Heat butter or margarine in a heavy skillet until it is hot enough to sizzle when a drop of water is added. Pour the egg mixture into the skillet, and cook over very low heat. As the mixture thickens, lift the edges lightly with a spatula or a fork (left) to let the uncooked part run underneath. Tilt the skillet if necessary. The omelet is done when it is golden brown on the bottom and the eggs will no longer flow. To remove the omelet, loosen the edges carefully (right), crease through the center with a spatula, fold it in half or roll it, and turn it out onto a hot platter.

An omelet should have a uniform light-brown appearance with a well-cooked, yet moist, center.

Courtesy The Borden Company

ACTIVITIES

Checking on the number of eggs you eat:

1. Find out how many eggs are used by your family each week. Compare the number with the number recommended in *A Daily Food Guide*.
2. Discuss why eggs are important in the diet.

Comparing the prices of eggs:

3. Weigh 1 dozen large eggs, 1 dozen medium eggs, and 1 dozen small eggs. Then compare the prices and the weights. Which is the best buy?

Finding out how eggs are graded in your state:

4. Make a report in class on grading eggs in your community and state. Are eggs graded by size or quality or both? Who does the grading?

Testing eggs for freshness:

5. Hard-cook four eggs of different grades, and notice the difference in the position of the yolk.
6. Demonstrate how eggs may be tested for freshness while still in the shell: *(a)* A fresh egg will lie on its side on the bottom of a pan of water. *(b)* An old or stale egg will float in a pan of water.
7. Explain the following statement: Eggs brought in by the farmer to the market or wholesaler are tested by a method known as "candling." Consult a dictionary or an encyclopedia to find the meaning of "candling."

Finding out about egg cookery:

8. Demonstrate how to break and separate an egg, as described on page 464.
9. Discuss precautions which should be taken in cooking eggs. Then make a list of the do's and don't's in egg cookery.
10. Demonstrate how to measure 1 tablespoon beaten egg, as shown on page 465.
11. Boil one egg at high temperature until it is hard-cooked. Cook another egg in simmering water according to the directions on page 260. Peel the eggs, and note the difference.
12. Ask your mother about the advantages and disadvantages of using Teflon utensils in egg cookery. Discuss your findings in class.

Serving eggs in various ways:

13. Find three recipes in which eggs are used, and bring them to class. Compare your recipes with those of your classmates. Then select three recipes which the class would like to try.
14. Plan five breakfast menus, each containing eggs prepared in a different way.
15. What is wrong with the statement: I had a hard-boiled egg for breakfast?

Courtesy Household Finance Corporation

Chapter 19 | **MEATS**

Meat is one of our most popular foods. Fortunately meat is good for us because of its high-quality (complete) protein. (See page 56.) In America, the four most common kinds of meat are beef (from mature cattle), veal (from young calves), pork (from hogs), and lamb (from young sheep). Meat from mature sheep is called "mutton."

Meat is the most expensive item in the food budget. Therefore, the following factors should be considered carefully:

1. *The selection:* The inspection, the grade, the appearance, and the cut of the meat should be checked when buying. (See page 266.)
2. *The cut:* Cuts of meat may be divided into two groups: tender cuts and less-tender cuts. (See pages 268 and 269.)
3. *The cost:* Low-cost cuts of meat have the same food value as more-expensive cuts and are just as flavorful if properly prepared. (See pages 267 and 273.)
4. *The time:* Tender cuts of meat usually can be cooked in a shorter time than less-tender cuts, but they are more expensive.
5. *The preparation:* Some meats should be cooked by moist heat, and others by dry heat. (See page 273.) Meat is juicier, more tender, more flavorful, and has less shrinkage when cooked at low rather than high temperature.

FOOD VALUE OF MEAT

Courtesy Swift and Company

Even though it costs more, a sirloin steak does not have any more food value than ground beef. In other words, the cost of a piece of meat is not the measure of its food value. All meat is an excellent source of many important nutrients (see page 49).

Proteins: Meat is one of the best sources of high-quality (complete) proteins, which are needed to build and repair the body and to replace worn-out tissue.

Fat: The fat in meat helps to give you energy and to keep you warm.

Minerals: Meat is the richest source of phosphorus, which is essential for building bones and teeth and for regulating the body processes. Meat also supplies two other minerals: iron and copper.

Courtesy American Sheep Producers Council, Inc.

Vitamins: Meat is an excellent source of three of the B vitamins: thiamine, riboflavin, and niacin. The fat of meat contains vitamin A.

The variety meats, such as liver, tongue, kidney, sweetbreads, and brains, are all very nutritious. Liver particularly is an excellent source of iron, which is needed to build rich, red blood. (See page 58.)

Courtesy "Forecast"   *Design Studio*

Check three things when selecting meat:

1. *The inspection stamp:* Federal law requires that all meat which is shipped from one state to another bear the United States government inspection stamp. This stamp indicates that the meat has passed federal inspection for sanitation and freedom from disease. Most state governments also require some type of inspection of meat sold within the state.

2. *The grade:* Grading is not required by law, but most meat is graded according to one of the following classifications: U.S. Prime (the highest grade, seldom sold in markets), U.S. Choice (the highest grade sold in most markets), U.S. Good (the most common grade found in most markets), U.S. Commercial (meat which has very little fat and practically no marbling), U.S. Utility (the lowest grade found in markets).

3. *The appearance:* Knowing what a good piece of meat looks like is a great help in buying. Good-quality beef is well streaked with creamy white fat. The lean part is firm, fine grained, and cherry red in color. Good-quality veal has a small amount of clear white fat. The lean part is fine grained and has a light grayish-pink color. Lamb is fine grained and has a clear white fat on the outside. The meat is pinkish red, and the bones have a reddish tint. As sheep grow older, the meat becomes darker in color and the bones become whiter and harder. Good-quality pork is firm, fine grained, and well streaked with fat. The color is a grayish pink in young animals and a delicate rose in older animals. Fresh pork usually comes from young animals.

BUYING MEAT

Courtesy Kroger Company

Whether you buy meat at a market where you are waited on or whether you select it yourself from a self-service counter, you should know how to buy meat properly. Wise buying can result in tasty meals at low cost.

A wise buyer knows the different cuts of meat that are sold, the amount of fat and bone that they contain, and the costs. Therefore, you should consider the amount of fat and bone in the various cuts as well as the cost when deciding on the kind and the amount of meat that you will need for a meal.

Sometimes it may be economical to buy a higher-cost meat than to buy a low-cost meat that contains a great deal of waste. Short ribs, for example, may be priced at less per pound than hamburger, but they yield only about one-third to one-half as many servings per pound.

Even though it is difficult to say exactly how much meat should be bought for a certain number of servings, the following guides may be helpful:

No Bone: Ground Meat, Boneless Stew, Liver
1 pound for 4 servings

Very Little Bone: Round Steak, Veal, Pork
1 pound for 2 to 3 servings

Fair Amount of Bone: Steaks, Chops, Shoulder and Loin Roasts
1 pound for 2 servings

Great Deal of Bone and Connective Tissue: Short Ribs, Spareribs
1 pound for 1 to 2 servings

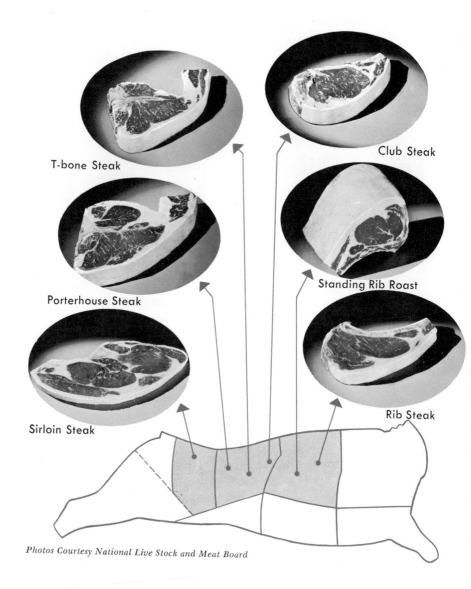

T-bone Steak

Club Steak

Porterhouse Steak

Standing Rib Roast

Sirloin Steak

Rib Steak

Photos Courtesy National Live Stock and Meat Board

The tender cuts of meat come from an area along the backbone where the animal does not use his muscles and connective tissues very much. The tenderness of meat also depends upon the age of the animal and the grade of the meat. (See page 266.) Meat with fat is more tender than meat with very little or no fat at all. Tender cuts of meat may be cooked by dry heat, which means that they may be broiled, roasted, or pan-fried. (See page 273.)

LESS-TENDER CUTS OF BEEF

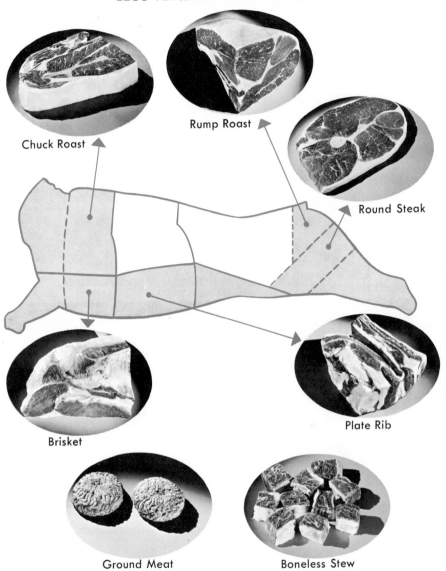

Chuck Roast

Rump Roast

Round Steak

Brisket

Plate Rib

Ground Meat

Boneless Stew

Photos Courtesy National Live Stock and Meat Board

Less-tender cuts of meat come from the parts of the animal which are exercised a lot, such as the legs, shoulder, and neck. Meat which is cut from these parts of the animal must be cooked by moist heat to make it tender. A less-tender cut of meat may also be made more tender by grinding, by pounding with a mallet, or by putting it through a cutting machine as in cubed meat. When this is done, it may be cooked by dry heat.

VEAL CUTS

Veal is meat from young calves that are from 2 to 14 weeks old. It is not considered tender because it has very little fat.

Long, slow cooking is needed in order to preserve the delicate flavor of veal and to make it tender.

Photos Courtesy National Live Stock and Meat Board

Arm Steak

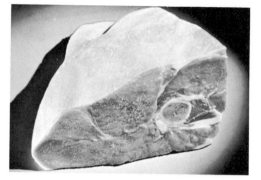

Rump Roast

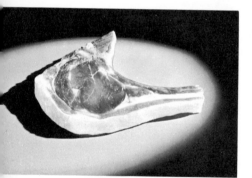

Rib Chop

City Chicken

LAMB CUTS

Leg of Lamb   Lamb Patties

Photos Courtesy National Live Stock and Meat Board

Pork may be bought fresh or cured. Some popular cuts of fresh pork are pork chops (rib or loin), spareribs, and roast pork (sirloin). Bacon and ham are favorite kinds of cured pork. Nearly all pork is tender and flavorful. However, all fresh pork should be cooked until well done.

Photos Courtesy National Live Stock and Meat Board

Sirloin Roast

Spareribs

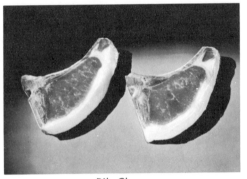

Rib Chops

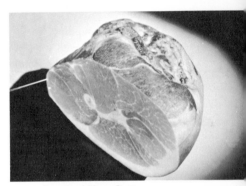

Smoked Ham Butt

Shoulder lamb chops (not shown here) cost less than rib or loin lamb chops and leg of lamb. Lamb shanks and lamb neck slices cost still less.

Rib Chops

Loin Chops

Photos Courtesy National Live Stock and Meat Board

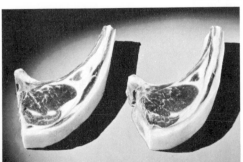

Courtesy Admiral Corporation

Courtesy Swift and Company

Fresh and Cured Meat

Remove the wrapping from meat as soon as you arrive home from the market. Cover it loosely with wax paper, leaving the ends open. Store it in the meat compartment or in the coldest part of the refrigerator. Cured meat, such as bacon and sausages, may be left in the package.

Ground meat, stew meat, and variety meats should be used within 24 hours. But steaks, chops, and roasts may be kept for 2 or 3 days if suitably refrigerated.

Frozen Meat

Place frozen meat in the freezer as soon as you bring it home from the market. It can be kept safely in the food freezer for several months but for only 2 or 3 weeks in the freezing compartment of the refrigerator. When steaks, chops, and ground meat are frozen, place pieces of moistureproof paper between the pieces or layers so that they can be easily separated before cooking.

Cooked Meat

Cooked meat will keep for 4 or 5 days if it is stored in the coldest part of the refrigerator. Place cooked meat in a covered dish or wrap it tightly in wax paper before putting it in the refrigerator. The larger the pieces, the better cooked meat will keep.

COOKING MEAT

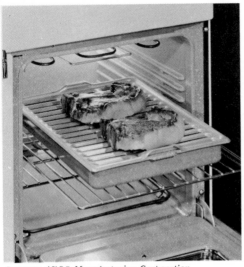

Dry-heat Method

Moist-heat Method

The dry-heat method, in which meat is cooked without moisture, or water, should be used for tender cuts (see page 268) which have a small amount of connective tissue and a moderate amount of fat. Broiling, pan-broiling, pan-frying, and roasting are examples of dry-heat cooking.

The moist-heat method, in which meat is cooked with moisture, or water, should be used for the less-tender cuts (see page 269). Since these cuts have little fat and a large amount of connective tissue, moist heat and long, slow cooking at a low temperature are necessary to soften the connective tissue. Pot-roasting, braising, stewing, and soup making are examples of moist-heat cooking.

Meat that is cooked at a constant low temperature is juicier, more tender, more flavorful, more attractive and appetizing, and has less shrinkage than meat that is cooked at a high temperature. Broiling, in which meat is cooked quickly at a high temperature, is an exception.

To make less-tender cuts of meat tender, sprinkle both sides of the meat evenly with a meat tenderizer, as you would sprinkle with salt. Then pierce the meat deeply at 1-inch intervals with a long-pronged fork.

BROILING MEAT

Suitable cuts for broiling are: tender beef steaks, lamb and mutton chops, sliced ham and bacon, ground beef and lamb patties, and liver.

1. Rub the broiler rack with fat to prevent the meat from sticking. Turn on the broiler (to "broil"). Then cut gashes in the fat edge to prevent the meat from curling.

2. When the meat is brown, about halfway through the cooking time, season on one side and turn with tongs. If you use a fork, be sure to put it into the fat. Never pierce the meat since this will allow the juices to escape. Cook to the degree of doneness desired: well done, medium, or rare.

3. Season, and serve immediately on a hot platter.

ROASTING MEAT

Suitable cuts for roasting are: all large, tender cuts of beef, veal, pork, and lamb.

1. Season with salt and pepper and place the meat, fat side up, on a rack in a pan. Insert a meat thermometer so that the bulb is in the center of the thickest part of the lean meat and does not touch bone or rest in fat.

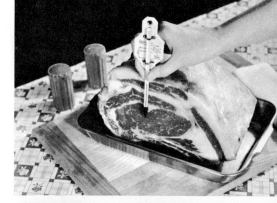

Courtesy National Live Stock and Meat Board

2. Place the pan in the center of the oven. Do not add water and do not cover. All meat except pork should be roasted in a 325° F. oven until the meat thermometer registers the degree of doneness desired.
    (See roasting timetable on page 519.)

Courtesy National Live Stock and Meat Board

3. Inexpensive cuts of meat may be cooked in aluminum foil. Lay the meat on the shiny surface of the foil. Seal it firmly, using a double fold. This type of meat should be cooked in a slow oven (300° to 325° F.)

Courtesy Reynolds Metals Company

MAKING A MEAT LOAF

Although ground meat is usually from less-tender cuts, it may be cooked by the dry-heat method. Grinding the meat breaks up its connective tissue, thus making it more tender.

Courtesy U·S. Bureau of Human Nutrition and Home Economics

Courtesy American Meat Institute

1. Combine the ground meat, the other ingredients, and the seasonings. Mix lightly because too much mixing will make the meat loaf tough. Shape the ingredients into a loaf, and bake in a moderate oven.

2. Remove the meat loaf from the oven, and place it on a hot platter. Slice it, and serve either plain or with gravy.

Ground meat will cook in a much shorter time than a meat loaf if it is baked in a ring mold, cooked in a muffin pan, or made into small patties of various shapes.

Courtesy National Live Stock and Meat Board

PAN-FRYING MEAT

Suitable meats for pan-frying are: ground-meat patties, any small, thin pieces of tender meat, and any meat which has been tenderized by pounding, scoring, cubing, or grinding.

Courtesy Procter and Gamble

To *pan-fry meat,* cook it in a heavy frying pan in a small amount of fat over moderate heat, turning occasionally until done. Do not cover. Remove and drain the meat on a paper towel for a few minutes before serving. Meat that is to be pan-fried may be rolled in flour first, if desired.

To *pan-fry bacon,* place it in a cold frying pan and cook over low heat, turning several times until each slice is crisp and evenly browned. Pour off the fat as the bacon cooks. Remove the slices one at a time, and drain on absorbent paper.

Courtesy Scott Paper Company

277

BRAISING MEAT

Suitable cuts for braising are: pot roasts, less-tender beef steaks, pork chops, veal chops, veal steaks, and veal cutlets.

1. Brown the meat slowly on both sides in a heavy utensil. The meat may or may not be coated with flour. When it is, fat should be added to the pan.

2. Add seasonings and a small amount of liquid, such as water, meat stock, canned tomatoes, or tomato juice.

3. Cover the pan tightly, and cook the meat at a low temperature either on top of the range or in the oven with the heat turned low. Do not allow it to boil. When the meat is done, remove excess fat from the pan and thicken the liquid for gravy.

Photos Courtesy Swift and Company

MAKING A STEW

Suitable cuts for stew are: less-tender cuts of beef, veal, and lamb. (See page 269.)

Photos Courtesy Swift and Company

1. Roll the pieces of meat in seasoned flour.

2. Brown the meat slowly and evenly in hot fat in a heavy kettle.

3. Add just enough water to cover the meat. Cover the pan with a tight-fitting lid, and simmer (do not boil) until the meat is done.

4. Add vegetables or noodles or dumplings during the last part of the cooking time, just before the meat is done.

5. When the meat and the vegetables are done, remove them from the pan and thicken the liquid for gravy. (See page 219.)

Photos Courtesy Swift and Company

Meat That Can Be Cooked Quickly

Frozen meats such as liver slices, thin steaks, cutlets, and meat patties can be cooked without defrosting. Because they can be cooked a few minutes after being bought or taken from the freezer, they save a great deal of time.

Meat That Has Not Been Defrosted

A roast in its frozen form takes one-third to one-half longer to cook than fresh meat. Thick frozen steaks and chops take almost twice as long to cook as fresh meat. Frozen meat must be cooked slowly so that the outside is not too well done by the time that the center is done. Most authorities recommend that meat be at least partially thawed before cooking.

Meat That Has Been Defrosted

Frozen meats that have been completely thawed can be cooked in the same way as fresh meat. Meat can be thawed: (1) in the refrigerator and (2) at room temperature. The method of thawing does not affect the flavor, the juiciness, or the tenderness of the meat, so the method may be selected according to convenience. The time that it takes to thaw meat depends upon the method used, the size of the piece of meat, and the way in which the meat is wrapped. After meat has been defrosted, it should be cooked immediately. Meat that has been defrosted should never be refrozen.

Courtesy Armour and Company

Kidneys

Beef and pork: Braise, cook in liquid
Veal and lamb: Broil, pan-broil, braise,
cook in liquid

Livers

Beef and pork: Roast, braise, fry
Veal and lamb: Broil, pan-broil, fry

Photos Courtesy National Live Stock and Meat Board

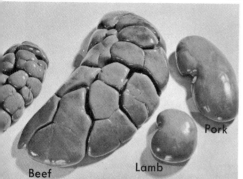

Hearts

Braise, cook in liquid

Tongues

Cook in liquid

Photos Courtesy National Live Stock and Meat Board

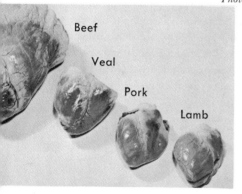

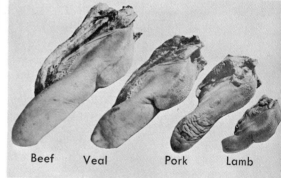

Sweetbreads

Broil, fry, braise, cook in liquid

Brains

Broil, fry, braise, cook in liquid

Photos Courtesy National Live Stock and Meat Board

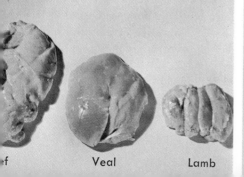

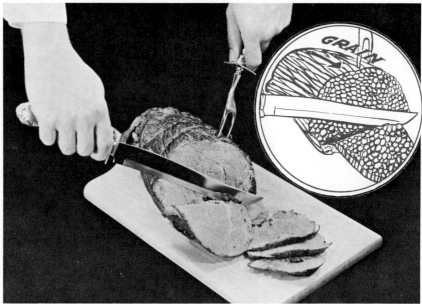

Courtesy West Bend Aluminum Company and Design Studio

To Carve Meat

Meat may be carved in the kitchen by the homemaker or at the table, depending upon the type of table service used (see page 25). A roast is easier to carve 15 to 20 minutes after it has been removed from the oven. It may be reheated if desired. When meat is carved at the table, it should be placed on a large platter so that there will be room for the slices as they are cut.

Some other suggestions for carving are these:

1. Use a fork to hold the meat steady on the platter.

2. Using a very sharp knife, draw it through the meat the full length of the blade rather than use a sawing motion.

3. Carve meat across the grain. The slices which result from this method of carving can be easily cut by those who are served.

To Serve Meat

Servings should be planned so that they will be of the same thickness and so that everyone will have some of the choice portions. Whether carved in the kitchen or at the table, the meat should look as attractive as possible. Bright-colored garnishes, such as parsley, carrots, mint jelly, or cranberry sauce, add to the appearance of a meat dish.

The platter on which the meat is to be served should be preheated so that the meat will be piping hot.

ACTIVITIES

Studying meat habits:
1. Discuss how the meat habits of people in other countries differ from ours.
2. How often is meat served in your home?
3. What are some of your favorite meat dishes?

Learning the cuts of meat:
4. Study charts showing various cuts of meat. Then visit a meat market if possible. Ask the butcher to demonstrate various ways of cutting meat. Also ask the butcher to show you the United States government inspection stamp on meat.
5. Mount pictures of various cuts of meat. Then divide your class into two groups, and have a contest to see which side can identify the most cuts of meat.
6. If possible, visit a commercial packing house. If this is impossible, perhaps one of your classmates has made such a trip and will tell the class about it.

Deciding on the best buy:
7. Discuss and compare the tender cuts of meat with the less-tender cuts as to cost, food value, flavor, and so on.
8. Compare the costs of canned, fresh, and frozen meat in your community. Give the advantages and the disadvantages of each.
9. Discuss the advantages and the disadvantages of buying a half or a quarter of beef and having it cut and wrapped for storage in a food locker or freezer.
10. Compare the prices per pound of loin lamb chops and shoulder lamb chops. Since both have the same food value, which would be the better buy if you wish to cut down on the amount that you spend for meat?

Comparing the methods of cooking meat:
11. Compare the dry- and moist-heat methods of cooking meat. List three cuts of meat that may be prepared by each method.
12. List 10 ways in which less-tender cuts of meat may be prepared.
13. Bring to class three recipes in which ground meat is used. Compare your recipes with those of your classmates. Then select three to be prepared in class.
14. How does each of the following help to make meat tender: (a) stewing, (b) tomato juice, (c) pounding, and (d) grinding?
15. List 10 dishes in which meat is combined with other foods. Discuss the advantages of combining meat with food such as noodles and vegetables.
16. Bring to class two of your favorite recipes for variety meats. Discuss what might be served with them, and select one to prepare in class. **283**

U.S. Fish and Wildlife Service   *Courtesy Armour and Company*

Chapter 20 | **POULTRY AND FISH**

"Poultry" is the term used for chickens, turkeys, ducks, geese, pigeons (squabs), guinea hens, and Rock Cornish hens. Chicken and turkey have long been the most popular and widely used of all kinds of poultry. Years ago, when poultry was more expensive than it is today, it was served only on special occasions. Today poultry is plentiful throughout the year, and many times it is less expensive than beef, lamb, and pork. It is suitable for simple, everyday meals and buffet suppers as well as for "company" meals.

"Fish" is a broad term which covers thousands of varieties of fish with bones, often called "finfish," and fish with a protective shell covering, called "shellfish." Trout, bass, mackerel, herring, whitefish, salmon, halibut, cod, and swordfish are some of the most common finfish. Shrimp, oysters, crabs, lobsters, clams, and scallops are shellfish. In the past, Americans did not eat nearly so much fish as people in other countries did. Today, because various kinds of fresh and frozen fish can be shipped safely and easily to all parts of the United States, a great deal of fish is consumed in America. Canned, smoked, and salted fish are also widely used. Fish is sometimes served at the beginning of a meal in the form of soup, a cocktail, or an appetizer, but it is most **284** often served as a main dish.

KINDS OF POULTRY

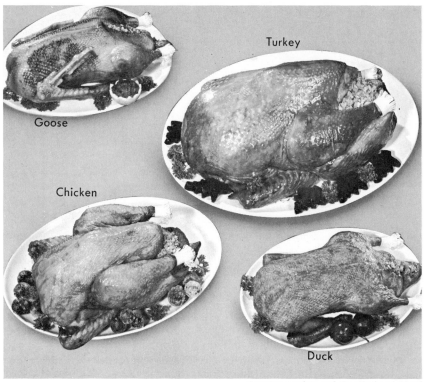

Goose

Turkey

Chicken

Duck

Courtesy Poultry and Egg National Board

Not only is poultry flavorful, but it is one of the most nutritious foods because it contains high-quality (complete) proteins and is rich in minerals and vitamins.

Of the four most common kinds of poultry used in American homes today, turkeys are the largest and ducks are the smallest. Turkeys and chickens have more white meat than dark and are slightly drier than ducks and geese, which have all dark meat. Ducks and geese have more of a wild flavor and usually have more fat than turkeys and chickens.

Courtesy Armour and Company

When poultry is served, it may be carved in the kitchen and brought in on a platter, or the whole bird may be brought to the table to be carved there by the father or the host.

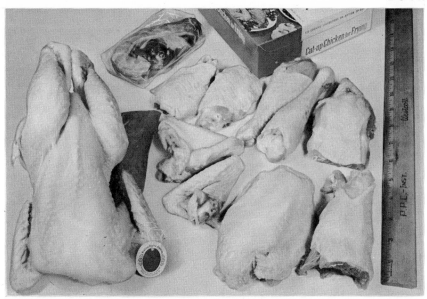

Courtesy Swift and Company

Fresh

When selecting fresh poultry, consider the grade, the brand name, and the appearance. Choose a clean bird that has a plump, full breast; plump legs; and no bruises or discolorations. Young poultry has smooth tender skin; soft tender meat; and a soft, flexible breastbone. Older poultry has coarse, thick skin and a firm breastbone. The following are common kinds of poultry and ways in which they may be used:

Broilers and fryers (8 to 9 weeks old, 1¾ to 3½ pounds dressed weight): Small birds are best for broiling. One-half a bird is usually allowed for each serving. For general frying purposes, poultry may be bought whole, quartered, or in pieces. Allow ½ to ¾ pound per serving.

Roasters or bakers (9 to 12 weeks old, 3½ to 4 pounds dressed weight): These birds are usually available fresh. If not, look for them in the frozen food department. They are cooked by roasting, braising, or frying. If fried, they should be covered and allowed to steam after browning, to ensure tenderness. Allow ½ to ¾ pound per serving.

Stewers (over 1 year old): These are usually heavy hens that are no longer in egg production. They should be cooked slowly in water for a long period, as in soups and stews. Allow ½ pound per serving.

Poultry spoils rapidly. Use it soon after it is bought. If the poultry is to be kept for any length of time, rewrap it loosely before putting it in the refrigerator. The loose wrap allows air to circulate and slow down spoilage.

POULTRY

Barbecued
Chicken

Frozen

Poultry can be purchased frozen — whole and wrapped in a plastic bag or cut up and packaged. Some frozen chicken is breaded and ready to be cooked. Still other frozen chicken is cooked and needs only to be heated. Frozen poultry can be kept for several months if it is stored in the freezer at 0° F. or below. But it can be kept for only 2 or 3 weeks if it is stored in the freezing compartment of the refrigerator.

Canned

Whole cooked poultry can be bought in large cans, and deboned poultry can be bought in large and small cans. Canned chicken or turkey may be used just as it comes from the can. Therefore, it is convenient to have on the shelf for an emergency (page 135), but it is too expensive for frequent use.

Cooked

Small barbecued or roasted chickens are available in many large city markets and delicatessens. These may be bought while still hot and served immediately, or they may be heated just before serving. Because they are cooked, they are more expensive per pound than uncooked fresh or frozen chickens.

Courtesy National Presto Industries, Inc.

Poultry of all kinds should be cooked at a low temperature so that the meat will be juicy, tender, and evenly cooked to the bone. Poultry that is overcooked is dry. The method used to cook poultry depends upon its age:

1. Young, tender broilers, fryers, and roasters should be cooked by the dry-heat method: broiled, fried, or roasted.
2. Older, less-tender poultry (1 year or more) should be cooked by the moist-heat method: braised or stewed. Poultry that is very old should be cooked slowly for a long time or cooked in a pressure saucepan.
3. Turkeys, geese, and ducks are usually roasted. Small, young turkeys (broilers) can be broiled, fried, or roasted.

U.S. Fish and Wildlife Service

The bony pieces of poultry may be stewed and used for soups, or the meat may be removed and used in chicken pies, salads, and sandwiches. The select pieces may then be fried or braised. Since leftover poultry can be used in many ways, it is often wise to buy more than the amount needed for one meal. The larger the bird, the more meat it has in proportion to the bone.

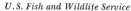

Courtesy Poultry and Egg National Board

To Stew Chicken

1. Leave the chicken whole or cut it into serving-size pieces.
2. Place the chicken in a deep saucepan. Add seasoning.
3. Add boiling water, and cover with a tight-fitting lid.
4. Simmer for several hours, or until the chicken is tender.

To Braise (Fricassee) Chicken

1. Coat each piece of chicken with flour.
2. Then brown the pieces of chicken in hot fat.
3. Add a small amount of liquid, and cook slowly in a covered pan.

Courtesy Poultry and Egg National Board

To Pan-fry Chicken

1. Shake the chicken and flour mixed with seasoning in a paper bag, or roll the chicken in the flour mixture until it is well coated.

Courtesy Poultry and Egg National Board

2. Place the coated pieces of chicken in hot fat about ½ inch deep. Cook the meaty pieces first. Brown each piece evenly. Reduce heat and cover. Cook slowly 20 to 40 minutes, depending on the size and the thickness of the pieces.

Courtesy Poultry and Egg National Board

3. The chicken is done if it is tender when pierced with a fork.

Courtesy Procter and Gamble

To Broil Chicken

1. Preheat the broiler.
2. Brush the chicken with butter or margarine, and place it skin side down on the broiler rack. Sprinkle with salt and pepper.
3. Place the broiler pan in the broiler 5 to 7 inches from the heat.
4. Baste and turn every 15 minutes until brown and tender — about 45 minutes.
5. Serve hot.

USDA Photo

To Barbecue Chicken

1. Baste broiled chicken with barbecue sauce each time it is turned.
2. If the chicken is barbecued over an open grill, start the fire about ½ hour before the chicken is to be put on so that it will cook slowly over the coals, not the flame.

Courtesy Ac'cent

To Roast Chicken

1. Clean the chicken, and rub the inside and the outside with salt.
2. Stuff lightly with your favorite dressing.
3. Rub the chicken all over with butter or fat, and baste during cooking.
4. Bake at 325° F. until tender. To test for doneness, move a leg. If it moves easily and the meat is soft when pressed between the fingers, the chicken is done.

Courtesy Poultry and Egg National Board

FOOD VALUE OF FISH

There are more than 100 varieties of edible finfish, all of which may be divided into two groups:

1. *Salt-water fish,* such as halibut, salmon, mackerel, cod, bluefish, flounder, haddock, and shad

2. *Fresh-water fish,* such as perch, bass, catfish, trout, pike, and carp

Fish is high in food 'value. It is listed in *A Daily Food Guide* (page 49) because . . .
. . . it is an excellent source of high-quality (complete) protein.
. . . it is an excellent source of the B vitamins — thiamine, riboflavin, and niacin.
. . . it is a good source of the minerals phosphorus, iron, and copper.

Also, . . .
. . . salt-water fish is a good source of iodine.
. . . canned fish (salmon, sardines, and so on) with softened bones that may be eaten is an excellent source of calcium and phosphorus.
. . . fish with fat, such as salmon, tuna, mackerel, trout, and shad, contains large amounts of vitamins A and D.

Many homemakers serve fish at least once a week because it is an economical source of protein, gives variety to the meals, and can usually be prepared in a short period of time.

Courtesy Florida Agricultural Extension Service

FORMS OF FISH

Whole or round fish is the term used for fish just as it comes from the water. Allow 1 pound per serving.

Drawn fish is the term used when the entrails have been removed. Allow ¾ pound per serving.

Dressed or pan-dressed fish has had the entrails, scales, and usually the head, tail, and fins removed. Allow ½ pound per serving.

Fillets are sides of fish cut lengthwise away from the backbone. Because the bone has been removed, fillets are often an economical choice. Allow ⅓ pound per serving.

Steaks are cross-section slices of large dressed fish. Allow ⅓ pound per serving.

Photos Courtesy Household Finance Corporation

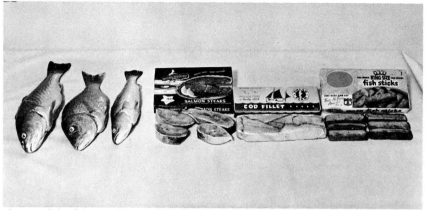

Courtesy Polunsky's

Fresh fish is delicately flavored. Because it spoils quickly, take care when buying fish to be sure that it is "fresh." A good fish has bright, clear eyes; firm, elastic flesh; tightly clinging scales with a sheen; and a fresh odor. To store fresh fish, clean and wrap it in wax paper or place it in a covered dish, and store it in the coldest part of the refrigerator. Use it within 24 hours.

Frozen fish (whole, fillets, steaks, or fish sticks) is available the year round. It should be kept frozen in the unopened package until it is to be used. To thaw and cook, follow the directions on the package.

Canned fish comes in a great variety. Because all canned fish has been cooked, it is ready to be served or to be used in dishes that require a slight amount of cooking. Therefore, canned fish is a good item for the emergency shelf. The most common kinds of canned fish are salmon, tuna, cod, and sardines.

Smoked, pickled, and salted fish are called "cured" fish. Some kinds are sold in bulk (smoked salmon, whitefish, and sturgeon; salt mackerel and herring), some in jars (pickled herring), and some in plastic bags (smoked herring and salmon; salt mackerel). All smoked, pickled, and salted fish should be kept under refrigeration. Because such fish is highly seasoned, it is generally used for appetizers.

Courtesy Polunsky's

SELECTING CANNED FISH

Solid-pack tuna (right) is more expensive than chunk tuna (center) or grated tuna (left). The food value of the three is the same. The most expensive canned salmon is deep red in color and has a higher oil content than less-expensive salmon. The higher-priced tuna and salmon are preferred for salads or when the fish is to be served plain. The less-expensive kinds can be used for casseroles, fish cakes, and other cooked dishes.

When canned fish is used for salads or sandwiches, the oil or liquid in the can should be removed. However, the oil may be used in place of fat for making the white sauce for creamed dishes and casseroles since it adds flavor and richness.

Canned fish should be broken or separated into flakes but not mashed or mixed too much.

Courtesy Ac'cent

COOKING FISH

Fish should be cooked just enough so that it may be easily broken or separated into flakes with a fork or the tip of a knife. When done, fish should be chalk white in color. It should also be moist and tender. The main problem in cooking fish is to bring out the flavor without drying out the fish. Like other protein foods, fish should be cooked at a low temperature. Because all fish is tender, it needs to be cooked for only a short time.

Some other suggestions for cooking fish are these:

1. Fat fish, such as salmon, mackerel, or shad, is best when cooked by dry heat — broiled, baked, or stuffed (page 297).

2. Lean fish, such as flounder, haddock, or cod, is especially suited to cooking by moist heat— boiling, steaming, poaching, or baking with a sauce. The secret is to allow the liquid to simmer but never to boil. Lean fish that is cooked by dry heat — broiled or baked — should be basted frequently with melted fat.

3. Both fat and lean fish may be fried.

Fish should be served soon after it has been prepared. Otherwise it will become dry and hard and lose some of its flavor.

Because fish has a mild flavor, it is frequently served with a highly seasoned sauce. Tomato, creole, lemon, white, and butter sauces may be cooked with the fish. Tartar or hollandaise sauce may be served on the fish after it is prepared.

Something colorful, crisp, or tart — celery, raw vegetables, cole slaw, or a tossed green salad — should be served with fish.

To Pan-fry Fish

1. Season serving-size pieces with salt and pepper. Dip them in milk or beaten egg. Roll them in corn meal, flour, or cracker crumbs until completely coated.
2. Fry the fish in a small amount of hot fat at moderate heat until golden brown. Turn the pieces carefully, and brown them on the other side.
3. Drain the fish on absorbent paper, and serve immediately on a heated platter.

Fish may also be fried in a deep frying kettle at 375° F. with enough fat to cover the fish. Fry only a single layer at a time. When the fish is golden brown, remove it and drain on absorbent paper.

Courtesy Agricultural Extension Service, Oklahoma State University

To Broil Fish

1. Place steaks, fillets, or small flat fish on a greased broiler about 2 to 3 inches from the heat. Baste with melted fat.
2. Broil the fish until light brown. Turn the fish carefully, brush again with melted fat, and brown on the other side. Small, thin pieces may be sufficiently cooked by broiling on one side only.
3. Serve the fish on a heated platter.

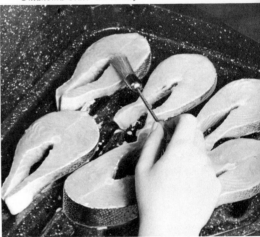

U.S. Fish and Wildlife Service

To Bake Fish

1. Sprinkle the fish with salt and pepper. Dip it in a mixture of melted butter, lemon juice, and minced onion.
2. Arrange the fish in a greased baking dish, and pour the rest of the mixture over it.
3. Bake the fish in a moderate oven (350° F.) for about 25 minutes, or until it is easily flaked but still moist. Baste the fish occasionally during baking.

U.S. Fish and Wildlife Service

SHELLFISH: THE MOLLUSKS

Oysters, clams, scallops, and mussels are called "mollusks." Mollusks are soft inside and have a hard outer shell. They may be bought in the shell, out of the shell, frozen (cooked or raw), and canned. Since fresh shellfish spoils easily, it should be kept under refrigeration until ready to be cooked.

Oysters in the shell are sold by the dozen. Out of the shell, they are sold according to size — small, medium, or large — in half-pint, pint, or quart containers. The liquid that comes with fresh oysters should be clear and fresh smelling (almost odorless). Oysters may be served raw on the half shell or in cocktails. They may be baked, broiled, fried, or scalloped. They may also be used in stews and in dressing for poultry.

Clams (soft shell and hard shell) are sold in the same way as oysters. Young, tender clams are known as littleneck clams or cherry stone clams. Frozen and canned clams are available in most markets, but fresh clams are not common except in the coastal areas where they are found. Clams are used mostly in the making of clam chowder. They may also be steamed in the shell and served with melted butter, and they may be fried. Small clams are served on the half shell or in stews.

Mussels are similar to oysters and clams, but they are not so common a food in America as they are in Europe.

Scallops are the muscle part that opens and closes the shell of the scallop. Small bay scallops are more tender and more delicately flavored than large deep-sea scallops. Fresh scallops are not available everywhere. Frozen scallops (breaded and ready to cook) and canned scallops can be bought in most markets. Scallops can be broiled, pan-fried, or fried in deep fat.

Courtesy Polunsky's

SHELLFISH: THE CRUSTACEANS

Lobsters, shrimp, crabs, and crayfish are called "crustaceans." While not so soft inside as the mollusks, crustaceans have a crustlike outer shell. Crayfish, sometimes called "crawfish," are found in fresh water. They may be used in place of shrimp or lobster in most recipes.

Lobsters are usually expensive. Fresh lobsters should be bought live. They should remain alive until they are dropped into boiling water to be cooked. In most areas only frozen or canned lobster is available. Frozen lobster tails are perhaps the most popular frozen form of lobster. Lobster may be boiled or broiled and served whole with melted butter. It may be served cold in a salad. It may also be creamed, such as lobster Newburg.

State Department of Sea and Shore Fisheries, Augusta, Maine

Shrimp vary in size from large to small. Raw shrimp are pearly gray, green, or brown. However, after being cooked (in the shell), they turn pink. Frozen breaded shrimp, which have been peeled, cleaned, and breaded, are ready for frying. Shrimp may be served as a cocktail or in salads. They may also be French-fried or broiled, or they may be cooked in a casserole, such as shrimp creole.

Courtesy Lipton Kitchens

Crabs are referred to as "hard-shell" crabs or "soft-shell" crabs. Crabs may be bought live, frozen, cooked in the shell, cooked and frozen, as fresh meat, or as canned meat. Crab meat is most commonly used for cocktails and salads. But it may also be served plain in chunks.

State Department of Sea and Shore Fisheries, Augusta, Maine

ACTIVITIES

Buying poultry:

1. With the help of your dictionary, compare and discuss the meaning of each of the following: *(a)* poultry, *(b)* fowl, and *(c)* bird.
2. Demonstrate that young chickens have a flexible breastbone and older chickens have a firm breastbone. Compare the skins of the two.
3. Compare the prices of older chickens with those of broilers and fryers.
4. Demonstrate how to cut up a chicken for frying.
5. Compare the prices of various cuts of chicken sold by the piece. For example, compare the price of breasts with that of wings or legs.

Cooking poultry:

6. Compare the cooking of poultry with that of beef and fish.
7. Suggest four different ways in which inexpensive pieces of chicken may be prepared.
8. Bring to class two recipes for using leftover chicken or turkey. Compare your recipes with those of your classmates.

Selecting and buying fish:

9. Name and describe four different kinds of fish sold in your local market. Compare the costs per pound. Discuss how you prepare each.
10. Compare the price of fresh fish with those of chicken and steak in your community. Then compare the price of fresh fish with those of frozen and canned fish.

Planning menus:

11. Plan four menus with each of the following prepared as a main dish: *(a)* pan-fried fish, *(b)* broiled fish, *(c)* baked fish, and *(d)* canned fish. Include in your menus potatoes, asparagus, tomatoes, carrots, celery, green salads, cucumbers, and radishes as a vegetable, a salad, or a garnish.
12. Find out how often fish is served in the homes of your classmates.

Cooking fish properly:

13. List precautions that should be taken when cooking fish.
14. Bring three fish recipes to class. Compare your recipes with those of your classmates. Select one to prepare in class. Decide on other foods to serve with the fish dish.

Studying about canned fish:

15. Buy a can of solid-pack tuna and a can of chunk-style tuna. Compare: *(a)* the amounts of oil and flaked tuna, *(b)* the prices, and *(c)* the flavors.
16. Buy five kinds of salmon. Read the labels, and compare the net weights and the prices. Open the cans, and compare: *(a)* appearances, *(b)* flavors, *(c)* colors, *(d)* amounts of fish, and *(e)* amounts of liquid.

Chapter 21 | CEREALS

Cereal is the name given to any grain that is used for food. Most cereal comes from wheat, corn, rye, oats, barley, and rice plants. Bread is the most common cereal food in America.

Many prepared cereals may be bought and eaten cold as breakfast foods. Others are bought whole or ground and cooked for hot cereal dishes. Cereal is the chief ingredient in bread, rolls, cakes, and cookies.

Much of the cereal grown in our country is ground into flour. Bread flour, made from hard wheat, is used for most rolls and bread. Cake flour, made from soft wheat, is used for cakes, crackers, and cookies. Flour made from durum wheat, an extra hard variety, is used in the production of macaroni, spaghetti, and noodles.

All-purpose flour, made by blending hard and soft wheat, is the flour that is generally used in our homes. It can be used satisfactorily in nearly all recipes.

Cereal is very important in the diet. It provides protein and vitamins, as well as calories. .

FOOD VALUE OF CEREALS

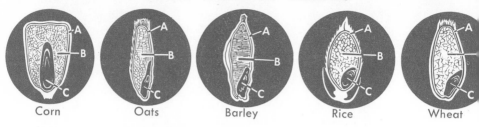

Corn　　Oats　　Barley　　Rice　　Wheat

Courtesy Cereal Institute, Inc.

Each grain of a cereal, as shown above, is made up of three parts:

A, the bran (cellulose, minerals, vitamin B, and proteins), which is the outer covering

B, the endosperm (starch and proteins), which is the large white center part of the grain

C, the germ (fat, proteins, minerals, and vitamins), from which the seed sprouts and which is the smallest but, nutritionally, the most important part of the grain

Some cereals are made from the whole grain — that is, the bran, the endosperm, and the germ — and some are made from only part of the grain.

Whole-grain cereals, made from the entire grain, contain all the nutrients found in the original grain itself. Therefore, they are much better for you than those made from only part of the grain.

Refined cereals have had the germ and some of the bran removed, leaving little food value other than the starch of the endosperm. The germ contains fat which becomes rancid. Therefore, it is removed to make the cereal keep better.

Restored cereals are refined cereals to which minerals and vitamins have been added.

Enriched cereals are refined cereals to which specific amounts of iron, thiamine, riboflavin, and niacin have been added. Sometimes calcium and vitamin D are also added to increase the food value.

Courtesy Evaporated Milk Association

The numerous ready-to-eat and precooked cereals that are available make possible a wide variety of flavors, textures, and combinations for the breakfast menu in a minimum of time. Many years ago all breakfast cereals were coarsely ground and had to be cooked, and sometimes soaked, for a long time. Today most cereals are precooked before packaging so that they may be cooked in a few minutes (see page 306). Ready-to-eat cereals are timesavers because they may be served just as they come from the box with milk or cream and sugar. For variety, two or more ready-to-eat cereals — flaked, rolled, shredded, puffed, baked, ground, sweetened, or flavored to taste — may be combined. Cereals may also be varied by the use of brown sugar, maple or corn sirup, honey, or molasses instead of sugar for sweetening. Fruits, whether fresh, frozen, dried, canned, or preserved, greatly improve the flavor of both cold and hot cereals. Fresh whole fruits and berries are favorites as a topping or combined with the cereal. Even though ready-to-eat cereals are good for you, they are not so nutritious as the same amount of a cooked cereal.

Courtesy Kellogg Company

Courtesy Cereal Institute, Inc.

Courtesy Evaporated Milk Association

Hot and cold breads

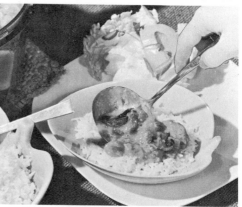

Courtesy National Presto Industries, Inc.

As a base for casseroles, stews, and sauces

Courtesy American Dairy Association

In cookies

Courtesy Cereal Institute, Inc.

For between-meal snacks

As a topping

Courtesy Ralston Purina Company

As a coating

Courtesy National Dairy Council

In meat loaf to extend the flavor of the meat

In combination with other foods

In puddings

As a garnish

As a stuffing

In candies

COOKING CEREALS

Courtesy Household Finance Corporation

A well-cooked cereal is free of lumps or raw parts, is well flavored without a starchy taste, and is not too stiff or too thin.

In cooking any cereal, it is best to follow the directions on the package. Cooking time varies according to the way in which the cereals have been manufactured. Since cereals are chiefly starch, they are cooked in large amounts of water so that the grains will absorb the water and increase in size.

Most cereals are prepared by slowly sprinkling the dry cereal into rapidly boiling salted water. If the whole amount is added at once, the cereal will be lumpy. The cereal should be stirred constantly until it begins to thicken (about 1 to 2 minutes). Then the heat should be lowered, and the cereal should be stirred occasionally until it is done. An inexperienced person may find it best to cook the cereal in the top part of a double boiler for the first few minutes and then place it over boiling water for the last part of the cooking time.

Dried fruits may be cooked with hot cereals, or stewed fruits may be used as a topping. Hot cereals may also be cooked with milk instead of water.

Courtesy American Dry Milk Institute, Inc.

To enrich the food value when cooking cereal, add ½ cup dry-milk solids for each cup of cereal.

Courtesy National Macaroni Institute

Macaroni, spaghetti, and noodles are often referred to as "macaroni products." There are some 150 different varieties of macaroni products in almost every shape and form. The best-quality macaroni products are made from durum wheat, which is the hardest wheat known.

307

COOKING MACARONI PRODUCTS

1. Cook macaroni products in a sauce-pan with a large amount of boiling salted water. Add the macaroni product gradually to rapidly boiling water so that the water will continue to boil.

(*NOTE:* Some macaroni products are enriched. They should be cooked in a small amount of boiling water.)

2. Cook the macaroni uncovered, stir-ring occasionally to prevent stick-ing, until tender. To test the tender-ness, press a piece of macaroni against the side of the saucepan with a fork. The tenderness desired will vary according to preference, but macaroni should never be cooked until it is soft and shapeless.

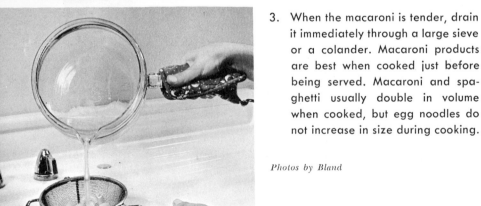

3. When the macaroni is tender, drain it immediately through a large sieve or a colander. Macaroni products are best when cooked just before being served. Macaroni and spa-ghetti usually double in volume when cooked, but egg noodles do not increase in size during cooking.

Photos by Bland

Courtesy Ac'cent

Macaroni products fit well into the menu from soup (noodles) and salad (macaroni) to main dishes (casseroles). Because of their bland flavor, they combine well with meat, fish, poultry, eggs, and cheese for casseroles salads, and top-of-the-stove dishes.

Macaroni products make it possible for leftovers to be brought to the table a second time with an entirely new look. They may be called "meat stretchers" or "extenders" because they can be served as the main course when combined with only a small amount of meat.

Macaroni products — particularly noodles — are sometimes served plain with only a seasoning of melted butter as an accompaniment to meat. However, they do not contain as many minerals and vitamins as do potatoes. They are best when served with a spicy cheese (macaroni) or a highly seasoned sauce (spaghetti) to offset their blandness.

For quick, convenient, easy-to-prepare meals, macaroni products may be purchased in ready-to-eat form, either canned or frozen.

Courtesy National Macaroni Institute

Courtesy Uncle Ben's Converted Rice

Regular white rice is polished after the hulls and the bran (see page 302) are removed. Since the hulls and the bran contain valuable minerals and vitamins, ordinary white rice is not so nutritious as it was before removal of the bran. Therefore, after polishing, many companies add minerals and vitamins to their rice. Such rice is labeled "enriched rice." It is more healthful than regular white rice. Enriched rice looks and tastes about the same as ordinary white rice.

Most companies recommend that rice not be washed before cooking nor rinsed afterward because the water causes a loss of natural and added minerals and vitamins.

Some rice has a short grain, and some has a long grain. Rice with a short grain is lower in price and usually cooks tender and moist. Long-grain varieties of rice cook more quickly and are drier than short-grain varieties. When cooked, they are loose and hold their shape.

Precooked rice has been partially cooked in the manufacture. Therefore, it can be cooked more quickly than regular rice. Some people find that precooked rice is more expensive and has less flavor than uncooked (or raw) rice.

Rice combines easily with other foods, such as meat, chicken, fish, or vegetables, in casserole main dishes. It makes a delicious side dish with gravy, meat, cheese, or tomato sauce. It can also be used in soups, salads, fruit desserts, and puddings. Serving rice with other foods not only adds nutritional value to the meal, but greatly reduces the cost per serving of a more expensive food.

ACTIVITIES

Studying about cereals:

1. Make a list on the board of the cereals that the members of your class eat most often. Opposite each cereal give the grain from which that cereal is made.
2. If possible, bring some cereal grains to class. Break the grains open, and look for the three parts: (a) bran, (b) endosperm, and (c) germ.
3. Name a ready-to-eat cereal which is manufactured in each of the following forms: (a) shredded, (b) flaked, (c) puffed, and (d) sugar-coated.
4. List ways in which each of the following cereal grains may be bought: (a) wheat, (b) oats, (c) rice, and (d) corn. For example, wheat may be bought as flour, as an uncooked cereal, or as a ready-to-eat cereal.

Buying cereals:

5. Make a list of the uncooked and the ready-to-eat cereals which are sold in your grocery store. Give the price of each, and tell if the label contains the words "refined," "restored," "enriched," or "made from whole grain."
6. Select five different ready-to-eat cereals. Measure the number of servings in each package. Then compare the costs.
7. Compare the cost of a precooked cereal with that of a ready-to-eat cereal.
8. Compare the cost of a ready-to-eat cereal in a large box with that of the same cereal in small individual boxes.
9. Collect labels from five different cereals, and compare them.
10. Post on the bulletin board six colored pictures showing attractive ways in which to serve cereal.
11. Prepare an uncooked cereal in the following three ways: (a) cooked in water, (b) cooked in a mixture of half water and half milk, and (c) cooked with dried milk added to the water. Then compare the tastes and food values.
12. Discuss ways of cooking and using rice.
13. Make a list of the grain foods (foods which come from grains) which you have eaten in the last three meals.

Pointing out the importance of eating cereals:

14. Make an attractive arrangement on the bulletin board to illustrate the importance of eating cereals. You may obtain your material from magazines, or you may write to the various companies that sell cereals for free literature.
15. Discuss ways of getting children to eat cereal. Perhaps the following suggestion will give you other ideas: Junior likes cereal because his dad eats it for breakfast every morning.

Chapter 22 | **BREADS**

Bread is called the "staff of life." In most families it is the principal source of carbohydrates, which supply energy. To obtain the nutrients you need, you should eat some bread every day, provided it is made from whole-grain or enriched flour (see page 315). Breads made with milk and eggs have more food value, of course, than breads made with water.

There are hundreds of kinds and varieties of breads, but all of them may be classified as either "quick breads" or "yeast breads." (See page 313.) Any kind of bread can be served at meals. Toast, muffins, griddlecakes, waffles, coffeecake, and sweet rolls are popular for breakfast. Sliced white, whole-wheat, or rye bread, sweet breads, and hot rolls are often served for lunch. Hard or soft rolls, corn bread, and hot biscuits are frequently preferred for dinner.

Regardless of the many forms of bread that may be bought in ready-to-serve form, with little or no preparation needed (bakery products, brown-and-serve rolls, canned biscuits, frozen rolls, and mixes), many homemakers make some of their own bread. With a little practice, it is easy to make good bread at home, and most **312** families enjoy hot breads fresh from the oven.

Courtesy Clabber Girl Baking Powder

Courtesy Malt-O-Meal

Quick breads may be divided into two groups: those made with batters (muffins, griddlecakes, and waffles) and those made with dough (rolled and dropped biscuits and dumplings). Baking powder, soda, and sometimes eggs are used to make quick breads rise. They are referred to as "leavening agents." The recipes on pages 526-531 give many varieties of quick breads.

Yeast breads are usually bought in a store because they take a long time to make at home. Yeast, which is the leavening agent in all yeast breads, requires time for rising and shaping. So, when yeast breads are made in the home, preparation must be started several hours before the bread is to be baked and served. (See page 324.)

Courtesy Wheat Flour Institute

TOAST

Toast is most often served for breakfast, but it is also frequently served at lunch as an accompaniment to soups and salads or as a base for a creamed dish. Toast may be made in the broiler, in the oven, or in an electric toaster at the table. When toast is made in the broiler, it must be watched carefully to keep it from burning. It may be buttered before it is brought to the table, or each person may butter his own toast. Regardless of how it is prepared, it should be served piping hot. For this reason, do not begin to toast bread until you are almost ready to serve. Neither should you stack buttered toast because the toast becomes soggy if allowed to stand. Turn to pages 524 and 525 for recipes for plain toast as well as such variations as cinnamon toast and orange toast. Muffins, rolls, or biscuits may be cut in half and toasted in the broiler.

Making tasty French toast is a good way to use bread which has become too hard to serve plain. (See recipe on page 525.) For other ways of using leftover bread and for making bread crumbs, see page 462.

INGREDIENTS USED IN MAKING BREADS

The five main ingredients that are used in making all breads are: (1) a flour or a meal, (2) a leavening agent, (3) a liquid, (4) seasoning, and (5) a fat.

Flour for breads is usually made of wheat. However, rye, soybean, and buckwheat flours are also used. Corn meal, oatmeal, and bran are used instead of, or in addition to, flour for some breads.

Whole-wheat flour, which is made from the entire wheat grain, is the most nutritious of all flours. However, it is not available in many stores because the fat in the wheat germ becomes rancid and does not keep well. For this reason, most flour is made from wheat from which the germ has been removed. The flour is then enriched, that is, vitamins and minerals are added to restore the food value of the whole grain. When buying flour, check to be sure that it has been enriched.

All-purpose flour can be used for quick breads, cakes, or pastries. Bread flour is best for making yeast breads. Cake and pastry flours are specially milled for making cakes and pastries. They can also be used for making quick breads, but they cannot be used for yeast breads. Self-rising flour is an all-purpose flour to which the leavening agent and salt have been added.

Leavening agents, such as baking powder, soda, yeast, and eggs, cause breads and cakes to rise and to be light and porous. Baking powder combined with a liquid or soda combined with sour milk or buttermilk forms a gas called "carbon dioxide." These gas bubbles expand when heated, causing the mixtures for biscuits, muffins, waffles, and griddlecakes to rise. Steam causes mixtures to rise, as in the case of popovers and cream puffs. As they bake, the liquid in the mixture turns to steam.

Eggs act as a leavening agent when beaten egg whites are folded into a mixture, as in waffles, sponge cake, angel food cake, soufflés, and puffy omelets. When egg whites and yolks are beaten together or egg yolks are used alone, they do little toward making a mixture rise. Eggs improve the flavor, the color, and the firmness of the product.

Yeast (either compressed or dry, granular yeast) is used as the leavening agent for yeast breads. As the yeast grows, it gives off carbon dioxide gas, thus causing the bread to rise. However, yeast is much slower than other leavening agents.

Liquids such as sweet milk, sour milk, or buttermilk add food value and improve the flavor and browning of the bread, whereas water does not. Dried or evaporated milk may also be used.

Fats — butter, fortified margarine, and shortenings — make breads tender, improve their flavor, and help to give them a crisp crust.

Seasonings — salt and sometimes sugar — improve the flavor of breads. Sugar helps to brown quick breads evenly. In yeast breads, sugar helps the yeast to grow and expand.

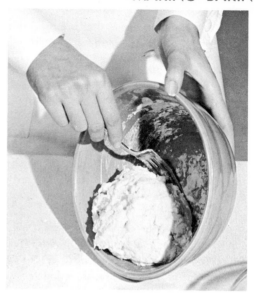

Photos Courtesy Wheat Flour Institute

Measure sifted flour. Sift again with baking powder and salt into a mixing bowl. Add the shortening, and cut it into the flour mixture with two knives or a pastry blender (left) until the mixture looks like coarse corn meal. Gradually add most of the milk, and stir. If the dough is not soft and easy to roll out (right), add the rest of the milk.

Sprinkle a little flour on a pastry board or a cloth and turn out the dough. Knead gently only a few times. To knead:

1. Fold the outside edge of the dough over on itself.
2. Press lightly with your fingers or with the heel of your hand.
3. Turn the dough around after each push.
4. Repeat the folding and pushing process until the dough is smooth.

Courtesy Wheat Flour Institute

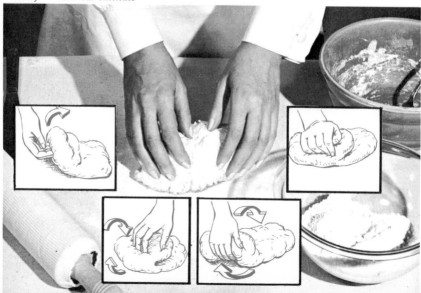

POWDER BISCUITS

Photos Courtesy Wheat Flour Institute

Roll the dough lightly with a floured or a stocking-covered rolling pin (above left), or pat lightly with a floured hand until the dough is about ½ inch thick.

Cut the dough with a biscuit cutter that has been dipped in flour (above right).

Place the biscuits 1 inch apart in a pan for crusty sides, as shown at the right in the picture below.

For soft sides, place the biscuits close together in the pan, as shown at the left in the picture below.

A good biscuit should be well shaped with straight sides, even tops, and a golden-brown color. It should double its size in baking but be light in weight. The inside of the biscuit should be creamy white, with a tender crumb, good flavor, and a fluffy-to-moist texture.

Courtesy Betty Crocker of General Mills

Courtesy Wheat Flour Institute

Measure sifted flour. Sift the flour again with baking powder, salt, and sugar into a mixing bowl. Add oil or cooled melted shortening to the beaten egg-and-milk mixture.

Add the milk-and-egg mixture to the dry ingredients all at once (below left). Stir quickly and only until the dry ingredients are moistened, leaving the mixture lumpy (below right). Do not beat or overmix.

Photos Courtesy Wheat Flour Institute

MUFFINS

Photos Courtesy Wheat Flour Institute

Fill greased muffin pans one-half to two-thirds full, using a rubber spatula or a spoon to push the batter off the mixing spoon (above left). When class periods are short, fill the muffin pans only half full so that the muffins will bake quickly. Wipe off any drops of batter spilled on the outside of the pans. Bake in a hot oven (425° F.) 20 to 25 minutes, or until golden brown (above right).

The top of a good muffin should be rough, not smooth. A muffin should have a good shape all over, with a rounded, golden-brown top which is free of peaks and knobs (below left). The inside should be creamy/white and have a light texture with small round holes (below right). If there are large holes or tunnels, it is not a good muffin because the batter was overmixed.

Courtesy Clabber Girl Baking Powder

319

MAKING GRIDDLECAKES

Courtesy General Foods Corporation

The batter for griddlecakes and waffles is made in the same way as is the batter for muffins. (See pages 318 and 319 and recipes on pages 526 and 527.) Heat the griddle while mixing the batter. To test the griddle, sprinkle a few drops of cold water on it. If the drops hiss and steam, the griddle is too hot. If they roll around, the griddle is not hot enough. If they dance about and evaporate, the griddle is just right for use.

Pour the batter from a pitcher or from the tip of a spoon onto the hot griddle, spacing the cakes a little distance apart (below left). Cook the cakes until the tops are full of little air bubbles, and turn them before the bubbles break (below right). Brown the other sides, and serve immediately with butter and sirup, jelly, or honey. Griddlecakes should be about the same size and shape, golden brown in color, light and tender in texture, and have a pleasing flavor.

Photos Courtesy Wesson Oil and Snowdrift Sales Company

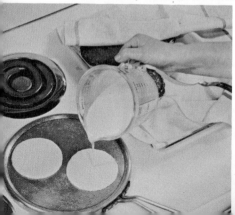

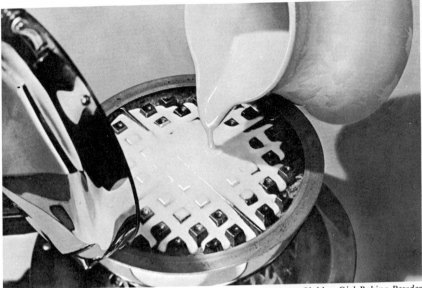

Courtesy Clabber Girl Baking Powder

Most waffle irons have a heat control. If your waffle iron does not, it can be tested in the same way as the griddle is for griddlecakes. When the waffle iron is hot, pour the batter in the center of a small waffle iron, or pour 1 to 2 tablespoons batter into the center of each section of a large waffle iron. Close the lid, and bake 3 to 5 minutes, or until the waffle iron stops steaming. Do not raise the cover while baking.

Lift the waffles out carefully with a fork. Serve piping hot. A good waffle should have a golden-brown color, be light, and have a crisp texture.

Courtesy Clabber Girl Baking Powder

Courtesy Flako Kitchens

Quick bread mixes (muffins, biscuits, corn bread, pancakes, and waffles) need only the addition of milk or water before shaping and baking. For some mixes, an egg is also needed. Quick breads made from mixes are more expensive than homemade products, but they are a wonderful timesaver. The directions for variations are found on the package.

Yeast bread mixes require the adding of a liquid, mixing, kneading, setting, and shaping of the dough before baking.

322

Courtesy The Borden Company

Canned biscuits may be baked just as they come from the can, or they may be reshaped and dressed up with a variety of seasonings before baking.

Frozen yeast rolls should be allowed to defrost and rise before baking, according to directions given on the box.

Frozen waffles merely need to be warmed in a toaster or a broiler before serving.

Brown-and-serve breads (rolls, sweet rolls, French bread, and coffeecakes) are completely prepared except for the finishing touch of heating and browning.

Bakery breads may be served just as they come from the store, or they may be wrapped in aluminum foil and heated in the oven.

Courtesy Wheat Flour Institute

323

1. Heat milk in a saucepan over low heat until scalded or until tiny bubbles appear around the edge. Add shortening (above left), salt, and sugar. Then stir. Cool until lukewarm. The temperature can be tested by putting a few drops on the inside of the wrist. (See page 117.)

2. Sift the flour. Then measure it while the milk is cooling. Pour lukewarm water into a large mixing bowl. Sprinkle dry yeast (above right) or crumble compressed yeast into the water. Let stand 5 to 10 minutes to soften. Then stir until the yeast is dissolved. Add the lukewarm milk.

3. Add half the flour, and mix (below left). Add the remaining flour, and continue to stir until the dough begins to form a ball and leave the inside of the bowl.

4. Turn the dough out onto a lightly floured board or cloth (below right).

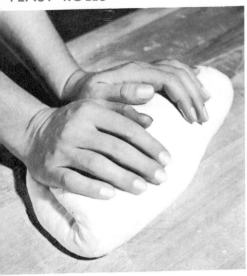

5. Knead the dough until it is smooth, adding more flour if necessary (above left).

6. Place the dough in a greased bowl. Grease the top of the dough, and cover the bowl with a clean cloth (above right). Then set the bowl in a warm place that is free from drafts to allow the dough to rise.

7. When the dough has doubled in size, press two fingers into it (below left). If the holes remain when you withdraw your fingers, punch the dough down in the bowl, pull it away from the edge, and fold it into the center of the bowl. Then let the dough rest 5 to 10 minutes.

8. Turn the dough out onto a lightly floured board, and knead it. Shape the dough into rolls, and place them on a lightly greased shallow baking pan (below right). Cover, and allow the rolls to rise. When the rolls have doubled in size, bake them in a 425° F. oven 10 to 12 minutes.

ACTIVITIES

Reviewing kinds of breads:
1. Explain the main difference between quick breads and yeast breads.
2. Devote half of the bulletin board to pictures of quick breads. On the other half, display pictures of yeast breads.
3. Visit a local bakery with your classmates. Take special notice of how the ingredients are measured and mixed. Examine the equipment and the ovens.

Realizing the food value of breads:
4. Study the drawing of a grain of wheat on page 302. Discuss which parts are used in making regular white flour and which parts are used in making whole-wheat flour.
5. Find out if your state has a law requiring that flour, corn meal, and bread be enriched. Discuss what "enrichment" means and what the advantages are.

Learning to be thrifty:
6. Compare the cost of biscuits that you make in the foods laboratory with that of ready-to-bake biscuits that you may buy.
7. Discuss ways of using leftover bread.
8. Demonstrate how to prepare bread crumbs. (See page 462.)

Exchanging ideas:
9. Demonstrate what happens when the following are mixed: (a) soda and sour milk and (b) baking powder and hot water.
10. Measure 1 cup flour without sifting it. Sift the flour, and then measure it again according to directions on page 438. How much did you have left over?
11. Discuss ways in which biscuit dough may be used. For example, it may be used to make dumplings.
12. When quick breads are prepared in class, select the first, second, and third best. Give your reasons for each choice.

Preparing quick breads:
13. Demonstrate the differences in the following: (a) drop biscuits, (b) rolled biscuits, and (c) cinnamon rolls made from biscuit dough.
14. Demonstrate how you can save time by patting out biscuit dough on a cookie sheet and cutting it into squares with a sharp knife or an ice cube divider from a refrigerator tray.
15. Plan to serve hot biscuits several times during the next month. Time yourself each time you make them to see if you can improve on your speed as well as on the quality of biscuits.
16. Study and compare the recipes for toast on pages 524-525. Have each group in class prepare a different kind of toast. Serve with hot chocolate, and discuss the differences.

Chapter 23 | # DESSERTS
—Cookies, Cakes, Frostings, Candies

There are many kinds of cookies, cakes, and candies. Most of them are not difficult to make if you know a few rules and follow the directions. Whether you use your own ingredients or a mix, the illustrations in this chapter should help you to learn the rules and to follow the directions.

Most cookies are of the following types: refrigerator, drop, molded, pressed, bar, rolled, and filled.

There are three types of cakes: (1) Butter cakes, often referred to as "shortened" cakes, are the most common type. They are made with butter, margarine, or shortening. (2) Sponge cakes and angel food cakes are made without fat. Eggs are used to make them rise. (3) Chiffon cakes are a combination of a butter cake and a sponge cake. They contain a large number of eggs, as do sponge cakes. They also contain oil or shortening, as do butter cakes.

There are three methods for making cakes which contain shortening: the conventional method, the one-bowl method, and the muffin method. If you understand these three methods, it will be easy to make any cake. Follow the directions given in the recipe, and do not try to combine one method with another. **327**

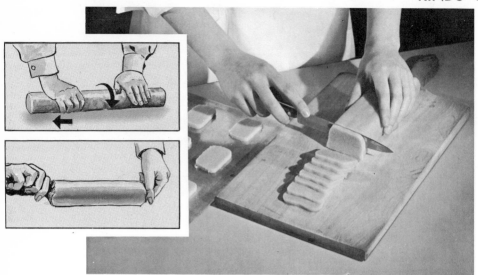

Courtesy Pillsbury Mills, Inc.

Refrigerator cookies are made from a stiff dough which has been pressed and rolled into a long roll, wrapped in wax paper, and placed in the refrigerator for several hours. Each cookie is then sliced off the chilled dough and baked. (See recipe on page 541.) The dough may be stored in the refrigerator for several weeks before it is used, or it may be frozen and stored in the food freezer for many months.

Drop cookies are considered one of the simplest and easiest kinds of cookies to make. After mixing, use a knife or another spoon to push the soft dough from the tip of a spoon onto a greased baking sheet, as shown below. Drop cookies are usually soft, but some chewy and crisp cookies are made by this method. Oatmeal cookies (page 542), brown sugar drops, chocolate chip cookies, and hermits are examples of drop cookies.

Courtesy Nestlé

Courtesy Mrs. Tucker's Shortening

Courtesy Spry

Molded cookies are made by shaping small pieces of stiff dough into balls with the hands. Before they are baked, the balls should be flattened with either a fork or the bottom of a glass which has been dipped into flour or covered with a damp cloth. Peanut butter cookies (page 543) are a good example of a molded cookie. Molded cookies can be made from the same dough that is used for rolled cookies (page 330).

Pressed cookies are made from a chilled dough which is placed in a cookie press and forced through an opening in the bottom to form a definite shape. The dough that is used in making pressed cookies must be smooth and moderately soft, or it will not go through the press. Yet the dough must be stiff enough to hold its shape. Cookie presses are sold with a variety of designs from which to choose. The manufacturers usually include a number of recipes in the package.

Courtesy Mirro

329

KINDS OF COOKIES

Courtesy Nestlé

Bar cookies, or "sheet" cookies, as they are sometimes called, are made by spreading a soft dough into a large greased pan and then baking. After they are baked and cooled slightly, they are cut into squares, bars, or diamonds. Bar cookies, like all other cookies, should be completely cooled on a cake rack before being stored. Brownies, coconut bars, and date bars are all examples of bar cookies.

Rolled cookies are made from a rather stiff dough that has been chilled and quickly rolled ⅛ inch thick on a lightly floured pastry cloth or board. The cookies can be cut with a cookie cutter (below left) or with a pastry wheel or a knife and lifted to the baking sheet with a spatula (below right).

Filled cookies are made by placing a filling between two layers of rolled dough. The edges are pressed together with a fork in order to seal them before baking.

Courtesy Spry   *Courtesy Pillsbury Mills, Inc.*

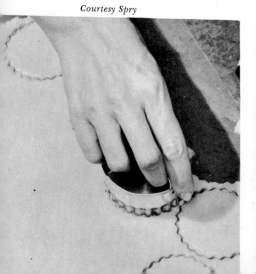

Pastry Wheel

BAKING AND COOLING COOKIES

Courtesy Mrs. Tucker's Shortening

1. Be sure that the cookies are the same size. Small ones will burn before large ones are done.
2. Use a baking sheet that is small enough to allow the air to circulate around it so that the cookies will not burn on the bottom before they are brown on the top.
3. Place the cookies 1 inch from the edge of the baking sheet to prevent those along the edge from becoming too brown.
4. Place the baking sheet in the center of the oven so that the cookies will brown evenly.
5. Check as soon as the minimum baking time is up.

Use a spatula to lift the cookies immediately from the baking sheet onto a cake rack to cool. If they are left on the baking sheet too long, they will stick to it and will be difficult to remove. Do not stack the cookies while they are still hot, but cool them separately before storing.

Courtesy Spry

KINDS OF CAKE

One-layer Cake

Two-layer Cake

Cupcakes

Loaf Cake

Upside-down Cake

Marble Cake

A good cake should be light in weight and well shaped without cracks or humps. When the cake is cut, the texture should be moist, tender, and velvety. It should have an even, fine grain with no large, loose holes or tunnels. The flavor should be well blended, pleasing, and free from undesirable flavor of rancid fat or old eggs.

Photos Courtesy Mrs. Tucker's Shortening

Check to make sure that you have the correct size pans (page 377) and that they are clean. Grease the pans lightly with a small piece of paper (above left) or a pastry brush. Dust the pans with flour. Then shake the flour over the pans (above right). Next, turn the pans over, and gently knock on the bottoms to remove excess flour.

Cake pans may be lined with clean smooth paper, such as wax paper or a lightweight wrapping paper. To cut paper to fit, place the pan on the paper, and trace around the pan with the point of a knife or the tip of a spatula (below left). Next, cut just inside the line. Two or more papers may be cut at once to save time.

Muffin pans should not be greased when paper cups are used for cupcakes (below right).

Photos Courtesy Mrs. Tucker's Shortening

Courtesy Mrs. Tucker's Shortening

The conventional method of making a cake is the method used in making the basic cake on page 544. It is sometimes called the "cake" method or the "creaming" method.

The following are the five steps in making a cake by the conventional method:

1. Measure sifted flour. Sift flour again with baking powder and salt. Add soda or spices when called for in the recipe.

2. Cream the shortening until soft and smooth by rubbing it against the side of the bowl with the back of a spoon (below left).

3. Slowly add the sugar (below right) about 2 tablespoons at a time, and continue creaming until light and fluffy.

Photos Courtesy Mrs. Tucker's Shortening

Courtesy Mrs. Tucker's Shortening

4. Add the unbeaten eggs one at a time, beating until smooth after each addition. If the recipe says that the eggs are to be beaten and then added, beat them with a rotary beater or with an electric mixer until they are thick, foamy, and lemon-colored.

5. Add the dry ingredients alternately with the milk (below left). To do this, add one-fourth of the dry ingredients, and stir until well blended. Add one-third of the milk (below right), and stir until none of the milk can be seen. Add another fourth of the dry ingredients, and continue adding dry ingredients and milk alternately until all have been added.

To mix a conventional-type cake in an electric mixer, follow these steps. However, be very careful to turn the beater to the lowest speed when adding the sifted dry ingredients alternately with the liquid ingredients. Beat only for the amount of time given in the recipe or only until the batter is smooth.

Photos Courtesy Mrs. Tucker's Shortening

MAKING A CAKE
(One-bowl Method)

The one-bowl method, also called the "quick-mix" method or "electric" method, is the quickest and easiest method of making cakes which contain shortening. It is used in the recipe for devil's food cake (page 545). Have all ingredients at room temperature.

1. Measure sifted flour. Sift again with the other dry ingredients (sugar, baking powder, and salt). Also add cocoa, soda, or spices when called for in the recipe.

2. Add the softened shortening and about two-thirds of the milk to the sifted dry ingredients.

3. Beat vigorously by hand about 2 minutes or 300 strokes. If an electric mixer is used, beat 2 minutes at medium speed. Scrape the bowl with a rubber spatula so that all the ingredients will be combined.

4. Add the remaining milk and the unbeaten eggs. Beat 300 strokes by hand or 2 minutes more at medium speed.

Photos Courtesy Spry

Courtesy Spry

Pour the same amount of batter into each pan so that the layers of the cake will be of the same thickness. Spread the batter so that it will be a little higher around the edges than in the middle. Then, when the cake rises, it will not be rounded up in the center. Check to make sure that the oven is at the correct temperature.

Place the pans as near the center of the oven as possible without having them touch each other or the walls of the oven. To allow the air to circulate around them properly, place the pans so that one is not directly above the other. Do not open the oven door until the cake is almost done. When you open the oven door, do so carefully, without letting it slam, because either cool air or a sudden jar will cause a cake to fall.

Photos Courtesy Robertshaw-Fulton Controls Company

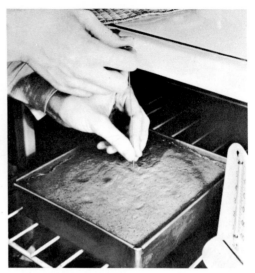

Courtesy Betty Crocker of General Mills   *Courtesy Swans Down Cake Flour*

One test for doneness (above left) is to press the cake lightly with your finger. If the dent disappears when you remove your finger, the cake is done.

Another test (above right) is to insert a wire cake tester or a toothpick. If it comes out clean, the cake is done. But if uncooked batter sticks to it, the cake needs more baking. Also, when a cake is done, the edges begin to pull away slightly from the sides of the pan.

To cool a cake, let it stand for about 10 minutes. Then loosen the edges from the sides of the pan with a spatula (below left). Next, place a cake rack on top of the cake. Turn the rack and the cake pan over (below right), and remove the cake pan from the cake.

If wax paper or a liner is used in the pan, pull it off the cake at once. Otherwise it will stick to the cake and will be difficult to remove later.

Courtesy Spry   *Courtesy Pillsbury Mills, Inc.*

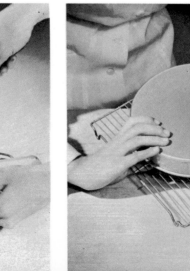

Courtesy Davila's Grocery Store

Chocolate, caramel, and fluffy white frostings may all be made quickly and easily from mixes by merely adding water and beating. As always, it is important that you follow the directions on the package.

Cream frosting (below left) is uncooked. It is made by mixing confectioners' sugar with one or more of the following: butter, cream, egg, or fruit juice. (See recipes on page 546.)

Double-boiler frosting (right) is made by beating an egg-white mixture over boiling water until it stands in peaks. It is then removed and beaten until it is thick enough to spread. (See recipes on page 547.)

Courtesy Swans Down Cake Flour   *Courtesy "Better Homes and Gardens"*

Courtesy Pillsbury Mills, Inc.

1. To protect the plate while frosting, place a collar of wax paper around the rim of the plate before putting the cake on it. When the cake is cool, brush the crumbs from the sides, and place one layer upside down on the plate. Spread the frosting all the way to the edge of the cake. Place the top layer right side up.

2. Spread the frosting on the sides of the cake, pulling from the bottom to the top with a spatula full of frosting.

3. Spread the frosting on top of the cake, and remove the paper collar which was put down to protect the plate.

Courtesy Pillsbury Mills, Inc.　　　　　　*Courtesy Wesson Oil and Snowdrift Sales Company*

Courtesy Sugar Information, Inc.

Candy may be soft, chewy, or hard. Even though there are hundreds of different kinds of candy, they may all be divided into two groups:

Noncrystalline candies, such as taffy, lollipops, brittles, butterscotch, and caramels, do not contain crystals. Lollipops, taffies, and brittles, such as peanut brittle, as well as the coating on taffy apples and popcorn balls are all hard, clear candies. Butterscotch and caramels are waxy or chewy in texture.

Crystalline candies, such as fudge, divinity, fondant, and panoche, contain tiny crystals. In well-made candy, these crystals are so tiny that you can scarcely feel them on your tongue.

For best results in making candy, use a heavy saucepan that is large enough to allow the candy to boil up without running over. One which holds about four times as much as the ingredients is best.

A wooden spoon is best for stirring and beating candy. For most candies, stir the sugar and the liquid until the sugar is dissolved before putting it on to heat, or stir the mixture over heat until the sugar is dissolved. A candy sirup made of sugar and water should not be stirred at all after it starts to boil. Other sirups, such as those which contain milk, cream, or chocolate, may be stirred occasionally to prevent scorching. Follow the recipe carefully as to whether the candy should boil slowly or rapidly.

Courtesy Test Kitchens of Grandma's Unsulphured Molasses

Courtesy "Better Homes and Gardens"

1. Cut chocolate squares into small pieces, and mix them with sugar, corn sirup, and milk in a large, heavy saucepan. Place the mixture over low heat, and stir until the sugar dissolves. Then stir only occasionally to prevent burning.

2. Cook the sirup gently until a little of the mixture forms a soft ball when dropped into cold water or until the sirup reaches 236° F. on a candy thermometer. Remove the saucepan from the heat before testing so that the sirup will not continue cooking. Otherwise, it might overcook while the test is being made.

Photos Courtesy "Better Homes and Gardens"

Put the candy thermometer into the sirup as soon as all the sugar has been dissolved. Never put a cold thermometer into boiling sirup. The bulb of the thermometer should be covered with the liquid, but it should not touch the bottom or the sides of the pan. When you have finished using it, put the thermometer into very hot water and cool it gradually.

To test candy without a thermometer, drop about ½ teaspoon of the hot sirup into a cup of cold water. Then shape it into a ball with the tip of your finger.

Photos Courtesy "Better Homes and Gardens"

3. Add butter or margarine. Set the sirup aside to cool without stirring until the thermometer reaches 110° F. or until the saucepan can be held comfortably in the palm of your hand.

4. Add vanilla. Beat with a wooden spoon until the fudge becomes creamy, loses its glossy appearance, and a small amount will hold its shape when dropped from a spoon.

5. Pour the fudge into a pan which has been lightly greased on the bottom and the sides with butter or margarine. Spread quickly.

6. When cool, cut the fudge into squares of the same size. Good fudge has a smooth and creamy texture, a glossy appearance, and a well-blended flavor.

Courtesy "Better Homes and Gardens"

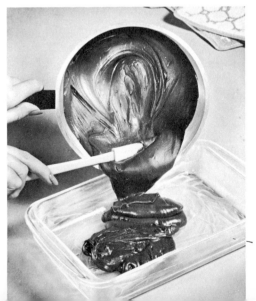

ACTIVITIES

Learning to make and serve good cookies:

1. Collect pictures of various kinds of cookies, such as refrigerator, dropped, and rolled. Mount them on the bulletin board.
2. Freeze refrigerator cookies before baking them. Then bake, and serve at a later date. Compare them with freshly made cookies.
3. Discuss the importance of having all cookies as near the same size as possible before they are baked. Describe an experience that you or a friend had when some of the cookies being baked burned before the others were done.
4. Compare spices used in cookies and cakes, such as ginger, cinnamon, anise, and cloves. Note differences in color, odor, and flavor.
5. Arrange pictures on the bulletin board showing ways to decorate cookies. Make rolled cookies (page 330), and decorate them with nuts, colored sugar, candied fruit, gumdrops, or cinnamon candies.
6. Make a score card for judging cookies. Remember that cookies should be fresh, attractive in appearance, tasty, well shaped, uniform in size, evenly baked, and good in texture. Some cookies are supposed to be crisp. Others are moist. Some are chewy. But no cookies are supposed to be tough, doughy, dry, or hard.

Studying cake making:

7. Study recipes of cakes made with shortening. Decide if they are made by the conventional method (pages 334 and 335) or the one-bowl method (page 336).
8. Discuss why the oven door should not be opened too often while a cake is baking.
9. Compare the cost of a bakery cake with the costs of a cake made from a prepared mix and a cake made from a recipe at home.
10. Visit a bakery. Compare the methods used in making many cakes with the method used at home in making only one cake.

Discussing cake frostings:

11. Describe the frosting that your mother makes most often for her cakes.
12. Compare the cost, the amount of time, and the results of frosting made from a mix with those of frosting made from your own ingredients.
13. Consult the chart on page 131. Compare the number of calories in a cake which has frosting with the number in a plain cake.

Getting ideas for making candy:

14. Bring to class two candy recipes which contain cereal. Select one to make in class.
15. Demonstrate the use of a candy thermometer.
16. Compare bubbles of fudge which has just started cooking with bubbles of fudge which is ready to be removed from the heat.

Courtesy National Canners Association

Chapter 24 | DESSERTS—Fruit, Custards, Puddings, Gelatin and Frozen Desserts, Pies

Desserts should be appealing in appearance and taste. They should fit in with the type of meal, the other foods served in the meal, the season of the year, and the likes and dislikes of the family. The time and the experience needed to prepare a dessert should be considered. Usually a simple dessert served in an attractive manner is more pleasing than an elaborate one.

A food used elsewhere in a meal should not be repeated in the dessert. Apple crumble would not be an appropriate dessert for a meal in which a Waldorf salad.is served. Neither should a gelatin dessert and a gelatin salad be served at the same meal.

A heavy, rich dessert — such as pie, bread pudding, steamed pudding, or cake à la mode — is enjoyable after a meal that is light and simple or during cold weather. Fresh fruits and gelatin or frozen desserts are appealing after a heavy meal or during warm weather.

Special attention is usually given to the dessert when there are guests for a meal—something homemade, something fancy, something new, or something that takes much time and experience to prepare.

345

Courtesy Florida Citrus Commission

Courtesy Westinghouse Electric Corporation

Fruit, the easiest dessert of all to prepare and serve, is attractive, tasty, and nutritious. It contains minerals and vitamins as well as sugar. A tray of attractively arranged whole fresh fruit, which has been washed and dried, may be used as a table decoration before being served as a dessert. Fresh, frozen, dried, and canned fruit can be served plain, with cream, or with a sauce.

Various kinds of fruit can be combined and served in a fruit cup, or they can be added to gelatin for a simple dessert. Fruit pies, tarts, cobblers, and dumplings are rich, heavy desserts. Upside-down cakes, fruit puddings, shortcakes, Betties, and crumbles are also richer fruit desserts than plain fruit which is served either raw or cooked.

Courtesy Florida Citrus Commission

Courtesy Armour and Company

Photos by Bland

To make a soft custard, sometimes referred to as "stirred custard," add scalded milk to beaten egg (above left). Then cook the mixture over low heat until it barely coats a spoon when dipped into the custard (above right). Remove from the heat and cool. Then chill in the refrigerator. Soft custards may be served plain or as a sauce over fruit, gelatin, cake, or pudding.

To make a baked custard, pour the milk-and-egg mixture into custard cups that have been placed in a pan of hot water (below left). Bake without stirring. To test for doneness, insert a knife in the center of one of the cups. If it comes out clean, the custard is done (below right). Cool the custard and serve it in the custard cups, or unmold it and serve it with whipped cream, a fruit sauce, or other dessert sauce and nuts.

Photos Courtesy "Practical Home Economics" and National Dairy Council

Courtesy Davila's Grocery Store

The many packaged pudding mixes that are available today make it possible to serve puddings with little preparation. Pudding is usually an inexpensive dessert. However, the ingredients to be added — such as the milk and any fruit, nuts, or candy added for variation — should be considered in the cost of the dessert.

Whether you use your own ingredients or a pudding mix, notice what the directions say about serving. Some puddings may be kept in a large dish and then served. Others should be put into serving dishes as soon as they are made so that they will not separate. A fruit sauce served over plain, bland puddings, such as cornstarch pudding (below left), adds to the flavor and the appearance. Other puddings, such as tapioca (below right), rice, and bread puddings, may be served with a dab of whipped cream and a cherry.

Courtesy Log Cabin Syrup　　　　　　　　　*Courtesy American Dairy Association*

Courtesy Knox Gelatine

Gelatin desserts may consist of plain gelatin, gelatin with fruit added (page 204), a combination of soft custard and cubes of gelatin, or whipped gelatin. Gelatin is used in such desserts as strawberry sponge (page 534), Bavarian cream, and refrigerator puddings. It is also used as a thickening agent in chiffon pies (page 351).

Whipped gelatin is made by beating plain gelatin when it begins to thicken. Gelatin is thick enough to be beaten when it is about as thick as an unbeaten egg white (below left). Do not wait until the gelatin becomes so stiff that the edges break apart. Gelatin should be beaten with a rotary beater until it is foamy (below right) and has increased to about twice its original amount. Then it should be chilled until firm.

Patteson

Bland

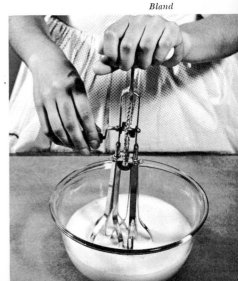

Courtesy American Dairy Asociation

Courtesy Evaporated Milk Association

Ice cream is a nutritious dessert because it is made from milk, cream, eggs, and sugar. Ice cream, as well as other frozen desserts, can be made at home from a recipe or from one of many prepared mixes. It may be frozen in a refrigerator tray or in a hand-operated or electric ice-cream freezer. However ice cream is made, it is important to follow the directions carefully and to have all the equipment well chilled. When frozen desserts are stored in the refrigerator or the freezer, the tray or the container should be covered to prevent layers of ice crystals from forming on the top.

Most commercial ice creams, sherbets, and other frozen mixtures consist of about 50 percent air. Sometimes, to increase the volume, still more air is added. So low-priced ice cream may not always be as good a buy as it appears. To be labeled "ice cream," the law requires that a frozen mixture contain a certain amount of butterfat (cream). Therefore, frozen mixtures that are similar to ice **350** cream but are made with vegetable fat cannot be sold as "ice cream."

PIES

Pies have often been called the favorite American dessert. Fortunately, anyone can learn to make good pies by following directions carefully. Whether you make a pie with your own ingredients or with a mix, keep in mind that a good pie has a crisp crust which is tender enough to break easily but is not so tender that it will crumble.

Courtesy Mrs. Tucker's Shortening

A good meringue pie (top) will hold its shape when cut, but the sides have a slight tendency to run from the crust. The meringue touches the pastry all around and is as deep at the edge as it is in the center. Meringue pies should not be served until they are completely cooled.

Courtesy Knox Gelatine

A good chiffon pie (center) has a light, airy filling which is slightly moist and rather thick. A chiffon pie should be kept well chilled until it is served.

A good fruit pie (bottom) has a sweet, tart taste and a crisp golden-brown crust. It is well shaped and is juicy without being runny. Fruit pies are best when served slightly warm.

Courtesy The Wesson People

1. Mix sugar, cornstarch, and salt in a mixing bowl. Scald the milk by heating it over boiling water.

2. Add the scalded milk to the sugar mixture, stirring constantly to prevent lumping.

3. Pour the mixture into the upper part of a double boiler.

Photos by Bland

PIE FILLING

4. Cook the mixture over boiling water, stirring constantly until thick.

5. Beat the egg yolk with a fork. Slowly add about half of the hot mixture to the beaten egg yolk. Then return the mixture to the double boiler.

6. Cook until the mixture forms a mound when dropped from a spoon. Add butter and vanilla. Cool, and serve as a pudding or a filling in a cream pie.

Photos by Bland

Photos Courtesy Pillsbury Mills, Inc.

1. Measure sifted flour. Sift flour again with salt. Add half the shortening, and cut it into the flour mixture with a pastry blender or two knives until the mixture looks like coarse corn meal. Add the remaining shortening, and cut it until the lumps are about the size of peas (above left).

2. Sprinkle the water over the flour mixture. Mix lightly with a fork. Press the dough lightly into a ball (above right).

3. Beginners find it easy to roll the dough between two sheets of wax paper. Lightly dampen the table top to keep the wax paper from slipping. Roll the dough until it is ⅛ inch thick and 1 inch larger than the piepan (below left).

4. Peel off the top layer of paper, and place the pastry over the piepan. Remove the other sheet of paper gently, and fit the pastry into the pan (below right).

Photos Courtesy Spry

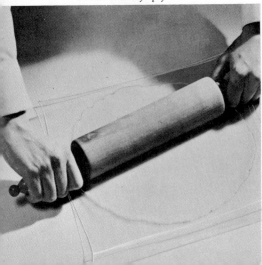 

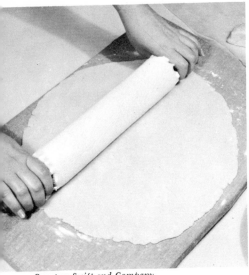

Courtesy Swift and Company

Courtesy Armour and Company

If you prefer to roll the dough on a floured board or cloth instead of between sheets of wax paper, roll it from the center to the edges with light strokes until it is ⅛ inch thick and about 1 inch larger around than the piepan (above left). Next, use the rolling pin to lift the pastry into the piepan (above right).

5. Pat and fit the pastry into the pan so that there will be no air spaces between it and the pan (below left). Do not stretch or pull the pastry, but ease it into the corners.

6. Cut off the edges of the dough, leaving a ½- to 1-inch overhang for a one-crust pie (below right). For a two-crust pie, trim the edges even with the rim of the pan.

Courtesy Betty Crocker of General Mills

Courtesy Spry

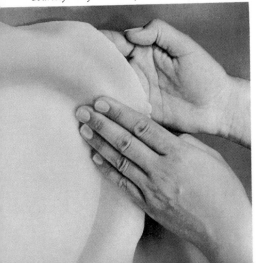

1. Build up a rim around the edge of the crust by folding the overhang under so that the edges come between the pastry and the rim of the pan (above left).

2. Flute the edges with the thumb of one hand and the thumb and the forefinger of the other (above right).

3. Use a fork to prick holes in the sides and the bottom of the pastry to prevent air blisters from forming while baking (below left).

4. Bake 10 to 15 minutes, or until golden brown.

5. Cool. Then add the filling (below right).

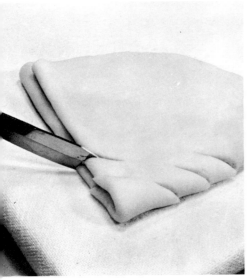

Photos Courtesy Betty Crocker of General Mills

1. Fit half the pastry into the piepan as shown on page 355. Add fruit filling according to the recipe.
2. Roll out the other part of the pie crust until it is about 1 inch wider than the top of the piepan. Fold in quarters, and make slits (above left) to allow steam to escape while the pie is baking. Moisten the edges of the lower crust with water.
3. Place the folded pastry on top of the pie filling, and unfold it (above right).
4. Trim the edges ½ inch beyond the edge of the pan. Fold the edge of the top crust under the edge of the bottom crust, and press together (below left). Flute the edges with the forefinger of one hand and the thumb and the forefinger of the other (below right), or use the method shown on page 356.

Photos Courtesy Pillsbury Mills, Inc.

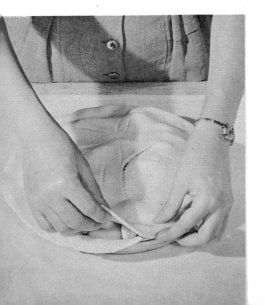

MAKING MERINGUE

1. Beat the egg whites and the salt in a large mixing bowl with a clean beater until frothy. Then add the sugar 1 tablespoon at a time.

2. Continue beating until the mixture stands in peaks when the beater is lifted but is not dry. Add vanilla, if desired.

3. Pile the meringue on top of the cooled pie filling, pushing it with the back of a spoon to make sure that it touches the crust all around the pie. Bake until delicately browned. Then cool at room temperature away from drafts.

Photos Courtesy Betty Crocker of General Mills

ACTIVITIES

Arousing interest in preparing desserts:
1. Keep a list of the desserts you eat for 1 week. With the help of your classmates, decide which desserts contained the most minerals and vitamins and which were most fattening.
2. Suggest five desserts which might be served to a family whose members are overweight.
3. Study the directions for measuring on page 437. Discuss the importance of measuring accurately.
4. Describe two fruit desserts that are served in your home. Describe two other desserts that your family enjoys.

Preparing fruit desserts:
5. Have a contest to see who can name, in 10 minutes, the most desserts which contain fruit.
6. Describe five fruit desserts that you might make in class.
7. List favorite fruit desserts of your classmates on the blackboard.

Preparing milk desserts:
8. Bring to class two dessert recipes which contain a large amount of milk. Select one recipe to prepare in class.
9. Explain the difference between a soft custard and a baked custard.

Preparing puddings:
10. Display in class various types of prepared puddings and desserts on the market, such as gelatins, puddings, and mixes. Discuss variations.
11. Make a collection of pictures of various kinds of puddings. Mount them on the bulletin board.
12. Ask each group in your class to prepare a pudding. Use several different brands of prepared mixes as well as your favorite pudding recipe. Compare the puddings as to: *(a)* cost, *(b)* flavor, *(c)* appearance, and *(d)* ease of preparation.

Preparing gelatin and frozen desserts:
13. Give a demonstration on whipping gelatin desserts. Display pictures of attractive gelatin desserts on the bulletin board.
14. Describe an ice-cream factory, a bakery, or the kitchen of a large restaurant you have visited.

Preparing pastry:
15. Discuss which of the illustrations on pages 354 and 355 would be helpful if you were making a pie crust from a mix.
16. List the new words that you have learned in making pastry.

Chapter 25 | BEVERAGES

Some beverages supply real food. Some are merely cool and refreshing. Still others are hot and stimulating. Selection of a beverage for a meal, a party, or just a snack should be given as much consideration as the main part of the menu.

Since there is a wide range of beverages, there is no need to serve the same one too frequently. Some of the most common beverages are milk, hot or iced chocolate, drinks made with fruit juices, hot or iced tea, hot or iced coffee, bouillon, powdered ade mixes, and bottled drinks. Most beverages are easy to prepare, but unfortunately many people neglect to do the little extra things that add so much.

A beverage should be served at its best. Iced drinks should be thoroughly chilled, and hot beverages should be piping hot. A beverage should be easy to drink and attractive in appearance. It should have a good flavor but should not be too sweet to satisfy thirst. Iced beverages are usually served in tall, sparkling glasses, while hot beverages are served in cups or mugs.

Water is also considered a beverage. It is very important for everyone to drink six to eight glasses of water every day either between meals or with meals. Water with meals, however, should not be used to wash down food.

Courtesy Carnation Company

Dairy bars which serve milk shakes, malts, and other "dressed up" milk drinks have become popular. Many people who do not care for plain milk enjoy the wide range of nutritious as well as tasty drinks that are made with milk. You can easily make your own by using milk as the basic ingredient and adding any one of the following: chocolate sirup, instant cocoa, malt, fruit or fruit juice, sherbet, ice cream, and so on. You can let ideas and imagination play a great part in finding the answer to the often-asked question, "What shall we have to drink?"

Courtesy United Fruit Company

To make a banana milk shake, beat one fully ripe banana with a rotary beater for each 2 cups of milk.

FRUIT DRINKS

Courtesy Florida Citrus Commission

Fruit drinks can be attractive and refreshing for parties or snacks as well as at meals. However, some are more nutritious than others. Fruit beverages made by squeezing the juice from fruit are the most nutritious. (See page 171.) When water and sugar are added to the fruit juice, it becomes a fruitade, such as orangeade and lemonade. Fruitades are not so high in food value as fruit juices. Bottled fruitades, such as orangeade, contain less food value than the fruitades that are made with fresh fruit. Fruit-flavored carbonated drinks and fruit-flavored powders which are dissolved in water contain still less minerals and vitamins in most cases. In some cases, they contain hardly any at all.

Fruit drinks may be served plain, with sherbet, or with a garnish, such as cherries, sprigs of mint, or slices, rings, or wedges of the fruit used in making the drink. In using garnishes, as in using anything else, it is always better to have too few rather than too many.

Courtesy "Better Homes and Gardens"

Courtesy Stix, Baer, and Fuller, St. Louis

Punch is a combination of three or more fruit juices as well as sugar, water, tea, or some other liquid. It has a combination of flavors rather than one outstanding flavor. Punch is served as a refreshment. It may be decorated with pieces of floating fruit. To prevent punch and other fruit drinks from becoming weak, freeze some of the punch or fruit juice and use it in place of part of the ice cubes.

Before using a punch bowl, allow cold water to stand in it for a few minutes. Then remove the water and pour in the punch. When you are serving the punch at a party, hold the cup over the punch bowl to prevent any of the punch from dripping on the table.

Photos by Patteson

Either hot chocolate or hot cocoa may be served with meals or between meals. When making hot cocoa, cook the sugar, salt, cocoa, and water over direct heat to cook the starch in the cocoa before adding the milk (above left). After adding the milk, finish cooking the cocoa over boiling water (above right). When making hot chocolate, melt the chocolate over hot water. Then add sugar, salt, and water, and cook over direct heat. Chocolate is richer than cocoa because it contains twice as much fat. Both contain a stimulant, but they are better for you than tea or coffee because of the milk. The scum which forms on hot cocoa or chocolate when it is allowed to stand contains proteins and should not be removed. Instead, beat with a rotary beater just before serving.

Cool refreshing chocolate drinks as well as hot ones may be quickly and easily made from the many mixes found in the market.

Photos by Patteson

Courtesy Instant Tender Leaf Tea

Tea, either hot or cold, is frequently served in the afternoons at social gatherings. It is also a favorite beverage at lunch, supper, or dinner.

Some suggestions for making good tea are:

1. Use a glass, china, or earthenware pot. A metal pot will affect the flavor.

2. Warm the teapot by rinsing it with boiling water.

3. Pour fresh boiling water over the tea leaves or the tea bags. Water that has been boiled for some time gives the tea a flat taste. Tea should never be boiled.

4. Do not let the tea leaves stand (steep) in hot water any longer than 5 minutes, preferably only 3 minutes. When the leaves steep longer than 5 minutes, tannin, or tannic acid, will dissolve into the tea, giving it a bitter taste. Tea contains a stimulant called theine. The longer the tea leaves stand in the water, the more of this stimulant will be dissolved.

Courtesy Tea Council

COFFEE

Vacuum   Percolator   Drip

Patteson

Good coffee should be piping hot, clear, and freshly made. It should have as small an amount of tannin (bitter taste) as possible. Here are some hints:

1. Wash the coffee maker with soapy water and rinse well after each use.
2. Use fresh coffee that has been ground to the correct fineness for the type of coffee maker that you are using. Store coffee in an airtight container.
3. Use fresh water. Never use water from the hot water faucet.
4. Keep the temperature of the coffee just below the boiling point. Less tannin will be dissolved.
5. Serve coffee as soon as it is made.

Coffee contains a stimulant called caffeine, which affects the kidneys, the heart, and the nervous system. For this reason and because it takes the place of much-needed milk, growing children should not drink coffee.

For iced coffee, pour hot coffee over cracked ice. For instant coffee, add boiling water.

Patteson

Iced Coffee   Instant Coffee

Bland

Naturally, milk and all drinks that are made with milk are better for you than coffee, tea, or other drinks which have little or no food value. But there are times when having a tasty, piping hot drink on a cold, miserable day or a cool, refreshing drink on an especially hot day can be delightful. There is an important point to remember. Keep a happy balance between beverages which are needed to balance your diet and those which you consume just because they give you a lift or are refreshing.

Courtesy Alamo Heights High School

367

Courtesy Glass Container Manufacturers Institute   *Courtesy California Lemon Products Industry*

A bottled beverage, a favorite dip, and snacks arranged in an attractive manner are often served when friends drop by after a movie or for some other informal get-together.

Lemonade and other simple beverages may be made at home and taken to the picnic grounds in a thermos jug. If bottled drinks are to be served at a picnic, be sure that they are packed in crushed ice. And don't forget the bottle opener! Always check the picnic grounds before you go on your picnic to make sure that there is plenty of fresh water. If not, take your own.

Paper cups are ideal for picnics and backyard suppers because there is no need to worry about breakage and washing dishes.

Courtesy Paper Cup and Container Institute

BEVERAGES AT PARTIES

When deciding what kind of beverage to serve at a party, consider how you are going to serve the refreshments. Beverages which are served in a cup or a small glass are easy to handle if the guests have to hold the refreshments in their laps or hold them while standing.

For other information on deciding which beverage to serve, turn to pages 8 and 9.

It is just as important that beverages be served graciously as it is that they be well prepared. If you are serving coffee, you might say, "May I serve you a cup of coffee?" As you finish pouring, say, "Do you care for cream and sugar?" (See pages 12 and 13.)

Photos Courtesy Stix, Baer, and Fuller, St. Louis

ACTIVITIES

Learning where beverages come from:
1. Arrange pictures on the bulletin board showing how the following are grown: *(a)* coffee, *(b)* tea, and *(c)* cocoa.
2. Make a report in class on the differences between cocoa and chocolate. If possible, illustrate your report with pictures showing how each is prepared for market.
3. List terms used in preparing different beverages.
4. Make a report in class on how black, green, and oolong teas differ.
5. List differences between fine, regular, and drip grind coffees.

Realizing the importance of drinking water:
6. Keep an account of the amount of water that you drink each day.
7. Make a report to the class on the precautions you should take when drinking water on a picnic or a hike.

Including milk in the diet:
8. Compare the prices of 1 quart of each of the following kinds of milk: *(a)* pasteurized, *(b)* canned, and *(c)* dried. Make cocoa with each, and note the differences.
9. Discuss the difference in food value of whole milk and chocolate milk bought in a carton.
10. Compare the food value of milk with that of coffee and tea.
11. List four ways in which you might influence your younger sister or brother to drink milk.

Getting variety in fruit beverages:
12. Keep an account for 1 week of the fruit beverages you drink. Compare the food values of these beverages.
13. Divide your class into teams, and have a contest to determine which team can name the most beverages made with fruit.
14. Have a class discussion on favorite fruit drinks. Compare recipes, and select one to prepare in class.

Preparing beverages:
15. Discuss precautions which should be taken in the preparation of cocoa, coffee, and tea.
16. Bring to class five beverage recipes which call for milk.
17. Demonstrate the various ways of making coffee which are illustrated on page 366.

Serving beverages:
18. Take turns serving coffee or punch at a make-believe tea or some similar entertainment.
19. List beverages which might be served at the various parties discussed in Chapter 1. Tell how you would serve each.

part **3**

YOUR MEALS IN
THE SCHOOL
KITCHEN

At the Range

At Mixing Unit

At the Sink

Courtesy "Kitchen Reporter"

Chapter 26 | **YOUR EQUIPMENT**

By having the correct equipment and knowing how to use it properly, you will save time, prevent accidents, and have better results.

The range, the refrigerator, and the small electrical appliances are the most expensive pieces of equipment found in the kitchen. Each will give better service if you follow the manufacturer's directions as to how to use it and how to care for it properly.

Small items of equipment are frequently referred to as "kitchen utensils." There are utensils for use in measuring, mixing and preparing, cutting and chopping, baking, cooking on top of the range, storing food, and cleaning. The utensils which are helpful to one homemaker may not be helpful to another. For example, one person may find a potato masher a necessity. A homemaker who uses a blender or an electric mixer to mash potatoes does not need a potato masher. However, you should know the names of all the equipment in the school kitchen and learn how to use and care for each.

Some of the equipment illustrated in this chapter is not the most efficient or expensive available. For example, can openers which are fastened to the wall or electric can openers are much easier to use than the one illustrated. However, they are expensive

and may not be found in each kitchen unit in school.

MEASURING EQUIPMENT

Supply pan (1), sometimes called a "utility tray," is used to carry the measuring equipment to the supply table and to bring the supplies back to your kitchen.

Liquid measuring cup (2) has a rim above the 1-cup mark to prevent spilling and a lip to make pouring easy. It is used for all liquids.

Pint or *quart measuring cup* (3) is used to measure large amounts of ingredients.

Dry measuring cup (4) is used to measure dry ingredients or shortening. Notice that it does not have a rim above the 1-cup mark so that ingredients may be measured level with the top.

Set of measuring cups (5) includes 1 cup, ½ cup, ⅓ cup, and ¼ cup. They are used to measure dry ingredients or shortening because each may be measured level with the top of the cup.

Measuring spoons (6) come in a set of 1 tablespoon, 1 teaspoon, ½ teaspoon, and ¼ teaspoon. They are used to measure less than ¼ cup of any ingredient.

Spoon (7) is used to put dry ingredients or shortening into a measuring cup.

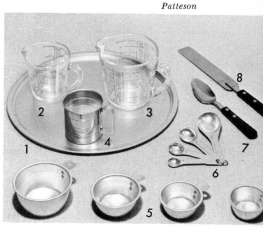

Patteson

Spatula (8) is used to level off ingredients in measuring cups or measuring spoons. It is also used to loosen the edges of a baked cake and to lift cookies or biscuits from a pan.

Scale (9) is used to measure ingredients in ounces and pounds.

Timer (10) is used to measure the length of time that a food is to cook.

Thermometers (11) are used to check the temperatures of candy, jelly, deep fat, meat, and the oven.

Courtesy Hanson

Patteson

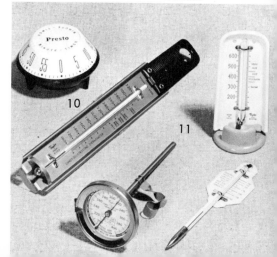

Patteson

Mixing bowls (1) should be large enough to hold ingredients while they are being mixed, but they should not be so large that food will be wasted.

Sifter (2) is used to sift flour and other dry ingredients.

Wire whip (3) is used to beat egg whites, sauces, and drinks.

Whisk beater (4) is a spoon-shaped beater made of many fine crisscross wires. It is used to beat egg whites into a larger amount than is possible with a rotary beater.

Rotary beater (5) is used to beat whole eggs, egg whites, and some batters and frostings.

Wooden spoon (6) is used to cream or beat cakes by hand, to mix other batters or doughs, and to stir hot mixtures, such as fudge, on top of the range.

Mixing spoon (7) is used to combine ingredients. The size should be in proportion to the mixing bowl or the saucepan in which it is used. If the handle is made of wood, it will not become hot when mixing ingredients on top of the range.

Slotted spoon (8) is used to lift poached eggs or fried foods, such as croquettes and fritters. It may also be used to cream butter and sugar mixtures.

Blending fork (9) is used for thorough mixing, as required for cakes, smooth sauces, and fluffy mashed potatoes.

Rubber scraper (10), often called "rubber spatula," is used to get the last drop of batter or cake icing out of a bowl or to clean plates before washing dishes. **374** It cannot be used to stir hot foods.

PREPARATION EQUIPMENT

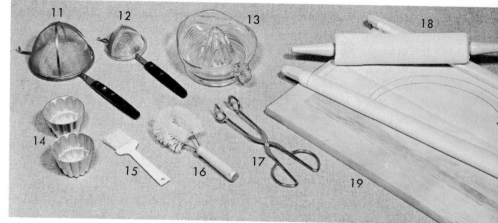

Strainer (11) is used to separate liquid from solid food. For example, a strainer is used to strain macaroni from the water in which it was cooked. It may also be used when washing berries, small fruits, and vegetables.

Tea strainer (12) is used to strain loose tea.

Fruit juice reamer (13), sometimes called a "juice extractor," is used to extract juice from lemons, oranges, and grapefruit.

Molds (14) are used for puddings and for gelatin salads and desserts.

Pastry brush (15) is used to apply milk or butter, for example, on food before baking to form a glaze.

Vegetable brush (16) is used to clean vegetables, such as potatoes, and fruits that have tough skin.

Tongs (17) are used to turn or lift meat or vegetables. They may be used in place of a fork when cooking on top of the range or for removing baked potatoes from the oven.

Rolling pin and pastry cloth (18) are used to roll dough for biscuits, cookies, or pastry.

Breadboard (19) may be used instead of a pastry cloth when rolling dough. It may also be used when crushing crackers or toast for crumbs. **375**

CUTTING AND CHOPPING EQUIPMENT

Butcher knife (1) is used for large or heavy cutting. Keep it sharp to save time.

French knife (2), sometimes called a "chopping knife," has a long, wide blade. It is used to chop and dice foods (see page 448).

Bread knife (3) has a saw-toothed blade, which makes a smooth edge when slicing bread or cutting sandwiches.

Cutting board (4) is used to protect the table when slicing or chopping food. It also prevents the edge of the knife from becoming dull.

Paring knife (5) has a short blade with a good point. It is used for removing skins and for cutting fruits and vegetables.

Parer (6), often called a "peeler," is used to remove a thin skin from carrots, potatoes, cucumbers, and other vegetables and fruits.

Fruit knife (7) has a curved edge. It is used to section citrus fruit (see page 468).

Scissors (8) may be used to mince dice, cube, and trim foods, such as parsley, candied fruit, marshmallows, or pastry dough (see pages 449 and 451).

Meat grinder (9) or food chopper has cutting knives of varied sizes. It is used to grind meat, bread crumbs, pickles, and so on.

Pastry blender (10) is used to cut shortening into dry ingredients when making biscuits or pastry. It is also used to blend liquids with dry ingredients.

Biscuit cutter (11) is used to cut biscuits, cookies, and sandwiches.

Grater (12) is used to grate or shred vegetables, cheese, and lemon or orange rind.

Can opener (13) is used to open cans. There are many kinds, but the ones which make a smooth edge on cans are best. The punch-type opener, which is used to pierce juice or milk cans, may or may not be attached to the can opener.

Lid flipper (14) is used to pry off most types of vacuum-sealed lids.

Jar opener (15) is used to open jars with screw tops.

Mallet (16) is used to pound raw meat, such as steak, to make it tender. The flat side is used to crack nuts and to crush ice. (See page 450.)

Masher (17) is used to mash potatoes, turnips, and other vegetables.

Courtesy Winn's Stores, Inc.

376

BAKING PANS AND OVEN DISHES

Round cake pan (1)   8 or 9 inches across and 1½ inches deep is the size used most often for baking layer cakes.

Square cake pan (2)   8 or 9 inches across and 1½ inches deep is the size used most often for baking a square one-layer or two-layer cake.

Oblong pan (3)   9x13 inches and 2 to 2½ inches deep will accommodate the amount of cake batter usually baked in two layers. It is also used for cobblers, baked apples, and puddings.

Loaf pan (4) is used for baking loaf bread or loaf cake, nut bread, pound cake, and fruit cake.

Tube cake pan (5) is used for baking chiffon cake, angel food cake, and some loaf cakes.

Muffin pans (6) with large, medium, or small cups are used for baking cupcakes, muffins, tarts, or pastry cups. The standard size of the cups is 2 inches across.

Cookie sheet (7), sometimes called a "baking sheet," has only one side to allow even browning when baking cookies or biscuits. It should be 1 to 2 inches smaller than the oven on all sides so that the heat can circulate around it and permit even baking.

Baking sheet (8) is sometimes called a "jelly roll pan" since it is used for baking jelly roll or a very thin sheet cake. It may also be used in the same way as a cookie sheet. However, the sides make it difficult to remove cookies.

Piepan (9),   8 or 9 inches across and 1½ inches deep, made of glass, enamel, or dark metal gives best results for a golden-brown pastry.

Cake rack (10) is used to cool pies, cakes, and cookies by allowing the air to circulate around them as they cool to prevent sweating.

Casserole (11) is used for baking and serving foods, such as a main dish or a pudding.

Custard cups (12) are used for baking custard, popovers, and rolls. Some desserts and salads may be molded in them.

Courtesy Wolff and Marx, Inc.

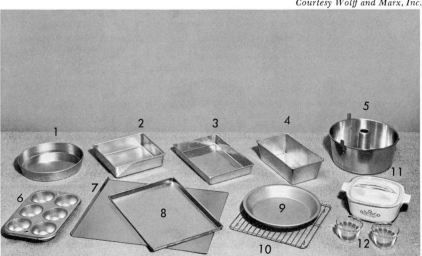

Courtesy Wolff and Marx, Inc.

Saucepan (1) has one long handle. It is used to cook sauces, fruits, and vegetables. When cooking fresh vegetables with little or no water, use a heavy saucepan with a tight-fitting lid.

Saucepan with a removable handle (2) may be used on top of the range. When the handle is removed, the saucepan can be used in the oven as a casserole.

Sauce pot (3) has handles on two sides. It is used in cooking bulky vegetables, soups, and stews. *Kettle* (not illustrated) is usually larger than a sauce pot. Like a Dutch oven, it has a bail handle which extends from one side to the other. It is used for making soups and stews and for canning.

Dutch oven (4) is used for long, slow cooking. Because of its heavy, tight-fitting lid, it holds a maximum amount of steam, which helps to make less-tender cuts of meat tender, such as a pot roast.

Double boiler (5) is used for low-heat cooking, such as cooking foods which burn easily, reheating a small amount of food, and keeping food hot.

Heavy skillet with a tight-fitting lid (6) is used for long, slow cooking, such as stewing and braising. It can also be used as a plain skillet without the lid.

Skillet (7), often called a "frying pan," is used for frying, sautéing, and pan-broiling.

Kitchen fork (8), sometimes called a "cooking fork," is used most often for turning and lifting meat. It can also be used to hold roasts and fowl for slicing and carving.

Egg turner (9) is used to lift eggs or bacon from a skillet. Notice the slots which allow the excess fat to run off.

Pancake turner (10) is used to turn pancakes, French toast, and so on.

Griddle (11) is used for cooking griddlecakes, French toast, bacon, and hamburgers. It should have a smooth surface and be heavy enough so that the
378 heat will spread evenly.

The utensils used in cooking on top of the range may be made of stainless steel (saucepan), superceramic (saucepan with removable handle), lightweight aluminum (sauce pot), heatproof glass (double boiler), hammered aluminum (skillet with tight-fitting lid), cast iron (skillet), heavy aluminum (griddle), copper bottom and aluminum sides (coffee maker), and enamelware.

When selecting utensils for cooking on top of the range, consider:

1. *The size:* If the container is too small, the food may boil over. If it is too large, the food may boil dry and burn.
2. *The lid:* Food can be cooked quickly and in little water in a utensil with a tight-fitting lid.
3. *The shape:* Utensils with straight sides require less heat and less space on the range than those with sides that flare out. Stirring the ingredients and cleaning the utensil will be easy if the container is slightly curved where the sides meet the bottom.
4. *The bottom:* A utensil with a flat bottom which covers the burner uses less fuel than, and will not turn over as easily as, a utensil with a small or rounded bottom.
5. *The handle:* If the handle is balanced with the utensil, it will not turn over easily whether it is full or empty.

Pressure saucepan (12), often called a "pressure cooker," is used to cook food quickly. There is no danger in using it if you follow the manufacturer's directions carefully. Select a recipe in the manufacturer's booklet or one which was planned to be cooked in a pressure saucepan. Use only the amount of water called for, and cook only the length of time suggested.

Teakettle (13) is used for heating water. For example, when making tea, always use freshly drawn water which has been heated to boiling.

Coffee maker (14) is used for making coffee on top of the range.

Asbestos mat (15) is used to protect the top of a cabinet or a table from hot utensils. When very little heat is needed, the asbestos mat can be placed on the range under the cooking utensil.

Kitchen mitt (16) is used to protect your hands when you lift hot dishes or utensils.

Pot holder (17) is used in the same way as a kitchen mitt.

Courtesy Wolff and Marx, Inc.   *Courtesy Winn's Stores, Inc.*

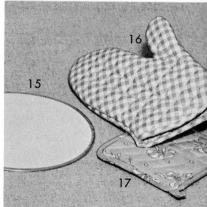

Courtesy Halamicek

Small electric appliances aid the homemaker in making her work easy as well as efficient if she uses them properly and gives them correct care. Therefore, it is most important that you read and understand the manufacturer's directions which come with an appliance. Even a simple error in use can sometimes cause much harm. General precautions in using small electric appliances are as follows:

1. Keep the appliance in a handy place so that it can be used frequently.
2. When you connect the plug to the outlet or remove it, hold the plug as shown in the picture of the toaster on page 381. Never pull the cord.
3. Avoid overloading a single circuit. (See picture on page 426.) ·
4. Have frayed cords repaired promptly.
5. Wash electric appliances, such as a coffee maker, a skillet, or a saucepan, carefully. Never let the motor or the heating element get wet unless the appliance is specially designed so that it can be placed in water.
6. Clean the outside of any electric appliance which cannot be washed, such as a toaster or a waffle iron, by wiping it with a damp cloth. Then dry and polish it with a dry, soft cloth.
7. Keep electric appliances covered when they are not in use.

The electric mixer, the toaster, and the waffle iron are probably the appliances that you will use most often at school. Therefore, specific instructions about each are given on page 381.

Electric Mixer

1. Measure all the ingredients and have everything ready before you start.
2. Use the correct speed, and time the beating period closely to avoid overmixing.
3. Use a rubber scraper if it is necessary to scrape the sides of the bowl.
4. Wash the beaters and the mixing bowls in warm soapy water as soon as you finish.

Waffle Iron

1. Use only the amount of batter that is suggested in the manufacturer's instructions.
2. Spread the batter evenly but not all the way to the edge.
3. Always open the waffle iron to allow it to cool when you have finished using it.
4. Remove loose crumbs with a stiff brush.

Electric Toaster

1. Use plain bread for toasting, never bread which has been buttered.
2. Brush the crumbs from the crumb tray frequently.
3. Be careful when connecting and disconnecting a toaster as well as any other appliance. Remember that the circuit should not be overloaded.

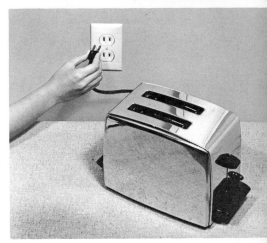

Photos Courtesy Halamicek

STORING FOOD IN THE REFRIGERATOR

Food which is used frequently should be arranged in the refrigerator so that it is easy to reach. Some food should be kept in a colder part than others. The coldest part of the refrigerator is the area near the freezing unit. Therefore, foods which spoil easily, such as meat, fish, and poultry, should be kept in the meat compartment, which is near the freezing unit. (See page 272.) Milk and cream should also be kept near the freezing unit. (See page 244.) Eggs (page 256), cooked meats, or cooked foods which contain milk and eggs should not be placed too far from the freezing unit, for they, too, are perishable. Leftover foods, pickles, jellies, nuts, and so on, should be kept in the center of the refrigerator. Fruits and vegetables are usually kept in the hydrator or the crisper. (See page 172.)

Courtesy Straus-Frank Company

CARE OF THE REFRIGERATOR

If you give the refrigerator proper care each day, the weekly cleaning will not be a problem. To keep the refrigerator clean:

1. Wipe off all milk bottles and other containers before storing them.
2. Wipe up anything that has been spilled as soon as you discover it. Never store anything in dishes or bottles which turn over easily.

Even if the refrigerator has an automatic defroster, it should be thoroughly cleaned every week. To clean the refrigerator:

1. Wash and dry the ice trays, and fill them with fresh water.
2. Wipe off containers of food, and check to make sure they are in place.
3. Throw away all foods that cannot be used. Check to make sure that each food has been placed in as small a dish as possible.

Refrigerators which do not have an automatic defroster should be defrosted whenever the frost on the freezing unit is over 1/4 inch thick. Otherwise, the refrigerator will not be as cold as it should be. To defrost the refrigerator:

1. Turn off the electric current.
2. Remove all ice trays and frozen foods from the freezing unit.
3. Wrap frozen foods in newspaper to keep them from thawing.
4. Put the drip tray in the proper place to catch the melted ice.
5. Place pans of hot water in the lower part of the freezing unit. Allow the ice to melt. Never use a sharp-pointed object to remove the ice.
6. Remove food in the lower part of the refrigerator.
7. Wipe out the inside of the freezing unit as well as the refrigerator with water to which 1 teaspoon baking soda has been added for each quart.
8. Turn on the current, and return the food to the refrigerator.

To get the best service from the refrigerator:

1. Study the booklet which is supplied by the manufacturer.
2. Keep the temperature between 35° and 45° F.
3. Allow hot food to cool before putting it in the refrigerator.
4. Open the door only when absolutely necessary, and keep it open for as short a time as possible.
5. Put leftovers in small dishes and use them as soon as possible to avoid overcrowding the refrigerator.
6. Remove food from paper bags before storing in the refrigerator.
7. Do not store unopened cans of food in the refrigerator unless they are to be chilled for the next meal.
8. Store foods in covered dishes or glass jars to prevent them from drying out and to prevent odors from spreading.
9. Avoid getting grease on the rubber band (gasket) around the door.
10. Decide on a definite place in which to keep each kind of food, and put the foods in the same places each time so that you will not waste time in looking for them.

USE AND CARE OF THE RANGE

Courtesy Dixie Products, Inc.

Low   Medium   High

On a gas range, the source of heat is called a "burner." On an electric range, the source of heat is called a "unit" or a "coil." The heat on either a gas or an electric range should be regulated according to what is being cooked and the size of the utensil. For a small utensil, such as a coffee maker, heat only the inside part of the burner or unit so that the heat will not extend beyond the utensil.

Note that gas ranges and electric ranges have a low heat for simmering, a medium heat for cooking gently, and a high heat for cooking rapidly. The low, medium, and high heats may each be adjusted to a slightly higher or lower degree. Some ranges also have a very low heat for keeping foods warm.

Often food is placed on high heat until it begins to cook. Then the heat is turned to low while the food cooks. Most foods cook just as quickly at medium or low heat as at high heat. Food cooked at medium or low heat will keep its shape, and there is less chance that the pan will boil dry or that the food will scorch. At moderate heat, fried food, such as fried chicken, is not likely to burn on the outside while it is raw in the center.

If you use the range correctly and give it the proper care each day, it will give good service and will last longer, and the weekly cleaning will be easy. Therefore, each time you use the range, remember the following:

1. Use utensils that are large enough to prevent food from boiling over either on top of the range or in the oven.
2. Keep a dish on top of the range to hold the spoon that you use in stirring food.
3. Avoid putting anything that is hot on the porcelain enameled surface or pulling cooking utensils across it. The heat may cause it to chip or crack.
4. Arrange pans in the oven so that the air can circulate around them.
5. Wipe the chromium trim with a damp cloth, and polish it with a dry cloth.

Courtesy General Electric Company

Many ranges have one thermostat-controlled top burner or unit. This unit can be set to operate at the exact degree of heat needed. Spill pans under all burners should be wiped after each use.

Wipe up all spilled foods with paper or a dry cloth as soon as possible. When the range has cooled after use, wash it with warm soapy water and rinse. Proper daily care will reduce the amount of weekly cleaning. However, special weekly cleaning is necessary. Grease collects in grooves, on the knobs, and on the accessories on the back panel. Check the instruction book to learn how

Courtesy Hotpoint Company

to remove the knobs and accessories for thorough cleaning. Special liquid cleansers and scouring pads which contain soap may be used to lessen the labor of cleaning different areas of the range. Follow the directions for using these cleansers and pads. For stubborn stains on enamel, use a special cleanser. Avoid using a coarse, gritty cleansing powder, which will scratch the enamel. Scouring pads are recommended for stubborn stains on areas of the range which cannot be cleaned with plain soap and water.

To clean the top of a gas range:
1. Remove the burners and the rack, and scrub them with warm soapy water or a scouring pad.
2. Clean the holes with a hairpin or a wire. Do not use a toothpick.
3. Rinse with clear hot water, and dry the rack. Turn the burners upside down in the oven.
4. Return the burners and the rack to the range as soon as they are dry.

To clean the units on an electric range:
1. Turn on the high heat so that any food on the units will burn off.
2. Cool, and then brush each unit with a soft nonmetallic brush. Never clean the unit with a metal brush, a fork, a knife, or a sharp metal tool.
3. You may use steel wool or a cloth on units which are enclosed.

To clean the oven:
1. Use a pancake turner immediately to remove food which has spilled in the oven.
2. Clean the oven thoroughly with a special cleanser when it is cool.
3. Wipe out the oven with soapy water. Rinse with clear water, and dry.
4. Turn on the oven for a few minutes to dry all parts so that they will not rust.

To clean the broiler:
1. Remove fat from the broiler pan. Then wipe the pan and the rack with paper.
2. Wash the broiler rack and the pan with hot soapy water, using a scouring pad.
3. Rinse and dry thoroughly.
4. Wipe the walls of the broiler. Then return the broiler pan and the rack. **385**

STORAGE EQUIPMENT

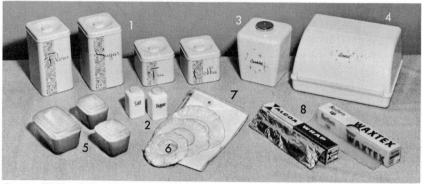

Courtesy Wolff and Marx, Inc.

Canister set (1) is used for storing staples, such as flour, sugar, coffee, and tea.
Salt and pepper shakers (2) are used for seasoning while cooking.
Cookie jar (3) is used for keeping cookies fresh.
Breadbox (4) is used for keeping bread fresh.
Refrigerator dishes (5) save space and prevent odors from spreading.
Bowl covers (6) are used to cover dishes which do not have lids.
Plastic bags (7) are used to keep vegetables crisp in the refrigerator.
Aluminum foil and wax paper (8) are used to cover dishes which do not have
lids or to wrap food to keep it from drying out.
Vegetable bin (see picture on page 163) is used to store potatoes, onions, and
other vegetables and fruits which do not need to be refrigerated.

CLEANING EQUIPMENT

Paper towels (1) may be used to dry your hands, to wipe out greasy pans, to
clean off bottle tops, and to wipe up spilled food.
Soap dish (2) is used to hold the soap so that the sink will be neat.
Newspaper (3) may be used for wiping out greasy skillets and for wrapping
garbage. It may also be used instead of a paper bag to line a garbage can.
Sink strainer (4) is used to hold peelings, seeds, egg shells, and other garbage
until they are put in the garbage can.
Scouring pads (5) are used to scrub pots and pans that are difficult to clean.
Dishpan (6) is used for washing dishes in warm soapy water.
Dishcloth (7) is used for washing dishes. *Dish towel* (8) is used for drying dishes.
Draining rack (9) is used to hold the dishes as they drain.
Tray (10) under the draining rack causes the water to run back into the sink.

Courtesy Wolff and Marx, Inc.

ACTIVITIES

Recognizing small kitchen utensils:
1. Arrange pictures of good kitchen utensils on the bulletin board. Learn the names of each.
2. Make a drawing of the placement of the utensils in the drawers and cabinets of the foods kitchen. Label each item.
3. Name three kitchen utensils which are seldom used in your home.
4. Discuss ways other than those listed in which each of the baking pans and oven dishes shown on page 377 may be used.

Using cutting and chopping equipment:
5. If you use a hand can opener at home, bring it to school and compare it with those of your classmates.
6. Demonstrate the uses of various pieces of kitchen equipment for cutting and chopping. Discuss safety precautions.

Cooking on top of the range:
7. List the advantages and the disadvantages of utensils made of: (a) aluminum, (b) enamel, (c) stainless steel, (d) cast iron, (e) tin, and (f) plastic.
8. Demonstrate how to use a double boiler (see page 364). Discuss the advantages and the disadvantages of using a double boiler.
9. Watch your teacher demonstrate the use of a pressure cooker.

Getting experience with small electrical appliances:
10. Make arrangements for the class to visit a store where electrical appliances are demonstrated. Examine the appliances on display.
11. Discuss the use, care, and storage of small electrical appliances.
12. Suggest as many different uses as you can for a waffle iron. For example, it may be used to make corn bread, cookies, and sandwiches as well as waffles.

Studying the range:
13. What precautions, in addition to those listed on page 385, should be taken in cleaning a range?
14. Check the gas burner in the school kitchen to see if it burns a blue flame or a yellow flame. Watch your teacher or the maintenance man adjust the burners so that they all burn a blue flame, which is hotter than a yellow flame.

Using the refrigerator:
15. Bring pictures of two types of refrigerators to class. Study them with regard to shape, size, and storage space for various foods.
16. Demonstrate the steps in defrosting and cleaning a refrigerator.
17. Discuss the advantage and the disadvantage of an automatic defroster. **387**

Chapter 27 | **WORKING TOGETHER**

You will work with people all of your life: in your own family, on committees, in an office, and so on. Working with your classmates in the kitchen at school is a good way to learn how to work with others happily and to respect other people's wishes and authority. As you and your friends learn to work together, you will also learn the following:

1. To share responsibilities and to work together as a group.
2. To have a place for everything and keep it there.
3. To plan menus and select recipes which can be prepared with the amount of money available.
4. To divide work evenly.
5. To plan and organize the work to have meals ready on time.
6. To prepare food quickly and easily.
7. To save time by immediately stopping whatever you are doing when the teacher taps the bell or calls the class to order.
8. To serve food attractively and correctly.
9. To recognize well-prepared food.
10. To clean up quickly and efficiently.
11. To evaluate work and to learn how to improve upon what has been done.

YOUR PERSONAL APPEARANCE IN THE KITCHEN

Looking attractive in the kitchen, whether at school or at home, is just as important as it is in any other place. To keep your hair arranged neatly so that it will not fall into your face and so that loose hairs will not fall into the food that you are preparing, tie your hair out of the way with a ribbon or pin it back securely with bobby pins. If you have long hair, you may prefer to wear a hairnet or a head band.

At school as well as at home, you should protect your clothing by wearing an apron. Your apron should . . .

. . . be one which you enjoy wearing — not "just any old thing."
. . . be becoming in color and be made of a material that launders easily.
. . . be made in a pleasing style which protects most of your dress.
. . . fit properly, look neat, and be easy to put on and remove.
. . . have pockets large enough for your handkerchief, and so on.

Boys usually wear large butcher aprons to protect their clothing. Most boys roll up their shirt sleeves while working in the kitchen to keep their cuffs from becoming soiled.

Dresses with short sleeves are easier to work in than dresses with long sleeves. Large bows, ruffles, flimsy material, and costume jewelry which gets in the way are out of place in the kitchen. They could be dangerous since they may catch fire easily or get caught in an electric mixer, a fan, or other moving equipment.

Never start cooking or handling food until you have washed your hands with warm soapy water. Rinse your hands, and then dry them with a paper towel or a hand towel. Never dry them with your apron or with the dish towel used for drying dishes. And, of course, all well-groomed persons keep their nails clean. Incidentally, a toothpick may be used to clean the nails.

Courtesy Stix, Baer, and Fuller, St. Louis

Courtesy National Presto Industries, Inc.

Your first experience in the kitchen was probably helping your mother or your grandmother to set the table or to cut up the ingredients for a salad. Later you may have learned to make a salad alone or to prepare some other dish. You may even have learned to prepare a simple meal all by yourself.

When you help your mother in the kitchen at home, you may have some problems when both of you need the same equipment and supplies at the same time. No doubt you work out these problems easily since they concern only the two of you.

In the school kitchen it is necessary for you to learn to share the work, the equipment, and the supplies with your classmates. Before you start to prepare food, you will need to learn where the various supplies and pieces of equipment are kept. It will be helpful to place labels made of masking tape in drawers, on shelves, and on cabinets which show the proper placement of the contents. There may also be a chart which shows the location of the equipment. The labels and the chart have two purposes: to help you to find the equipment and to help you to return the equipment to its proper place after you have used it.

Patteson

Most school kitchens are divided into several small kitchens which are often called "units." Your class will probably be divided into groups of four or six girls who will work together in these small kitchens. Of course, it may sometimes be necessary to have a practice lesson and to work in groups of two in order to develop skill in preparing a certain recipe, such as muffins.

To become acquainted with the school kitchen, you may choose as your first lesson to serve a simple snack using foods that are already prepared, such as tomato juice and cheese crackers. As your next lesson, you might serve something that is easy to prepare, such as instant cocoa and graham crackers topped with toasted marshmallows or banana milk shake and cookies that have been purchased.

Once you have become acquainted with the school kitchen and the general routine of working with your classmates, you may start preparing simple meals with recipes that are easy to use. Each lesson will be a little more difficult than the previous one. But no lesson will be so difficult that you cannot do your best work.

From time to time, your teacher may give a demonstration to teach you how to follow a certain recipe, how to set the table, how to hold your knife and fork when eating, and so on. Sometimes your teacher may ask you to prepare a recipe up to a certain point. Then she will demonstrate the steps which may be difficult for you, such as how to knead biscuits (see page 316). The more closely you pay attention to each thing your teacher does, the easier it will be for you when you try to do it yourself.

Patteson

SCHEDULING THE WORK

A schedule, often referred to as a "work plan," is a list of things that you want to get done in a certain amount of time, such as during the term, during the week, or during one day. You will have your individual schedule at school as well as the one you have at home (see page 396).

Term schedule: With the help of your teacher, you and your classmates will make a schedule for the amount of time that you want to spend on each topic that you will study during the term.

Weekly schedule: You and your classmates will plan together what you want to study during the week or how you can plan, prepare, and serve a simple meal. Your weekly schedule might be something like this:

Monday: Divide the class into family groups. Plan the meal to be served, considering other meals that might be eaten during the day. Select and copy recipes if necessary. Plan a schedule. Make a market order. (See pages 395–397.)

Tuesday: Watch a film or a demonstration, study recipes to be used, or have a practice lesson. Each of these activities will help you to develop skill and speed in using recipes so that you will have well-prepared food when you serve your meal. Buy groceries.

Wednesday: Measure dry ingredients, or start preparing food which cannot be completed in one class period. Discuss the recipes to be prepared the next day (see pages 398 and 399).

Thursday: Prepare and serve the meal (see page 401).

Friday: List the things that were done especially well during the week. Discuss ways in which the meal might have been improved (see page 404). Decide what you wish to study and do the next week.

Edison

DIVIDING THE WORK

For work in the school kitchen to run smoothly, each girl should understand what she is to do and she should do it willingly and promptly.

Each girl in each class group may be known as a member of a family; as a host, a hostess, a waitress, or a guest; or as first, second, third, or fourth girl. In some classes there are a cook and an assistant cook in each group, and the other girls set the table and wash the dishes or observe the girls who are cooking (page 415). If your class is divided into family groups, the members of each group will be known as Father, Mother, Big Sister, or Little Sister. Their work might be divided something like this:

Father: Makes the market order and buys the groceries. Prepares the cereal or the vegetables. Washes the dishes used in cooking. Acts as host during the meal. Washes the dishes after the meal.

Mother: Acts as chairman of the family in planning the meal. Prepares the main dish and the salad. Acts as hostess during the meal. Cleans the cabinets and the stove. Puts the dishes away.

Big Sister: Draws the plan for setting the table. Plans the centerpiece. Sets the table. Prepares the beverage. Acts as waitress during the meal. Clears the table, stacks the dirty dishes, and helps to put the clean dishes away.

Little Sister: Acts as chairman in planning the schedule of the work to be done each day (page 392) and assigns a girl to do each job. Has the schedule checked by the teacher. Prepares the bread, the fruit, or the dessert. Acts as a guest during the meal. Rinses and dries the dishes.

It may be necessary to adjust the duties from time to time if you find that some of the girls have more work to do than others. But if everyone is a good sport, these problems can easily be adjusted.

Edison

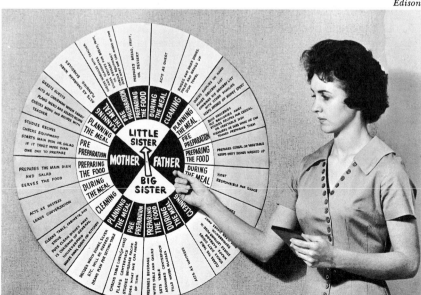

393

Edison

As you and your classmates work together in planning the menus to be prepared in class, you will find it helpful to study or at least to review a number of pages in this book so that you will be able to answer the following questions about each menu:

1. Is the menu written correctly? (See page 65.)
2. Have you had enough experience to prepare all the foods in the menu, or would it be better to prepare fewer dishes until you have had more experience?
3. Can the food be prepared and served in the amount of time that you have? (See page 398.)
4. Can part of the food be prepared one day and mixed, baked, or cooked the next? (See page 399.)
5. Can the menu be prepared without too many last-minute details?
6. Can the menu be prepared with the amount of money that you have to spend? (See page 395.)
7. Did you consult A *Daily Food Guide* (pages 48–52) when planning the menu?
8. Is there variety in color, size and shape, texture, flavor, and method of preparation? (See pages 70–73.)
9. Will the oven be needed for more than one dish? If so, can both dishes be cooked at the same temperature? Or can you bake the casserole first, for example, and then bake the biscuits while the casserole is being served?
10. Have you selected recipes which you understand and can follow easily? (See page 433.)

MAKING THE MARKET ORDER

When you prepare meals at school, your family group may be given a certain amount of money to spend for groceries. Then one or two members of your group will do the shopping, or perhaps one student or the teacher may buy the groceries for the entire class. Whatever plan you follow, it will be necessary for each family group to make a detailed market order of the groceries to be bought. You will also need to make a list of the staples that you plan to use, such as flour, salt, and sugar. Then you or someone else can check to make sure that you have enough of the staples in the school kitchen. A list of the groceries to be bought is not enough. You will also need to know . . .

. . . whether fresh, frozen, dried, or canned food is to be bought.

. . . the kind of apples, potatoes, and so on, that are needed since different kinds are used for different purposes.

. . . the brand, the grade, and so on.

. . . the amount of food to buy: size of the can and number of pounds.

. . . possible substitutes for foods that are too expensive or foods that are not available in the store.

It is not necessary to give all the above information about each item. But do give enough information so that the person who buys the groceries will know what you want. (See the market order below.) For example, if the shopper buys a large can of sliced pineapple instead of the small can of crushed pineapple that you ordered, it will cost more than you intended to spend and it will not be what you need.

STAPLES TO BE USED	MARKET ORDER			
	Groceries to Be Bought	Amount	Cost	Other Information
	Canned and bottled			
	Staples			
	Bakery foods			
	Dairy products and eggs			
	Meat and fish			
	Fruits and vegetables			
	Frozen foods			

Daily schedule: Since most class periods are only 55 minutes, make every minute count, especially on the day that you prepare and serve your meal. Your schedule for that day might be something like this:

Put books away and prepare to work	4 minutes
Roll call and announcements	3 minutes
Prepare the meal	20 minutes
Eat	15 minutes
Clean up	10 minutes
Prepare to leave	3 minutes

Individual schedule when working with other girls: Write a schedule of each thing that you are to do and when you are to do it. For example, suppose that your family group plans to serve a breakfast of grapefruit juice, scrambled eggs, toast, jelly, and milk and that your job is to prepare and serve the juice and toast. Put the grapefruit juice in the refrigerator to chill the day before the breakfast. Then prepare a schedule for the next day like the following:

9:00   Wash hands and put on apron.
9:04   Listen to announcements, and answer the roll call.
9:07   Get out the supplies and the equipment, and turn on the broiler.
9:10   Pour the grapefruit juice, and put it on the table.
9:15   Make the toast in the broiler.
9:20   Spread the butter on the toast, and serve.
9:27   Act as a guest while eating.
9:42   Rinse the dishes, and dry the dishes.
9:52   Get ready to go to the next class.
9:55   Go to the next class.

Always have your plans checked by your teacher to save time and to make sure that there are no errors.

Courtesy Stix, Baer, and Fuller, St. Louis

396

INDIVIDUAL SCHEDULE

Making a schedule: Before you make your individual schedule for preparing and serving a meal in the school kitchen, review the schedules that are given on page 396. Then you and your classmates will need to decide on the answers to the following questions:

1. What foods will you prepare and serve? (See pages 391 and 394.)
2. What will you have to do in addition to preparing the food, such as arranging flowers?
3. What jobs will each person do? (See page 393.)
4. How long will each job take?
5. When should each job be done? Review the weekly schedule on page 392 and the daily schedule on page 396. Then decide on the answers to:
   a. What work can be done the day before the meal?
   b. Which food will take the longest time to prepare?
   c. At what time should you start preparing each dish?
   d. Which foods will require last-minute details?
   e. What can be done ahead of time to avoid last-minute details?

Individual schedule when working alone: If you were to prepare a breakfast of grapefruit juice, scrambled eggs, toast, jelly, and milk at home, you would have to include in your working schedule the jobs that the other girls in your family group would do if the meal were prepared and served in class. That is, in addition to preparing and serving the fruit juice and the toast, you would have to set the table, prepare the eggs, serve the jelly and the milk, clear the table after the meal, wash the dishes, and so on. You would probably also make coffee for your mother and father. To save time, you might decide to make the toast in the electric toaster at the table.

Patteson

Preparing and serving meals in a 55-minute period is often a problem if you are to serve the food correctly and enjoy yourself without feeling rushed. Perhaps the following suggestions will help you to do some of the work on the day before the meal is to be served:

1. Read and study the recipe carefully, and make sure that you understand each step. (See page 433.)
2. Check to see that you have all the supplies that you will need.
3. Decide on which utensils you will need.
4. Make sure that you understand how to turn on the oven, how to use the electric appliances, and so on.
5. Watch a demonstration by the teacher to make sure that you understand how to prepare the recipe that you are to use the next day.
6. Have a "tasting party." The teacher will prepare a roast or broil a steak. Then each of you can have a taste. If the roast is not too expensive, it can be cooked as a demonstration for the entire class one day and be heated and served as a part of the meal the next day.
7. Prepare such foods as breads as a practice lesson. Then reheat them in the top part of a double boiler, or cut them in half, spread with butter, and toast.
8. Some foods which are prepared as a practice lesson may be frozen until it is time to serve the meal.
9. Decide on the quickest method for preparing the food. For example, individual meat loaves bake more quickly than one large loaf.

Baked potatoes take less of the cook's time than French-fried potatoes, but they take longer to cook. Corn bread baked in a pan takes less of the cook's time than muffins. Muffin pans which are only half full will bake more quickly than those which are two-thirds full. Drop cookies or drop biscuits can be made more quickly than rolled ones.

Courtesy Stix, Baer, and Fuller, St. Louis

THE FOOD

Additional suggestions for partially preparing the food one day and finishing the preparation the next are as follows:

1. Meat dishes which require long, slow cooking may be partially cooked one day and then completed the next. For example, the meat for stew may be cooked one day. Then the vegetables can be added the next day.
2. Meat pie may be prepared with the exception of the topping.
3. Chicken which is to be used in creamed or casserole dishes, in salads, or in sandwiches may be cooked, and the bones may be removed.
4. Eggs may be hard-cooked for use in salads, sandwiches, and so on.
5. Many casseroles may be made and kept in the refrigerator.
6. Cheese may be grated and stored in a covered jar.
7. Bread crumbs may be made and stored in a jar.
8. Nuts, pickles, or any food not injured by standing may be chopped.
9. Some sandwich fillings can be made, or at least partially prepared, one day and spread on bread the next day.
10. The core may be removed from lettuce, and the leaves may be separated. Other salad greens or vegetables may be washed and stored in a plastic bag in the refrigerator to keep them crisp and fresh.
11. Carrot sticks and celery may be cut and stored in a jar.
12. Mayonnaise or salad dressing may be made. The sauce for the meat or the dessert may also be prepared and stored in the refrigerator.
13. Congealed salads or desserts may be prepared and put into molds.
14. Potatoes may be washed so that they will be ready to be put in the oven 30 minutes before class time.
15. Pie crust may be rolled, shaped, and baked one day. Or the unbaked dough may be kept in the refrigerator and then baked the next day.
16. Pie filling may be prepared, cooled, and added to the baked crust one day. Meringue may be added the next day, and the pie may be baked and served.

Patteson

Dry ingredients for quick breads, biscuits, or cakes may be measured the day before the meal and stored in a jar. Then on the day of the meal, add the liquid and the remaining ingredients, and bake.

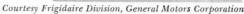

Courtesy Frigidaire Division, General Motors Corporation

On the day before the meal, meat patties may be shaped and stored in the refrigerator with a piece of wax paper between the patties.

399

A

C

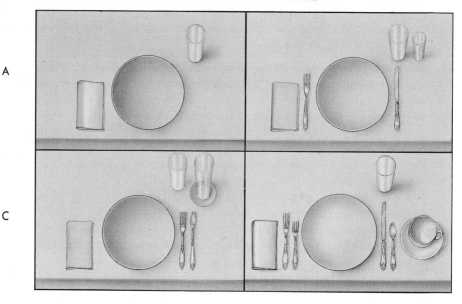

A. *Snack menu:* Sandwich, potato chips, and beverage
B. *Breakfast menu:* Fruit juice, scrambled eggs, jelly, toast, butter, and milk
C. *Lunch menu:* Fruit plate, buttered rolls, and iced beverage
D. *Dinner menu:* Meat, vegetable, salad, and bread served on plate, pie, and hot beverage.

The way in which the table is set depends upon the menu. (See page 24.) The girl who has charge of setting the table will need to do these things:

1. Decide which pieces of china, silver, and glassware will be needed as soon as the menu has been planned.
2. Draw a plan (table cover) showing how the table is to be set. The drawing need not be elaborate, but it should be clear enough so that the teacher will know that the girl understands just what she is to do. Pages 19-21 will help her with her plans.
3. Check the table linen if it is to be used. Most classes prefer to use place mats which do not need to be laundered.
4. Plan a centerpiece and assemble the materials needed. Before arranging the centerpiece, she will find it helpful to review pages 22 and 23.
5. Have her plans checked by the teacher.
6. Set the table, using both hands and taking as few steps as possible. For example, she may pick up and put down the forks with her left hand and the knives with her right hand.

SERVING THE MEAL

Before serving a snack or a meal, the hostess and the waitress will need to make decisions concerning the following questions:

1. Will there be time for the host to serve the main dish? (See page 25.)
2. Or should all the food be put in serving dishes and passed at the table?
3. Is the main dish, such as a casserole, too hot to pass?
4. Would it be better to serve the individual plates before they are put on the table in order to save time?
5. If serving dishes are used, which ones would be best?
6. Which serving dishes should be placed on asbestos mats?
7. Should the salad be put in a large bowl and passed at the table, or should it be served in individual dishes? (See pages 198-200.)
8. What can be done to serve the food attractively? (See page 463.)
9. If food drips on the side of a plate or a dish, who should wipe it off?
10. What should be put on the table first? Last?
11. Should the beverage be put on the table when everyone sits down?
12. Should the girls be given an extra serving of the beverage? If so, should the waitress serve it or should it be on the table to be served by the hostess?
13. What should be served with the beverage, such as sugar and lemon for the tea?
14. Should the dessert be put on the table at the beginning of the meal, or will there be time to clear the table and serve the dessert?
15. What dishes should be arranged in the kitchen so that the dessert can be served quickly?
16. Who should make sure that everything is on the table?
17. What can be done ahead of time so that the waitress will not have to leave the table any more than is necessary during the meal?

Edison

Scrape and rinse the dishes that are especially soiled. Soak in cold water dishes that contained cereal, egg, or flour mixtures. Soak in hot water greasy dishes and those that were used for sugar mixtures.

If the pans or skillets are badly burned, fill them with water. Add a little baking soda, and boil them until clean.

Stack the dishes by putting similar things together. Place the glasses next to the sink since they should be washed first. Place the silverware next and then the china. Pots, pans, and other utensils should be last. Smaller and least-soiled cooking utensils should be placed so that they will be washed before the large, greasy utensils.

Photos Courtesy Wooster Rubber Company

WASHING THE DISHES

1. Fill the sink or the dishpan half full with hot soapy water. The amount of soap or detergent that you should use depends upon the hardness of the water.

2. Put only a few dishes into the sink or the dishpan at one time.

3. Hold each dish in your left hand and the sponge or the dishcloth in your right hand as you wash dishes.

4. Rinse the dishes with plenty of very hot water. Glasses, cups, jars, and bottles should be rinsed inside and out. Plates, saucers, and so on, should be rinsed on both sides.

5. Place the dishes in the dish drainer at an angle at which they will drain best. For example, turn glasses and cups upside down after they have been scalded. Stand plates, saucers, and so on, at almost a right angle.

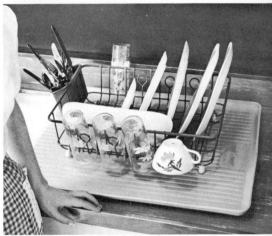

Photos Courtesy Wooster Rubber Company

6. Dry the dishes with a clean dish towel, and put them in their proper places.

7. Hang up the dish towel neatly when you finish drying the dishes.

8. Pour the dishwater through a sink strainer unless you have a garbage disposal. Otherwise you may clog the sink.

9. Use soapy water to clean the sink, rubbing it hard. If the sink is especially dirty, use soda or a fine scouring powder. Use a bleach to remove stains.

10. Clean the table and the cabinet tops thoroughly, giving special attention to the edge of the table. Any food left on the table or in cracks is apt to attract insects.

403

EVALUATING YOURSELF

Your success in preparing a meal at school depends largely upon how well you work with others. Before you leave the room, check yourself on the following questions as though you were grading someone else:

1. Was I ready to start work on time, with my books and wraps put away?
2. Was I clean and neat in appearance?
3. Did I follow the teacher's instructions?
4. Was I friendly, pleasant, and courteous to my classmates?
5. Did I do my share of the work?
6. Did I make the best use of my time?
7. Did I help others when they needed help?
8. Did I willingly assume the responsibilities of my partner who was absent?
9. Did I find things to do without being told?
10. Did I follow the rules of the class?
11. Did I disagree courteously when I had to disagree?
12. Did I take more than my share of the supplies, such as nuts, dates, or other foods that I especially like?
13. Did I keep my working area clean and orderly?
14. Did I use a minimum number of dishes and utensils while cooking?
15. Did I practice safety habits?
16. Did I finish my work on time?
17. Did I prepare my share of the food properly, season it well, and serve it at the correct temperature? Did it have an appealing flavor and an attractive appearance?
18. What could I have done to improve the food that I prepared?
19. Did I practice good table manners?
20. Did I contribute to an interesting conversation at the table?
21. Was I a good listener?
22. Did I do my part in helping to put the kitchen in order after the meal?
23. Did I do my best to help earn the highest grade for my group?

Courtesy Stix, Baer, and Fuller, St. Louis

ACTIVITIES

Becoming acquainted in the school kitchen:
1. Browse around the school kitchen to get a general idea of where everything is located.
2. Have a contest in learning the names of your classmates.
3. Make a poster illustrating class courtesy.
4. Select three pictures of aprons which would be appropriate for use in a foods class.

Sharing work:
5. Make a list or arrange a display on the bulletin board showing how girls in class help at home.
6. Compare the work you do in the school kitchen with what you do at home.
7. Discuss the importance of sharing the work in the school kitchen.
8. Decide how girls who do extra work should be repaid.
9. Discuss ways of dealing with students who do not do their share.

Selecting a partner:
10. Describe a person with whom you enjoy working. Do not give her name. Allow your classmates to guess whom you have described.
11. Select the girl with whom most of you would enjoy working. Then have a class discussion about why you would prefer to work with her rather than any other girl.
12. Make a list of the characteristics that you want in a partner.

Dividing the work:
13. Pretend that two of you are making oatmeal cookies together. Study the recipe on page 542. Then decide what each of you might do.
14. Pretend that you and your classmates work in groups of four. Decide on a plan for dividing the work in your class similar to the one on page 392.

Preparing and serving the meal:
15. Plan a simple meal that you and your classmates might prepare in class.
16. Make a market order for the meal. Then work out a schedule.
17. Set up some basic rules to be followed when preparing and serving meals in class.
18. Decide what should be done with a girl who is indifferent to errors because "I didn't do it."
19. List ways in which you may judge your own work as well as your classmates' work.
20. List the new terms that you have learned in studying this chapter. Compare your list with those of other members of the class.

Chapter 28 | **MANAGING YOUR MEALS**

Homemakers who are good managers seem to be able to keep everything spic and span without effort. They have more free time than those who do not keep their homes nearly so neat. Because they organize their work, they do not tire as easily as poor managers.

Some homemakers sit and think or talk about all there is to be done without acting. Others waste time because they cannot decide what to do first. Still others waste time because they jump from one job to another without any system.

In a poorly arranged kitchen, even though she may not realize it, the homemaker has to take unnecessary steps. In a kitchen which is arranged in good order, the homemaker can work quickly and easily without extra steps.

Having a place for everything and keeping it there are the first steps toward being a good manager. Not only must your equipment and supplies be arranged so that they are near the place where you plan to use them, but they must also be kept in an orderly manner.

Last, but by no means least, a good manager must plan her work. Good planning has as much to do with the success of a meal as any other one thing.

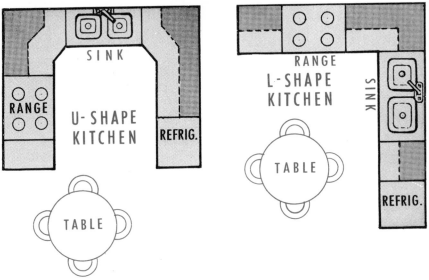

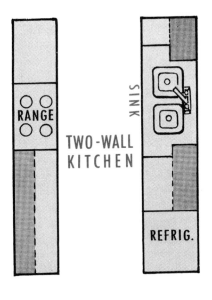

Most kitchens are in the shape of an L with the cabinets arranged along two adjoining walls (top right) or in the shape of a U (top left). Two-wall (left) and one-wall (above) kitchens do not have much storage space. They are usually found in small homes and apartments. Regardless of the shape of your kitchen, you should arrange your equipment and supplies in the following five centers for convenience and ease in working: preparation and mixing center, cooking center, cleaning center, serving center, and planning center.

407

Courtesy A. J. Martin

Preparation and Mixing Center

The preparation and mixing center is usually located between the refrigerator and the range. You can save many steps if you keep supplies, utensils, and equipment for preparing and mixing food near the place where you use them most often. For example, utensils which are used in cleaning, peeling, paring, and cutting fruits or vegetables should be kept between the sink and the refrigerator.

Ingredients such as flour, sugar, and baking powder, as well as cocoa, spices, and shortening, should be stored in cabinets in the mixing center, where breads and cakes are mixed. Measuring spoons and cups, mixing bowls, sifter, and mixing spoons should all be within easy reach. Other utensils and equipment, such as cookie sheets, cake pans, casserole dishes, a blender, and an electric mixer, should also be nearby. You can save additional steps if you keep pieces of equipment that you use together, such as a rolling pin and a breadboard, in the same place. Likewise, the utensils and the ingredients that you use in making salads should be stored close together. Canned food should be kept near the place where it will be used most often.

There are no exact rules as to where supplies and utensils should be kept in every kitchen. Many homemakers, however, arrange everything so that as they prepare a meal, they can easily go from one job to another, moving from right to left. For example, after the boy in the picture removed the carrots from the refrigerator, he could have washed them at the sink, cut them in the preparation center, cooked them at the range, and then served them without retracing his steps. This is an efficient arrangement of kitchen centers.

Courtesy A. J. Martin

Cooking Center

The cooking center, which includes all supplies and utensils used in cooking food, is planned around the range. Small utensils which are used at the range, such as a pancake turner, a cooking fork, and spoons for stirring and tasting, as well as such large utensils as a griddle, a skillet, and covers for pans, should be kept near the range. Since water is usually added to saucepans before they are put on the range to heat, they may be stored near the sink instead of the range.

Patteson

Cleaning Center

Most cleaning takes place in the area of the sink. Hence, all supplies and equipment that are used for scraping, washing, rinsing, and drying dishes should be near the sink. The cabinet in which the dishes are stored is often at the left of the sink because dishes are usually washed from right to left. The platters and other serving dishes, however, should be kept near the range, where they can be reached easily when the food is ready to be served.

Serving Center

One counter near the range which is not too far from the dining room or the breakfast table may be used as a serving center. Then hot food may be served and taken to the table piping hot. Utensils needed for serving should be nearby. The sugar bowl, salt and pepper shakers, paper napkins, and place mats should all be kept in the serving center. Electric appliances which are used on the table, such as the toaster and the waffle iron, are frequently stored in the serving center.

Sometimes the preparation and mixing center is also used as the serving center. For example, the counter next to the refrigerator might be used for putting the salad on individual plates as well as for serving an iced beverage or a dessert which is kept in the refrigerator.

Planning Center

Every homemaker should have a planning center or "business center," as it is often called, where she can plan her work and keep recipes and bills. (See picture on page 406.) There should be a notebook for writing recipes, menus, notes, and so on, as well as a pad and pencil for keeping a list of the groceries and supplies needed. A chalk board above the planning center can be used for writing all kinds of reminders to various members of the family. Many homemakers also have a calendar, some small change, a radio, and a clock in the planning center.

The planning center need not be elaborate to be handy. Papers and records can be kept in a drawer and recipe files and cookbooks on a shelf. The breakfast table or a counter top above the drawer could double as a desk for planning menus and other writing. It is important to have a place for everything, to keep the center in order, and to have a pad and pencil handy for making a list of groceries and supplies which need to be replaced.

Courtesy A. J. Martin

410

FOOD STORAGE

Even though all food should be kept near the place where it will be used and should be arranged so that it can be seen easily and reached conveniently, special precautions should be taken in storing various kinds of food. Unopened canned foods, whether in tin cans or glass jars, should be stored in a dark, cool, dry place. Many homemakers prefer to keep their canned goods on low rather than on high shelves in the kitchen because low places are usually cooler. At no time should canned foods be stored near the range, steam pipes, or anything damp. Once canned foods have been opened, whether left in the can or put into another container, they must be kept in the refrigerator.

For ease in finding canned goods, the same kinds of food should be put together. For example, the fruit should be stored together, the vegetables together, and so on. Small cans may be arranged on shelves of different levels to save space and to permit the labels to be seen easily. Tall cans on the same shelf with smaller cans should be placed in the back. All should be arranged so that the labels can be seen.

Spices will keep their flavor longer if the containers are kept tightly closed. Dry staple foods, such as baking powder, coffee, and cocoa, may be left in the original containers, but they should also be kept tightly covered or closed. A metal, plastic, or glass container with a tight-fitting lid is best for flour, sugar, or tea because it keeps out insects as well as moisture. Likewise, cereals, such as rice and rolled oats, should be kept in covered containers.

The containers in which bread and cakes are kept should have small holes for ventilation. A breadbox should be washed and aired frequently to prevent bread that is stored in it from molding. Crackers and ready-to-eat cereals should be kept in closed containers in a dry place. If crackers lose their crispness, place them in the oven for a few minutes.

Patteson

If you work in an orderly manner, not only will you save time, but you will produce good results and your kitchen will be neat. Naturally, you can work quickly and easily in a kitchen when you do not have to waste time in picking up and putting away things that are out of place. Here are some rules to keep in mind:

1. Have a place for everything, and keep it there.
2. Keep drawers and cabinet doors closed except when you wish to remove or replace something.
3. Keep the place where you work as neat as possible by keeping unneeded supplies and utensils out of the way.
4. Keep your work toward the center of the table to avoid spilling food on the floor.
5. Work quickly, but do not go about your work so fast that you become careless. When you do spill anything, clean it up immediately.
6. Use utensils that are large enough so that food will not boil over in the oven or on top of the range.
7. Stir food gently to prevent it from spattering.
8. Put a small dish on the range to hold the spoons that you use in stirring or tasting the food which is cooking.
9. Regulate the heat and watch cooking food carefully to avoid burning.
10. Use no more utensils than are necessary, and keep your working space clean by stacking dirty dishes out of the way. Often if you rinse a dish, you can use it for something else.
11. Clean up as you work. Use a sink strainer or a newspaper spread on the table for the waste when you peel or pare fruits or vegetables. If you do not have a garbage disposal, deposit the waste in the garbage can.
12. Line the garbage can with newspaper or put a large paper bag in it so that it will be easy to keep clean.
13. Keep the garbage can covered, and empty it each day. When necessary, wash it with warm soapy water.
14. It is unwise to sweep during the time that food is being prepared. When you clean the kitchen, be sure that you clean under and behind everything.

Courtesy "Electrical Merchandising"   *Patteson*

Courtesy Robert May's Kitchens

Dovetailing means doing two or more things at the same time. In meal preparation, dovetailing is necessary if all the foods for the meal are to be ready at the same time, with the hot foods hot and the cold foods cold. Examples of ways in which you may dovetail tasks in meal preparation are these:

1. When you are having scrambled eggs and bacon, prepare the eggs while the bacon is cooking.
2. Boil the water for potatoes while you peel the potatoes.
3. Scrape carrots or prepare another vegetable while the potatoes are cooking.
4. Prepare a salad or a dessert while the rest of the food for the meal is cooking.

Dovetailing saves time in serving a meal and in cleaning up after a meal. For instance, you can set the table or wash some of the utensils that you use in food preparation while the food for the meal is cooking.

Courtesy Joske's

To make sure that you do not allow anything that is cooking to burn while you are doing something else, use an automatic timer, or write down the time that the food being cooked should be done.

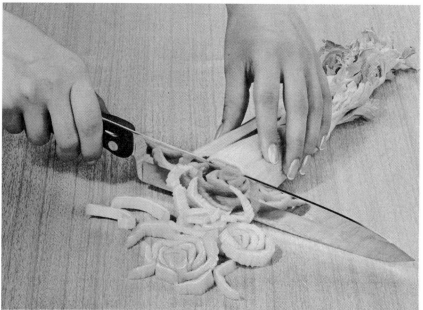

Courtesy Cutco

Many businesses hire experts to make time and motion studies of their employees to find out how they can save time in their work. You, too, can make a time and motion study of your own work or of a friend's work. For example, do you cut several pieces of celery or other vegetables at once rather than a slice at a time? Some methods of making a cake are much quicker than others. For this reason, when you select a recipe, you should consider the amount of time that it will take you to make it. Examine the time and motion study of cake making pictured below.

If your partner watches you do a certain job, she will probably notice immediately if you are taking unnecessary steps and wasting time even though you may not know that you are doing so. You can, in turn, watch her. As you do, you will find it helpful to make a list of the ways in which she might improve upon her job. It is surprising how much time you will save in a month or a year if you save only a few minutes at each meal.

Some classes are divided into groups with a cook, an assistant cook, a guest, and a waitress (see page 393). The girl who acts as guest at a meal may be assigned to observe the others as they work. She should look for ways in which they might improve upon what they are doing.

Courtesy The Pillsbury Company

Courtesy Stix, Baer, and Fuller, St. Louis

If you are asked to observe another girl and to suggest how she could save time, you might notice the following:

1. Did she make more than one trip to get supplies?
2. Was the extra trip necessary?
3. Did she waste time in getting the supplies?
4. How many times did she open the refrigerator door, or did she get everything she needed at once?
5. Did she gather all the needed ingredients and equipment before she started to work?
6. Did she get her supplies without spilling anything or bumping into the other girls?
7. Did she dovetail her work by doing two or more things at once?
8. List two specific things that she did in order to save time.
9. Did she do each job in the quickest and easiest manner as well as to the best of her ability?
10. Did she put things away as soon as she finished using them?
11. Did she ask unnecessary questions?
12. Did she take unnecessary steps? If so, where?
13. Could she have combined any of the jobs?
14. Did she use the most appropriate equipment?
15. Did she open the oven door more frequently than necessary?
16. Did she use two hands whenever possible, such as when she took dishes from the cabinet or when she removed things from the refrigerator? **415**

TIMESAVERS

Most homemakers look for ways of doing their work in a quick, efficient way. You have already learned how you can save time and steps by arranging supplies and equipment conveniently, by keeping things orderly, by making a schedule, by learning to do two or more things at once, and by changing your work habits. Still other ways are as follows:

1. Read the instructions, and learn how to use equipment properly.
2. Keep the electric mixer and other appliances in a convenient place.
3. Keep your knives razor-sharp. Dull knives cause you to waste time.
4. Dates and parsley can be cut more quickly with scissors than with a knife.
5. Grate the rind of a lemon or an orange first when a recipe calls for both grated rind and juice.
6. Rub a crust of bread over the grater to clean it after grating cheese.
7. Wash the grater with a brush instead of a dishcloth.
8. Put a damp cloth under a mixing bowl to keep it from moving around while you are beating ingredients in it.
9. Coat pieces of food with flour by shaking them in a paper bag containing flour rather than by rolling each piece in a dish of flour.
10. After frying foods, pour fat into a container immediately. Warm fat pours more easily than fat which has been allowed to stand.

Patteson

You may save time in meal preparation by...

...using paper cups for muffins.

...using a rubber scraper to remove ingredients from a cup or a bowl.

...keeping a spoon rest on top of the range to hold the spoons that you use in stirring.

Courtesy Swift and Company

Patteson

GENERAL RESPONSIBILITIES

In addition to planning, preparing, and serving a meal, there are a number of duties or responsibilities which need to be carried out each day, once every other day, or once a week. With the help of your teacher, you and your classmates will be able to work out a plan for carrying out the responsibilities of the class in the school kitchen. To keep the class running smoothly, it will probably be necessary to assign one or more general responsibilities to each member. After making a list of the duties, you will need to decide who will:

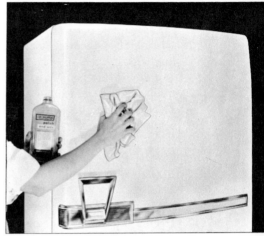

Cleaning the refrigerator once a week is one of the responsibilities in every homemaking department.

1. Act as president, vice-president, and secretary.

2. Act as hostess when your class has a guest. How should she introduce the guest? What should she do to see that the guest is comfortable.

3. Take charge of the bulletin board and the display case.

4. Check the cabinets to see that all the dishes and utensils are in order at the end of the period.

5. Empty the garbage can and see that it is kept clean.

6. Make sure that all chairs are in their proper places at the end of the period and that the floor is clean.

7. Take charge of all books, magazines, and booklets.

8. Check the lockers to make sure that aprons, notebooks, and other equipment have been put away properly and that each door is closed.

9. Assist the teacher when she gives a demonstration by getting out the supplies, utensils, and other equipment and then putting them away.

10. Clean the refrigerator and see that all food is kept in the correct place.

11. See that each group keeps the range clean and that all ovens are turned off at the end of the period.

12. Get out supplies and put them away.

13. Adjust the windows and make sure that the room is kept at the correct temperature.

417

ACTIVITIES

Arranging the kitchen:

1. Bring to class a picture of each of the following types of kitchens: (a) L-shaped, (b) U-shaped, (c) two-wall, and (d) one-wall.
2. Discuss the advantages and disadvantages of the various shapes of kitchens.
3. Describe a kitchen which, because it is poorly arranged, causes the homemaker to take many steps.
4. Notice the way in which spices and canned foods are stored in your school kitchen. Decide if there is any way of improving upon it.

Being orderly:

5. Explain the statement: A place for everything and everything in its place.
6. Make a list of do's and don't's to be followed in the foods laboratory.
7. Decide on a way of dealing with girls who leave dirty dishes or the cabinet drawers out of order, thus causing a delay in starting the next class.

Developing good working habits:

8. Demonstrate how much time you can save by going straight to your locker when you enter the school kitchen instead of stopping to visit with first one and then another friend.
9. Give a talk on the importance of working together without friction or confusion.
10. Study the discussion of dovetailing on page 413. Then check girls in your group to see how often they do two things at once when preparing a meal.

Saving time:

11. Discuss how much time can be saved if every girl stops what she is doing and listens as soon as the teacher calls the class to order.
12. Suggest ways for you and other members of your class to save time.
13. Discuss the list of timesavers on page 416. Describe additional timesavers your mother uses.

Assuming general responsibilities:

14. Make a list of general duties or responsibilities that are required in the school kitchen, such as those given on page 417.
15. Discuss the time required for each of the housekeeping duties in the school kitchen.
16. Divide the duties in the school kitchen among various members of the class. Ask each girl to describe her responsibilities to the class so that there will be no misunderstanding about what she is to do.

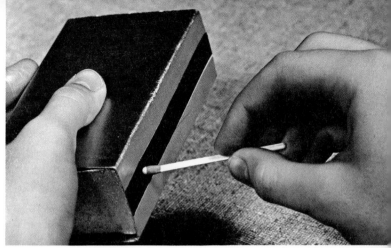

Chapter 29 | SAFETY IN THE KITCHEN

An attractive kitchen looks like a perfectly safe place in which to work. Yet serious accidents occur more frequently in the kitchen than in any other room in the home.

Most of the accidents which occur in the kitchen can be prevented. A safe kitchen is convenient and orderly. Unfortunately, many people are inclined to think that their kitchens are safe without taking time to check on the various items that might be dangerous and cause accidents. Such accidents are cuts, falls, burns, electric shock, poisoning, and bumps caused by swinging doors and open cabinets and drawers.

The most frequent causes of kitchen accidents are haste, carelessness, poor work habits, lack of training, poor arrangement of cabinets or equipment, poor equipment, poor lighting, and unsuitable clothing.

Preventing kitchen accidents is a steady job — something to keep in mind at all times. For example, always strike a match away from you. Do not turn on a burner until you are ready to use it. Do not reach over an open flame. No doubt you can think of other safety measures. As you study this chapter, you will learn still others.

419

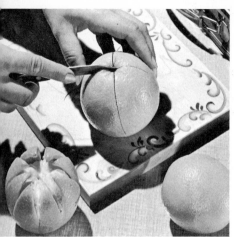

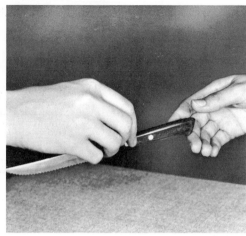

Courtesy Sunkist Growers

Patteson

When you use a knife, keep your fingers out of the way and cut away from you. Hold the knife and the food that you are cutting in such a way that you will not cut your fingers if the knife slips. Use a cutting board to protect the table.

When you hand a knife to someone, hold it so that the other person can take hold of the handle. Keep a firm grip on the knife until the other person grasps it securely.

When you wash or dry a knife, hold it by the handle with the sharp edge away from the hand in which you are holding the sponge or the dish towel. Never allow a knife to lie loose in the dishwater.

When you store a knife, put it in a separate compartment in a drawer, in a knife rack, or in a knife holder. Do not let it lie loose in a drawer.

Photos by Patteson

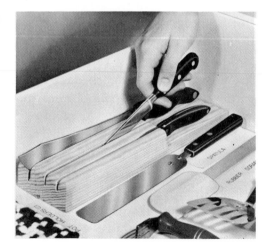

Photos Courtesy Libby, McNiell and Libby

When you open a can or a jar, use the proper utensil. Never use a knife to open a can or a jar.

Use a punch-type can opener to open cans that contain liquid. For a jar with a screw top use a jar opener, and for a jar with a vacuum-sealed lid use a lid flipper. (See page 376.)

When glasses stick together, put the bottom glass into hot water and pour cold water into the top glass. Then you will be able to pull the glasses apart without trouble.

When you break a glass or a dish, sweep up all the broken pieces immediately and wrap them in several thicknesses of newspaper. Then carefully clean up any small bits of glass or china that are left on the surface with a damp paper towel.

Courtesy Wooster Rubber Company　　　　　　　　　　　　　　　*Patteson*

TO AVOID FALLS

To reach something on a high shelf, stand on a well-constructed stepladder or stepstool. Never stand on a box or on books placed on a chair or a table.

Turn on water faucets slowly to avoid getting water on the floor as well as on yourself.

Wipe up immediately anything that you spill on the floor. Grease, soapy water, food, and liquids spilled on the floor can make it slippery and cause someone to fall.

Electric cords should be kept out of the way. If they are allowed to lie on the floor, someone may stumble or fall over them.

Courtesy Stix, Baer, and Fuller, St. Louis

It is unwise to carry such large bundles that you cannot see where you are going.

If you drop something, stop and pick it up at once. Someone might fall over it.

Carry sharp objects, such as knives or scissors, with the point down. But do not carry them at all when you are in a hurry.

If it is necessary to carry hot liquids from one part of a room to another, be sure that the containers are covered.

Patteson

TO PREVENT BURNS

Turn the handle of a saucepan inward or toward the back of the range. In this position, the saucepan cannot be reached by children or be knocked off the range by someone who passes by hurriedly.

Patteson

When you take the lid off a saucepan, lift the far side of the lid first so that the steam will rise away from you.

Courtesy American Gas Association

When you pour hot liquids from a saucepan, hold the lid in place to prevent the food from spilling out. Stand in such a way that the steam will not burn your face or your arm. To keep from burning your fingers, use a dry well-padded pot holder. Never use your apron, a dish towel, or a paper towel.

Patteson

When you turn chicken or meat that you are frying, hold the lid of the pan in front of you to prevent the hot grease from hitting you. Never reach across a lighted burner.

Courtesy Lone Star Gas Company

Before you add a liquid to hot fat in a skillet, remove the skillet from the heat and put it on an asbestos mat (below left). Otherwise the fat may bubble over the sides of the pan and catch fire. Asbestos mats are also used to protect the table.

When frying food in deep fat, use a deep pan so that the fat will be at least 3 inches from the top (below right). See that the food is as dry as possible before dropping it into the hot fat because moisture will cause the fat to boil up more than usual. Fat that overflows may start to burn.

Courtesy Saladmaster   *Courtesy Wolff and Marx, Inc.*

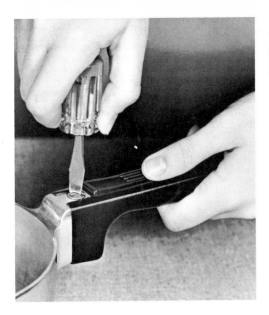

Photos by Patteson

If the handles on pans become loose, use a screwdriver to tighten them (above left). Loose handles may slip, causing you to spill hot liquid on yourself or on someone else.

Never fill a saucepan so full that it is likely to boil over and put out the gas flame (above right). If this does happen, turn off the heat and open a window. Escaping gas is dangerous because it may be ignited by the flame of another burner or may cause asphyxiation.

When grease in a skillet or a broiler catches fire, turn off the heat at once. Then smother the fire with baking soda, baking powder, flour, or salt (below left).

If you cook over an open fire at a picnic, throw sand or water on the burning embers before you leave (below right).

Courtesy Church and Dwight Company, Inc.   *Courtesy National Girl Scout News Bureau*

CARE IN USING ELECTRIC APPLIANCES

Be sure that electric appliances are disconnected before you pour water into them (above). With some appliances, care must be taken not to get water in or on the electric connection. Other electric appliances are designed so that they can be put into water safely. Follow the manufacturers' instructions.

When you turn on a light switch or use an electric appliance, be sure that your hands are dry. If your hands are wet or if you are standing on a wet floor, you are likely to get a shock.

When you connect or disconnect an electric appliance, hold the plug rather than the wire (below left). Do not bend or make a knot in an electric cord.

Avoid overloading a circuit (below right).

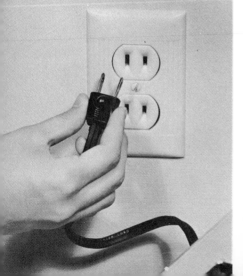
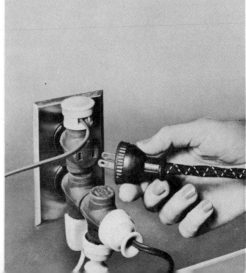

TO DEVELOP SANITARY HABITS

Photos Courtesy South San Antonio High School

Cleanliness, a good safety measure against the spread of germs, is especially important in the kitchen.

The following are some sanitary habits that you should develop for use in the school kitchen as well as in your kitchen at home:

1. Before you start to prepare food, make sure that your hands are clean by washing them with plenty of soap and water.

2. When you are ill, do not handle food that other people are to eat.

3. Be especially careful to cover your mouth with a handkerchief or a tissue when you cough. If you use your hand to cover a cough, wash your hands immediately.

4. Do not get close to other people or, better still, stay home when you have a bad cold or an illness that may be contagious.

5. When you taste a food that you are cooking, use a clean spoon rather than the one you have used in stirring. When you are not using them, keep your stirring and tasting spoons on a saucer nearby.

Finding insects in the home is not a disgrace. They can easily crawl into the kitchen or be carried into the house with the groceries. But it is a disgrace to allow the insects to stay. Start trying to get rid of them immediately.

To prevent the breeding of ants, roaches, and other insects:

1. Remove all garbage every day.
2. Keep the kitchen clean and all food tightly covered or stored.
3. Study the labels on various insecticides to decide which will be most effective in getting rid of the type of pest you have.
4. Read the directions, and follow them carefully.
5. Wash your hands as soon as you have finished using the insecticide.

Courtesy Real-Kill

Insecticides, lye, fly poison, kerosene, disinfectants, and cleaning fluids should not be kept under the kitchen sink, especially if there are children in the family. Instead, keep them on a high shelf or in a locked cabinet.

Patteson

428

Courtesy Johnson and Johnson

There should be a first-aid kit in every home for meeting emergencies that may occur in spite of all precautions. The first-aid kit should be kept in a convenient, yet out-of-the-way, place so that children will not be able to reach it and so that other members of the family will be able to find what they want quickly and easily.

People who have not had much experience in treating injuries should practice first aid only on minor injuries, such as small cuts or minor burns. If you are not absolutely sure of the correct thing to do or if the injury appears to be serious, call a doctor immediately.

REMEMBER, IT PAYS TO PLAY SAFE IN THE KITCHEN!

ACTIVITIES

Learning to be safe:

1. Discuss ways in which one girl's carelessness in the school kitchen might hurt another girl.
2. List safety precautions which you and your classmates should take.
3. Take turns observing the girls in your foods class to see what can be done to eliminate habits which might cause accidents.
4. Have a slogan or poster contest on safety regulations to be observed in the school kitchen.
5. Inspect your kitchen at home with the help of your mother. Then decide what might be done to make it safer than it is.

Preventing accidents:

6. Tell about a bad fall that you or a friend had which might have been prevented.
7. Describe an accident that you have had or have seen because a cupboard door or a drawer was left open.
8. Discuss what should be done if a glass breaks in the dishwater.

Observing fire regulations:

9. Discuss what should be done in case of a fire in your classroom. Do you have a fire blanket and a fire extinguisher? How do you use them?
10. Decide what you should do during a fire drill. Who should close the windows? Who should turn off the burners and ovens? Who should lead the way out of the room? Who should be the last to leave the room?
11. Discuss what might happen if a pot holder or a piece of paper were left too near a pilot light on a range.
12. Demonstrate how to light a gas burner which does not have an automatic pilot light by taking the following steps: *(a)* Strike a match. *(b)* Hold the match over or to the side of the burner. *(c)* Slowly turn on the gas. *(d)* Light the burner. *(e)* Put out the match. *(f)* Adjust the flame.
13. Watch your teacher demonstrate how to light and regulate the oven.

Developing good habits:

14. Decide on the best way to ventilate your school kitchen.
15. Discuss ways of labeling poisons, such as tying a bell around the bottle, drawing a skull and bones on the bottle with bright-red nail polish, or putting several rubber bands around the neck of the bottle to indicate that the bottle contains poison.

part **4** YOUR RECIPES AND
HOW TO USE THEM

HOW TO DO IT

Everyone loves good food, and everyone admires the person who can cook well. Many years ago people learned how to cook by watching someone else. Today anyone can learn to cook by following a good recipe accurately and by practicing.

Have you ever wondered why food prepared by one person is so much more attractive and tasty than that prepared by someone else who has used the same recipe? Could it be that, for best results, you must know how to use a recipe correctly? Using a recipe correctly depends largely upon your knowledge and skill...

. . . in selecting the recipe.

. . . in selecting the ingredients.

. . . in deciding which equipment to use.

. . . in preheating the oven to the correct temperature and in using the right amount of heat when cooking on top of the range.

. . . in understanding the terms used in the recipe.

. . . in measuring the ingredients.

. . . in following the directions.

. . . in applying basic principles of cooking.

. . . in managing so that the food is ready to serve at the right time and at the correct temperature.

HOW TO SELECT A RECIPE

Many people have the reputation for being a good cook merely because they prepare certain dishes especially well. You, too, can have such a reputation if you will learn to use a few basic recipes well. Then, little by little, you can add more and more recipes to your collection.

When selecting a recipe, you should consider the following:

1. *The amount of experience that you have had:* The first recipes you use should be very simple and easy to understand. Then, as you gain experience, you can select more difficult recipes.
2. *How the recipe will fit in with the rest of the meal:* See page 64.
3. *The ingredients called for in the recipe:* Have you all of the ingredients, or will you have to buy some?
4. *The equipment:* Have you the correct equipment? What is the best size of mixing bowl, cake pan, saucepan, and so on, to use?
5. *The cost:* Foods which are expensive are not necessarily the best.
6. *The length of time that is needed to prepare and serve the recipe:* Can the recipe be partially prepared one day and cooked the next day so that it can be used in short class periods? (See page 399.)
7. *The number of people to be served:* Can the proportions in the recipe be changed to suit the size of your family? (See page 436.)
8. *The oven:* Will the oven be needed for cooking more than one dish? If so, can the dishes be cooked at the same temperature?
9. *The source:* Did you obtain the recipe from a reliable source?

Always check the recipe after you have copied it to make sure that you have made no errors.

Patteson

Julio G. Huante

For best results, use only the ingredients that are called for in the recipe, especially if you are using it for the first time. When in doubt, always check to make sure that you are using the correct ingredients. For example, if a recipe calls for gelatin, would you use sweetened or unsweetened gelatin? Your choice could mean the success or failure of your recipe.

Sweetened gelatin: Sweetened gelatin, or ready-mixed gelatin, contains sugar and flavoring. Only hot water needs to be added to it. Fruit juice or sirup from canned fruits may be used in place of part of the water.

Gelatin: Plain gelatin, which comes in boxes of four envelopes, may be bought in granulated or powdered form. It should first be softened in cold water and then dissolved in boiling water. Since plain gelatin is unsweetened and has no flavor, sugar, fruit juice, or some other flavoring, and a few grains of salt may be added.

Courtesy Knox Gelatine

HOW TO SELECT THE EQUIPMENT

Selecting the correct equipment is as important as selecting the correct ingredients. Food cooked in a saucepan without a lid requires more water than food cooked in one with a lid. The tighter the lid, the less water is needed. Hence, recipes often vary the amount of water to be used. Many foods do not require any water when cooked in a saucepan with a very tight-fitting lid.

Using a cooking utensil of the correct size is also important. To prevent the loss of vitamins, vegetables should be cooked in as small a utensil as possible. Rice, macaroni, and other cereal products swell when cooked. Hence, a large cooking utensil is needed. Candy and frosting boil up to a large amount. Therefore, they, too, should be cooked in a large saucepan. Cakes rise after being put into the oven. If a cake pan is too large, the layer will be thin. If the cake pan is too small, the batter will run over. A cake baked in a pan of the correct size, however, will be gently rounded and even with the edge of the pan (below left). To measure a cake pan, measure from one side to the other, and then measure the depth (below right).

Too large   Too small   Just right

HOW TO UNDERSTAND THE RECIPE

Table of measurements: When it is necessary to change from one type of measurement to another, you will need to know the following:

3 teaspoons = 1 tablespoon		4 quarts = 1 gallon
16 tablespoons = 1 cup		4 tablespoons = ¼ cup
1 cup = ½ pint		2 tablespoons = ⅛ cup
2 cups = 1 pint		16 ounces = 1 pound
2 pints = 1 quart		8 ounces = ½ pound

Changing the amount: Since measurements for two, four, and six servings are listed in the recipes in this book, it will not be necessary for you to change the proportions. In other books, some recipes are for four servings, other recipes are for six servings, and some are for eight or more servings. When using such recipes, it may be necessary to change the proportions to suit your needs. If you do, change all proportions before you start, and write them down. Then recheck your work so that there will be no error. To divide a recipe in half, divide each amount by 2. To divide it into thirds, divide each amount by 3. For measurements less than 1 cup, change the proportions into tablespoons and then divide by ½, ⅓, ¼, and so on. To save time, measure fractions of a cup rather than tablespoons.

1 cup = 16 tablespoons		⅓ cup = 5⅓ tablespoons
½ cup = 8 tablespoons		⅔ cup = 10⅔ tablespoons
¼ cup = 4 tablespoons		⅛ cup = 2 tablespoons
¾ cup = 12 tablespoons		

⅜ cup = 6 tablespoons or ¼ cup plus 2 tablespoons
⅝ cup = 10 tablespoons or ½ cup plus 2 tablespoons
⅞ cup = 14 tablespoons or ¾ cup plus 2 tablespoons

The servings for four and six in the recipes on pages 476-548 are smaller than average family-size servings. Hence, you may wish to increase the amounts when you use the recipes at home.

Abbreviations: Abbreviations are not used in the recipes in this book. In other books the following abbreviations are used most frequently:

teaspoon	*t* or *tsp.*	pint	*pt.*	ounce	*oz.*
tablespoon	*T* or *tbsp.*	quart	*qt.*	few grains	*f.g.*
cup	C	pound	*lb.* or #	speck	*spk.*

Equivalents: When you are deciding on the amount to buy, the following list of equivalents should be helpful:

1 pound cheese (American or Cheddar) = 4 cups grated
1 can (14½ ounces) evaporated milk = 1⅔ cups
¼ pound chopped nuts = 1 cup
¼ pound marshmallows = 16 large marshmallows
9 finely crumbled salted crackers = 1 cup crumbs
11 finely crumbled graham crackers = 1 cup crumbs
1 medium lemon = 3 tablespoons juice

HOW TO MEASURE ACCURATELY

For best results, use standard measuring cups, spoons, and so on, when measuring ingredients, not just any cup or spoon.

Use measuring spoons when measuring less than ¼ cup (4 tablespoons equal ¼ cup). Use a dry measuring cup when measuring flour, sugar, meal, and other dry ingredients. Use a liquid measuring cup when measuring milk, water, fruit juice, and other liquids.

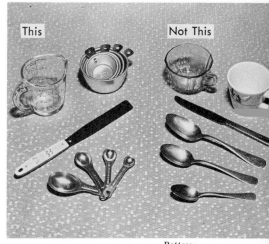

Patteson

Patteson

When measuring amounts not marked on the dry measuring cups, remember the equivalent measurements listed on page 436.

Patteson

437

Sift white flour before measuring. Stir whole-wheat flour and presifted flour with a fork before measuring.

Courtesy Betty Crocker of General Mills

Put flour into a dry measuring cup until the cup is more than full. Do not shake the cup or tap it on the table. If you do, the flour will "pack" and you will have too much.

Level off the cup of flour with a spatula or the back edge of a knife. When you empty the cup, tap the bottom to be sure that you have removed all the flour.

Courtesy Betty Crocker of General Mills

When measuring less than ¼ cup, it is not necessary to sift the flour. Instead, fill the measuring spoon to overflowing. Then level it off with a spatula or the back edge of a knife (below left). To measure ½ tablespoon flour, first measure 1 tablespoon. Next divide the amount in half, and push out the un-wanted part (below right).

Courtesy Betty Crocker of General Mills

Photos below by Patteson

DRY INGREDIENTS

Put sugar into a dry measuring cup. Level off the cup of sugar with a spatula or the back edge of a knife. If at all lumpy, the sugar should be sifted first.

Courtesy Betty Crocker of General Mills

Put brown sugar into a dry measuring cup. Pack it just firmly enough with the back of a spoon for it to hold the shape of the cup when turned out. If brown sugar is lumpy, press it through a coarse sieve, heat it in a warm oven for a few minutes, or roll out hard lumps with a rolling pin.

Courtesy Western Beet Sugar

Sift confectioners' or powdered sugar to remove lumps. Using a small sifter, you may sift the sugar right into a dry measuring cup. Otherwise use a tablespoon to lift the sugar carefully into the cup until it is more than full. Do not shake the cup, as that will cause the sugar to "pack." Next, level off the cup with a spatula or the back edge of a knife.

Cocoa, baking powder, and soda should be stirred before they are measured if there are any lumps (below right). Use your measuring spoons for measuring, not for stirring (below left).

Patteson

Courtesy Pillsbury Mills, Inc.

Patteson

439

HOW TO MEASURE SHORTENING

Photos by Patteson

To measure ½ cup shortening by the cold-water method, first measure ½ cup water (above left).

Add shortening a little at a time (above right) until the water rises to the 1-cup mark when the shortening is pushed under the water (below left).

Pour off the water. There will be ½ cup shortening in the cup (below right).

When measuring various amounts of shortening, keep the following in mind:

For ¾ cup shortening, use ¼ cup water.
For ⅔ cup shortening, use ⅓ cup water.
For ⅓ cup shortening, use ⅔ cup water.
For ¼ cup shortening, use ¾ cup water.

Photos by Patteson

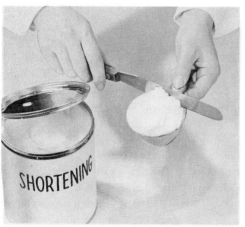 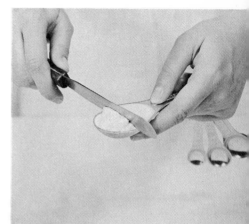

To measure shortening in a graduated measuring cup or spoon, pack it so that all air spaces are pressed out. Then level it off with a spatula or the back edge of a knife (above left).

When measuring less than ¼ cup, use a tablespoon. Hold your finger under the bowl of the spoon as you dip it into the shortening and as you level it off to avoid bending or breaking the handle (above right).

Shortening is easy to measure when it is at room temperature.

HOW TO MEASURE GRATED CHEESE AND GROUND MEAT

Shredded or grated cheese, ground meat, or chopped meat should be packed lightly into the measuring cup.

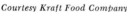

HOW TO MEASURE BUTTER, MARGARINE, AND CHOCOLATE

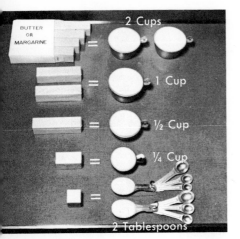

Butter and margarine are usually bought in 1-pound packages of four sticks which weigh ¼ pound each. When measuring butter or margarine, you will find it helpful to remember:

4 sticks, or 1 pound = 2 cups
2 sticks, or ½ pound = 1 cup
1 stick, or ¼ pound = ½ cup
      ½ stick = ¼ cup or 4 tablespoons
      ¼ stick = 2 tablespoons

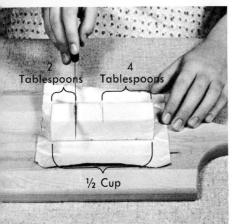

When a recipe calls for ½ cup butter or margarine, use one stick (¼ pound). For ¼ cup or 4 tablespoons, divide the stick in half. For only 2 tablespoons, use ¼ stick of butter or margarine.

Most chocolate comes in 1-ounce squares or blocks. In other words, each square equals 1 ounce. Each square is marked down the center and can be broken evenly and easily into ½-ounce sections. For ¼ ounce, cut a ½-ounce section in half.

Photos by Patteson

HOW TO MEASURE LIQUIDS

Julio G. Huante

Patteson

To measure a liquid, place the cup on a flat surface and pour the liquid to the desired line. Always check the measurement at eye level.

Pour thick liquids, such as honey, sirup, or molasses, into the measuring spoon or cup. Level off the top or check the amount carefully just before the cup mark is reached since thick liquids tend to pile up. Use a rubber scraper to remove all the liquid from the cup.

Patteson

Patteson

443

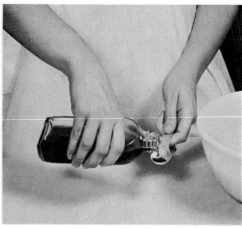

Patteson   *Courtesy Betty Crocker of General Mills*

To measure a tablespoon of a thin liquid, such as milk or water, dip the measuring spoon into the liquid and lift it out. Make sure that it is completely full (above left).

When measuring flavoring, hold the measuring spoon to one side of the mixing bowl as you pour the flavoring into the spoon. Otherwise, you might spill some and get too much flavoring into whatever you are making (above right).

HOW TO MEASURE SPICES

To measure spices, dip a small measuring spoon into the ingredient. Then level it off with the edge of the can or a spatula. Hold a large spoon over wax paper or a small plate, and shake the spice into it.

To measure less than ¼ teaspoon, use your fingers or divide ¼ teaspoon in half. Each half equals ⅛ teaspoon. When ⅛ teaspoon is divided in half, each part equals $1/16$ teaspoon, which is usually referred to as a "few grains," a "speck," a "dash," or a "pinch."

Photos by Patteson

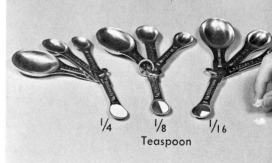

¼   ⅛ $1/16$
Teaspoon

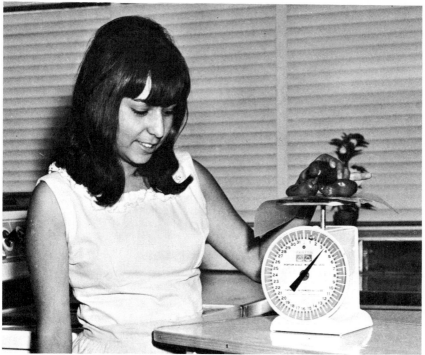

Courtesy Las Cruces, New Mexico Public Schools

Before putting food on a scale to be weighed, check to make sure that the pointer is even with the zero on the dial.

If it is necessary to weigh food in a bowl or a container, put the empty bowl or container which is to hold the food on the scale. Then turn the dial until the pointer is even with the zero (below left). If you follow this method, the weight of the bowl will not be added to the weight of the food. Add shortening, nuts, or whatever food you wish to measure until the pointer indicates the amount called for in the recipe (below right).

Photos Courtesy Hanson

Patteson

Peel: To pull off the outer skin or rind. For example, you peel a banana, an orange, or a cooked potato.

Pare: To cut off the skin or rind with a knife. For example, you pare an apple or a raw potato.

Courtesy Cutco

Scrape: To remove the skin by rubbing it with the sharp edge of a knife.

Break: To divide lettuce or other salad greens into pieces (below left).

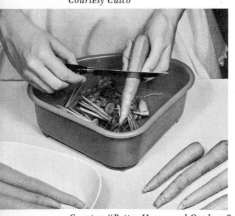

Tear: To pull salad greens into pieces.

Slice: To cut across into flat pieces (below right). See picture of celery being sliced on page 414.

Courtesy "Better Homes and Gardens Salad Book"

Patteson

Courtesy Cutco

PREPARATION TERMS

Cut into strips: To cut into long, narrow pieces. To cut strips of a potato, first cut it into lengthwise slices. Hold the slices together, and turn the potato over. Again cut lengthwise slices to make long, narrow strips (right).

Julienne: To cut into thin, matchlike strips.

Patteson

Dice: To cut into small pieces of uniform size and shape. To dice a potato, first cut long strips. Then hold the long strips together as you cut crosswise to make cubes.

Cube: To cut into pieces of uniform size. Meat may be cut into 1- to 2-inch cubes, but most foods are cut into ¼- to ½-inch cubes.

Patteson

Cut into halves: To cut into two equal parts. To cut crosswise, hold one end of the fruit and cut across it (below left). To cut lengthwise, hold both ends of the fruit, and cut the long way (below right).

Wedge: To cut into the shape of a wedge. This means that each piece is thick at one end and thin at the other.

Photos by Patteson   *Courtesy The Aluminum Cooking Utensil Co., Inc.*

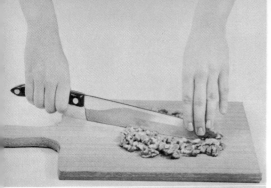

Chop: To cut into small, uneven pieces with a knife or a chopper. To use a French (chopping) knife, hold the tip of the blade with your left hand as you move the handle up and down in a semicircle with your right hand. Celery, carrots, onions, and parsley may be chopped in this manner. They may also be chopped in a chopping bowl.

Courtesy Cutco

Chop finely: See *mince* (page 449).

Patteson

Shred: To cut into thin, narrow strips with a knife or a shredder. For steamed cabbage, use coarsely shredded cabbage. For cole slaw, use finely shredded cabbage cut with a knife or shredder. When using a shredder, rub the food in one direction only.

Patteson

Grate: To rub food against a grater in a circular motion or back and forth to cut it into fine pieces. To grate lemon rind, rub it against the grater, removing only the colored part of the rind.

Patteson

448

Mince: To cut or chop into tiny pieces. To mince parsley with scissors, hold the leaves of several stalks between the thumb and the forefinger of your left hand as you cut tiny pieces.

To mince onion, slice off the end of the onion. Then make small squares, cutting into the onion as deep as you like. Next, cut thin slices crosswise so that the minced onion will drop off. Another way to cut onion very fine is to rub it on a medium-sized grater. For onion juice, slice off the end of the onion and scrape juice from the center with a teaspoon.

Grind: To put food through a food chopper, sometimes called a "meat grinder."

Flake: To separate fish into small pieces (see picture on page 295) or to break fish apart lightly with a fork (see picture on page 296).

Mash: To press food into a pulp or into small pieces with an up-and-down or beating motion of a fork, a potato masher, or a pastry blender.

Patteson

449

Purée: To rub food, such as cooked vegetables and fruits, through a sieve or a food mill to make a smooth semiliquid mixture for use in soups or sauces or as food for babies. (See page 119.) The food may also be put in an electric blender.

Pound: To beat meat with a mallet or the edge of a saucer to break the connective tissues and make the meat more tender. Sometimes flour is rubbed or pounded into the meat to absorb the juices.

Rub bowl: To move a clove of garlic back and forth across a bowl to give a garlic flavor to a vegetable or meat salad. Using a garlic press to distribute garlic juice over the salad, if you have one, is easier than rubbing a bowl.

Toss: To mix lightly by lifting the ingredients for a salad with a spoon and a fork or with two forks to avoid bruising the ingredients.

Marinate: To let food, such as meat and salad ingredients, stand in French dressing or an oil-acid mixture to add flavor.

Soak: To put food in enough liquid to cover for a specified length of time.

Slit: To cut a long, narrow opening without cutting all the way through.

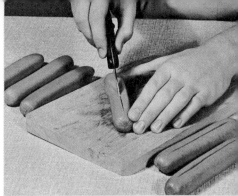

Gash: To cut a deep opening, as in a baked potato.

Snip: To cut a small amount with one short stroke.

Pierce: To stick a fork into a food, such as a baked potato, to allow the steam to escape. See picture of pastry being pierced on page 356.

Core: To remove the seeds and the core of an apple. To do this, insert an apple corer about two-thirds of the way down toward the blossom end. Hold the apple firmly, and twist the apple corer to remove the core.

Cut sticky foods: To cut sticky foods, such as dates, raisins, or marshmallows, use scissors or a knife. Dip the cutting utensil into water or powdered sugar frequently.

Pit: To remove the pit or the seed from dates, prunes, cherries, or other fruits.

Cream: To rub, mash, or work shortening, or shortening and sugar, against the side of a bowl with the back of a spoon until it is smooth and creamy.

Soften: To cream butter, margarine, or shortening until it is smooth and creamy, or to let it stand at room temperature until it is soft.

Courtesy Betty Crocker of General Mills

Stir: To move a spoon round and round in a bowl, a double boiler, or a saucepan to mix the ingredients. When you stir food in a double boiler or in a saucepan over heat, the spoon should touch the bottom and the sides to prevent the food from sticking.

Patteson

Blend: To mix two or more ingredients until you cannot tell one ingredient from another. You may use either a stirring motion or a creaming motion.

Beat: To make the mixture smooth and light by lifting it over and over. When beating by hand with a spoon, a fork, or a wire whip, tilt the bowl slightly. When using a rotary beater, move it back and forth across the bowl. When using an electric mixer, use a rubber scraper. (See picture on page 333.)

Whip: To beat rapidly with a whisk beater (below left), a rotary beater (below right), or an electric mixer to incorporate air and to increase volume in egg whites, whipping cream, or whipped gelatin.

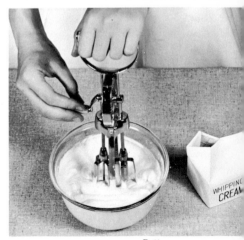

Courtesy Betty Crocker of General Mills

Fold: To add beaten egg whites or whipped cream to a mixture without losing the air that has been beaten into them. To do this, gently push a whisk beater, a spoon, or a rubber scraper down through the mixture, across the bottom of the bowl, and then up and over the top. Repeat this folding process, turning the bowl often, until the egg whites or the whipped cream disappear into the mixture.

Courtesy "Better Homes and Gardens"

Cut in: To combine shortening and dry ingredients when making biscuits or pastry. Use a pastry blender or two knives, and cut the shortening again and again. You may use your fingertips, but the heat of your hand will soften the shortening and prevent the pastry from being flaky, especially if you work slowly.

Press: To pack or push down on a mixture or an ingredient.

Patteson

454

Courtesy "Better Homes and Gardens"

Dip: To put food into something and take it out quickly. For example, to dip meat or fish into an egg-and-milk mixture (below left).

Bread: To cover food with bread crumbs. For example, before the meat for breaded steak is cooked, it is dipped into an egg-and-milk mixture and then into fine bread crumbs. (See recipe on page 513.)

Coat: To cover all sides of a food with a mixture — such as one made with egg and milk — or with only one ingredient — such as flour, bread crumbs, icing, sugar, or crushed nuts.

Roll in flour: To coat a food with flour. (See picture on page 280.)

Dredge: To coat with a dry ingredient, such as flour, fine bread crumbs, sugar, or meal. The food may be sprinkled, dipped, or rolled in one of the ingredients. (See picture on page 290.)

Sprinkle: To scatter sugar, flour, and so on, over food (below right).

Dust: To sprinkle lightly with flour or sugar.

Flour: To sprinkle or cover lightly with flour.

Sift: To put dry ingredients through a sifter. (See picture on page 436.)

Batter: A mixture of flour, a liquid, and other ingredients that will pour or drop. Griddlecakes (page 320), waffles (page 321), and popovers are made with a *pour batter.* Muffins (page 319) and cakes are made with a *drop batter.*

Dough: A mixture of flour, a liquid, and other ingredients which is thick enough to hold its shape when dropped from a spoon, as in drop biscuits, or thick enough to be kneaded and rolled, as in rolled biscuits (page 317). Biscuits and drop cookies are made with a *soft dough* (pages 316 and 328). Yeast bread is made with a *stiff dough* (page 324).

Patteson

Courtesy Betty Crocker of General Mills

455

Simmer: To cook just below the boiling point. Small bubbles form on the bottom of the saucepan and slowly rise to the surface.

Boil gently: To cook in a liquid when medium-sized bubbles appear at the bottom of the saucepan and then rise to the top and break on the surface.

Boil rapidly: To cook in a liquid when large bubbles rise rapidly and break all over the surface. Food cooks just as quickly in gently boiling water as in rapidly boiling water. Besides, the food does not break up so easily and less fuel is used.

Bland

Blanch or scald: To pour boiling water over a food or to dip the food into boiling water and then into cold water to loosen the skins of tomatoes and peaches, for example, or to get some foods ready for the freezer.

Lukewarm: Milk or another liquid is lukewarm when a few drops placed on the inside of the arm are pleasantly warm, neither too hot nor too cold.

Scald: To heat a liquid, usually milk, in the upper part of a double boiler until tiny bubbles appear around the edge. If a scum forms on top of the milk, beat it with a rotary beater because the scum contains valuable proteins.

Courtesy Wooster Rubber Company

456

Scald also means "to pour boiling water" over dishes, and so on.

Steam: To cook food by steam in a covered steamer rather than in boiling water. The steam from the boiling water below rises through the holes in the steamer to cook the food. Food cooked in a pressure saucepan is also cooked by steam. Because of the pressure saucepan's tight-fitting lid, the steam becomes much hotter and cooks the food more quickly than in a steamer or by boiling.

Courtesy Saladmaster

Poach: To cook eggs, fish, and other foods in a hot liquid just below the boiling point.

Steep: To cover tea leaves or the like with boiling water and allow to stand, to extract the flavor, color, and aroma from the leaves.

Melt: To change a solid to a liquid by heating, as in melting chocolate or butter. To melt chocolate, put it in a custard cup or a small bowl and place the cup or bowl in a strainer over hot, not boiling, water.

Courtesy "Better Homes and Gardens"

Tea Council of U.S.A., Inc.

Patteson

Courtesy Fearn Food, Inc.

Baste: To moisten food while it is being baked to prevent it from drying out. This may be done by pouring a liquid over the food with a spoon or by using a brush (page 297) or a baster.

Brush: To use a brush, folded paper, or a cloth to spread a thin coat of melted butter, oil, or beaten egg on food.

Grease: To rub food or a pan lightly with shortening or salad oil. (See picture on page 336.)

Spread: To cover with a thin layer, as to spread butter or mayonnaise on bread when making sandwiches. (See picture on page 228.)

Dot: To put small pieces of butter, cheese, and nuts, for example, on top of food. (See picture on page 174.)

Drain: To pour off fat, liquid, or drippings from a food (left); to allow food which has been cooked in fat to drain on a paper towel (below).

Drippings: The fat or juice which comes out of meat, such as bacon or a roast, while it is cooking.

Courtesy Armour and Company

Courtesy Scott Paper Company

Preheat: To heat an oven to the correct temperature before putting in the food to cook.

Bake: To cook in an oven.

Toast: To brown by direct heat, as to toast bread (page 314), marshmallows, or coconut.

Roast: To cook meat or poultry uncovered in an oven without added moisture. (See picture on page 275.)

Broil: To cook by direct heat under a broiler or over the hot coals of an open fire. (See pictures on page 274.)

Pan-broil: To cook meat uncovered in a lightly greased or ungreased skillet on top of a range. Pour off the fat as it accumulates so that the food will not fry.

Barbecue: To baste meat from time to time with a highly seasoned sauce as it cooks by direct heat over coals, in an oven, or under a broiler. Turn the meat frequently so that all sides will brown evenly. (See picture on page 291.)

Fry: To cook in hot fat without water or a cover.

Pan-fry or sauté: To cook in a small amount of fat. (See picture on page 277.)

Shallow-fry: To cook in enough hot fat to cover food partially. (See picture on page 290.)

Deep-fat-fry: To cook in enough hot fat to cover food completely. (See picture on page 424.)

Braise: To brown meat or vegetables in a small amount of hot fat and then cook slowly in a covered pan with a small amount of liquid. (See picture on page 278.)

Fricassee: To cook poultry, rabbit, or veal by braising. The meat is usually cut into pieces and served in gravy or sauce. (See picture on page 289.)

Sear: To brown meat quickly on all sides at a high temperature to develop flavor and improve the appearance.

Stew: To cook food for a long time in a small amount of liquid at a simmering temperature. Stewed fruit and stewed meat are examples. (See pictures on pages 279 and 289.)

Season: To add salt, pepper, spices, herbs, or other seasonings to improve the flavor of food.

Season to taste: To season according to the individual preference. Since some people prefer more seasoning than others, recipes often say, "Season to taste."

Tender: Food is tender when it is easily cut or soft enough so that a fork can be stuck into it easily. Many foods are tested for doneness with a fork.

Test for doneness: There are ways of making sure that foods are ready to be served. See the following pages: vegetables, page 188; sauce, page 218; meat, page 275; fried chicken, page 290; roast or baked chicken, page 291; fish, page 296; macaroni, page 308; cake, page 338; candy, page 342; baked custard, page 347; soft custard, page 347; cream pie, page 353.

Undiluted   Water   Diluted
Evaporated Milk   Evaporated Milk

Patteson

HOW TO PREPARE
FORMS OF MILK

1 cup undiluted evaporated milk plus 1 cup water makes 2 cups diluted milk. Diluted evaporated milk may be used when recipes call for milk.

⅓ Cup   ¾ Cup   1 Cup

Patteson

⅓ cup nonfat dry-milk powder plus ¾ cup water equals 1 cup nonfat milk. If dry-milk powder is mixed with water the night before it is to be used, the flavor will be improved. For a richer-tasting drink, mix nonfat milk with fresh whole milk.

Sour Milk

Patteson

To make sour milk, add 1 tablespoon vinegar to 1 cup sweet milk. Use in recipes which call for sour milk or buttermilk.

To whip nonfat dry milk, sprinkle an equal amount of nonfat dry-milk powder over ice-cold water or fruit juice. Beat with a rotary beater or an electric mixer until thick.

Courtesy American Dry Milk Institute, Inc.

HOW TO WHIP
EVAPORATED MILK

Put the bowl and the beaters in the refrigerator to chill.

Patteson

Pour the amount of undiluted evaporated milk called for in the recipe into an ice-cube tray. Put the tray in the freezing compartment of the refrigerator.

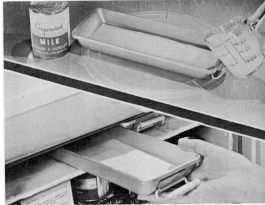

Courtesy Evaporated Milk Association

Chill the tray of evaporated milk until tiny ice crystals begin to form around the edges of the milk. Then pour the ice-cold evaporated milk into the chilled bowl, and beat until it begins to thicken.

Courtesy Evaporated Milk Association

Add lemon juice and sugar according to the recipe. Recipes usually call for about 2 tablespoons lemon juice and 2 tablespoons sugar for each cup of evaporated milk. Beat until very stiff, and serve immediately.

Courtesy Evaporated Milk Association

461

HOW TO USE LEFTOVER BREAD

Courtesy American Institute of Baking

Patteson

Soft bread crumbs: To make soft bread crumbs, tear day-old bread into small pieces with your fingers or a fork. Soft bread crumbs are used in bread pudding, poultry stuffing, and meat loaf. They are often used as a thickening for sauces.

Dry bread crumbs: To make dry bread crumbs, put bread in a very slow oven (250° F.) until it is crisp or leave the bread overnight in an oven which has a pilot. Crush crisp bread with a rolling pin. To save time, put the crisp bread in a paper bag before crushing. Dry bread crumbs may be used to coat foods which are to be cooked in fat. They may also be used for scalloped dishes.

Croutons: To make toasted bread cubes, or croutons, to be served with soup, first cut buttered or unbuttered bread into strips. Then cut the bread in the opposite direction to form cubes (below left). Toast in a slow oven (300° F.) until the bread cubes are golden brown on all sides, turning occasionally (below right). Croutons may also be sautéed, that is, pan-fried in a small amount of butter or margarine, until they are golden brown.

Photos Courtesy American Institute of Baking

HOW TO MAKE TOAST SHELLS

To make toast shells, remove the outside crust from bread and spread one side with melted butter or margarine.

Put the bread slices in muffin pans with the buttered sides down. Press the bread into the shape of the muffin pan.

Bake in a moderate oven (350° F.) for 20 minutes, or until toast shells are a delicate brown.

Fill the toasted patty shells with creamed meat, eggs, or vegetables, and serve.

Photos Courtesy Kraft Foods Company

463

Photos by Patteson

How to break an egg: Hold the egg firmly, and give it a quick hard lick on the edge of a bowl or with a knife.

How to pull the shell apart: Hold the egg with the cracked side up just above a bowl. Put your thumbs on each side of the crack, and carefully pull the shell open. Break one egg at a time into a separate bowl to make sure that each is fresh.

How to separate the yolk from the white: As you pull the shell apart, hold it so that the yolk remains in one half of the shell and the white slips over the sides of the shell into the bowl (below left). Pour the yolk into the other half of the shell, being careful not to break it, and allow the remaining egg white to run into the bowl (below right).

Photos by Patteson

HOW TO MEASURE BEATEN EGGS

Most recipes call for a certain number of eggs without saying what size egg. Many recipes in this book require only part of an egg. Hence, it is suggested that you use a certain number of tablespoons of egg.

To measure part of an egg: Break the whole egg into a small bowl, and beat with a fork or a rotary beater until it is a uniform yellow color. Then dip the measuring spoon to the bottom of the cup or bowl so that you have a tablespoon of egg rather than only foam.

Julio G. Huante

NUMBER OF TABLESPOONS IN ONE EGG

SIZE OF EGG	MINIMUM WEIGHT PER DOZEN	AVERAGE VOLUME PER EGG
Jumbo	30 ounces	5 tablespoons
Extra large	27 ounces	4½ tablespoons
Large	24 ounces	4 tablespoons
Medium	21 ounces	3½ tablespoons
Small	18 ounces	3 tablespoons
Peewee	15 ounces	2½ tablespoons

HOW TO BEAT EGG WHITES

Do not remove the eggs from the refrigerator until you are ready to separate the egg whites from the yolks. Eggs separate more easily when they are cold. Do not return the egg whites to the refrigerator because egg whites at room temperature will beat up to a larger volume than those which have just been taken from the refrigerator. The bowl should have a rounded bottom so that the bottom of the beaters will be covered. Keep the beaters moving over the entire bowl so that all of the egg whites will be beaten.

Patteson

Photos by Patteson

Slightly beaten egg whites have large air bubbles, are transparent, and flow easily when one side of the bowl is lifted (above left).

Foamy or frothy egg whites are light and thick but do not quite hold their shape when the beater is lifted (above right).

Stiffly beaten egg whites have soft rounded peaks which droop over slightly when the beater is lifted (below left). They are very white and have smaller air cells than the foamy egg whites. The surface is moist and glossy.

Very stiffly beaten egg whites will stand in pointed peaks when the beater is lifted (below right). They have tiny air cells and will slowly slide to one side of the bowl when it is tilted or will not slide at all. The surface is glossy, but not so glossy as the stiffly beaten egg whites, which have rounded peaks.

Photos by Patteson

Photos Courtesy Wesson Oil and Snowdift Sales Company

Wash leafy vegetables under running water (above left), or lift them up and down in a pan of cold water, changing the water as often as necessary. (See picture on page 186.) Wash celery, carrots, and other sturdy vegetables by rubbing them with your hands or with a vegetable brush under running water.

Dry vegetables if they are to be used in a salad. Otherwise the salad will be watery. You can remove most of the excess water from salad greens by shaking them. To remove additional water, shake the salad greens in a clean towel (above right), or pat them dry with a paper towel. Drain or pat sturdy vegetables.

To separate the leaves of a head of lettuce, cut the core out of the center of the head with the point of a knife (below left). Then hold the lettuce under cold running water so that the force of the water will separate the leaves without breaking them (below right). If only a few leaves are needed or if pieces of the lettuce are to be used, remove only the end of the core. Then pull off the number of leaves or the amount of lettuce needed.

Julio G. Huante   *Courtesy Wesson Oil and Snowdrift Sales Company*

Julio G. Huante

Wash and dry a grapefruit which has been chilled. Then hold the stem end of the grapefruit firmly with one hand, and cut the grapefruit in half crosswise. Remove the seeds.

Cut around each section separately, using a fruit knife or a sharp paring knife (below left).

Remove the center core by cutting it out with scissors or a sharp knife (below right).

Photos Courtesy Florida Citrus Commission

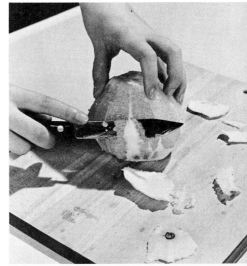

Photos Courtesy Florida Citrus Commission

Hold the fruit firmly as you remove the skin with a sharp knife by cutting it in strips from the top, the stem end, to the bottom. Cut deep enough to remove the white membrane.

To remove the sections, cut on each side of the white membrane which separates the sections. Then lift out the sections, and remove the seeds. To slice an orange, hold it firmly but not too tightly with your left hand, and cut slices with a sharp knife.

Courtesy Florida Citrus Commission   *Courtesy Sunkist Growers*

Courtesy Wesson Oil and Snowdrift Sales Company

To make radish roses: Cut off the root end, but leave part of the top, if desired. Cut down the sides close to the skin in four or five places to form petals. Chill the radish in ice water, and the petals will open like a rose.

To make radish chrysanthemums: Slice off the root end. Then make small squares by cutting into the radish first one way and then another, but do not cut clear through. Drop the radish into ice water so that it will spread out like a chrysanthemum.

To make radish accordions: Remove both ends. Cut into the radish as if you were slicing it, but do not cut clear through. Chill the radish in ice water so that it will fan out like an accordion.

To make green pepper rings: Cut into circles. Then remove the center and the seeds.

To make green pepper sticks: Remove the stem and the seeds. Then cut into lengthwise strips.

To make scalloped slices: Pull the tines of a fork down the side of a cucumber or a peeled banana. Repeat all the way around. Cut into crosswise slices.

Photos by Patteson

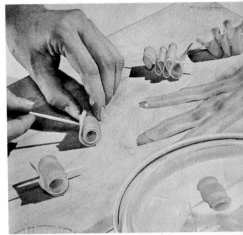

Photos Courtesy "Better Homes and Gardens Salad Book"

To make carrot curls: Wash carrots and remove the skins. Cut into thin lengthwise slices with a parer. Roll up long slices, and fasten them with toothpicks. Drop the slices into ice water to make them crisp. Remove the toothpicks before serving.

To make carrot zigzags: Put thin lengthwise slices of carrot on toothpicks in accordion style. Chill the slices in ice water 2 to 3 hours to make them hold their shape. Remove the toothpicks before serving.

To make celery curls: Cut celery stalks into 2- to 3-inch pieces. Make narrow parallel cuts in the ends of each piece. Leave about ½ inch in the center uncut. Put the pieces in ice water to make the ends curl.

To make tomato flowers: Cut a tomato across as though you were cutting wedges, but do not cut the base. Pull the tomato open partially or completely, and fill it with chicken salad or cottage cheese. (See pages 288 and 493.)

Photos by Patteson

Courtesy Sunkist Growers

To make lemon garnishes: Slice a lemon crosswise. Then cut into various shapes as shown. Because of their color and sharp flavor, garnishes made from lemons may be used on many foods.

To cut melon balls: Roll a ball cutter or a measuring spoon from right to left and left to right as it cuts into a cantaloupe, a honeydew melon, or a watermelon. Turn the handle completely around to make sure that all sides have been cut. Then lift out the melon ball.

To use a cutter: Cut bright-colored vegetables, fruits, pimentos, cranberry jelly, or candied fruit into different shapes, and place the pieces on various foods to add a special touch of color.

Courtesy "Better Homes and Gardens Salad Book"

Patteson

SUMMARY OF PRINCIPLES OF COOKERY

As you develop a better understanding of the principles of cookery, following a recipe will be easier, the results will be better, the food will be more nutritious, and you will be less likely to make errors. Some of the most common principles of cookery you have learned while studying this book are:

1. Fruit should be cooked slowly. If you wish fresh fruit to hold its shape, add sugar at the beginning of the cooking. Otherwise, do not add sugar until just before removing the fruit from the heat. (See page 175.)

2. To save minerals and vitamins, vegetables should be cooked in large pieces in a small amount of water only until tender in a pan with a lid. However, to prevent green vegetables from turning dark, the lid should be left off for the first 2 to 3 minutes.

3. To prevent lumps, flour or cornstarch should be mixed with sugar or melted fat before a liquid is added.

4. Milk is usually cooked in a double boiler because it scorches easily.

5. Egg whites cannot be beaten stiffly if egg yolk or fat is present.

6. Egg whites will beat up to a larger volume (amount) if they are at room temperature than they will if they are cold.

7. Add hot mixture to beaten egg rather than add the beaten egg to the hot mixture.

8. Eggs and cheese should be cooked at a low temperature because high heat toughens the proteins in these foods.

9. Tender cuts of meat are cooked by dry heat, such as baking or broiling.

10. Less-tender cuts of meat are cooked by moist heat, such as braising or stewing.

11. Meat shrinks less if cooked at a low temperature than if cooked at a high temperature.

12. Poultry, like meat, should be cooked at a low temperature so that it will be juicy, tender, and evenly cooked to the bone.

13. Fish should be cooked just long enough to be easily broken or separated into flakes.

14. Most starchy foods, such as rice and macaroni, should be cooked in a large amount of water because starchy foods absorb water.

15. Cereals should be added to rapidly boiling water to keep the particles separated.

16. Sift white flour before measuring it. Stir whole-wheat flour and presifted flour with a fork before measuring.

17. Many failures are caused by too little or too much stirring. For example, the dry ingredients for muffins should be stirred only until moistened. Otherwise the muffins will have tunnels.

18. Soak unsweetened gelatin in cold water before adding hot liquid. Otherwise the gelatin will not dissolve.

19. When making the sirup for hot cocoa, cook the cocoa and the sugar in a small amount of water to swell the starch grains and give the cocoa a better flavor.

Courtesy Robert May's Kitchens

Always read a recipe several times before you start to prepare the food. Stop and think through each step to be sure that you understand perfectly what you are to do. If terms that you do not understand are used in the recipe, look them up.

Turn on the oven if the food is to be roasted, baked, or broiled. Be sure that you set the heat regulator so that the oven will be at the correct temperature by the time it is needed.

Courtesy Robert May's Kitchens

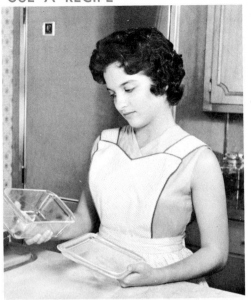

Courtesy Robert May's Kitchens

Get out all the equipment you will need, being careful to select utensils of the correct size. Grease the baking pan, the casserole dish, or other cooking pan, and put it aside out of the way. Put the ingredients which you will need on the table. If possible, measure all the ingredients. Check to make sure that you have everything that you need.

Prepare foods that require special preparation, such as chopping, grating, mincing, melting, or precooking, before you start mixing unless the recipe tells you to do this while something else is cooking.

Courtesy Robert May's Kitchens

475

FRUITS

AMBROSIA

4 student servings		6 student servings
3	MEDIUM ORANGES	5
2 tablespoons	CONFECTIONERS' SUGAR	3 tablespoons
½ cup	SHREDDED COCONUT	¾ cup

STEPS IN PREPARATION

1. Wash and dry the chilled oranges.

2. Remove the skin with a sharp knife by cutting it in strips from the top, the stem end, to the bottom. Cut deep enough to remove the white membrane, as shown in the picture on page 469.

3. Cut the oranges into sections, working over a bowl to catch the juice. Remove the seeds as the sections are cut.

4. Place part of the orange sections in a dessert dish, and sprinkle with the confectioners' sugar and coconut. Repeat by adding another layer of each.

5. Chill, if time permits, and serve as a dessert.

---

2 student servings: 2 small oranges; 1 tablespoon confectioners' sugar; ¼ cup shredded coconut

---

HINTS

1. The oranges may be sliced crosswise instead of being cut into sections.

2. Ambrosia may be placed on lettuce or other salad greens and served as a salad if the sugar is omitted.

3. Toasted coconut, salted peanuts, or almonds may be substituted for the plain coconut. Pineapple chunks or sliced bananas may be substituted for part of the orange sections.

GRAPEFRUIT HALVES

Prepare chilled grapefruit halves as shown in the picture on page 468. Place each half on a serving dish, and garnish with half a maraschino cherry or sprig of mint, if desired. Serve plain, with sugar, or with salt.

FRUIT CUP

4 student servings		6 student servings
1	MEDIUM ORANGE	1½
½	MEDIUM APPLE	1
1	MEDIUM BANANA	1½
½ cup	FRUIT COCKTAIL (canned)	¾ cup
1 cup	PINEAPPLE CHUNKS or SEEDLESS GRAPES	1½ cups

STEPS IN PREPARATION

1. Chill the fruit.

2. Wash and dry the orange, apple, and banana.

3. Remove the skin from the orange, and cut it into sections or pieces, as shown in the pictures on page 469. Remove the seeds.

4. Cut the apple into quarters, remove the core, and cut into ½-inch pieces.

5. Put the orange, apple, drained fruit cocktail, and pineapple chunks or seedless grapes in a mixing bowl.

6. Peel the banana and slice it. Mix lightly with the other fruit.

7. Chill, if time permits.

8. Serve in chilled fruit cups as a dessert or an appetizer.

---

2 student servings: ½ medium orange; ¼ large apple; ½ medium banana; ¼ cup fruit cocktail (canned); ½ cup pineapple chunks or seedless grapes

---

HINTS

1. Fruit cup may be garnished with a fresh strawberry, a maraschino cherry, a sprig of mint, or a few whole blueberries or red raspberries.

2. The following combinations of ingredients may be used in a fruit cup:
   Fresh or canned peaches, pears, and raspberries
   Grapefruit and orange sections
   Bananas with fresh cherries or grapes
   Fresh pineapple chunks and strawberries

3. Fruit cup may be placed on lettuce or other salad greens and served as a salad if it is drained. (See picture on page 198.)

STEWED PRUNES or APRICOTS

4 student servings   **6 student servings**

4 student servings		6 student servings
1 cup	DRIED PRUNES or APRICOTS	1½ cups
1½ cup	WARM WATER	2 cups
2 to 4 tablespoons	SUGAR (if desired)	¼ to ⅓ cup

STEPS IN PREPARATION

1. Wash the dried fruit under running water.

2. Put the washed fruit in a saucepan, and add just enough warm water to cover. Soak 1 to 2 hours, or until the fruit is plump.
   (*NOTE:* Tenderized dried fruits do not have to be soaked, but they should be cooked according to the directions on the package.)

3. Cover the saucepan in which the fruit has been soaked, and cook the fruit slowly 20 to 40 minutes, or until it is tender when pierced with a fork.

4. Add the sugar, if desired, and cook 1 minute, or until the sugar dissolves.

5. Serve (see picture on page 179), or store in a covered glass jar in the refrigerator.

---

2 student servings: ½ cup dried prunes or apricots; ⅔ cup warm water; 1 to 2 tablespoons sugar (if desired)

HINTS

1. To improve the flavor of prunes, add lemon juice (1 tablespoon for each cup) or a small piece of lemon rind at the same time that the sugar is added.

2. For variety in flavor, cook together two or more different kinds of dried fruits.

3. To prepare stuffed prunes for a salad, remove the stones, and fill the centers with cream cheese softened with a little cream.

4. Stewed prunes or apricots may be served with cereal or quick breads. They may be used in muffins and puddings and as a garnish for meat.

APPLESAUCE

4 student servings		6 student servings
4	TART APPLES	6
½ cup	WATER	¾ cup
¼ to ⅓ cup	SUGAR	⅓ to ½ cup
few grains	NUTMEG, CLOVES, and/or CINNAMON (if desired)	⅛ teaspoon

STEPS IN PREPARATION

1. Wash and dry the apples, and cut away any bad spots.

2. Pare them thinly, cut into quarters, and remove the cores.

3. Put the apples in a saucepan, and add the water.

4. Cover and cook slowly 15 to 20 minutes, or until the apples are soft when mashed with a fork against the side of the saucepan.

5. Remove from the heat, and mash with a fork.

6. Add the sugar, and simmer 1 to 2 minutes, or until the sugar dissolves. (*NOTE:* The amount of sugar added depends upon how tart the apples are and upon the sweetness desired.)

7. Add the nutmeg, cloves, and/or cinnamon, if desired.

8. Serve hot or cold. (See picture on page 175.)

---

2 student servings: 2 tart apples; ¼ cup water; 2 to 3 tablespoons sugar; few grains nutmeg, cloves, and/or cinnamon (if desired)

HINTS

1. For a more nutritious applesauce which is also pink in color, leave the skins on when the apples are cooked, and put the cooked apples through a coarse sieve or strainer. (See picture on page 450.)

2. Sweet apples may be used instead of tart apples if lemon juice (2 teaspoons for 4 apples) is added.

479

APPLE CRUMBLE

4 student servings		6 student servings
2	TART APPLES	3
2 tablespoons	WATER	3 tablespoons
⅓ cup (sifted)	ALL-PURPOSE FLOUR	½ cup (sifted)
½ cup	SUGAR	¾ cup
½ teaspoon	SALT	¾ teaspoon
½ teaspoon	CINNAMON	¾ teaspoon
2½ tablespoons	BUTTER or MARGARINE	¼ cup

STEPS IN PREPARATION

1. Turn on the oven, and set the temperature control at 375° F. for a moderate oven.

2. Wash and dry the apples, and cut away any bad spots.

3. Pare them thinly, cut into quarters, and remove the cores.

4. Slice the apples thinly into a greased baking dish, and sprinkle the water over them.

5. Sift the flour, measure it, and put it in a mixing bowl.

6. Add the sugar, salt, cinnamon, and butter or margarine to the flour. Work them together with a fork until crumbly. Spread this mixture over the apples.

7. Bake 30 minutes, or until the apples are tender and the crust is brown.

8. Serve warm with cream.

---

2 student servings: 1 tart apple; 1 tablespoon water; 3 tablespoons sifted all-purpose flour; ¼ cup sugar; ¼ teaspoon salt; ¼ teaspoon cinnamon; 1½ tablespoons butter or margarine

---

HINTS

1. For variety, substitute rolled oats for half the flour.
2. To add sweetness, substitute graham cracker crumbs for flour.
3. If desired, add 1 tablespoon raisins or mincemeat for each apple.

VEGETABLES

TIMETABLE FOR COOKING FRESH VEGETABLES*

The length of time required for cooking a given vegetable by any method cannot be stated exactly because the time differs with the variety and maturity of each, the length of time and the temperature at which the vegetable has been held since it was harvested, and the size of the pieces into which it has been cut. Each vegetable should be cooked for the shortest time necessary to give a palatable product.

The amount of water required for cooking a given vegetable cannot be stated exactly because food cooked in a saucepan without a lid requires more water than food cooked in one with a lid. The tighter the lid, the less water is needed. Hence, recipes often vary the amount of water to be used. Many foods cooked in saucepans with very tight-fitting lids need no water at all.

VEGETABLE	TIME IN MINUTES		
	Boiling	Steaming	Pressure Saucepan (15 pounds pressure)
Asparagus, whole	10 to 20	12 to 30	½ to 1½
Beans, lima, green	20 to 25	25 to 35	1 to 2
Beans, snap, whole	15 to 30	20 to 35	1½ to 3
Beets, new, whole	30 to 45	40 to 60	5 to 10
Broccoli, heavy stalks, split	10 to 15	15 to 20	1½ to 3
Brussels sprouts, whole	10 to 20	10 to 20	1 to 2
Cabbage, green, quartered	10 to 15	15	2 to 3
Cabbage, shredded	3 to 10	8 to 12	½ to 1½
Carrots, young, whole	15 to 25	20 to 30	3 to 5
Carrots, sliced	10 to 20	15 to 25	1½ to 3
Cauliflower, whole	15 to 20	25 to 30	10
Cauliflower, flowerets	8 to 15	10 to 20	1½ to 3
Celery, diced	15 to 18	25 to 30	2 to 3
Corn, on cob	5 to 15	10 to 15	0 to 1½
Okra, sliced	10 to 15	20	3 to 4
Peas, green	8 to 20	10 to 20	0 to 1
Potatoes, white, medium, whole	25 to 40	30 to 45	8 to 11
Potatoes, quartered	20 to 25	20 to 30	3 to 5
Spinach	3 to 10	5 to 12	0 to 1½
Squash, summer, sliced	10 to 20	15 to 20	1½ to 3
Sweetpotatoes, whole	25 to 35	30 to 35	5 to 8

*Adapted from *Handbook of Food Preparation* by the American Home Economics Association.

BUTTERED POTATOES

4 student servings	MEDIUM POTATOES	6 student servings
2 to 3	MEDIUM POTATOES	4 to 5
1 to 1¼ cups	WATER	1 to 1½ cups
½ teaspoon	SALT	¾ teaspoon
1½ tablespoons	BUTTER or MARGARINE	2 tablespoons

STEPS IN PREPARATION

1. Wash the potatoes with a vegetable brush.

2. Pare them very thinly, and cut into quarters. (See picture on page 186.)

3. Put the water in a saucepan, and heat. As soon as the water comes to a boil, add the potatoes and salt. (See pictures on page 187.)

4. Cover the saucepan with a tight-fitting lid. Lower the heat as soon as the water starts to boil again.

5. Boil gently 15 to 25 minutes, or until the potatoes are soft when pierced with a fork. (See picture on page 188.)
   (*NOTE:* If there is any liquid left—but there shouldn't be—save it for soups or sauces, or place the uncovered saucepan over high heat until the liquid evaporates.)

6. Add the butter or margarine, and serve immediately.

2 student servings: 1 to 2 medium potatoes; ¾ to 1 cup water; ¼ teaspoon salt; 1 tablespoon butter or margarine

HINT: Add finely chopped parsley just before serving. Do not reheat.

MASHED POTATOES

4 student servings	MILK	6 student servings
3 tablespoons	MILK	⅓ cup

Follow the recipe for **Buttered Potatoes,** but in Step 5 shake the uncovered saucepan over the heat to dry the potatoes thoroughly. Mash the potatoes with a potato masher, pastry blender, or electric mixer. Then add the butter or margarine. Next add milk. Place over very low heat, and beat until the potatoes are light and fluffy. Serve immediately.

BUTTERED CARROTS

4 student servings		6 student servings
4	MEDIUM CARROTS	6
¾ cup	WATER	1 cup
½ teaspoon	SALT	¾ teaspoon
1½ tablespoons	BUTTER or MARGARINE	2 tablespoons

STEPS IN PREPARATION

1. Wash the carrots with a vegetable brush.
   (*NOTE:* Young carrots may be cooked in their skins. If the carrots are old, remove the skins by scraping them with a knife.)

2. Cut the carrots into strips or slices. (See pictures on pages 446 and 447.)

3. Put the water in a saucepan, and heat. As soon as the water comes to a boil, add the carrots and salt.

4. Cover the saucepan with a tight-fitting lid. Lower the heat as soon as the water starts to boil again. (See picture on page 187.)

5. Boil gently 15 to 20 minutes, or until the carrots are tender. (See picture on page 188.)
   (*NOTE:* If there is any liquid left—but there shouldn't be—save it for soups or sauces, or place the uncovered saucepan over high heat until the liquid evaporates.)

6. Add the butter or margarine, and serve immediately.

---

2 student servings: 2 medium carrots; ½ to ¾ cup water; ¼ teaspoon salt; 2 teaspoons butter or margarine

---

HINT: Add finely chopped parsley just before serving. Do not reheat.

CREAMED CARROTS

4 student servings		6 student servings
⅔ cup	MEDIUM WHITE SAUCE	1 cup

Follow the recipe for **Buttered Carrots,** but in Step 6 omit the butter or margarine, and add **Medium White Sauce** (page 501).

BUTTERED SPINACH

4 student servings		6 student servings
1 pound	**SPINACH**	1½ pounds
¼ teaspoon	**SALT**	½ teaspoon
1½ tablespoons	**BUTTER or MARGARINE**	2 tablespoons

STEPS IN PREPARATION

1. Remove any discolored leaves, roots, and tough stems.

2. Wash the spinach under running water or dip the leaves up and down in a large bowl of water until they are free of sand. (See picture on page 186.)

3. Put the spinach in a saucepan, and add the salt.
   (*NOTE:* It is not necessary to add water, because the water which clings to the leaves is sufficient for cooking.)

4. Cover the saucepan with a tight-fitting lid, and cook over low heat 5 to 8 minutes, or until the spinach is tender.
   (*NOTE:* If there is any liquid left—but there shouldn't be—save it for soups or sauces, or place the uncovered saucepan over high heat until the liquid evaporates.)

5. Add the butter or margarine, and serve immediately.

---

2 student servings: ½ pound spinach; few grains salt; 2 teaspoons butter or margarine

---

HINTS

1. Spinach may be garnished with hard-cooked eggs.
2. To improve the flavor of spinach, add lemon juice or vinegar "to taste" when it is served.
3. For variety, in Step 3 add 1 tablespoon finely chopped onion for each pound of spinach. In Step 5 use bacon drippings instead of butter or margarine. Sprinkle crumbled, crisp bacon over the top before serving.
4. In Step 4 drain the cooked spinach when it is almost tender. Add a few drops of lemon juice, and spread the spinach in a thin layer in a baking dish. Sprinkle with grated cheese, and place in the broiler until the cheese melts.

STEAMED CABBAGE

4 student servings	SHREDDED CABBAGE	6 student servings
2 to 3 cups (½ pound)	SHREDDED CABBAGE	3 to 4 cups (¾ pound)
⅓ cup	WATER	½ cup
½ teaspoon	SALT	¾ teaspoon
1½ tablespoons	BUTTER or MARGARINE	2 tablespoons

STEPS IN PREPARATION

1. Wash the cabbage and shred it. (See picture on page 448.)

2. Put the water in a saucepan, and heat. As soon as the water comes to a boil, add the cabbage and salt.

3. Cover the saucepan with a tight-fitting lid. Lower the heat as soon as the water starts to boil again.

4. Boil gently 5 to 10 minutes, or until the cabbage is tender but still crisp. (*NOTE:* If there is any liquid left—but there shouldn't be—save it for soups or sauces, or place the uncovered saucepan over high heat until the liquid evaporates.)

5. Add the butter or margarine, and serve immediately.

---

2 student servings: 1½ cups (¼ pound) shredded cabbage; ¼ cup water; ¼ teaspoon salt; 2 teaspoons butter or margarine

---

CABBAGE AU GRATIN

4 student servings		6 student servings
⅔ cup	MEDIUM WHITE SAUCE	1 cup
3 tablespoons	BUTTERED BREAD CRUMBS	¼ cup
3 tablespoons	GRATED AMERICAN CHEESE	¼ cup

Follow the recipe for **Steamed Cabbage,** but in Step 5 omit the butter or margarine, and put the cooked cabbage in a greased casserole. Then add **Medium White Sauce** (page 501). Sprinkle bread crumbs and grated cheese over the top. Bake in a hot oven (400° F.) 15 to 20 minutes.

CREAMED GREEN PEAS

4 student servings		6 student servings
⅓ cup	WATER	½ cup
1 package (10-ounce)	GREEN PEAS (frozen)	1½ packages (10-ounce)
½ teaspoon	SALT	¾ teaspoon
⅔ cup	MEDIUM WHITE SAUCE (page 501)	1 cup

STEPS IN PREPARATION

1. Put the water in a saucepan, and heat. As soon as the water comes to a boil, add the frozen peas and salt. (See picture on page 189.)

2. Bring quickly to a boil over high heat. Separate the peas with a fork as they thaw.

3. Cover the saucepan with a tight-fitting lid. Lower the heat as soon as the water starts to boil again.

4. Boil gently 5 to 8 minutes, or until the peas are tender.
   (*NOTE:* If there is any water left—but there shouldn't be—save it for soups or sauces, or place the uncovered saucepan over high heat until the liquid evaporates.)

5. Make **Medium White Sauce** while the peas are cooking.

6. Add the white sauce to the cooked peas, and serve immediately. (See picture on page 241.)

---

2 student servings: ⅓ cup water; ½ package (10-ounce) frozen green peas; ¼ teaspoon salt; ⅓ cup **Medium White Sauce** (page 501)

BUTTERED GREEN PEAS

4 student servings		6 student servings
1½ tablespoons	BUTTER or MARGARINE	2 tablespoons

Follow the recipe for **Creamed Green Peas,** but in Step 5 omit the white sauce, and add butter or margarine.

GREEN BEANS WITH BACON

4 student servings		6 student servings
2	BACON SLICES	3
⅓ cup	CHOPPED ONION	½ cup
2½ tablespoons	CHOPPED GREEN PEPPER	¼ cup
1⅓ cups	GREEN BEANS (canned)	2 cups (1-pound can)
⅓ cup	LIQUID FROM CAN	½ cup
¼ teaspoon	SALT	½ teaspoon

STEPS IN PREPARATION

1. Cut the bacon into 1-inch pieces.
2. Put the pieces in a skillet, and fry them until they are light brown but not crisp.
3. Add the onion and the green pepper. Cook 1 to 2 minutes, or until the onion is light yellow.
4. Remove from the heat. Add the green beans, the liquid from the can, and the salt.
5. Boil gently until the beans are hot and most of the liquid has evaporated.
6. Serve hot.

---

2 student servings: 1 bacon slice; 2½ tablespoons chopped onion; 1½ tablespoons chopped green pepper; ⅔ cup green beans (canned); ¼ cup liquid from can; ⅛ teaspoon salt

---

GREEN BEANS WITH MOCK HOLLANDAISE SAUCE

Heat canned green beans according to the directions for preparing canned vegetables on page 190. Serve with **Mock Hollandaise Sauce** (page 502).

(*NOTE:* For other suggestions on how to prepare canned vegetables, turn to page 139.)

HARVARD BEETS

4 student servings		6 student servings
¼ teaspoon	SALT	½ teaspoon
2 teaspoons	CORNSTARCH	1 tablespoon
¼ cup	SUGAR	⅓ cup
⅓ cup	VINEGAR	½ cup
2 cups	SLICED or CUBED BEETS (cooked or canned)	3 cups
1 tablespoon	BUTTER or MARGARINE	2 tablespoons

STEPS IN PREPARATION

1. Fill the lower part of a double boiler about one-third full of water. Heat to boiling.

2. Mix the salt, cornstarch, and sugar in the upper part of the double boiler.

3. Add the vinegar slowly, stirring until it makes a smooth paste.

4. Place the upper part of the double boiler over the boiling water. Cook the mixture, stirring constantly, until it is thick and smooth.

5. Add the beets and the butter or margarine to the sauce. Mix lightly.

6. Cover and let stand over the boiling water 15 to 20 minutes, or until the sauce becomes red.

7. Serve hot.

---

2 student servings: ⅛ teaspoon salt; 1 teaspoon cornstarch; 2 tablespoons sugar; 2½ tablespoons vinegar; 1 cup sliced or cubed beets (cooked or canned); 2 teaspoons butter or margarine

---

PICKLED BEETS

Mix ⅓ cup vinegar, ⅓ cup water, 3 tablespoons sugar, 2 whole cloves, and ¼ teaspoon salt in a saucepan. Boil 2 minutes. Pour the liquid over 1½ cups cooked or canned beets which have been sliced or cubed. Let stand for at least 24 hours. (Serves 4)

SCALLOPED TOMATOES

4 student servings		6 student servings
2 slices	TOAST	3 slices
1⅓ cups	TOMATOES (canned)	2 cups
2 teaspoons	FINELY CHOPPED ONION	1 tablespoon
½ teaspoon	SALT	1 teaspoon
2 tablespoons	BUTTER or MARGARINE	3 tablespoons

STEPS IN PREPARATION

1. Turn on the oven, and set the temperature control at 375° F. for a moderate oven.

2. Cut the toast into 1-inch squares.

3. Put a layer of the tomatoes in a casserole.

4. Add a layer of the toast.

5. Repeat Steps 3 and 4 until all the tomatoes and toast have been used. The toast should be the top layer.

6. Sprinkle the onion and salt over the top.

7. Dot with the butter or margarine.

8. Bake 15 to 20 minutes, or until most of the liquid has cooked out.

9. Serve hot in the casserole. (See picture on page 193.)

---

2 student servings: 1 slice toast; ⅔ cup tomatoes (canned); 1 teaspoon finely chopped onion; ¼ teaspoon salt; 1 tablespoon butter or margarine

---

BROILED TOMATOES

Cut firm, fresh, unpeeled tomatoes in half crosswise. Spread the cut surface with melted butter. Sprinkle with salt, pepper, and dry bread crumbs. Arrange the tomatoes in a shallow baking pan. Place the pan in the broiler so that the tops of the tomatoes are 2 to 3 inches from the heating unit. Cook 8 to 10 minutes, or until the tomatoes are light brown.

CAMP-STYLE BEANS

4 student servings		6 student servings
2	BACON SLICES	3
2 tablespoons	CHOPPED ONION	3 tablespoons
⅔ cup	TOMATOES (canned)	1 cup
¼ teaspoon	SALT	½ teaspoon
⅛ teaspoon	PEPPER	¼ teaspoon
1⅓ cups	PORK AND BEANS (canned)	2 cups

STEPS IN PREPARATION

1. Cut the bacon into ½-inch pieces.

2. Put the pieces in a skillet, and place the skillet over low heat.

3. Fry the bacon slowly until most of the fat has been cooked out, but do not let the bacon become crisp. Pour off part of the bacon drippings, leaving about a tablespoon in the skillet.

4. Add onion. Cook 1 to 2 minutes, or until the onion is light yellow.

5. Remove from the heat, and add the tomatoes, salt, and pepper. Cook 5 minutes, and then add the beans.

6. Cook over low heat 15 minutes, or until the liquid has cooked down and is thick.

7. Serve hot as a main luncheon dish or for outdoor meals.

---

2 student servings: 1 bacon slice; 1 tablespoon chopped onion; ⅓ cup tomatoes (canned); ⅛ teaspoon salt; few grains pepper; ⅔ cup pork and beans (canned)

(*NOTE:* If time does not allow complete preparation in one period, prepare the mixture one day and bake the next as a **Bean Casserole**.)

BEAN CASSEROLE

Follow Steps 1 to 5 in the recipe for **Camp-style Beans.** Pour the mixture into a casserole, and bake in a moderate oven (350° F.) 30 minutes.

SALADS AND SALAD DRESSINGS

SEAFOOD SALAD

4 student servings		6 student servings
1 cup	TUNA, SALMON, CRAB MEAT, or SHRIMP	1½ cups
1 teaspoon	LEMON JUICE	2 teaspoons
1 teaspoon	FINELY CHOPPED ONION	1½ teaspoons
1 cup	CHOPPED CELERY	1½ cups
2 tablespoons	CHOPPED GREEN PEPPER	3 tablespoons
⅛ teaspoon	SALT	¼ teaspoon
¼ cup	MAYONNAISE or SALAD DRESSING	⅓ cup
	LETTUCE or other SALAD GREENS	

STEPS IN PREPARATION

1. Drain the liquid or oil from the seafood.

2. Put the seafood in a mixing bowl, and flake or break it into small pieces with a fork. (See picture on page 295.)

3. Add the lemon juice, onion, celery, green pepper, salt, and just enough mayonnaise or salad dressing to moisten.

4. Toss gently with two forks.

5. Serve on lettuce or other salad greens with additional dressing, if desired.

2 student servings: ½ cup tuna, salmon, crab meat, or shrimp; ½ teaspoon lemon juice; ½ teaspoon finely chopped onion; ½ cup chopped celery; 1 tablespoon chopped green pepper; few grains salt; 2 tablespoons mayonnaise or salad dressing; lettuce or other salad greens

HINTS

1. Seafood salad may be used as a filling for sandwiches, provided it is not too moist and the ingredients are cut into smaller pieces. (Salad amount for 4 fills 6 sandwiches.)
2. One 7-ounce can of most seafood equals 1 cup.

POTATO SALAD

4 student servings		6 student servings
2 to 3	COOKED POTATOES	4
1	HARD-COOKED EGG (page 510)	2
2 tablespoons	CHOPPED PIMENTO	3 tablespoons
2 tablespoons	CHOPPED CELERY	3 tablespoons
2 tablespoons	CHOPPED PICKLE	3 tablespoons
1 tablespoon	FINELY CHOPPED ONION	2 tablespoons
½ teaspoon	SALT	1 teaspoon
¼ to ⅓ cup	MAYONNAISE or SALAD DRESSING	⅓ to ½ cup
	LETTUCE or other SALAD GREENS	

STEPS IN PREPARATION

1. Peel the cooked potatoes and the **Hard-cooked Egg,** and cut them into ½-inch pieces.

2. Add the pimento, celery, pickle, onion, and salt.

3. Add the mayonnaise or salad dressing, and mix lightly, being careful not to break the pieces of potato.
   (*NOTE:* The flavor of the potato salad will be improved if it is chilled.)

4. Serve on lettuce or other salad greens.

---

2 student servings: 1 cooked potato; ½ **Hard-cooked Egg** (page 510); 1 tablespoon chopped pimento; 1 tablespoon chopped celery; 1 tablespoon chopped pickle; 2 teaspoons finely chopped onion; ¼ teaspoon salt; 2 to 3 tablespoons mayonnaise or salad dressing; lettuce or other salad greens

---

HINTS

1. To improve the flavor of potato salad, add a small amount of vinegar or prepared mustard to the mayonnaise or salad dressing.
2. For a very moist potato salad, mix mayonnaise or salad dressing with an equal amount of milk before it is added to the salad.

TOMATO AND COTTAGE CHEESE SALAD

4 student servings		6 student servings
2	MEDIUM TOMATOES	3
1 cup	COTTAGE CHEESE	1½ cups
1 tablespoon	MAYONNAISE or SALAD DRESSING	1½ tablespoons
2 teaspoons	FINELY CHOPPED GREEN ONION	1 tablespoon
2 tablespoons	CHOPPED GREEN PEPPER	3 tablespoons
2 tablespoons	CHOPPED CELERY	3 tablespoons
⅛ teaspoon	SALT	¼ teaspoon
few grains	PEPPER	few grains
	LETTUCE or other SALAD GREENS	

STEPS IN PREPARATION

1. Chill tomatoes which have been washed.
2. Drain the cottage cheese, if necessary. Mix the cottage cheese, mayonnaise or salad dressing, onion, green pepper, celery, salt, and pepper.
3. Slice the tomatoes, and arrange on lettuce or other salad greens.
4. Put the cottage cheese mixture on top of the sliced tomatoes.

---

2 student servings: 1 medium tomato; ½ cup cottage cheese; 2 teaspoons mayonnaise or salad dressing; 1 teaspoon finely chopped green onion; 1 tablespoon chopped green pepper; 1 tablespoon chopped celery; few grains salt; few grains pepper; lettuce or other salad greens

---

STUFFED TOMATO SALAD

Allow 1 medium tomato for each person. Remove core and cut each almost through into 6 sections so that it will open like a flower. (See picture on page 471.) Place on lettuce or other salad greens. Open the tomato, and fill with the cottage cheese mixture above, **Seafood Salad** (page 491), or **Chicken Salad Sandwich Filling** (page 504). See picture on page 203.

TOSSED VEGETABLE SALAD

4 student servings		6 student servings
⅔ stalk	CELERY	1 stalk
½	CARROT	1 small
2	SMALL TOMATOES	3
½	MEDIUM HEAD LETTUCE	¾
½ teaspoon	SALT	¾ teaspoon
2 tablespoons	FRENCH DRESSING (page 500)	3 tablespoons

STEPS IN PREPARATION

1. Wash the chilled vegetables in cold water, and dry them. (See picture on page 467.)

2. Slice the celery crosswise.

3. Scrape the carrot, and cut it into very thin slices.

4. Cut the tomatoes into wedges.

5. Tear the lettuce into pieces.

6. Put the celery, carrot, tomatoes, and lettuce in a salad bowl. Add the salt.

7. Pour the **French Dressing** over the vegetables slowly.

8. Toss gently with two forks, as shown in the picture on page 202.

9. Serve immediately in a salad bowl or on individual salad plates. (See picture on page 111.)

---

2 student servings: ⅓ stalk celery; ¼ carrot; 1 small tomato; ¼ medium head lettuce; ¼ teaspoon salt; 1 tablespoon **French Dressing** (page 500)

HINTS

1. To give a garlic flavor to salad, rub the salad bowl with a clove of garlic. (See picture on page 450.)
2. The following vegetables may be substituted for any one of the above ingredients: radishes, cauliflower, green pepper, avocado.
3. A tossed green salad may be made by using three or four different kinds of salad greens, tossed together with French dressing, and garnished with tomato wedges, sliced radishes, green pepper rings, or sliced cucumbers.

COLE SLAW

4 student servings		6 student servings
⅔	SMALL HEAD CABBAGE	1
2 teaspoons	VINEGAR	1 tablespoon
2 teaspoons	SUGAR	1 tablespoon
¼ teaspoon	SALT	½ teaspoon
2 tablespoons	SWEET CREAM or MAYONNAISE	3 tablespoons

STEPS IN PREPARATION

1. Cut the chilled cabbage in half, then in quarters and remove the core.

2. Shred the cabbage very fine, as shown in the picture on page 448.

3. Make a dressing by stirring the vinegar, sugar, and salt together until the sugar dissolves. Add the sweet cream or mayonnaise, and mix well.

4. Pour the dressing over the shredded cabbage.

5. Toss gently with two forks.

6. Serve in a salad bowl.

---

2 student servings: ⅓ small head cabbage; 1 teaspoon vinegar; 1 teaspoon sugar; ⅛ teaspoon salt; 1 tablespoon sweet cream or mayonnaise

---

HINT: If time permits, chill the shredded cabbage in ice water 10 to 30 minutes, or until it is crisp. Drain and dry the cabbage between two clean towels.

CABBAGE-PEPPER SLAW

Mix 1 tablespoon tarragon vinegar, ¼ cup mayonnaise, 1 tablespoon sugar, ½ teaspoon salt, and 1 teaspoon prepared mustard in a mixing bowl. Add 2 cups shredded cabbage, ¼ cup chopped green pepper, and ½ teaspoon celery seed. Mix lightly. (Serves 4)

CABBAGE AND PIMENTO

Combine 1½ cups shredded cabbage, 2 tablespoons chopped pimento, 6 olives (chopped), 2 tablespoons finely chopped onion, and ½ cup chopped celery. Add ¼ cup mayonnaise, and mix lightly. (Serves 4)

HEALTH SALAD

4 student servings		6 student servings
2	MEDIUM CARROTS	3
1	SMALL APPLE	1½
½ cup	CRUSHED PINEAPPLE (drained)	¾ cup
2 tablespoons	SEEDLESS RAISINS or CHOPPED DATES	3 tablespoons
2 to 3 tablespoons	MAYONNAISE or SALAD DRESSING	3 to 5 tablespoons
	LETTUCE or other SALAD GREENS	

STEPS IN PREPARATION

1. Wash the chilled carrots and the apple in cold water, and dry them. Scrape the carrots and pare the apple, if desired.
2. Shred the carrots and chop the apple into a salad bowl. Add the pineapple and raisins.
3. Add just enough mayonnaise or salad dressing to moisten.
4. Mix gently with a fork.
5. Serve in a salad bowl or on individual salad plates on lettuce or other salad greens.

---

2 student servings: 1 medium carrot; ½ small apple; ¼ cup crushed pineapple (drained); 1 tablespoon raisins; 1 to 2 tablespoons mayonnaise or salad dressing; lettuce or other salad greens

---

SUGGESTED FRUIT

MIXED FRUIT: Combine 3 bananas (sliced), 1 cup fruit cocktail, and ⅓ cup chopped peanuts. Add ¼ cup mayonnaise and 1 tablespoon lemon juice. Mix lightly. (Serves 4)

ORANGE AND CARROT: Combine 1½ cups orange sections (drained), 1½ cups shredded carrot, and ½ cup seedless raisins. Add 2 to 3 tablespoons French dressing, and mix lightly. (Serves 4)

PINEAPPLE AND CABBAGE: Combine 2 cups shredded cabbage, ½ cup crushed pineapple (drained), and ½ cup small marshmallows. Add ¼ cup mayonnaise, and mix lightly. (Serves 4)

WALDORF SALAD

4 student servings		6 student servings
2	MEDIUM APPLES	3
2 teaspoons	LEMON JUICE	1 tablespoon
½ cup	CHOPPED CELERY	¾ cup
2 to 4 tablespoons	MAYONNAISE or SALAD DRESSING	¼ to ⅓ cup
2 tablespoons	CHOPPED NUTS	3 tablespoons
	LETTUCE or other SALAD GREENS	

STEPS IN PREPARATION

1. Wash and dry the chilled apples.
2. Pare the apples thinly, if desired. If red apples are being used, leave the skins on.
3. Cut the apples into quarters, remove the cores, and cut into ½-inch pieces.
4. Sprinkle the lemon juice over the apples to prevent them from turning dark.
5. Add the celery and mayonnaise or salad dressing to the apples.
6. Mix gently with a fork.
7. Serve in a salad bowl or on lettuce or other salad greens.
8. Sprinkle the nuts over the salad, and serve.

2 student servings: 1 medium apple; 1 teaspoon lemon juice; ¼ cup chopped celery; 1 to 2 tablespoons mayonnaise or salad dressing; 1 tablespoon chopped nuts; lettuce or other salad greens

SALAD COMBINATIONS

APPLE AND CELERY: Combine 1 large apple (chopped), 2 tablespoons lemon juice, ½ cup diced celery, ½ cup seedless raisins, and ½ cup pineapple wedges. Add ¼ cup mayonnaise, and mix lightly. (Serves 4)

BANANA AND RAISIN: Combine 4 bananas (sliced), ¼ cup seedless raisins, and ½ apple (chopped with red skin on). Add 2 tablespoons salad dressing, and mix lightly. (Serves 4)

ORANGE AND PINEAPPLE: Combine 1½ cups orange sections (drained), ½ cup pineapple wedges, and ½ cup shredded coconut. Add 2 tablespoons poppy-seed salad dressing, and mix lightly. (Serves 4)

BEET AND GREEN ONION: Combine 1 cup diced cooked beets, 1 cup sliced celery, 2 tablespoons thinly sliced green onions, and $\frac{1}{4}$ teaspoon salt. Add 2 tablespoons French dressing, and mix lightly. (Serves 4)

CARROT AND RAISIN: Combine 4 medium carrots (grated) and $\frac{1}{2}$ cup seedless raisins. Toss with $\frac{1}{4}$ cup mayonnaise. (Serves 4)

CAULIFLOWER AND GREEN PEPPER: Combine 1 cup sliced raw cauliflower, $\frac{2}{3}$ cup sliced celery, 3 tablespoons chopped green pepper, 2 tablespoons chopped sweet pickle, and few grains salt. Add $\frac{1}{4}$ cup French dressing, and mix lightly. (Serves 4)

CHEF'S SALAD BOWL: Combine $\frac{1}{4}$ small head lettuce (shredded), $\frac{1}{4}$ cucumber (sliced), $\frac{1}{4}$ cup sliced radishes, 1 small tomato (wedges), 1 green onion (sliced), $\frac{1}{4}$ cup sliced celery, and $\frac{1}{4}$ cup shredded carrot. Add $\frac{1}{4}$ cup French dressing and 1 tablespoon chili sauce. Mix lightly. (Serves 4)

GREEN BEAN AND PIMENTO: Combine 2 cups green beans (drained), 1 pimento (chopped), 3 tablespoons finely chopped onion, and $\frac{1}{4}$ cup sliced celery. Add $\frac{1}{4}$ cup French dressing, and mix lightly. (Serves 4)

KIDNEY BEAN: Mix $\frac{1}{4}$ teaspoon prepared mustard, $\frac{1}{4}$ teaspoon salt, and 2 to 3 tablespoons mayonnaise in a mixing bowl. Add $1\frac{1}{2}$ cups cooked kidney beans (drained), $\frac{1}{2}$ cup chopped celery, 1 teaspoon chopped onion, and 3 tablespoons pickle relish. Mix lightly. (Serves 4)

LETTUCE AND CARROT: Combine 1 cup lettuce (broken into pieces), 2 carrots (shredded), and 1 cup sliced celery. Add 2 to 3 tablespoons French dressing, and toss lightly. (Serves 4)

LIMA BEAN: Combine 2 cups lima beans (drained), 1 hard-cooked egg (chopped), 1 tablespoon finely chopped onion, 3 tablespoons pickle relish, and $\frac{1}{4}$ teaspoon salt. Add $\frac{1}{4}$ cup mayonnaise, and mix lightly. (Serves 4)

MIXED VEGETABLE: Combine $\frac{1}{2}$ cup thinly sliced celery, $\frac{1}{2}$ cup thinly sliced radishes, 1 cup thinly sliced cucumber, $\frac{1}{2}$ green pepper (chopped) , 1 raw carrot (thinly sliced), and 1 green onion (thinly sliced). Add $\frac{1}{4}$ cup French dressing, and mix lightly. (Serves 4)

PEAS AND CHEESE: Mix 1 tablespoon French dressing and $\frac{1}{4}$ cup mayonnaise in a mixing bowl. Add 1 cup cooked green peas, 1 cup sliced celery, and $\frac{1}{2}$ cup diced American cheese. Mix lightly. (Serves 4)

SPINACH: Combine 4 cups fresh spinach (torn into pieces), $\frac{1}{2}$ cup sliced radishes, and $\frac{1}{3}$ cup sliced green onions. Add $\frac{1}{4}$ cup French dressing, and toss lightly. (Serves 4)

GOLDEN SALAD

4 student servings		6 student servings
⅓ cup (⅔ package)	LEMON-FLAVORED GELATIN	½ cup (1 package)
⅔ cup	HOT WATER	1 cup
⅔ cup	PINEAPPLE JUICE	1 cup
¼ teaspoon	SALT	½ teaspoon
⅔ cup	GRATED CARROT	1 cup
⅔ cup	CRUSHED PINEAPPLE (drained)	1 cup
	LETTUCE or other SALAD GREENS	

STEPS IN PREPARATION

1. Put the gelatin in a mixing bowl. (See picture on page 434.)

2. Add the hot water, and stir until the gelatin completely dissolves.

3. Add the pineapple juice and salt.

4. Place in the refrigerator, and chill until the gelatin begins to thicken, as shown in the picture on page 349.

5. Add the carrot and pineapple to the gelatin. (See picture on page 204.)

6. Pour the gelatin mixture into molds which have been rinsed in cold water or lightly rubbed inside with vegetable oil.

7. Chill in the refrigerator until firm.

8. Unmold according to the directions on page 204.

9. Serve on individual salad plates on lettuce or other salad greens. (See picture on page 199.)

---

2 student servings: 3 tablespoons lemon-flavored gelatin; ⅓ cup hot water; ⅓ cup pineapple juice; ⅛ teaspoon salt; ⅓ cup grated carrot; ⅓ cup crushed pineapple (drained); lettuce or other salad greens

---

HINT: Because raw pineapple prevents gelatin from setting, it should never be used in gelatin salads or desserts.

FRENCH DRESSING
(½ Cup)

½ teaspoon	SUGAR
½ teaspoon	PAPRIKA
½ teaspoon	SALT
¼ cup	VINEGAR or LEMON JUICE
¼ cup	SALAD OIL

STEPS IN PREPARATION
1. Put all ingredients into a jar with a tight-fitting cover.
2. Shake vigorously until all ingredients are blended.
   (*NOTE:* If desired, a garlic clove or ¼ teaspoon grated onion may be added just before shaking. Remove garlic before serving.)
3. Serve immediately or store in the refrigerator.
4. Reshake before adding to a salad.

TOMATO DRESSING

Follow the recipe for **French Dressing,** but in Step 1 add 3 tablespoons catsup.

ROQUEFORT DRESSING

Follow the recipe for **French Dressing,** but in Step 1 add 3 tablespoons Roquefort cheese or Blue cheese.

VARIATIONS OF MAYONNAISE AND SALAD DRESSINGS

THOUSAND ISLAND DRESSING: To each cup mayonnaise or salad dressing add 3 tablespoons chili sauce, 1 hard-cooked egg (finely chopped), and 2 tablespoons finely chopped olives.

RUSSIAN DRESSING: To each cup mayonnaise or salad dressing add 3 tablespoons chili sauce and 1 teaspoon grated onion.

WHIPPED CREAM DRESSING: To each cup mayonnaise or salad dressing add ½ cup heavy cream (whipped).

PICKLE RELISH DRESSING: To each cup mayonnaise or salad dressing add ¼ cup tart pickle relish. If desired, 1 to 2 teaspoons horseradish may be added.

SAUCES AND SOUPS

WHITE SAUCE
(1 cup)*

INGREDIENTS	THIN	MEDIUM	THICK
BUTTER or MARGARINE	1 tablespoon	2 tablespoons	3 tablespoons
FLOUR	1 tablespoon	2 tablespoons	3 tablespoons
SALT	½ teaspoon	½ teaspoon	½ teaspoon
MILK	1 cup	1 cup	1 cup

STEPS IN PREPARATION

Method I

1. Fill the lower part of a double boiler about one-third full of water. Heat to boiling. (See picture on page 218.)

2. Put the butter or margarine in the upper part of the double boiler, and place it over the boiling water. Heat until the butter or margarine melts.

3. Add the flour and salt. Stir until the mixture is a smooth paste.

4. Add the milk slowly, stirring constantly.

5. Cook until the white sauce is thick and smooth, continuing to stir.

Method II

The more experienced cook may make white sauce over direct heat if she uses a heavy saucepan over low heat and stirs the mixture constantly.

Method III

1. Pour half of the milk into a jar, and add the flour. Cover and shake until the flour and milk are thoroughly mixed and entirely smooth. (See picture on page 219.)

2. Put the milk-and-flour mixture in a heavy saucepan or in the upper part of a double boiler. Add the remaining milk.

3. Cook over very low heat or over boiling water, stirring constantly, until the sauce is thick and smooth. Stir in the butter or margarine and salt.

(*NOTE:* This method is used to thicken stews.)

*To make ⅔ cup medium white sauce, use 4 teaspoons butter or margarine, 4 teaspoons flour, ¼ teaspoon salt, and ⅔ cup milk.

CHEESE SAUCE

Follow the recipe for **Medium White Sauce,** but in the last step add ½ cup grated American cheese, and stir until the cheese is melted. Serve over vegetables, eggs, fish, or ground meat patties.

EGG SAUCE

Follow the recipe for **Medium White Sauce,** but in the last step add 2 hard-cooked eggs (chopped). Carefully stir the egg into the white sauce. Serve over cooked fish.

MUSHROOM SAUCE

Follow Method I for **Medium White Sauce,** but in Step 2 add ½ cup sliced mushrooms and 1 teaspoon finely chopped onion to the melted butter or margarine. Cook about 5 minutes, or until the onion is very light yellow. Add the flour, and continue to follow the steps in Method I.

MOCK HOLLANDAISE SAUCE

Follow Method I for **Medium White Sauce,** but in the last step slowly add the white sauce to 2 beaten egg yolks, stirring constantly. Gradually stir in 2 tablespoons melted butter or margarine and 3 tablespoons lemon juice. Serve at once over asparagus, broccoli, green beans, or fish. (See picture on page 221.)

CREAM OF VEGETABLE SOUP

To 1 cup **Thin White Sauce** (page 501) add ⅔ cup spinach, mushrooms, corn, split peas, or asparagus which has been mashed with a fork, put through a sieve, or cut into small pieces. Heat thoroughly, and season as desired. Serve in warm bowls, and sprinkle with paprika, grated cheese, chopped parsley, or croutons, if desired. This amount serves 2. For 4 servings, double the amount.

CREAM OF TOMATO SOUP

4 student servings		6 student servings
1½ cups	THIN WHITE SAUCE (page 501)	2 cups
1½ cups	TOMATOES (canned)	2½ cups
2 teaspoons	FINELY CHOPPED ONION	1 tablespoon
⅛ teaspoon	CELERY SEED	¼ teaspoon
¼ teaspoon	SALT	½ teaspoon
¼ teaspoon	SUGAR	½ teaspoon
¼	BAY LEAF or DRIED BASIL	½
2	WHOLE CLOVES	3

STEPS IN PREPARATION

1. Make **Thin White Sauce.**

2. Put the tomatoes, onion, celery seed, salt, sugar, bay leaf or dried basil, and whole cloves in a saucepan, and simmer over low heat 10 minutes.

3. Strain the tomato mixture by pouring it through a sieve and pressing the tomatoes against the sieve with a spoon.

4. Stir the tomato liquid into the white sauce slowly.
   (*NOTE:* If the soup curdles, beat with a rotary beater until smooth.)

5. Serve immediately in warm bowls with croutons, bread sticks, or crackers. (See pictures on pages 208 and 212.)

---

2 student servings: 1 cup **Thin White Sauce** (page 501); 1 cup tomatoes (canned); 1 teaspoon finely chopped onion; few grains celery seed; ⅛ teaspoon salt; ⅛ teaspoon sugar; small piece bay leaf or dried basil; 1 whole clove

---

CHICKEN–VEGETABLE SOUP

Add 1½ cups chicken broth (the water in which chicken was cooked) to 1 can vegetable soup. Boil gently 3 minutes. (Serves 4)

SANDWICH FILLINGS AND SPREADS

CHICKEN SALAD SANDWICH FILLING

4 student servings		6 student servings
⅔ cup	CHOPPED COOKED CHICKEN	1 cup
1	CHOPPED HARD-COOKED EGG (page 510)	2
⅓ cup	FINELY CHOPPED CELERY	½ cup
½ teaspoon	SALT	¾ teaspoon
¼ cup	MAYONNAISE or SALAD DRESSING	⅓ cup
2 tablespoons	CHOPPED PICKLE	3 tablespoons

STEPS IN PREPARATION

1. Combine the chicken, egg, and celery in a mixing bowl.

2. Mix the salt, mayonnaise or salad dressing, and pickle until well blended.

3. Add the mayonnaise mixture to the chicken, and mix lightly.

4. Make sandwiches according to the directions on pages 228 and 229.

---

2 student servings: ⅓ cup chopped cooked chicken; ½ chopped **Hard-cooked Egg** (page 510); 3 tablespoons finely chopped celery; ¼ teaspoon salt; 2 tablespoons mayonnaise or salad dressing; 1 tablespoon chopped pickle

HINTS
1. Green pepper or onion may be added, if desired.
2. Chicken salad sandwich filling may be tossed together and served as a salad on lettuce or other salad greens if the ingredients are cut into larger pieces. (See picture on page 203.)

BEEF or HAM SANDWICH FILLING

Follow the recipe for **Chicken Salad Sandwich Filling,** but in Step 1 substitute chopped cooked beef or ham for the chicken.

CHICKEN AND HAM: Combine ⅔ cup chopped cooked chicken and ½ cup chopped cooked ham. Add 3 olives (chopped), 2 to 3 tablespoons mayonnaise or salad dressing, and ½ teaspoon lemon juice. Mix lightly. (Fills 4 sandwiches)

DEVILED MEAT: Combine 1¼ cup chopped cooked beef or pork with 2 tablespoons catsup or chili sauce, ½ teaspoon Worcestershire sauce, ¼ teaspoon paprika, ½ teaspoon grated onion, ½ teaspoon salt, and 3 tablespoons mayonnaise or salad dressing. Mix lightly. (Fills 4 sandwiches)

TUNA SPREAD: Combine 1 cup canned tuna (flaked), 2 tablespoons chopped celery, 1 teaspoon lemon juice, ¼ teaspoon salt, 3 tablespoons mayonnaise or salad dressing. Mix lightly. (Fills 4 sandwiches)

HAM AND EGG: Combine ½ cup finely chopped cooked ham, 2 hard-cooked eggs (chopped), ½ teaspoon prepared mustard, 1 tablespoon finely chopped onion, ½ teaspoon Worcestershire sauce, and 2 to 3 tablespoons mayonnaise or salad dressing. Mix lightly. (Fills 4 sandwiches)

EGG AND DEVILED HAM: Combine 2 hard-cooked eggs (chopped), ⅓ cup deviled ham, 1 tablespoon Worcestershire sauce, and 3 to 4 tablespoons finely chopped pickle. Mix lightly. (Fills 4 sandwiches)

EGG AND BACON: Combine 4 hard-cooked eggs (chopped), 4 slices cooked, crisp bacon (chopped), and ¼ cup mayonnaise or salad dressing. Mix lightly. Spread on buttered bread. (Fills 4 sandwiches)

CORNED BEEF AND CHEESE: Combine ¼ cup chopped sharp American cheese with 2 tablespoons mayonnaise or salad dressing. Add ½ cup finely chopped corned beef, ¼ cup finely chopped sour pickles, 1 tablespoon grated onion, and 2 tablespoons finely chopped celery or parsley. Season with salt, paprika, or Worcestershire sauce. Mix well. (Fills 4 sandwiches)

CELERY AND CHEESE: Combine 1 cup grated American cheese, ⅓ cup chopped celery, 1½ teaspoons chopped onion, and 1½ teaspoons chopped pimentos. Add ¼ teaspoon salt and ⅓ cup mayonnaise or salad dressing. Mix well. (Fills 4 sandwiches)

PIMENTO CHEESE: Combine 1 cup grated American cheese, 3 tablespoons chopped pimento, and 3 tablespoons mayonnaise or salad dressing. Mix well. (Fills 4 sandwiches)

PEANUT BUTTER AND BACON: Crumble 4 slices cooked, crisp bacon. Combine 2 tablespoons mayonnaise or salad dressing, 2 teaspoons lemon juice, and ½ cup peanut butter. Fold in the bacon, ¼ cup finely chopped apples, and ¼ cup finely chopped celery. Mix just enough to blend the ingredients. (Fills 4 sandwiches)

PEANUT BUTTER, BANANA, AND JELLY: Mash 1 very ripe banana. Add ¼ cup peanut butter and 1 tablespoon currant jelly. Mix just enough to blend the ingredients. (Fills 4 sandwiches)

PEANUT BUTTER AND CARROTS: Combine ¼ cup peanut butter, ½ cup grated raw carrot, ¼ cup seedless raisins, and 2 tablespoons mayonnaise or salad dressing. Mix just enough to blend the ingredients. (Fills 4 sandwiches)

PEANUT BUTTER AND DATES: Combine ½ cup crunchy peanut butter, ¼ cup finely chopped pitted dates, and ⅓ cup orange juice. Mix just enough to blend the ingredients. (Fills 4 sandwiches)

PEANUT BUTTER AND PINEAPPLE: Combine ½ cup peanut butter and ½ cup canned crushed pineapple (drained). Mix just enough to blend the ingredients. (Fills 4 sandwiches)

CREAM CHEESE AND BACON: Soften one 3-ounce package cream cheese with 1 tablespoon milk. Add 2 tablespoons chopped green pepper, 3 slices cooked, crisp bacon (crumbled), and 1 teaspoon finely chopped onion. Mix well. Spread on bread or crackers.

CREAM CHEESE AND MARMALADE: Combine one 3-ounce package cream cheese with 2 tablespoons orange marmalade, ¼ cup chopped nuts, and grated rind of 1 orange. Mix well. Spread on bread or toast rounds.

CREAM CHEESE AND NUTS: Combine one 3-ounce package cream cheese, ¼ cup minced parsley, ¼ cup chopped salted nuts, ½ teaspoon lemon juice, and few grains salt. Mix well. Spread on bread or crackers.

CREAM CHEESE AND OLIVES: Combine one 3-ounce package cream cheese, 1 tablespoon chopped pimentos, 1½ tablespoons chopped olives, and 2 teaspoons chopped nuts. Mix well. Spread on bread or crackers.

CREAM CHEESE AND PINEAPPLE: Combine one 3-ounce package cream cheese, 1 cup crushed pineapple (drained), 1 tablespoon grated carrot, and ⅛ teaspoon salt. Mix well. Spread on bread or crackers.

EGGS

SCRAMBLED EGGS

4 student servings		6 student servings
4	EGGS	6
¼ cup	MILK	⅓ cup
¼ teaspoon	SALT	½ teaspoon
⅛ teaspoon	PEPPER	¼ teaspoon
2 teaspoons	BUTTER, MARGARINE, or BACON DRIPPINGS	1 tablespoon

STEPS IN PREPARATION

1. Break the eggs, one at a time, into a saucer or shallow dish before putting them in a mixing bowl.

2. Add the milk, salt, and pepper. Beat with a fork until the yellows and whites are blended.

3. Melt the butter, margarine, or bacon drippings in a heavy skillet.

4. Reduce the heat, and pour the eggs into the skillet.

5. Cook over very low heat, stirring occasionally by scraping the bottom and sides of the skillet as the mixture thickens, 4 to 8 minutes, or until the eggs are cooked through but still moist.

6. Serve hot with buttered toast. (See picture on page 257.)

---

2 student servings: 2 eggs; 2 tablespoons milk; few grains salt; few grains pepper; 1 teaspoon butter, margarine, or bacon drippings

---

HINTS

1. Scrambled eggs may be made in a double boiler by placing eggs with milk and seasonings in the upper part and cooking over boiling water until done.

2. To improve the flavor of scrambled eggs, in Step 3 add pieces of ham, dried beef, or crisp bacon to the melted butter or margarine.

3. For variety, put the scrambled eggs on hot toast just before they are done. Sprinkle with grated cheese (1 tablespoon for each egg). Heat in the oven until the cheese melts.

FRIED EGGS

4 student servings	BUTTER, MARGARINE, or BACON DRIPPINGS	6 student servings
1 to 2 tablespoons		2 to 4 tablespoons
4	EGGS	6

STEPS IN PREPARATION

Method I

1. Melt the butter, margarine, or bacon drippings in a heavy skillet. Heat over low heat until hot enough to make a drop of water sizzle.
2. Break the eggs, one at a time, into a saucer or shallow dish.
3. Lower the saucer close to the fat, and slip each egg into the skillet, being very careful not to break the yolk. (See picture on page 261.)
4. Cook the eggs slowly 3 to 4 minutes, or until the whites are firm. (See picture on page 259.) To coat the top of the eggs, dip the hot butter or fat over them with a spoon until a thin white film forms over the yolk, or turn the eggs over and cook them on the other side.
5. Lift the eggs out of the skillet with a broad spatula, and place on a hot dish.
6. Serve immediately, allowing each person to season as desired.

Method II

1. Use just enough butter, margarine, or bacon drippings to coat the skillet.
2. Follow the directions in Steps 1 through 3 of Method I.
3. Cook the eggs over low heat for 1 minute, or until the edges turn white.
4. Add ½ teaspoon cold water for each egg, and cover immediately with a tight-fitting lid. (See pictures on page 261.)
5. Cook 1 to 2 minutes if a soft yolk is desired, or 2 to 3 minutes for a well-cooked egg yolk.
6. Lift the eggs out of the skillet with a broad spatula, and place on a hot dish.
7. Serve immediately, allowing each person to season as desired.

---

2 student servings: 2 teaspoons butter, margarine, or bacon drippings; 2 eggs

PLAIN OMELET

4 student servings		6 student servings
4	EGGS	6
¼ cup	MILK	⅓ cup
½ teaspoon	SALT	¾ teaspoon
⅛ teaspoon	PEPPER	¼ teaspoon
1 tablespoon	BUTTER or MARGARINE	1½ tablespoons

STEPS IN PREPARATION

1. Break the eggs, one at a time, into a saucer or shallow dish before putting them in a mixing bowl. Beat slightly with a fork.
2. Add the milk, salt, and pepper to the eggs. Mix only until well blended.
3. Heat the butter or margarine in a heavy skillet until moderately hot.
4. Pour the eggs into the skillet, and cook them over very low heat.
5. Lift the edges of the egg mixture gently with a spatula or fork as it thickens to let the uncooked part run underneath. Tilt the skillet slightly. (See picture on page 262.)
6. Turn off the heat when the omelet is done, or when the eggs are set and do not flow. The omelet should be golden brown on the bottom.
7. Loosen the edges carefully, crease through the center with a spatula, fold in half or roll, and turn out onto a hot platter.
8. Serve immediately.

---

2 student servings: 2 eggs; 2 tablespoons milk; ¼ teaspoon salt; few grains pepper; 2 teaspoons butter or margarine

---

HINT: The size of the skillet should vary according to the number of eggs. For 2 eggs, use a 6- or 7-inch skillet. For 4 eggs, use an 8-inch skillet. For 6 eggs, use a 10-inch skillet.

OMELET VARIATIONS

Follow the recipe for **Plain Omelet,** but in Step 6 add 1 or 2 tablespoons of the following for each 2 eggs used: grated cheese, mushrooms, ham, bacon, or jelly.

SOFT-COOKED EGGS
(Cold-water Method)

4 student servings		6 student servings
4	**EGGS**	6
1 quart	**WATER**	1 quart

STEPS IN PREPARATION

1. Put the eggs in a saucepan, and cover them completely with cold or lukewarm water.
2. Heat the water to boiling. Cover the saucepan with a tight-fitting lid.
3. Turn off the heat, and let the eggs stand 2 to 5 minutes, depending upon the softness or hardness desired.
4. Pour off the hot water. Add cold water for a few seconds to stop the cooking and to make the eggs easier to handle.
5. Serve the egg immediately in the shell, or remove the egg from the shell and serve in a dish.

2 student servings: 2 eggs; 2 to 3 cups water

HARD-COOKED EGGS
(Cold-water Method)

4 student servings		6 student servings
4	**EGGS**	6
1 quart	**WATER**	1 quart

STEPS IN PREPARATION

1. Put the eggs in a saucepan, and cover them completely with cold or lukewarm water.
2. Heat the water to boiling. Cover the saucepan with a tight-fitting lid.
3. Turn off the heat, and let the eggs stand 15 to 20 minutes. If more than 4 eggs are cooked, reduce the heat and keep the water just below simmering.
4. Pour off the hot water. Cool the eggs in cold water immediately to stop the cooking and to make it easier to remove the shells.
5. Remove the egg shells according to the directions on page 260.

2 student servings: 2 eggs; 2 to 3 cups water

(Boiling-water Method)
See pictures on page 260.

DEVILED EGGS

4 student servings		6 student servings
4	HARD-COOKED EGGS	6
¼ teaspoon	SALT	½ teaspoon
few grains	PEPPER	⅛ teaspoon
½ teaspoon	PREPARED MUSTARD	1 teaspoon
1 tablespoon	MAYONNAISE or SALAD DRESSING	1½ tablespoons
1 teaspoon	VINEGAR (if desired)	1½ teaspoons

STEPS IN PREPARATION

1. Remove the shells from the **Hard-cooked Eggs** according to the directions on page 260.

2. Cut the eggs in half lengthwise or crosswise.

3. Take out the yolks with a spoon, and put them in a mixing bowl, being very careful not to break the whites.

4. Mash the yolks with a fork. Add the salt, pepper, mustard, mayonnaise or salad dressing, and vinegar if desired. Mix until smooth.

5. Refill the whites neatly with the egg-yolk mixture, heaping it up lightly. Chill, if time permits.

6. Serve as a main dish, a salad, or an accompaniment.

---

2 student servings: 2 Hard-cooked Eggs; ⅛ teaspoon salt; few grains pepper; ¼ teaspoon prepared mustard; 2 teaspoons mayonnaise or salad dressing; ½ teaspoon vinegar (if desired)

HINTS

1. Any of the following ingredients may be added to the filling for deviled eggs: chopped ham, pickles, olives, celery, pimentos.

2. Deviled eggs may be garnished with a dash of paprika, chopped parsley, strips of pimento, or slices of ripe olives.

3. To pack deviled eggs for picnics or school lunches, smooth the egg-yolk mixture so that it is level with the egg white, put the halves together, and wrap in wax paper, twisting the ends of the paper.

MEATS, POULTRY, AND FISH

PAN-BROILED BACON

4 student servings   **6 student servings**

BACON SLICES

STEPS IN PREPARATION

1. Lay the bacon slices in a cold skillet. (See picture on page 277.)

2. Place the skillet over moderately low heat, turning the bacon as it cooks. Cook 6 to 8 minutes, or until the bacon is brown and crisp but not dry and brittle. Pour off excess fat as it accumulates.

3. Remove the bacon slices, one at a time, and drain them on paper toweling or brown paper.

4. Serve on a hot platter.

LIVER AND BACON

4 student servings		6 student servings
⅔ pound	CALF'S LIVER	1 pound
½ teaspoon	SALT	¾ teaspoon
¼ cup	FLOUR	⅓ cup
4	BACON SLICES	6

STEPS IN PREPARATION

1. Cut liver into individual pieces for serving.

2. Mix salt and flour in a flat dish or pan. Roll each slice of liver in the flour until it is well coated. (See picture on page 279.)

3. Pan-broil the bacon, leaving a small amount of fat in the skillet.

4. Put the liver slices in the hot bacon fat, and pan-fry over moderate heat 2 to 4 minutes, or until light brown.

5. Turn and brown on the other side.

6. Serve on a hot platter with the crisp bacon. (See picture on page 107.)

2 student servings: ⅓ pound calf's liver; ¼ teaspoon salt; 2 tablespoons flour; 2 bacon slices

BREADED STEAKS

4 student servings		6 student servings
⅔ pound	CUBED STEAKS or VEAL CUTLETS	1 pound
1 small	EGG	1
2 tablespoons	MILK	3 tablespoons
½ teaspoon	SALT	1 teaspoon
few grains	PEPPER	⅛ teaspoon
2 tablespoons	FLOUR	¼ cup
½ cup	DRIED BREAD CRUMBS	¾ cup
3 tablespoons	OIL or SHORTENING	¼ cup

STEPS IN PREPARATION

1. Cut the meat into individual pieces for serving if it has not been done.

2. Break the egg into a shallow dish, and beat it with a fork. Add the milk, salt, and pepper. Mix well.

3. Roll each piece of meat in the flour, dip it into the egg-and-milk mixture, and roll it in the bread crumbs until it is well coated.

4. Heat the oil or shortening in a heavy skillet over medium heat.

5. Put the pieces of meat in the hot skillet, and brown them on both sides. Cover and cook over low heat 15 to 20 minutes.

6. Serve hot. **Mushroom Sauce** (page 502) or cream gravy may be added. (See picture on page 219.)

---

2 student servings: ⅓ pound cubed steaks or veal cutlets; 2 tablespoons beaten egg; 1 tablespoon milk; ¼ teaspoon salt; few grains pepper; 1 tablespoon flour; ¼ cup dried bread crumbs; 2 tablespoons oil or shortening

---

HINT: To make your own cubed steaks, buy round steak and tenderize it at home by beating it with a meat mallet, removing the tough membrane, and cutting it into individual pieces for serving. (See picture on page 450.)

PAN-FRIED HAMBURGER STEAKS

4 student servings		6 student servings
1⅓ cups (⅔ pound)	GROUND BEEF	2 cups (1 pound)
½ teaspoon	SALT	¾ teaspoon
⅛ teaspoon	PEPPER	¼ teaspoon
1 teaspoon	FINELY CHOPPED ONION (if desired)	1½ teaspoons
4	BACON SLICES	6

STEPS IN PREPARATION

1. Put the ground beef, salt, and pepper in a mixing bowl, and add the onion, if desired. Mix lightly.

2. Shape into round, flat patties about ½ inch thick. Do not pack too tightly.

3. Wrap a slice of bacon loosely around the side of each patty. Hold the bacon in place with a toothpick.

4. Grease a skillet lightly, and heat.

5. Put the meat patties in the hot skillet, and cook them over moderate heat 6 to 8 minutes, or until brown.
    (*NOTE:* Do not flatten or pat the meat with a pancake turner as it cooks, because this will press out the juices. See picture on page 277.)

6. Turn the meat patties, and continue to cook them until they are well browned. Reduce the heat, and cook the meat patties slowly, turning occasionally, 10 to 15 minutes, or until they are done.

7. Serve hot. Tomato sauce or cream gravy may be added.

---

2 student servings: ⅔ cup (⅓ pound) ground beef; ¼ teaspoon salt; few grains pepper; ½ teaspoon finely chopped onion (if desired); 2 bacon slices

---

(*NOTE:* If time does not allow for complete preparation in one class period, Steps 1 through 3 may be done one day and Steps 4 through 7 another day.)

BROILED HAMBURGER STEAKS

Follow the recipe for **Pan-fried Hamburger Steaks,** but in Step 4 place the hamburger steaks on the broiler rack 2 to 3 inches from the heating unit. (See pictures of broiled steak on page 274 for direction on broiling.)

OVEN TEMPERATURES

TEMPERATURE (degrees F.)	TERM
250 and 275	Very slow
300 and 325	Slow
350 and 375	Moderate
400 and 425	Hot
450 and 475	Very hot
500 and 525	Extremely hot

TIMETABLE FOR BROILING MEATS*

KIND AND CUT	APPROXIMATE THICKNESS (inches)	APPROXIMATE TOTAL COOKING TIME IN MINUTES		
		Rare	Medium	Well Done
Beef steaks				
Rib, club, tenderloin,	¾ to 1	10	14	18
porterhouse, T-bone, sirloin	1½	16	20	26
Ground beef patties	¾	8	12	14
Lamb chops	¾		12	14
Rib, loin, shoulder	1½		18	22
Ham, slice				
Uncooked	1			20
Cooked	1			10

(NOTE: Do not broil veal or fresh pork.)

*Adapted from *Handbook of Food Preparation* by the American Home Economics Association.

CHEESE PUPPIES

4 student servings		6 student servings
4	FRANKFURTERS	6
4	CHEESE STRIPS (4x½x¼ inches)	6
2	BACON SLICES	3
8	TOOTHPICKS	12

STEPS IN PREPARATION

1. Slit frankfurters lengthwise to within ½ inch of each end, being careful not to cut all the way through.

2. Turn on the broiler, and set the temperature control at "Broil."

3. Put one cheese strip in each frankfurter.

4. Cut the bacon in half crosswise, and place one piece on each frankfurter over the cheese. Hold the bacon in place at each end with a toothpick.

5. Arrange the frankfurters in a shallow baking pan with the bacon side up.

6. Place the pan in the broiler so the tops of the frankfurters are 3 inches from the heating unit.

7. Broil under direct heat until the bacon is crisp and the cheese is melted.

8. Serve hot.

---

2 student servings: 2 frankfurters; 2 cheese strips (4x½x¼ inches); 1 bacon slice; 4 toothpicks

---

HINTS

1. Mustard may be spread in the slit of the frankfurter before it is filled with the cheese.

2. The bacon may be partially cooked before it is placed on the frankfurter in Step 4.

3. For broiling cheese puppies over a campfire, use one whole slice of bacon wrapped around the frankfurter and fastened at each end with a toothpick.

BEEF STEW

4 student servings		6 student servings
⅔ pound	LEAN BEEF	1 pound
1 tablespoon	FLOUR	2 tablespoons
1 teaspoon	SALT	1½ teaspoons
⅛ teaspoon	PEPPER	¼ teaspoon
1 tablespoon	OIL or SHORTENING	2 tablespoons
⅔ cup	TOMATO SAUCE	1 cup
1 cup	HOT WATER	1 to 1½ cups
4	SMALL ONIONS	6
2	MEDIUM CARROTS	3
2	MEDIUM POTATOES	3

STEPS IN PREPARATION

1. Cut the beef into 2-inch cubes. (See picture on page 447.)
2. Mix the flour, salt, and pepper in a flat dish or pan. Roll each piece of meat in the seasoned flour until it is well coated. (See picture on page 279.)
3. Place the oil or shortening in a heavy skillet over moderate heat.
4. Brown the meat slowly on all sides in the hot fat, stirring occasionally.
5. Add the tomato sauce and enough hot water to cover the meat.
6. Cover the skillet or kettle with a tight-fitting lid. Lower the heat, and simmer 1 to 1½ hours, or until the meat is almost tender.
7. Peel the onions, scrape the carrots, and pare the potatoes. Cut all into quarters.
8. Add the onions, carrots, and potatoes to the meat, and cook 20 minutes, or until the vegetables are tender.
9. Serve in a warm dish, garnished with parsley or celery leaves.

---

2 student servings: ⅓ pound lean beef; 2 teaspoons flour; ½ teaspoon salt; few grains pepper; 2 teaspoons oil or shortening; ⅓ cup tomato sauce; ¾ cup hot water; 2 small onions; 1 medium carrot; 1 medium potato

---

(*NOTE:* If time does not allow for complete preparation in one class period, Steps 1-6 may be done one day and Steps 7-9 another day.)

HINTS

1. One 8-ounce can of tomato sauce equals 1 cup.
2. Lamb may be substituted for beef to make lamb stew.
3. To make a meat pie, put the stew in a baking dish, top it with baking powder biscuits, pastry, or mashed potatoes, and bake. (See picture on page 90.)

MEAT LOAF

4 student servings		6 student servings
2 tablespoons (1 small egg)	BEATEN EGG	1
⅓ cup	SOFT BREAD CRUMBS	½ cup
⅓ cup	MILK	½ cup
1 cup (½ pound)	GROUND BEEF	1½ cups (¾ pound)
2 tablespoons	CHOPPED ONION	3 tablespoons
½ teaspoon	SALT	¾ teaspoon
⅛ teaspoon	PEPPER	¼ teaspoon

STEPS IN PREPARATION

1. Turn on the oven, and set the temperature control at 350° F. for a moderate oven.

2. Put the beaten egg, bread crumbs, and milk in a mixing bowl.

3. Add the beef, onion, salt, and pepper to the bread-crumb mixture, and mix lightly.

   (*NOTE:* Too much mixing will toughen the loaf.)

4. Press the meat lightly into a greased loaf pan, or shape the meat into an oblong loaf on a greased pan. (See pictures on page 276.)

   (*NOTE:* To shorten the cooking time, shape into individual loaves, or fill muffin pans about two-thirds full, as shown in the picture on page 145.)

5. Bake 30 minutes to 1 hour, depending upon the size of the loaf.

6. Serve hot or cold. Tomato sauce may be added.

---

2 student servings: 1 tablespoon beaten egg; 3 tablespoons soft bread crumbs; 3 tablespoons milk; ½ cup (¼ pound) ground beef; 1 tablespoon chopped onion; ¼ teaspoon salt; few grains pepper

---

(*NOTE:* If time does not allow for complete preparation in one class period, Steps 2 through 4 may be done one day and Steps 5 and 6 another day.)

TIMETABLE FOR ROASTING MEATS*

KIND AND CUT	APPROXIMATE WEIGHT	INTERNAL TEMPERATURE	APPROXIMATE TOTAL COOKING TIME AT 325° F.
Beef	(pounds)		(hours)
Standing ribs**	4	140° F. (rare)	1¾
(10-inch ribs)		160° F. (medium)	2
		170° F. (well done)	2½
	6	140° F. (rare)	2
		160° F. (medium)	2½
		170° F. (well done)	3⅓
Rolled ribs	4	140° F. (rare)	2
		160° F. (medium)	2½
		170° F. (well done)	3
	6	140° F. (rare)	3
		160° F. (medium)	3¼
		170° F. (well done)	4
Rolled rump	5	140° F. (rare)	2¼
		160° F. (medium)	3
		170° F. (well done)	3¼
Sirloin tip	3	140° F. (rare)	1½
		160° F. (medium)	2
		170° F. (well done)	2¼
Lamb			
Leg (half)	3 to 4	180° F. (well done)	2½ to 3
Rolled shoulder	3	180° F. (well done)	2½
	5	180° F. (well done)	3
Veal			
Leg	5	170° F. (well done)	2½ to 3
	8	170° F. (well done)	3½
Loin	5	170° F. (well done)	3
Shoulder	6	170° F. (well done)	3½
Pork, fresh			
Leg (fresh ham)	6	185° F. (well done)	4
Cushion shoulder	5	185° F. (well done)	3½
Shoulder butt	5	185° F. (well done)	3½
Pork, cured			
Ham, whole	12	160° F. (well done)	3½
Picnic shoulder	6	170° F. (well done)	3½

*Adapted from *Handbook of Food Preparation* by the American Home Economics Association.

**Standing ribs, 8-inch ribs, allow 30 minutes longer.

CHICKEN SPAGHETTI

4 student servings		6 student servings
1 cup	COOKED CHICKEN	1½ cups
1½ cups	CHICKEN BROTH	2 cups
⅓ cup	TOMATO SOUP	½ cup
½ clove	FINELY CHOPPED GARLIC	¾ clove
2 tablespoons	CHOPPED ONION	3 tablespoons
1	WHOLE CLOVE	2
2 tablespoons	MUSHROOMS (canned) (if desired)	3 tablespoons
½ teaspoon	SALT	¾ teaspoon
½ cup (2 ounces)	BROKEN SPAGHETTI	¾ cup (3 ounces)

STEPS IN PREPARATION

1. Cut the chicken into 1-inch pieces.

2. Put the chicken, chicken broth, tomato soup, garlic, onion, and whole clove in a saucepan. Add the mushrooms, if desired.

3. Cook over moderate heat 10 minutes. Season with salt.

4. Add the uncooked spaghetti to the chicken mixture. Boil gently for 10 minutes, or until the spaghetti is tender when mashed against the side of the saucepan with a fork. (See picture on page 308.)

5. Serve hot.

---

2 student servings: ½ cup cooked chicken; 1 cup chicken broth; ¼ cup tomato soup; ¼ clove finely chopped garlic; 1 tablespoon chopped onion; 1 whole clove; 1 tablespoon canned mushrooms (if desired); ¼ teaspoon salt; ¼ cup (1 ounce) broken spaghetti

---

HINTS

1. Canned consommé or chicken bouillon cubes may be substituted for the chicken broth.

2. One can of tomato soup measures 1¼ cups.

BROILED FISH FILLETS

4 student servings		6 student servings
1 pound	**FISH FILLETS** (fresh or frozen)	1½ pounds
¼ teaspoon	**SALT**	½ teaspoon
2 tablespoons	**BUTTER or MARGARINE**	3 tablespoons
2 teaspoons	**LEMON JUICE**	1 tablespoon

STEPS IN PREPARATION

1. Let the fish thaw partially if it is frozen.

2. Turn on the broiler, and set the temperature control at "Broil."

3. Sprinkle the fish with salt.

4. Melt the butter or margarine in a small saucepan. Add lemon juice.

5. Arrange the fish, with the skin side down, on a greased baking pan or a broiler rack.

6. Place the pan in the broiler so the top of the fish is about 3 inches from the heating unit.

7. Baste the fish with the lemon-and-butter sauce occasionally while it cooks. It is not necessary to turn fillets unless they are more than 1 inch thick. (See picture on page 297.)

8. Broil the fish 6 to 10 minutes, or until it is brown and easily flaked with a fork but still moist. (See picture on page 296.)

9. Serve on a hot platter.

---

2 student servings: ½ pound fish fillets (fresh or frozen); ⅛ teaspoon salt; 1 tablespoon butter or margarine; 1 teaspoon lemon juice

---

HINTS

1. Fish fillets may be garnished with finely chopped parsley or lemon slices.
2. Any of the following ingredients may be added to the lemon-and-melted-butter mixture for 6 servings: 1 tablespoon finely chopped onion, 1 teaspoon Worcestershire sauce, 1 teaspoon mustard, or 1 tablespoon catsup.

DRIED BEEF RABBIT

4 student servings		6 student servings
1⅓ cups	MEDIUM WHITE SAUCE (page 501)	2 cups
1⅓ cups	GRATED AMERICAN CHEESE	2 cups
4 ounces	DRIED BEEF	6 ounces
4 slices	CRISP TOAST	6 slices

STEPS IN PREPARATION

1. Make **Medium White Sauce,** omitting the salt.

2. Add the cheese to the white sauce, and stir until it melts.

3. Tear the dried beef into pieces with the fingers.

4. Add the dried beef to the white sauce, and mix lightly.

5. Serve hot on toast, **Baking Powder Biscuits** (page 528), **Waffles** (page 527), fluffy rice, or baked potatoes. See picture on page 249.

2 student servings: ⅔ cup **Medium White Sauce** (page 501); ⅔ cup grated American cheese; 2 ounces dried beef; 2 slices crisp toast

CREAMED HAM or CHICKEN

4 student servings		6 student servings
1⅓ cups	COOKED HAM or CHICKEN	2 cups

Follow the recipe for **Dried Beef Rabbit,** but omit the cheese and dried beef, and use cooked ham or chicken cut into ½-inch pieces. Add it to the white sauce, and season with salt. Serve on crisp toast.

CREAMED CHEESE ON TOAST

Follow the recipe for **Dried Beef Rabbit,** but in Step 4 omit the dried beef. Season with salt, a few grains of dry mustard, and paprika. Add more grated cheese, if desired. Serve on hot, crisp, toast.

CREAMED TUNA

4 student servings		6 student servings
⅔ cup	FLAKED TUNA	1 cup
1 tablespoon	LEMON JUICE	2 tablespoons
2 teaspoons	GRATED ONION	1 tablespoon

Follow the recipe for **Dried Beef Rabbit,** but omit the cheese and dried beef, and add flaked tuna, lemon juice, and onion to the white sauce. Season with salt. Serve on crisp toast. Chopped pimento or celery may be added for color and texture contrast.

TUNA CASSEROLE

4 student servings		6 student servings
⅔ cup	CREAM OF MUSHROOM SOUP	1 cup
⅓ cup	MILK	½ cup
⅔ cup	TUNA	1 cup
⅔ cup	COOKED GREEN PEAS	1 cup
⅔ cup	CRUSHED POTATO CHIPS	1 cup

STEPS IN PREPARATION

1. Turn on the oven, and set the temperature control at 350° F. for a moderate oven.

2. Put the mushroom soup in a small casserole, add the milk, and stir until well blended.

3. Drain liquid from the tuna (see picture on page 295) and green peas.

4. Add the tuna, green peas, and about three-fourths of the potato chips to the soup, and mix well.

5. Sprinkle the remaining potato chips over the top.

6. Bake 25 minutes.

7. Serve hot in the casserole.

2 student servings: ⅓ cup cream of mushroom soup; 2 tablespoons milk; ⅓ cup tuna; ⅓ cup cooked green peas; ⅓ cup crushed potato chips

BREADS

BUTTERED TOAST
(Broiler Method)

4 student servings		6 student servings
4 slices	DAY-OLD BREAD	6 slices
4 teaspoons	BUTTER or MARGARINE	2 tablespoons

STEPS IN PREPARATION

1. Turn on the broiler, and place the broiler rack so it is 2 to 4 inches from the heating unit.
2. Place the bread on the broiler rack,* and toast it to a golden brown on one side. Watch carefully to prevent burning.
3. Turn and brown on the other side.
   (*NOTE:* For dry, crisp toast, brown the bread slowly. For toast that is soft inside, brown the bread quickly.)
4. Spread butter or margarine evenly over the toast, and serve it hot.

*Bread may also be arranged on a baking sheet and toasted in a hot oven with the temperature control at its highest point.

---

2 student servings: 2 slices day-old bread; 2 teaspoons butter or margarine

---

CINNAMON TOAST

4 student servings		6 student servings
2 tablespoons	SUGAR	3 tablespoons
½ teaspoon	CINNAMON	¾ teaspoon
4 slices	DAY-OLD BREAD	6 slices
4 teaspoons	SOFT BUTTER or MARGARINE	2 tablespoons

STEPS IN PREPARATION

1. Mix the sugar and cinnamon.
2. Make buttered toast according to the directions above.
3. Sprinkle the sugar-and-cinnamon mixture over the buttered side of the toast.
4. Return the toast to the broiler, and heat until the sugar melts.
5. Serve hot.

---

2 student servings: 1 tablespoon sugar; ¼ teaspoon cinnamon; 2 slices day-old bread; 2 teaspoons soft butter or margarine.

ORANGE TOAST

4 student servings		6 student servings
2 teaspoons	ORANGE JUICE	1 tablespoon
2 teaspoons	ORANGE RIND	1 tablespoon
¼ cup	SUGAR	⅓ cup

Follow the recipe for **Cinnamon Toast,** but in Step 3 substitute the above mixture for the sugar-and-cinnamon mixture.

FRENCH TOAST

4 student servings		6 student servings
1	EGG	2
⅓ cup	MILK	½ cup
⅛ teaspoon	SALT	¼ teaspoon
4 teaspoons	BUTTER or MARGARINE	2 tablespoons
4 slices	DAY-OLD BREAD	6 slices

STEPS IN PREPARATION

1. Break the egg into a shallow dish or pan.

2. Beat the egg slightly with a fork, add the milk and salt, and mix.

3. Melt 1 teaspoon butter or margarine in a heavy skillet or griddle for each slice of bread that you will cook at the same time.

4. Dip each side of the bread quickly into the egg-and-milk mixture so it is coated but not soaked with the mixture.

5. Put the bread in the hot skillet, and cook it over low heat until it is golden brown on one side.

6. Turn and brown on the other side.

7. Serve hot with sirup, jam, jelly, or confectioners' sugar. (See picture on page 314.)

2 student servings: 2 tablespoons beaten egg; 3 tablespoons milk; few grains salt; 2 teaspoons butter or margarine; 2 slices day-old bread

GRIDDLECAKES

4 student servings (4 griddlecakes)		6 student servings (6 griddlecakes)
1 cup (sifted)	ALL-PURPOSE FLOUR	1½ cups (sifted)
1¾ teaspoons	BAKING POWDER	2½ teaspoons
4 teaspoons	SUGAR	2 tablespoons
½ teaspoon	SALT	¾ teaspoon
2 tablespoons (1 small egg)	BEATEN EGG	1
⅔ to ¾ cup	MILK	1¼ cups
2 tablespoons	OIL or MELTED SHORTENING	3 tablespoons

STEPS IN PREPARATION

1. Sift the flour with the baking powder, sugar, and salt into a mixing bowl. (See picture on page 438.)
2. Mix the beaten egg, milk, and oil or cooled melted shortening.
3. Heat the griddle or skillet.
4. Add the egg-and-milk mixture to the dry ingredients all at once, and stir quickly until the dry ingredients are moistened. Do not beat or overmix, because the mixture should be lumpy.
5. Test the griddle or skillet by sprinkling a few drops of cold water on it. If the drops dance about and evaporate, the griddle is ready. (See picture on page 320.)
6. Pour the batter onto the hot griddle from a pitcher or from the tip of a large spoon, making each cake 3 to 4 inches across.
7. Cook until the top is full of little air bubbles and the under side is golden brown. Turn with a pancake turner before bubbles break.
8. Brown the other side. Turn only one time.
9. Serve at once with butter or margarine and sirup, jelly, or honey.

---

2 student servings (2 griddlecakes): ½ cup sifted all-purpose flour; 1 teaspoon baking powder; 2 teaspoons sugar; ¼ teaspoon salt; 1 tablespoon beaten egg; ⅓ to ½ cup milk; 1 tablespoon oil or melted shortening

---

(*NOTE:* If time does not allow for complete preparation in one class period, Step 1 may be done one day and Steps 2 through 9 another day.)

WAFFLES

4 student servings (4 waffles)		6 student servings (6 waffles)
1 cup (sifted)	ALL-PURPOSE FLOUR	1½ cups (sifted)
1 teaspoon	BAKING POWDER	2 teaspoons
¼ teaspoon	SALT	½ teaspoon
1½ teaspoons	SUGAR	2 teaspoons
1	EGG	2
⅔ cup	MILK	1 cup
4 tablespoons	OIL or MELTED SHORTENING	6 tablespoons

STEPS IN PREPARATION

1. Sift flour with baking powder, salt, and sugar into a mixing bowl.

2. Separate the egg yolk from the egg white. (See picture on page 464.)

3. Beat the egg yolk until it is light and foamy, and stir in the milk and the oil or cooled melted shortening.

4. Start heating the waffle iron.

5. Add the egg-and-milk mixture to the dry ingredients all at once, and stir quickly until the dry ingredients are moistened.

6. Beat the egg white until it stands in stiff peaks when the beater is lifted. (See picture on page 466.)

7. Fold egg white into the batter until all egg white has disappeared.

8. Pour 1 to 2 tablespoons of the batter into the center of each section of the waffle iron when it is hot. (See picture on page 321.)

9. Close the cover, and bake 3 to 5 minutes, or until the waffle iron stops steaming and the waffle is golden brown. Do not raise the cover while baking.

10. Remove the waffle with a fork.

11. Serve immediately with butter or margarine and sirup, jam, or honey.

---

2 student servings (2 waffles): ½ cup sifted all-purpose flour; ½ teaspoon baking powder; ⅛ teaspoon salt; ½ teaspoon sugar; 1 small egg; ⅓ cup milk; 2 tablespoons oil or melted shortening

BAKING POWDER BISCUITS

4 student servings (8 medium biscuits)		6 student servings (12 medium biscuits)
1 cup (sifted)	ALL-PURPOSE FLOUR	1½ cups (sifted)
1½ teaspoons	BAKING POWDER	2¼ teaspoons
½ teaspoon	SALT	¾ teaspoon
2 tablespoons	SHORTENING	3 tablespoons
⅓ cup	MILK	½ cup

STEPS IN PREPARATION

1. Turn on the oven, and set the temperature control at 450° F. for a very hot oven.

2. Sift the flour with the baking powder and salt into a mixing bowl. (See picture on page 438.)

3. Add the shortening and cut into the flour mixture with a pastry blender or two knives until the mixture looks like coarse corn meal. (See picture on page 316.)

4. Add gradually just enough milk to make a soft dough, and stir.

   (*NOTE:* If more milk is needed to make a soft dough as shown in the picture on page 316, add extra milk, 1 tablespoon at a time.)

5. Sprinkle flour on a pastry board or cloth, and turn out the dough.

6. Knead the dough gently a few times until it is smooth. (See picture on page 316.)

7. Pat or roll the dough lightly until it is about ½ inch thick. (See picture on page 317.)

8. Cut the biscuits with a biscuit cutter that has been dipped in flour.

9. Place the biscuits on an ungreased shallow baking pan about 1 inch apart. (See pictures on page 317.)

10. Bake 12 to 15 minutes, or until golden brown.

---

2 student servings (4 to 6 medium biscuits): ⅔ cup sifted all-purpose flour; 1 teaspoon baking powder; ¼ teaspoon salt; 1 tablespoon shortening; ¼ cup milk

---

(*NOTE:* If time does not allow for complete preparation in one class period, Steps 2 and 3 may be done one day and Steps 4 to 10 another day.)

PLAIN MUFFINS

4 student servings (8 small muffins)		6 student servings (12 small muffins)
1 cup (sifted)	ALL-PURPOSE FLOUR	1½ cups (sifted)
1½ teaspoons	BAKING POWDER	2¼ teaspoons
¼ teaspoon	SALT	½ teaspoon
1 tablespoon	SUGAR	1½ tablespoons
2 tablespoons (1 small egg)	BEATEN EGG	1
½ cup	MILK	¾ cup
2 tablespoons	OIL or MELTED SHORTENING	3 tablespoons

STEPS IN PREPARATION

1. Turn on the oven, and set the temperature control at 425° F. for a hot oven.

2. Prepare the muffin pan by greasing the bottoms and sides with shortening or oil.

3. Sift the flour with the baking powder, salt, and sugar into a mixing bowl. (See picture on page 438.)

4. Mix the beaten egg, milk, and oil or cooled melted shortening. (See picture on page 318.)

5. Add the egg-and-milk mixture to the dry ingredients all at once, and stir quickly until the dry ingredients are moistened. Do not overmix or beat, because the mixture should be lumpy.

6. Fill the greased muffin pans one-half to two-thirds full.

7. Bake 20 to 25 minutes, or until golden brown.

---

2 student servings (4 small muffins): ⅔ cup sifted all-purpose flour; 1 teaspoon baking powder; ⅛ teaspoon salt; 2 teaspoons sugar; 1 tablespoon beaten egg; ⅓ cup milk; 1 tablespoon oil or melted shortening

---

(*NOTE:* If time does not allow for complete preparation in one class period, Step 3 may be done one day and the other steps another day.)

BEVERAGES

COCOA

4 student servings		6 student servings
2 tablespoons	SUGAR	3 tablespoons
2 tablespoons	COCOA	3 tablespoons
few grains	SALT	⅛ teaspoon
⅔ cup	WATER	1 cup
2 cups	MILK	3 cups

STEPS IN PREPARATION

1. Fill the lower part of a double boiler about one-third full of water. Heat to boiling.

2. Mix the sugar, cocoa, and salt in the upper part of the double boiler.

3. Add the water to the cocoa mixture, and stir until it is smooth.

4. Boil 3 minutes over direct heat, stirring constantly. (See picture on page 364.)

5. Add the milk, and place the upper part of the double boiler over the boiling water.

6. Heat 10 minutes, or until the mixture is hot. Do not let it boil.

7. Beat with a rotary beater just before serving, until it is smooth and foamy.

8. Serve plain, with marshmallows, or with whipped cream. (See picture on page 8.)

---

2 student servings: 1 tablespoon sugar; 1 tablespoon cocoa; few grains salt; ⅓ cup water; 1 cup milk

---

(*NOTE:* If time does not allow for complete preparation in one class period, Steps 2 through 4 may be done one day and Steps 5 through 8 another day.)

HINT: To prepare instant cocoa, often called "ready-to-serve" cocoa, follow the directions given on the label of the can.

LEMONADE

4 student servings		6 student servings
⅔ cup	WATER	1 cup
⅔ cup	SUGAR	1 cup
⅔ cup (3 to 4 lemons)	LEMON JUICE (fresh or frozen)	1 cup (5 to 6 lemons)
2½ cups	COLD WATER	3½ cups

STEPS IN PREPARATION

1. Put the water and sugar in a saucepan, and stir.
2. Boil the water-and-sugar mixture 1 to 2 minutes, or until the sugar dissolves. Cool.
3. Squeeze the juice from the lemons while the sirup is cooling. Strain and pour into a pitcher.
4. Add the cold water and cooled sugar sirup to the lemon juice, and mix well.
5. Pour into glasses filled with ice cubes.
6. Garnish with slices of lemon, sprigs of mint, or maraschino cherries.

---

2 student servings: ⅓ cup water; ⅓ cup sugar; ⅓ cup lemon juice (fresh or frozen); 1½ cups cold water

---

LIMEADE

Follow the recipe for **Lemonade,** but in Step 3 substitute lime juice in place of lemon juice. A few drops of green coloring may be added.

ORANGEADE

4 student servings		6 student servings
1⅓ cups	ORANGE JUICE	2 cups
2 to 3 tablespoons	LEMON JUICE	¼ cup

Follow the recipe for **Lemonade,** but use the above amounts of orange and lemon juice.

DESSERTS

STRAWBERRY or RASPBERRY SPONGE

4 student servings		6 student servings
⅔ cup	STRAWBERRIES or RASPBERRIES (fresh or frozen)	1 cup
⅓ cup	COLD WATER	½ cup
2 teaspoons	UNFLAVORED GELATIN	1 tablespoon
⅓ cup	SUGAR	½ cup
1 tablespoon	LEMON JUICE	1½ tablespoons
1	EGG WHITE	2

STEPS IN PREPARATION

1. Crush the berries with a fork, if fresh. Defrost the berries, if frozen.

2. Fill the lower part of a double boiler about one-third full of water. Heat to boiling.

3. Pour the cold water into the upper part of the double boiler. Sprinkle the gelatin over the water, and soak 5 to 10 minutes.

4. Place the upper part of the double boiler over the boiling water. Stir until the gelatin dissolves.

5. Add the sugar, and stir until it dissolves.

6. Remove from the heat. Add the lemon juice and the berries.

7. Cool quickly by placing the upper part of the double boiler in a bowl of ice and water. Chill until slightly thickened, as shown in the picture on page 349.

8. Beat the egg white until it stands in soft, rounded peaks when the beater is lifted.

9. Beat the gelatin mixture with a rotary beater until it is light and fluffy.

10. Fold the egg white into the gelatin mixture.

11. Turn into individual molds, custard cups, or serving dishes, and chill in the refrigerator.

12. Serve with **Soft Custard** (page 536), whipped cream, or crushed sweetened berries.

TAPIOCA CREAM

4 student servings		6 student servings
2 small	EGG YOLKS	2
1⅓ cups	MILK	2 cups
¼ cup	SUGAR	⅓ cup
2 tablespoons	QUICK-COOKING TAPIOCA	3 tablespoons
⅛ teaspoon	SALT	¼ teaspoon
½ teaspoon	VANILLA	1 teaspoon
2	EGG WHITES	2

STEPS IN PREPARATION

1. Put the egg yolks in a saucepan, and beat with a rotary beater until well blended.

2. Add the milk to the beaten egg yolks slowly.

3. Stir in about half of the sugar. Add the tapioca and the salt.

4. Cook over low heat, stirring constantly, 5 to 8 minutes, or until the mixture comes to a boil.

5. Remove from the heat, and add the vanilla.

6. Beat the egg whites in a mixing bowl until foamy. Gradually add the remaining sugar and continue beating until the egg whites stand in soft, rounded peaks when the beater is lifted. (See picture on page 466.)

7. Add the hot tapioca mixture to the beaten egg whites, stirring constantly.

8. Cool the mixture, stirring once after 15 or 20 minutes.

9. Chill.

10. Serve plain or with fruit or cream.

---

2 student servings: 1 egg yolk; ⅔ cup milk; 2 tablespoons sugar; 1 tablespoon quick-cooking tapioca; few grains salt; ¼ teaspoon vanilla; 1 egg white

---

HINT: For variety, in Step 7 add ¼ cup semisweet chocolate pieces or ¼ cup crushed peanut brittle for 6 servings.

SOFT CUSTARD

4 student servings		6 student servings
1⅓ cups	MILK	2 cups
2	EGGS	3
¼ cup	SUGAR	⅓ cup
⅛ teaspoon	SALT	¼ teaspoon
1 teaspoon	VANILLA	1½ teaspoons

STEPS IN PREPARATION

1. Fill the lower part of a double boiler about one-third full of water. Heat to boiling.
2. Pour the milk in the upper part of the double boiler, and place it over the boiling water. Heat the milk, without stirring, until scalded, or until tiny bubbles form around the edge. (See picture on page 456.)
3. Break the eggs into a mixing bowl. Beat with a fork or a rotary beater until well blended. Stir in the sugar and salt.
4. Add the scalded milk gradually to the beaten eggs, stirring constantly.
5. Pour the egg-and-milk mixture into the upper part of the double boiler. Cook slowly over the hot water, stirring constantly, 5 to 7 minutes, or until the mixture coats a metal spoon. (See picture on page 347.)
6. Remove from the heat. Cool quickly by placing the pan in cold water. Add vanilla. Then chill in the refrigerator.
7. Serve with whipped cream or as a sauce over cake, fruit, or puddings.

---

2 student servings: ⅔ cup milk; 1 egg; 2 tablespoons sugar; few grains salt; ½ teaspoon vanilla

---

BAKED CUSTARD

1. Follow the recipe for **Soft Custard,** but in Step 5 pour the milk-and-egg mixture into custard cups which have been placed in a shallow baking pan. (See picture on page 347.)
2. Sprinkle a little nutmeg over each cup. Pour hot water carefully into the baking pan until it is even with the custard in the cup.
3. Bake 30 to 40 minutes in a 350° F. oven. Test for doneness by inserting a silver knife in the center of the custard. If the knife comes out clean, the custard is done. Remove from the heat immediately.
4. Serve warm, or chill and serve cold. Serve in custard cups, or unmold by running a spatula around the inside of each cup, inverting on a dessert plate. (See picture on page 113.)

PASTRY
(8-inch Pie Shell)

1 crust		2 crusts
1 cup (sifted)	ALL-PURPOSE FLOUR	1½ cups (sifted)
½ teaspoon	SALT	¾ teaspoon
⅓ cup	SHORTENING	½ cup
2 tablespoons	COLD WATER	3 tablespoons

STEPS IN PREPARATION OF A 1-CRUST PIE

1. Turn on the oven, and set the temperature control at 450° F. for a very hot oven.
2. Sift the flour with the salt into a mixing bowl.
3. Add half the shortening, and cut it into the flour mixture with a pastry blender or two knives until the mixture looks like coarse corn meal.
4. Add the remaining shortening, and cut it in until the lumps are about the size of large peas, as shown in the picture on page 354.
5. Sprinkle the water over the flour mixture 1 tablespoon at a time. Mix lightly until the mixture sticks together and cleans the bowl.
6. Roll the dough between two sheets of wax paper, as shown in the picture on page 354, or roll the dough on a floured board, as shown in the pictures on page 355. Roll from the center to the edge with light strokes until the dough is ⅛ inch thick and is 1 inch larger around than the piepan.
7. Pat and fit the dough into the piepan without stretching or pulling it, as shown in the pictures on page 355.
8. Cut off the edges, leaving a ½- to 1-inch overhang for a single crust.
9. Build up a rim around the edge of the crust, and flute the edges, as shown in the picture on page 356. Then prick holes in the side and bottom of the pastry.
10. Bake 10 to 15 minutes, or until golden brown.
11. Cool. Then add the filling. (See picture on page 356.)

STEPS IN PREPARATION OF A 2-CRUST PIE

1. Measure the ingredients listed above for a 2-crust pie.
2. Follow Steps 2 through 5 for a 1-crust pie.
3. Divide the dough about in half.
4. Follow Steps 6 and 7 for a 1-crust pie for rolling the bottom crust and putting it in the piepan. Cut off the edges even with the rim of the pan.
5. Turn on the oven, and set the temperature control at 425° F.
6. Prepare the filling.
7. Cover the filling with pastry according to directions on page 357.
8. Bake 40 to 50 minutes, or until the crust is nicely browned.

CREAM PIE
(8-inch Pie)

2 cups	MILK
½ cup	SUGAR
¼ cup	CORNSTARCH
⅛ teaspoon	SALT
2	EGG YOLKS
1 tablespoon	BUTTER or MARGARINE
1 teaspoon	VANILLA

STEPS IN PREPARATION

1. Bake pastry for a 1-crust pie according to the directions on page 537.

2. Fill the lower part of a double boiler about one-third full of water. Heat to boiling.

3. Pour the milk into the upper part of the double boiler, and place over the boiling water. Heat the milk, without stirring, until scalded, or until tiny bubbles form around the edge. (See picture on page 456.)

4. Put the sugar, cornstarch, and salt in a mixing bowl, and mix lightly. (See picture on page 352.)

5. Add the scalded milk gradually to the sugar mixture, stirring constantly to prevent lumping.

6. Pour the mixture into the upper part of the double boiler. Cook over the boiling water, stirring constantly, about 15 minutes, or until thick.

7. Cover and cook 10 minutes longer, stirring occasionally. (See picture on page 353.)

8. Beat the egg yolks with a fork.

9. Add about half of the hot mixture slowly to the beaten egg yolks, stirring constantly. (See picture on page 353.)

10. Stir the egg mixture into the hot mixture that is left in the top of the double boiler. Cook 2 to 5 minutes longer, or until the mixture forms a mound when dropped from a spoon.

11. Add the butter or margarine and vanilla. Cool.

12. Pour the cooled filling into a baked pie shell. Cover with meringue. (See page 540.) Bake in a moderate oven (350° F.) 12 to 15 minutes.

VANILLA PUDDING

Prepare filling for a cream pie according to the directions on page 538. Chill, and serve as a dessert with crushed fruit, whipped cream, or ice cream. (See pictures on page 348.)

CREAM PIE VARIATIONS AND PUDDINGS

CHOCOLATE CREAM PIE or PUDDING: Follow the recipe for **Cream Pie,** but in Step 3 add 2 squares unsweetened chocolate, cut into small pieces, to the scalded milk, and in Step 4 increase the amount of sugar to ⅔ cup. Use as a pie filling covered with meringue, or add nuts and serve as a pudding.

BANANA CREAM PIE or PUDDING: Follow the recipe for **Cream Pie,** but in Step 12 peel 2 bananas, and slice them crosswise into the cooled pie shell. Then pour the cooled filling over the bananas, and cover with whipped cream. For banana pudding, combine sliced bananas and cream pie filling. Chill and serve with cream.

BUTTERSCOTCH CREAM PIE or PUDDING: Follow the recipe for **Cream Pie,** but in Step 4 substitute brown sugar for granulated sugar, and in Step 11 increase the amount of butter to 2 tablespoons. Use as a pie filling, or chill and serve as a pudding topped with whipped cream.

PINEAPPLE CREAM PIE or PUDDING: Follow the recipe for **Cream Pie,** but in Step 12 add ½ cup drained crushed pineapple to the cooled filling just before pouring it into the pie shell, or chill and serve as a pudding.

COCONUT CREAM PIE or PUDDING: Follow the recipe for **Cream Pie,** but in Step 12 fold ¾ cup shredded coconut into the filling just before pouring it into the pie shell. The meringue may be sprinkled with a small amount of the coconut just before it is browned. Coconut cream pie filling may also be served as a pudding.

MERINGUE
(For 8-inch Pie)

2	EGG WHITES
⅛ teaspoon	SALT
4 tablespoons	SUGAR
¼ teaspoon	VANILLA (if desired)

STEPS IN PREPARATION

1. Turn on the oven, and set the temperature control at 350° F. for a moderate oven.

2. Put the egg whites* in a large mixing bowl, and add the salt.

3. Beat the egg whites until foamy or frothy, as shown in the picture on page 466.

4. Add the sugar, 1 tablespoon at a time, and continue beating until the sugar dissolves and until the egg whites stand in pointed peaks when the beater is lifted but are not dry. (See picture on page 358.)

5. Add vanilla, if desired.

6. Pile the meringue on top of the cooled pie filling, being sure that it touches the crust all around. Pile higher in the center.

7. Bake 12 to 15 minutes, or until light brown.

8. Remove from the oven.

9. Cool at room temperature away from any draft, to prevent shrinking and weeping.

---

*Egg whites will not whip to a stiff foam if any egg yolk or fat is present. Egg whites that are at room temperature are easier to whip.

REFRIGERATOR COOKIES

3 to 4 dozen		4 to 6 dozen
½ cup	BUTTER or MARGARINE	¾ cup
1 cup	SUGAR	1½ cups
1	EGG	2
1 teaspoon	VANILLA	1½ teaspoons
2 cups (sifted)	ALL-PURPOSE FLOUR	3 cups (sifted)
½ teaspoon	SALT	¾ teaspoon
½ teaspoon	SODA	¾ teaspoon
½ cup	FINELY CHOPPED NUTS (if desired)	¾ cup

STEPS IN PREPARATION

1. Cream the butter or margarine until soft and smooth by rubbing it against the side of the bowl with the back of a spoon. Slowly add the sugar, and continue creaming until light and fluffy.
2. Beat the egg with a rotary beater.
3. Add the egg and vanilla to the sugar mixture. Stir until smooth.
4. Sift the flour with the salt and soda into a mixing bowl or onto wax paper. (See picture on page 438.)
5. Add the sifted dry ingredients gradually to the egg mixture, and mix thoroughly. Add the nuts, if desired.
6. Press the dough together with the hands. Shape into long rolls about 2 inches in diameter. (See picture on page 328.)
7. Wrap in wax paper. Chill overnight or for several hours until firm.
8. Turn on the oven, and set the temperature control at 375° F. for a moderate oven.
9. Cut the dough into thin, uniform slices about ⅛ inch thick.
10. Place the cookies about 1 inch apart on an ungreased baking sheet.
11. Bake 10 to 12 minutes, or until lightly browned.
12. Remove the cookies from the baking sheet with a spatula, and cool on a cake rack.

---

18 to 24 cookies: ¼ cup butter or margarine; ½ cup sugar; 2 tablespoons beaten egg; ½ teaspoon vanilla; 1 cup sifted all-purpose flour; ¼ teaspoon salt; ¼ teaspoon soda; ¼ cup finely chopped nuts (if desired)

OATMEAL COOKIES

20 cookies		40 cookies
½ cup (sifted)	ALL-PURPOSE FLOUR	1 cup (sifted)
¼ teaspoon	SODA	½ teaspoon
¼ teaspoon	SALT	½ teaspoon
½ teaspoon	CINNAMON	1 teaspoon
¼ cup	BROWN SUGAR	½ cup
2 tablespoons	GRANULATED SUGAR	¼ cup
¼ cup	SHORTENING	½ cup
2 tablespoons (1 small egg)	BEATEN EGG	1
1 tablespoon	MILK	2 tablespoons
1 cup	QUICK-COOKING ROLLED OATS	2 cups
½ cup	RAISINS	1 cup

STEPS IN PREPARATION

1. Turn on the oven, and set the temperature control at 375° F. for a moderate oven.
2. Prepare the baking sheet by lightly greasing it with shortening.
3. Sift the flour with the soda, salt, and cinnamon into a mixing bowl.
4. Add the brown sugar, granulated sugar, shortening, beaten egg, and milk.
5. Beat vigorously by hand for 50 strokes. (For a larger recipe, beat 100 strokes.)
6. Stir in the rolled oats and raisins.
7. Drop by rounded teaspoonfuls, about 2 inches apart, on the prepared baking sheet. (See picture on page 328.)
8. Bake 12 to 15 minutes, or until golden brown.
9. Remove the cookies from the baking sheet with a spatula, and cool on a cake rack. (See picture on page 331.)

---

10 cookies: ¼ cup sifted all-purpose flour; ⅛ teaspoon soda; ⅛ teaspoon salt; ¼ teaspoon cinnamon; 2 tablespoons brown sugar; 1 tablespoon granulated sugar; 2 tablespoons shortening; 1 tablespoon beaten egg; 2 to 3 teaspoons milk; ½ cup quick-cooking rolled oats; ¼ cup raisins

---

PEANUT BUTTER COOKIES

1 ½ to 2 dozen		3 dozen
¾ cup (sifted)	ALL-PURPOSE FLOUR	1 ½ cups (sifted)
½ teaspoon	SODA	1 teaspoon
few grains	SALT	few grains
¼ cup	BUTTER or MARGARINE	½ cup
¼ cup	BROWN SUGAR	½ cup
¼ cup	GRANULATED SUGAR	½ cup
¼ cup	PEANUT BUTTER	½ cup
2 tablespoons (1 small egg)	BEATEN EGG	1

STEPS IN PREPARATION

1. Turn on the oven, and set the temperature control at 375° F. for a moderate oven.
2. Prepare the baking sheet by lightly greasing it with shortening.
3. Sift the flour with the soda and salt into a mixing bowl or onto wax paper.
4. Cream the butter or margarine until soft and smooth by rubbing it against the side of the bowl with the back of a spoon. Slowly add the brown sugar and the granulated sugar, and continue creaming until light and fluffy. Add the peanut butter, and mix well.
5. Add the beaten egg to the sugar mixture, and stir until smooth.
6. Add the sifted dry ingredients gradually to the egg mixture, and mix thoroughly.
7. Shape into balls the size of a walnut, and place on the prepared baking sheet 2 inches apart. (See picture on page 329.)
8. Flatten each cookie by pressing it with a fork.
9. Bake 15 minutes, or until golden brown.
10. Remove the cookies from the baking sheet with a spatula, and cool on a cake rack. (See picture on page 331.)

½ **to 1 dozen cookies:** ⅓ cup sifted all-purpose flour; ¼ teaspoon soda; few grains salt; 2 tablespoons butter or margarine; 2 tablespoons brown sugar; 2 tablespoons granulated sugar; 2 tablespoons peanut butter; 1 tablespoon beaten egg

---

BASIC CAKE
(Conventional Method)

One 8-inch layer		Two 8-inch layers
1 cup (sifted)	CAKE FLOUR	2 cups (sifted)
1 teaspoon	BAKING POWDER	2 teaspoons
⅛ teaspoon	SALT	¼ teaspoon
⅓ cup	SHORTENING	⅔ cup
⅔ cup	SUGAR	1⅓ cups
2	EGGS	3
⅓ cup	MILK	⅔ cup
½ teaspoon	VANILLA	1 teaspoon

STEPS IN PREPARATION

1. Turn on the oven, and set the temperature control at 375° F. for a moderate oven.
2. Prepare the cake pan by lightly greasing the bottom and side with shortening. Dust the pan lightly with flour until it is well coated, and turn it over to shake out the excess flour. (See pictures on page 333.)
3. Sift the flour with the baking powder and salt into a mixing bowl or onto wax paper. (See picture on page 334.)
4. Cream the shortening until soft and smooth by rubbing it against the side of the bowl with the back of a spoon. Slowly add the sugar, and continue creaming until light and fluffy.
5. Add the unbeaten eggs, one at a time, beating well after each addition.
6. Add one-fourth of the dry ingredients, and beat until well blended. Add one-third of the milk, and stir until smooth. Add another fourth of the dry ingredients, and continue adding first one and then the other until all have been added, being sure to add dry ingredients last.
7. Add the vanilla.
8. Pour the batter into the prepared cake pan. (See picture on page 337.)
9. Bake 25 to 30 minutes, or until brown. (See pictures on pages 337 and 338.)
10. Remove from the oven. Leave the cake in the pan 7 minutes. Loosen from the sides and turn onto a cake rack. (See picture on page 338.)
11. Cool. Brush off the crumbs, and frost with **Double-boiler Frosting** or **Butter Cream Frosting** (pages 546 and 547). See pictures on page 340.

---

2 student servings (4 to 6 cupcakes): ½ cup sifted cake flour; ½ teaspoon baking powder; few grains salt; 2½ tablespoons shortening; ⅓ cup sugar; 1 egg; 3 tablespoons milk; ¼ teaspoon vanilla. Bake in hot oven (400° F.) 18 to 20 minutes

DEVIL'S FOOD CAKE
(One-bowl Method)

Two 8-inch layers

1½ cups (sifted)	CAKE FLOUR
1¼ cups	SUGAR
½ cup	COCOA
¾ teaspoon	SALT
1¼ teaspoons	SODA
⅔ cup	SHORTENING
1 cup	BUTTERMILK or SOUR MILK
2	EGGS
1 teaspoon	VANILLA

STEPS IN PREPARATION

1. Turn on the oven, and set the temperature control at 350° F. for a moderate oven.
2. Prepare the cake pans by lining them with wax paper or by lightly greasing the bottoms and sides with shortening. Dust the pans lightly with flour until they are well coated, and turn them over to shake out the excess flour. (See pictures on page 333.)
3. Sift the flour with the sugar, cocoa, salt, and soda into a large mixing bowl. (See the picture on page 336.)
4. Add shortening and about two-thirds of the buttermilk or sour milk.
5. Beat vigorously by hand about 2 minutes, or 300 strokes. If an electric mixer is used, beat 2 minutes on medium speed, scraping the bowl constantly.
6. Add the remaining buttermilk or sour milk, unbeaten eggs, and vanilla. (See picture on page 336.)
7. Beat 2 minutes more, or another 300 strokes.
8. Pour the batter into the prepared cake pans, being sure to put the same amount of batter in each pan. Then spread out evenly in the pans. (See picture on page 337.)
9. Bake 30 to 35 minutes, or until done. To test for doneness, see the picture on page 338.
10. Remove from the oven. Let the cake stand in the pans 5 to 10 minutes. Loosen from the sides with a spatula, and turn onto a cake rack.
11. Cool. Brush off the crumbs, and frost with **Double-boiler Frosting** or **Butter Cream Frosting** (pages 546 and 547). See pictures on page 340.

BUTTER CREAM FROSTING

1 layer		2 layers
3 tablespoons	BUTTER or MARGARINE	⅓ cup
1½ cups (sifted)	CONFECTIONERS' SUGAR	3 cups (sifted)
1 to 2 tablespoons	CREAM	3 to 4 tablespoons
¾ teaspoon	VANILLA	1½ teaspoons

STEPS IN PREPARATION

1. Cream the butter or margarine until soft and smooth by rubbing it against the side of the bowl with the back of a spoon.

2. Add the sifted confectioners' sugar slowly to the butter or margarine alternately with the cream, mixing well. Add just enough cream to make a frosting that will spread smoothly.

3. Add the vanilla, and beat until light and fluffy. (See picture on page 339.)

4. Spread the frosting on the cake according to the pictures on page 340.

2 student servings (4 to 6 cupcakes): 1½ tablespoons butter or margarine; ¾ cup sifted confectioners' sugar; 2 to 3 teaspoons cream; ¼ teaspoon vanilla

CHOCOLATE FROSTING

1 layer		2 layers
2½ tablespoons	COCOA	⅓ cup

Follow the recipe for **Butter Cream Frosting,** but in Step 2 sift cocoa with the confectioners' sugar before adding it to the butter or margarine.

PINEAPPLE FROSTING

1 layer		2 layers
2½ tablespoons	CRUSHED PINEAPPLE (drained)	⅓ cup

Follow the recipe for **Butter Cream Frosting,** but in Step 2 substitute drained crushed pineapple for the cream, and in Step 3 omit the vanilla.

DOUBLE-BOILER FROSTING
(For 2 Layers)

2	EGG WHITES
1½ cups	SUGAR
⅓ cup	COLD WATER
few grains	SALT
2 teaspoons	CORN SIRUP
1 teaspoon	VANILLA

STEPS IN PREPARATION

1. Fill the lower part of a double boiler about one-third full of water. Heat to boiling.

2. Put the egg whites, sugar, cold water, salt, and corn sirup in the upper part of the double boiler, and mix thoroughly.

3. Place the upper part of the double boiler over the boiling water. Beat constantly with a rotary beater 5 to 7 minutes, or until the frosting stands up in stiff peaks. When an electric mixer is used, beat at high speed only 4 to 6 minutes. (See picture on page 339.) Move the beater from side to side and top to bottom while beating.

4. Remove from the boiling water, add the vanilla, and beat 2 to 3 minutes, or until thick enough to spread.

5. Frost the cake according to the directions on page 340.

SEAFOAM FROSTING

Follow the recipe for **Double-boiler Frosting,** but in Step 2 omit the corn sirup, and substitute the same amount of brown sugar for the granulated sugar.

ORANGE MIST FROSTING

Follow the recipe for **Double-boiler Frosting,** but in Step 2 omit the corn sirup, and substitute ¼ cup orange juice and 2 tablespoons lemon juice for the water. In Step 4 substitute 1 teaspoon grated orange rind for the vanilla.

FUDGE

4 student servings (¾ pound)		6 student servings (1 pound)
1½ squares	UNSWEETENED CHOCOLATE	2 squares
1½ cups	SUGAR	2 cups
1 tablespoon	CORN SIRUP	4 teaspoons
½ cup	EVAPORATED MILK	⅔ cup
1½ tablespoons	BUTTER or MARGARINE	2 tablespoons
½ teaspoon	VANILLA	¾ teaspoon
½ cup	CHOPPED NUTS	¾ cup

STEPS IN PREPARATION

1. Cut the chocolate squares into small pieces.
2. Put the chocolate pieces, sugar, corn sirup, and undiluted evaporated milk in a heavy saucepan.
3. Place over very low heat, and stir until the chocolate melts and the sugar dissolves. (See picture on page 342.)
4. Continue cooking the mixture until it reaches 236° F. on a candy thermometer, or until a little of the mixture dropped in cold water forms a soft ball. Stir occasionally to prevent burning.
5. Remove from the heat, add the butter or margarine, and set aside to cool without stirring. (See picture on page 343.)
6. Cool to 110° F., or until the saucepan can be held comfortably on the palm of the hand.
7. Prepare a pan by lightly greasing the bottom and sides with butter or margarine.
8. Add the vanilla. Beat with a wooden spoon until the fudge becomes creamy, loses its glossy appearance, and holds its shape when dropped from a spoon.
9. Stir in the nuts, and quickly pour the fudge into a buttered pan.
10. Cut into squares when firm and cool.

---

2 student servings (½ pound): 1 square unsweetened chocolate; 1 cup sugar; 2 teaspoons corn sirup; ⅓ cup evaporated milk; 1 tablespoon butter or margarine; ¼ teaspoon vanilla; ¼ cup chopped nuts

---

ILLUSTRATED COOKING PROCEDURES

CHECK YOUR VOCABULARY

Be sure you know the meaning and spelling of the following terms:

1. *Let's Have a Party*
   decorations
   entertainment
   host
   hostess
   invitation
   party theme
   refreshments

2. *Setting the Table*
   centerpiece
   china
   cover
   glassware
   place mats
   silverware
   table linen

3. *Mealtime Manners*
   cafeteria
   guest of honor
   informal
   main course
   manners
   restaurant

4. *Your Food Needs*
   calories
   carbohydrates
   daily food guide
   fats
   minerals
   nutrients
   proteins
   vitamins

5. *Planning Your Meals*
   au gratin
   budget
   meat substitute
   menu
   nutrition

   variety

6. *Breakfast*
   breakfast patterns
   electric appliance
   time-savers
   variations
   well-balanced diet

7. *Lunch or Supper*
   casserole
   cold-meat plate
   fruit plate
   leftovers
   luncheon patterns
   scalloped
   vegetable plate

8. *Dinner*
   appetizer
   dinner patterns
   garnish
   main dish
   melba toast
   salad
   starchy vegetable

9. *Special Meals*
   baby sitter
   food habits
   formula
   infant
   light diet
   liquid diet
   soft diet
   weight control

10. *Meals in a Hurry*
    dehydrated
    emergency shelf
    frozen foods
    homemaking

   mixes
   powdered
   precooked foods
   TV dinners

11. *Buying Your Foods*
    advertisements
    delicatessen
    family income
    food specials
    market list
    nonessential food
    supermarket

12. *Fruit*
    citrus fruits
    dried fruits
    quick energy
    quick frozen
    roughage
    varieties

13. *Vegetables*
    crispness
    leafy
    legumes
    mild-flavored
    root
    strong-flavored
    watery

14. *Salads*
    curly endive
    head lettuce
    leaf lettuce
    marinate
    mayonnaise
    salad dressing
    seasoning

15. *Soups and Sauces*
    bisque

bouillon
cocktail sauce
consommé
stock
tartar sauce
white sauce

16. *Sandwiches*
dainty
grilled
hearty
hot
ribbon
rolled
sawing motion

17. *Milk and Milk Products*
butterfat
buttermilk
evaporated milk
homogenized milk
nonfat dry milk
pasturized milk
raw milk
skim milk
whole milk

18. *Eggs*
cartons
dried eggs
food value
frozen eggs
grades of eggs
white
yolk

19. *Meats*
beef
carve
complete protein
grading
lamb
meat thermometer
pork
variety meats

20. *Poultry and Fish*
broilers
drawn fish
fillets
fryers
roasters
shell fish
stewers

21. *Cereals*
bran
endosperm
enriched
extenders
germ
grain
refined

22. *Breads*
batter
dough
enriched flour
leavening agents
quick breads
yeast breads

23. *Desserts*
butter cakes
chiffon cakes
crystalline
noncrystalline
texture

24. *Desserts*
Bavarian cream
cake à la mode
chiffon pie
cobbler
custard
frozen mixture
sherbet

25. *Beverages*
bottled drinks
chilled
dairy bars

lemonade
scum
stimulant
thermos jug

26. *Your Equipment*
aluminum foil
baking pans
blending fork
bread knife
cake rack
cannister set
measuring
mixing
oven dishes
range
refrigerator
vegetable brush

27. *Working Together*
committee
demonstration
evaluate
organize
responsibilities
schedule

28. *Managing Your Meals*
cleaning center
cooking center
dovetailing
orderliness
planning center
preparation
serving center

29. *Safety in the Kitchen*
accidents
asbestos mats
circuit
disinfectants
insecticides
sanitary habits
stepstool

551

SELECTED STUDENT REFERENCES

Betty Crocker's New Picture Cook Book, McGraw-Hill Book Company, Inc., New York, 1961

Building Your Home Life, Inez Wallace and Bernice McCullar, J. B. Lippincott Company, Philadelphia, 1966

Experiences with Foods, L. Belle Pollard, Ginn and Company, Boston, 1964

Exploring Home and Family Living, Henrietta Fleck, Louise Fernandez, and Evelyn Munves, Prentice-Hall, Inc., Englewood Cliffs, N.J., 1965

Food for Modern Living, Irene E. McDermott, Mabel B. Trilling, and Florence W. Nicholas, J. B. Lippincot Company, Philadelphia, 1967

Foods in Homemaking, Marion Cronan and June Atwood, Chas. A. Bennett Company, Inc., Peoria, Ill., 1965

Guide for Today's Home Living, H. M. Hatcher and M. E. Andrews, D. C. Heath and Company, 1966

Guide to Modern Meals, Dorothy E. Shank, Natalie K. Fitch, and Pauline A. Chapman, McGraw-Hill Book Co., New York, 1964

Homemaking for Teen-agers, Book I, Irene E. McDermott and Florence W. Nicholas, Chas. A. Bennett Company, Inc., Peoria, Ill., 1966

Junior Homemaking, Evelyn G. Jones and Helen A. Burnham, J. B. Lippincott Company, Philadelphia, 1963

Keys to Safety in Homemaking, Detroit Public Schools, McGraw-Hill Book Company, New York, 1966

Manners Made Easy, Mary Beery, McGraw-Hill Book Co., New York, 1966

Mealtime, Bess V. Oerke, Chas. A. Bennett Company, Inc., Peoria, Ill., 1967

Meal Planning and Table Service, Beth Bailey McLean, Chas A. Bennett Company, Inc., Peoria, Ill., 1964

Setting Your Table, Helen Sprackling, M. Barrows and Company, Inc., New York, 1960 .

Teen Guide to Homemaking, Marion S. Barclay and Frances Champion, McGraw-Hill Book Company, Inc., New York, 1967

Teenage Living, Nell Giles Ahern, Houghton Mifflin Company, Boston, 1966

Tomorrow's Homemaker, Dora S. Lewis, Anna K. Banks, Marie Banks, and Adele G. Columbia, The Macmillan Company, New York, 1960

You and Your Food, Ruth B. White, Prentice-Hall, Inc. Englewood Cliffs, N. J., 1966

Young Living, Nanalle Clayton, Chas. A. Bennett Company, Inc., Peoria, Ill., 1963

Your Foods Book, Florence L. Harris and Rex Todd Withers, D. C. Heath and Company, Boston, 1966

Your Home and You, Carlotta C. Greer and Ellen P. Gibbs, Allyn and Bacon, Inc., Englewood Cliffs, N. J., 1965

GENERAL INDEX

559

560

RECIPE INDEX